D0948827

Amazonian Indians from Prehistory to the Present

Amazonian Indians
from Prehistory to the Present

Anthropological Perspectives

Edited by

ANNA ROOSEVELT

THE UNIVERSITY OF ARIZONA PRESS
Tucson & London

The University of Arizona Press
Copyright © 1994
The Arizona Board of Regents
All rights reserved
Manufactured in the United States of America

99 98 97 96 95 94   6 5 4 3 2 1

Library of Congress Cataloging-in-Publication Data

Amazonian Indians from prehistory to the present : anthropological
   perspectives / edited by Anna Roosevelt.
       p.   cm.
   Includes bibliographical references and index.
   ISBN 0-8165-1436-4 (alk. paper)
     1. Indians of South America—Amazon River Regions—History.
   2. Indians of South America—Amazon River Region—Social life and
   customs.   3. Ethnohistory—Amazon River Region.   4. Subsistence
   economy—Amazon River Region.   5. Human ecology—Amazon River
   Region.   6. Amazon River Region—Social conditions.   I. Roosevelt,
   Anna Curtenius.
   F2519.1.A6A465   1994
   981'.100498—dc20   94-18716
                                                                       CIP

British Cataloguing-in-Publication Data
A catalogue record for this book is available from the British Library.

Parts of chapter 16 originally appeared in the article "Similarity and Variation in Plant
Names in Five Tupí-Guaraní Languages (Eastern Amazonia)," by William Balée and
Denny Moore, in the *Bulletin of the Florida Museum of Natural History (Biological Sciences)*
35 (1991): 209–62, and are reproduced here by permission of the bulletin. Chapter 13
was published in a somewhat different form in *Ethnohistory* 38 (1991): 338–413 and is
reproduced here by permission of Duke University Press.

Contents

List of Contributors   ix

Preface   xiii

1   Amazonian Anthropology: Strategy for a New Synthesis   1
    Anna C. Roosevelt

PART I   FIRST TRANSFORMATIONS

2   The Ancient Amerindian Polities of the Amazon, the Orinoco,
and the Atlantic Coast: A Preliminary Analysis of Their Passage
from Antiquity to Extinction   33
    Neil Lancelot Whitehead

3   The Impact of Conquest on Contemporary Indigenous Peoples of the
Guiana Shield: The System of Orinoco Regional Interdependence   55
    Nelly Arvelo-Jiménez and Horacio Biord

4   Social Organization and Political Power in the Amazon Floodplain:
The Ethnohistorical Sources   79
    Antonio Porro

5 The Evidence for the Nature of the Process of Indigenous
   Deculturation and Destabilization in the Brazilian Amazon
   in the Last Three Hundred Years: Preliminary Data   95
   Adélia Engrácia de Oliveira

PART II   HABITAT AND HUMAN BIOLOGY IN PERSPECTIVE

6 Health and Demography of Native Amazonians: Historical
   Perspective and Current Status   123
   Warren M. Hern

7 Diet and Nutritional Status of Amazonian Peoples   151
   Darna L. Dufour

8 Hunting and Fishing in Amazonia: Hold the Answers, What Are
   the Questions?   177
   Stephen Beckerman

PART III   SOCIETY, ECOLOGY, AND COSMOLOGY IN CONTEXT

9 Homeostasis as a Cultural System: The Jivaro Case   203
   Philippe Descola

10 Farming, Feuding, and Female Status: The Achuar Case   225
   Pita Kelekna

11 Subsistence Strategy, Social Organization, and Warfare in Central
   Brazil in the Context of European Penetration   249
   Nancy M. Flowers

12 Environmental and Social Implications of Pre- and Postcontact
   Situations on Brazilian Indians: The Kayapó and a
   New Amazonian Synthesis   271
   Darrell Addison Posey

13 Beyond Resistance: Comparative Study of Utopian Renewal
   in Amazonia   287
   Michael F. Brown

PART IV   STRATEGIES FOR INTEGRATIVE RESEARCH

14 The Eastern Bororo from an Archaeological Perspective   315
   Irmhild Wüst

15 Genetic Relatedness and Language Distributions in Amazonia   343
   Harriet E. Manelis Klein

16 Language, Culture, and Environment: Tupí-Guaraní Plant Names
    Over Time   363
      William Balée and Denny Moore

PART V   ADAPTATION TODAY

17 Becoming Indians: The Politics of Tukanoan Ethnicity   383
      Jean E. Jackson

    Index   407

Contributors

NELLY ARVELO-JIMÉNEZ received her Ph.D. from Cornell University in anthropology. Since 1993 she has been Professor Emeritus of Anthropology at the Venezuelan Institute for Scientific Investigations. She became Savage Professor of International Relations and Peace at the University of Oregon in 1994. She has published four books, twenty-eight chapters in books, and forty papers in anthropological journals.

WILLIAM BALÉE, Associate Professor of Anthropology at Tulane University, New Orleans, Louisiana, 70118, took his Ph.D. in Anthropology at Columbia University in 1984. He is author of *Footprints of the Forest: Ka'apor Ethnobotany* (Columbia University Press) and coeditor of *Resource Management in Amazonia: Indigenous and Folk Strategies* (New York Botanical Garden).

STEPHEN BECKERMAN received his Ph.D. in cultural anthropology from the University of New Mexico in 1975; he is now an associate professor at the Pennsylvania State University. Since 1970, he has conducted fieldwork with the Barí of the southwestern Maracaibo Basin; his publications deal with the Barí, their ecological relations, and other aspects of human ecology.

HORACIO BIORD was for ten years Research Assistant in the Laboratory of Ethnology, Department of Anthropology, Venezuelan Institute for Scientific Research (IVIC). He is a graduate student in linguistics at the Catholic University of Caracas. He teaches linguistics at the Catholic University and the Metropolitan University, also in Caracas, and has published several papers on South American linguistics.

MICHAEL F. BROWN is Professor of Anthropology and Chair, Department of Anthropology and Sociology, Williams College, Williamstown, Massachusetts. His books include *Tsewa's Gift: Magic and Meaning in an Amazonian Society* (1986) and *War of Shadows: The Struggle for Utopia in the Peruvian Amazon* (1991), the latter co-authored with Eduardo Fernández.

PHILIPPE DESCOLA is Directeur d'études at the Ecole des Hautes Etudes en Sciences Sociales, Paris, and member of the Laboratoire d'Anthropologie Sociale at the Collège de France. He is the author of *In the Society of Nature: A Native Ecology in Amazonia* (1994), *Les Lances du Crépuscule: Relations Jivaros* (1994), and co-author of *Les Idées de l'Anthropologie* (1988) and *Dictionnaire de l'Ethnologie et de l'Anthropologie* (1981).

DARNA L. DUFOUR is an Associate Professor of Anthropology at the University of Colorado, Boulder. Her research has focused on the nutritional ecology of native Amazonians, and more recently the nutrition of economically deprived urban women in Colombia. Her published articles include "Insects as Food: A Case Study from the Northwest Amazon" (*American Anthropologist* 1987), "Effectiveness of Cassava Detoxification Techniques Used by Indigenous Peoples in Northwest Amazonia" (*Interciencia* 1989), and "People in the Tropical Rainforests of Amazonia" (*BioScience* 1990).

NANCY M. FLOWERS is Adjunct Associate Professor of Anthropology at Hunter College, City University of New York. She began studying the Xavante Indians in 1976 as a participant in the project "Human Ecology in Central Brazil," organized by Dr. Daniel R. Gross. At the same time she did research for her doctoral dissertation, "Forager-Farmers: The Xavante Indians of Central Brazil." She received the Ph.D. from the Graduate Center, City University of New York. She has continued her study of the Xavante and returned in 1990, with Brazilian colleagues, to do further fieldwork. Her interests include human ecology, demography, nutrition, and ethnohistory.

WARREN M. HERN is a physician and epidemiologist who is Associate Professor Adjunct, Department of Anthropology, University of Colorado–Boulder and the University of Colorado–Denver, and Associate Clinical Professor, Department of Preventive Medicine and Biometrics, University of Colorado Health Sciences Center in Denver. He has conducted research on the health effects of cultural change among the Shipibo of the Peruvian Amazon since 1964.

JEAN E. JACKSON is Professor of Anthropology in the Anthropology/Archaeology Program at MIT. Her earlier research in Mexico, Guatemala, and the Colombian Amazon focused on birth spacing, anthropological linguistics, patrilineal descent, and gender. More recent research interests include the epistemology of anthropological fieldnotes, ethnic nationalism, Indian rights movements, and chronic pain.

PITA KELEKNA completed her doctoral work in anthropology at the University of New Mexico in 1981 and is author of several articles on the Jivaroan Achuara. Her research interests are symbolism, gender asymmetry, and incipient hierarchy in social organization. She resides in New York City and is a member of the Ecological Systems and Cultural Evolution seminar at Columbia University.

HARRIET E. MANELIS KLEIN is Professor of Anthropology at Montclair State College. She received a Ph.D. from Columbia in 1973, and her research activities and publications have centered on the linguistic study of various Central and South American Indian groups. *South American Indian Languages: Retrospect and Prospect* (coeditor Louisa R. Stark) and *Una Gramática de la Lengua Toba* are two of the books she has written. She is president-elect of the Society for Linguistic Anthropology.

DENNY MOORE, Director of the Linguistics Division of the Museu Paraense Emílio Goeldi, Caixa Postal 399, 66040 Belém, Pará, Brazil, took his Ph.D. in Anthropology at the City University of New York in 1984. He analyzed the syntax of the Gavião language of Rondônia, Brazil. He is currently involved in a major comparative study of Tupian languages. His publications have appeared in the *International Journal of American Linguistics* and *América Indígena* as well as in other journals and books.

ADÉLIA ENGRÁCIA DE OLIVEIRA is a Senior Researcher of the Brazilian National Research Council (CNPq) working in research and administration at the Museu Paraense Emílio Goeldi in Belém, where she is the head of the Human Sciences Department. She has worked for the last twenty-five years in Brazilian Amazonia with indigenous cultures in the regions of the Xingu, Negro, and Madeira Rivers. She has also worked with *caboclos* of the Negro and Tocantins Rivers and is now conducting interdisciplinary research on human occupation in Amazonia.

ANTONIO PORRO, born in Italy (1940), lives in São Paulo, Brazil. His Ph.D. in Social Anthropology (1977) is from the University of São Paulo. He is the author of several papers and books on Maya history and religion and on the ethnohistory of the sixteenth- and seventeenth-century tribes of the middle and upper Amazon River.

DARRELL ADDISON POSEY is currently Visiting Scholar at The Institute for Social and Cultural Anthropology and Senior Member of St. Antony's College, Oxford University, England. He is Titled Researcher of the Brazilian National Council for Science and Technology (CNPq) and Head of the Program of Ethnobiology of the Goeldi Museum, Belém, Brazil. He is one of the founders and Past President of the International Society for Ethnobiology and currently serves as Executive Director of The Global Coalition for Biological and Cultural Diversity. He received his Ph.D. in anthropology from the University of Georgia.

NEIL LANCELOT WHITEHEAD is currently Assistant Professor of Anthropology, University of Wisconsin–Madison. He has held appointments at the Universities of Oxford and Leiden and is the author of several works on the historical anthropology of Amazonia and the Caribbean.

IRMHILD WÜST was born in Erlangen, Germany, and emigrated to Brazil in 1967. Since 1972 she has worked as an archaeologist in central Brazil, concentrating on precolonial agricultural societies and contemporary Indian groups, including the Bororo, Karajá, and Shavante. She received her Ph.D. in Social Anthropology from the Universidade de São Paulo in 1990. Currently, she is Titular Professor of Archaeology at the Universidade Federal de Goiás.

Preface

What significant changes have taken place in the cultures and the conditions of life of indigenous Amazonian populations through the millennia? Why did the changes happen, and what are their implications for our explanations of people's lifeways? What are the significant variations in indigenous lifeways through the enormous expanse of Amazonia? What factors need to be taken into consideration to explain the cultural forms and adaptations in different regions? What are the reasons for the significant contrasts in the subsistence and demography of prehistoric and ethnographic (i.e., postconquest) Indians, and what are their implications for cultural and ecological explanations? What stereotypes about Amazonian environments need to be corrected? What are the significant regional differences in resource potential, and what is their impact on regional cultures?

Chapter 1 explores these questions in an overview of the indigenous occupation of Greater Amazonia from earliest prehistory to the present day. In it I outline some of the significant variations in cultural and ecological adaptations through time and space, documenting some earlier peoples and cultures that are very different from those that exist today. Based on these findings, I recommend directions for future research on the interrelationships between conceptual and material culture, using a research strategy that integrates the theories and methods of social anthropology, archaeology, physical anthropology, and linguistics.

Part I: First Transformations

The first part of our book traces the important ethnohistorical transition, a period of convulsive change in indigenous societies during the European conquest and colonization of Amazonia from the sixteenth through twentieth centuries. During this time, many groups had to adapt to greatly changed circumstances, some forms of society disappeared, and new ones came into being. In Chapter 2, Neil Whitehead analyzes the transformations of Orinoco and Guianan societies in the northeastern lowlands during the early part of the conquest period. He shows that the invasions spelled immediate decline for some groups and gave others opportunities to develop trade and militarism in new directions over expanded territories, at least temporarily. Eventually, however, complex indigenous social forms disappeared as the colonization expanded.

In Chapter 3, Nelly Arvelo-Jiménez and Horacio Biord outline the effects of the later stages of conquest on the interactions among the peoples of the interior of the Orinoco and Guiana Shield in Venezuela. They argue that preconquest craft production, trade, ritual, and political interaction were conducted so as to encourage interethnic exchange. As conquest and colonization progressed, this indigenous system of interaction was transformed structurally and functionally through mechanisms such as imposed settlement change and debt peonage.

In Chapter 4, Antonio Porro gives a picture of chiefly floodplain societies of the western part of the Brazilian Amazon at the time of first contact and traces the early changes that took place as native populations declined and societies were disrupted by the intrusions of the conquerors. With numerous quotations from eyewitness accounts, he shows that, over time, paramount leaders disappeared, their realms disintegrated, and the size and number of native settlements shrank substantially as the conquest of Amazonia progressed.

The process of conquest in the lower Amazon over the last 300 years is detailed by Adélia de Oliveira in Chapter 5 in an analysis of the changes that took place in indigenous societies as the colonial administration developed in the eastern part of what is now the Brazilian Amazon. Important factors that she highlights in the process were demographic decline due to disease, warfare, and forced labor, and a loss of indigenous identity through political disintegration, deculturation through missionization, and enforced miscegenation.

Part II: Habitat and Human Biology in Perspective

What do we know about the subsistence, health, and reproductive strategies of Amazonian Indians over time and space, and what impact have historical, political, and socioeconomic factors had on these characteristics? Part 2 of our book presents current knowledge of the nutrition, health, and demography of Amazonian Indians and discusses the role of animal capture in subsistence adaptations. The results of this review show that high-quality data is sorely lacking for the most part but suggest some interesting contrasts over space and time. Future research to interpret human biology in Amazonia over the long term will benefit from systematic, long-term collaborative studies by a wide range of specialists in genetics, child development, nutrition, disease, and demography.

In Chapter 6, Warren Hern surveys the available data on the health status of indigenous Amazonians, especially in regard to demography and infectious disease. He suggests that there has been considerable dynamism in the state of Amazonian populations and points to some possible trends for the near future. Although some Amazonian populations have recently rebounded from severe conquest-related declines, he feels that overall populations will continue to decline.

In Chapter 7, Darna Dufour surveys the diet and nutrition of Amazonian Indians across the region and characterizes the common form of subsistence: slash-and-burn cultivation of starchy crops. The data that she brings together suggest that although most adults have adequate diets, many Amazonian Indian children may be suffering from undernutrition, which leads to depressed growth curves and subsequent stature reduction in adults.

In Chapter 8, Steve Beckerman's survey of hunting-and-gathering practices in Amazonia suggests the need to rethink our research questions about subsistence. Framed in the light of current debates about resources, population, and subsistence technology in Amazonia, his review traces some aspects of human ecological variation through Amazonia. Finding little evidence that foraging patterns are shaped by overall resource inadequacy, he suggests future research to investigate a wider range of factors, including seasonality and the wider socioeconomic context of foraging.

Part III: Society, Ecology, and Cosmology in Context

What influence has Amazonian people's changing ecological, economic, and social contexts had on their ideology and organization? And what impact, in turn, have organizational and ideological systems had on people's conditions of life? Why do present-day societies organize themselves and conceive of the world in different ways from prehistoric societies? What has been the impact of the interaction with whites on indigenous lifeways, particularly in regard to organization, warfare, and distribution? Can the different histories of contact help explain variations seen in indigenous cultures and their trajectories of development? The third part of our book presents five case studies that attempt to trace the relationship between an ecological, organizational, or ideological characteristic of an Amazonian society and one or more other factors in the lifeways or contexts of the people.

In Chapter 9, Philippe Descola argues that the Jivaroan Achuar of Ecuador have successfully adapted to the conquest through a process of cultural ecological stability rather than rapid cultural change. Thus we can see how some Amazonian societies have adapted to the intrusion of outsiders by maintaining rather than abandoning their lifeways. He cautions, however, that cultural stability was a possible adaptation for the Jivaro only because they escaped direct military conquest and close involvement with colonial and national market economies.

In Chapter 10, Pita Kelekna examines a fascinating aspect of Amazonian societies: the relationship of gender status to other facets of lifeways. In her research she isolates patterns of subsistence and warfare as an especially strong influence on gender relations and traces the working out of these interactions among the Jivaroan Achuar of the upper Amazon in Peru, relatives of the Ecuadorian Achuar. Although this topic has been little researched, it promises to be an important one in the future, given the importance of gender in Amazonian Indian culture and the evidence for variation in gender over time and space. Nancy Flowers examines the Xavante of Central Brazil in Chapter 11 and finds evidence of the continuing influence of contact on native subsistence and settlement patterns. She finds that the great flexibility of the Xavante's seminomadism and the huge extent of their interaction system helped them to avoid missionization and enslavement.

Darrell Posey, in Chapter 12, takes the Northern Kayapó of central Brazil from their earliest known history to today, tracing a long trajectory of cultural, ecological, and demographic adaptation to contact. Through collaboration with native informants, Posey gained insights into an ancient forest management complex that had escaped anthropologists' attention before. Also of interest is his hypothesis that mortality from the new epidemic diseases led to increased internal conflict as people struggled to understand the increased death rates in traditional ways.

Michael Brown, in Chapter 13, traces utopian millenarian movements in the upper Amazon to a time before the inception of recent contact processes, to which these movements are often considered a response. He finds evidence that central elements of these cults have firm indigenous roots in precontact lifeways, particularly in the cultural complex of indigenous paramount chiefship. Brown's tracing of the actual history of the millenarian cults uncovered evidence that contradicts the intuitively appealing explanation that the movements were adaptations to contact.

Part IV: Strategies for Integrative Research

How can we investigate the important changes that have taken place in the characteristics of societies during the long trajectory of the indigenous occupation of Amazonia? What methods can reveal comparable cross-disciplinary information about the changing relationships among different aspects of lifeways? The next three chapters describe longitudinal research in one or more subdisciplines of anthropology aimed at gleaning information about the nature and reasons for changes in Amazonian Indian ways of life through time. They show the value of systematic comparisons made with an awareness of the possibility of significant change.

In Chapter 14, Wüst relates the results of her innovative ethnoarchaeological research on the cultural history of the Bororo and their neighbors. Far from being prepottery hunter-gatherers, as they have been characterized in the past, the Bororo turn out to be pottery-using maize horticulturalists who entered the region as recently as the eighteenth century. She attributes their loss of pottery and deemphasis on plant cultivation in the historical period to the disruptive effects of European conquest on settlement patterns, demography, and crafts. Such historical-archaeological analyses as Wüst's are widely applicable for testing evolutionary theories based on present indigenous distributions.

In Chapter 15, Harriet Klein reviews some traditional techniques of historical linguistics and their potential for the study of lowland South American Indian societies. Her focus is on glottochronology, a much-criticized technique of language analysis popular in the past, especially among archaeologists working in Amazonia. Although its use has been marred by uncritical methods of data collection and a reliance on untested theories, Klein shows that it could be of great value for charting and analyzing transformations in language. The potential of historical linguistics should encourage archival and ethnographic research using new audio and computer technology to create high-quality databases for different times and places.

In Chapter 16, Balée and Moore present the results of a case study that exemplifies the value of research on language change through space and time. Gathering detailed information on variation in plant vocabulary in Tupí-Guaraní languages through time, they uncover significant patterns stemming from evolutionary changes in the role of plants in human adaptation in lowland South America. Similar methods applied to vocabulary in other important areas of culture, such as social and political organization, could yield knowledge of significant long-term trends in social evolution.

Part V: Adaptation Today

How, specifically, are Amazonian Indians using ethnicity and other cultural mechanisms to adapt to unavoidable contacts today? What is their current status, and what are the prospects for maintaining their access to resources and their freedom to develop their cultures in the face of increasing pressure from national cultures, organizations, and populations?

In the final essay in the book, Chapter 17, Jean Jackson shows how the Tukanoan speakers of the northwest Amazon construct new complexes of indigenous imagery in their creation of identities that are appropriate for organizing politically for interactions with outsiders. Out of tradition, new cultural forms are arising as Amazonian peoples deal dynamically with membership in the larger world.

Amazonian Indians from Prehistory to the Present

I

Amazonian Anthropology

Strategy for a New Synthesis

ANNA C. ROOSEVELT

This is a book about the changing relationships among human organization, ideology, and ecology during the approximately 12,000 years of indigenous occupation in Amazonia. The results of the past twenty years of research in the area reveal significant changes in human societies and their conditions of life through the millennia, but the implications of these changes have not yet been incorporated into Amazonian anthropology. The dynamism of the native occupation has become evident through cross-field research, but our confinement in our subfields is hindering its integration into a comprehensive understanding of Amazonian peoples and cultures. The new knowledge encourages a reorientation of theoretical interest in anthropology, and research into its implications will require methodological retooling as well. A central problem for the future is to develop for Amazonia a pragmatic research strategy that integrates the four fields of anthropology, uses both qualitative and quantitative approaches, and combines the materialist and idealist theoretical approaches, which have sometimes been opposed in the past. Such a strategy of anthropological synthesis can help us reach better explanations for the diversity of Amazonian peoples.

The Amazonian Environment

The two new bodies of evidence most important for reevaluating the anthropology of the Amazon in recent times have to do with the nature of the environment and the complex trajectory of indigenous occupation.

Amazonia as a habitat has long been the focus of a debate about the impact of the tropical rain forest environment on aboriginal cultural development in the Americas. A popular view—whether implicit or explicit—has been that this is a nutrient-poor environment that has limited indigenous population growth and cultural development in comparison with other areas because of its leached soils, dense vegetation, and sparse game (Jennings 1964; Meggers 1971; Steward, ed. 1946–50). In reality, because of particular geological and climatic conditions (Franzinelli and Latrubesse 1992), although large parts of the area are indeed very poor in resources, other parts hold some of the richest habitats in the world for the subsistence of humans with preindustrial technologies. Rainfall, rather than being uniformly high, varies regionally from isolated highs of 4,000 to 3,000 mm a year to moderate to low levels of between 1,500 and 2,500 mm a year over large areas. The seasonality of the climate has led to extensive floodplain development in areas with headwaters in weatherable rock, and such floodplains possess abundant aquatic fauna and flora, vast areas of silty alluvial soils, and extensive fluvial forests and savannas rich in edible fruits and fauna (see references in Roosevelt 1980, 1988, 1989, 1990a,b, 1991a,b, 1992a,b). The floodplain lakes of Amazonia, for example, have been shown to have very high primary production levels and rates of turnover (Junk 1970, 1973). Even the upland tropical forests, long branded unsuitable for the support of dense, sedentary human populations because of their poor soils on ancient, nutrient-poor geological substrate, are now known to include areas of limestones and mafic igneous rocks with high-nutrient soils. The Ecuadorian Amazon, for example, is blanketed with soils developed from nutrient-rich volcanic ash, and the Peruvian Amazon has large zones of soils developed on limestones (Franzinelli and Latrubesse 1992). In Brazil, outcrops of limestones and diabase dikes occur above the Amazon mainstream from Manaus to Belém (Projeto Radambrasil 1976). The forests and rivers of such upland areas are much more productive of food resources than those of the tropical rain forests on acid, leached soils.

Beyond the spatial diversity in resource abundance in Amazonia, the paleontological and archaeological records of both floodplains and upland forests show considerable change in temperature, rainfall, hydrology, sedimentation, and wildlife through time (Bush et al. 1989; Campbell and Frailey 1984; Campbell et al. 1985; Colinvaux et al. 1990; Franzinelli and Latrubesse 1992). Existing evidence from paleoecology suggests a period of increased seasonality in the late Pleistocene about 12,000–10,000 years ago, followed by a period of high temperatures, rain, and river levels in the early Holocene, between 10,000 and 5,000 years ago. Since then, water levels and rainfall have fluctuated at somewhat lower levels in patterns similar to today's Amazonian climates. Although the timing and extent of post-Pleistocene environmental change is not yet clear, it has been suggested that human populations were affected by them (Meggers 1975, 1977). Human settlement patterns keyed to hydrological and vegetation patterns would certainly be expected to have shifted during these times, although there is no clear evidence yet of any such process.

This Amazon environment was thus no homeostatic "counterfeit paradise" that hindered native occupations but a heterogeneous, often lush homeland that has been inhabited by human populations for more than 11,000 years. Although there is empirical evidence for high resource potential and changing human ecological adaptation in some lowland areas, only a few voices have called out this message and discussed its implications for anthropology (Allen 1968; Brochado 1980; Lathrap 1970; Magalis 1975; Roosevelt 1980, 1989, 1990a, 1991b, 1992b), and it is not usually accounted for in consensual interpretations of Amazonian ethnology, which characteristically tend to present today's native cultures as ancient traditional adaptations to the tropical forest environment (see references in Hames and Vickers 1983).

The Prehistoric Occupation

Cumulative archaeological and ethnohistoric evidence presented in Chapters 1–5 in this book and other sources (Brochado 1980; Hartt 1883, 1885; Lathrap 1970; Meggers and Evans 1983; Porro 1981, 1983–84, 1987; Roosevelt 1980, 1987, 1989, 1990b, 1991a, 1992a, n.d., Roosevelt et al. 1991 and n.d.; Whitehead 1988; de Oliveira 1988) reveals that this diverse habitat supported a great variety of peoples and cultures in a long, dynamic trajectory of development. This new understanding of culture history in Amazonia is directly contrary to the earlier idea, cited above, that due to the difficult tropical forest environment, indigenous human cultures from the centers of urban civilization—Mesoamerica and the Central Andes—had developed a common "tropical forest culture" of village societies relying on slash-and-burn horticulture, hunting, and fishing. In contrast, the archaeological findings from Amazonia document diverse occupations by humans, including some of the earliest foragers, farmers, and villagers yet known in the New World and culminating in populous indigenous complex societies in some areas in late prehistoric times. Rather than merely the product of influence or invasions from the outside (Evans and Meggers 1960, 1968; Meggers and Evans 1957), some lowland cultures were innovative, and some had considerable influence elsewhere in the Americas.

Early Foragers

The earliest known Amazonian cultures appear as early as those in other parts of the Americas and were technologically and aesthetically complex. They are found in a range of habitats, in both uplands and floodplains and in rain forests, savannas, gallery forests, and swamps. Although rainfall and hydrology appear to have fluctuated substantially during the period, the plant remains and fauna known from the archaeological sites are all of tropical species still found at or near the sites today, which means that the earliest Amazonian Indians that we know about had already adapted to tropical habitats.

The presence of bands of Paleoindian hunter-gatherers in Amazonia is indicated by numerous prepottery sites with terminal Pleistocene radiocarbon dates (uncalibrated) between about 11,400 and 10,000 years ago (Bryan 1983; Miller 1987; Roosevelt et al. n.d.; Schmitz 1987, 1990; Simoes 1976). The most common formal chipped-stone tools of these early complexes vary from large and small (5 to 13 cm in length), finely chipped, tanged spear points, found in central and northern Amazonia, to the large, crudely chipped, heavily worn scrapers found in the south. So far, the earliest dated lithics are from the Santarém–Monte Alegre area of the lower Amazon, where two successive Paleoindian cultures have radiocarbon dates from 11,400 to 10,000 B.P. The lithics include triangular stemmed points of hyaline quartz or chalcedony as well as other forms, such as knives, gravers, and scrapers. Finds of large, finely chipped spear points in the Guiana Shield suggest Paleoindian occupations in these areas also, although they are as yet undated (Boomert 1980; Cruxent and Rouse 1958–59; Roosevelt 1989, 1990b; Roosevelt et al. n.d.). These northern points vary from large, willow-leaf-shaped points of quartzite in Venezuelan Guyana to large, long flint points with parallel-sided fluted stems in Guyana and the Rio Negro drainage in Brazil. These early point complexes usually include some specimens that are expertly made and finely retouched with pressure flaking. Later preceramic complexes of the Guiana and Brazilian shields have smaller (4–8 cm length), thicker, and more crudely chipped points or complexes lacking points, dated between 10,000 and 7,000 B.P. (Barse 1990; Boomert 1980; Lopes Frois and Silveira n.d.;

Schmitz 1987, 1990; Schmitz et al. 1981–84; Simoes et al. 1985).

It is apparent that the small, presumably mobile, forager bands who made the stone tools also created a corpus of rock art. Panels of polychrome paintings of animals, humans, and/or geometric motifs abound at early preceramic rock shelters, caves, and outcrops south of the Amazon mainstream (Schmitz 1987, 1990; Schmitz et al. 1981–84), and a few have been found in the Guiana Shield (e.g., Roosevelt 1989). The dated Pleistocene points mentioned above were in fact recovered from one of several painted caves on the north bank of the main channel of the lower Amazon (Hartt 1971; Roosevelt 1990b; Roosevelt et al. n.d.) and were recovered from strata with abundant specimens of red pigment of the same chemical composition as the paint on the cave walls.

The size of some of the early points and finds of extinct fauna with willow-leaf points at a few sites on the Venezuelan coast north of the Orinoco River suggest a possible focus on large game in some cultures, but many of the early lowland sites have the remains of small game, fish, shellfish, palm seeds, and pits of tree fruits. The change in shape and the reduction in size of stone tools in the early Holocene may signal changes in subsistence adaptations and rock procurement as the modern climate began. Tools and technology for hunting large game may have become less important as people settled down in particular regions and intensified their resource use.

Early in the modern climate period, people specializing in fishing and shellfishing established villages along the banks of the middle and lower Amazon and the Atlantic estuaries, and began to use pottery. Their stone tools—mainly rare flakes, use-worn stone grinders, and abraders—appear crude and unspecialized compared to the earlier chipped tools and the ground and polished stone tools of later peoples. Several of the large ceramic-age shell middens in this area have produced radiocarbon and thermoluminescence dates from 8000 to 6000 B.P. (uncalibrated), making them the earliest pottery-age sites in the Americas (Roosevelt 1990b; Roosevelt et al. 1991 and n.d.; Simoes 1981; Guyanese and Brazilian sites, Radiocarbon date list, Smithsonian Institution Archives). These cultures are therefore difficult to interpret as intrusions from outside the Amazon. Far from being simple and crude, some of this early pottery was decorated with curvilinear and punctate incised designs.

During this time, landscapes in some areas of Amazonia were transformed by high rainfall and fluctuating river levels, and the ecological adaptations of the groups in distinct habitats diverge in some ways. Apparently people in the uplands between the large rivers had not yet taken up pottery (e.g., Lopes Frois and Silveira n.d.), and were dispersed in smaller habitation sites than

those of the riverbank peoples. While subsistence near the floodplains appears to have been focused upon fish and shellfish, between the rivers people
continued to pursue a broad-spectrum subsistence of small-game hunting,
fishing, and collecting of tree fruits and aquatic fauna.

Tribal and Village Horticulturalists

Between about 4,500 and 2,000 years ago, people with a lifeway in some
ways quite similar to that of present-day Indians established villages along
the major floodplains of Amazonia. In some areas, ceramic griddles and stone
grater chips came into use, possibly for processing the crop manioc, as did
ground-stone axes, perhaps for slash-and-burn cultivation. With this lifeway
came pottery decorated with incised and modeled geometric and/or animal
images sometimes with red and white painting (Boomert 1983; Cruxent and
Rouse 1957–58; Hilbert 1959; Lathrap 1970; Roosevelt 1978, 1980, 1990b,
n.d.; Roosevelt et al. n.d.; Bolivian sites, Smithsonian Radiocarbon Datelist, nos. SI-4113 to SI-4119, National Archives; Vargas 1981). Rare items
recovered from some sites include wooden spear-throwers preserved by water-
logging, small (ca. 0.5 cm), thick, crudely chipped stemmed quartz points,
possibly for spear-throwers, biomorphic tubular smoking or snuffing pipes of
pottery, and small carved stone ornaments and spindle whorls.

In some areas, such as the Ucayali Basin and the middle Orinoco, starchy
roots and fish appear to have been staple foods at this time, to judge from the
evidence of the ceramic griddles, human bone chemistry, and food remains
(Roosevelt 1980, 1989; Roosevelt et al. n.d.; van der Merwe et al. 1981).
The modest size of the early archaeological sites of this culture (between 1 and
2 ha) and their considerable depth (from one-half to more than 1 meter) indicate a pattern of small but stable settlements. By the period 3000–2000 B.P.,
however, people in the middle and lower Orinoco were living in large villages
of many hectares. In the floodplains of the Bolivian Amazon and at the
mouth of the Amazon, people of related ceramic traditions built the earliest-
known earthen mounds in Amazonia (Smithsonian Radiocarbon datelist,
nos. SI-4113 to SI-4119, Smithsonian Archives; Roosevelt 1991a). The structure and layout of the early villages and mounds have not yet been studied
for community organization and regional integration, but the sharing of artis-
tic styles and subsistence patterns over wide areas suggests the existence of
interregional affiliations.

Chiefdom Societies

By about 2,000 years ago, new cultural and demographic configurations co-
alesced, and they transformed the lifeways of people in much of the Greater

Amazonian floodplain and certain parts of the uplands by the time of the arrival of Europeans in the sixteenth and seventeenth centuries (Athens 1989; Brochado 1980; Erickson 1980; Porras 1987; Roosevelt 1980, 1987, 1993, n.d.; Spencer and Redman 1991). These later peoples made elaborately painted, modeled, and incised pottery, figurines, and large effigies of people—sometimes predominantly female. The images portray personages wearing ornaments and decorated clothing, sitting on stools, and sometimes playing musical instruments. In this period the dead were often buried in large cemeteries, commonly as secondary interments encased in large, decorated urns.

This occupation of the region seems to have been denser and more permanent than earlier ones, to judge from the many large, deep black-soil middens, numerous traces of houses and hearths, abundant artifacts, and in some areas, extensive monumental earthworks. Bioarchaeological studies and ethnohistorical reports indicate a widespread shift to economies of native seed crops and intensive small-species fishing at this time, and by about 1,000 years ago maize had become a staple in several areas in both floodplains and uplands (Bush et al. 1989; Roosevelt 1980, 1989, 1990b, 1991a; Roosevelt et al. n.d.). Based on their large populations, public works, differentiated settlements, elaborate ceremonial art, long-distance trade, and elitist symbolism, these societies are often judged to have been complex chiefdoms. Indeed, European observers in these areas in the sixteenth and early seventeenth centuries described paramount chieftaincies with large domains, organized, large-scale warfare and diplomacy, elite ranking based on descent from deified human ancestors sometimes identified as female, and far-flung interregional trade and tribute systems (Bettendorf 1910; Carvajal 1934; de Heriarte 1934; Nimuendaju 1949; Roosevelt 1980, 1987; Whitehead 1988).

The Prehistoric Population

The human population of the basin during prehistoric times is now known to have been sizable (Denevan 1976; Porro, this volume; Roosevelt 1980, 1989, 1990b, 1991a; Whitehead 1988). Rather than being universally sparse, shifting, and dispersed on the land, as is often the case today, populations in several areas grew rapidly during the late prehistoric period and settled in extensive villages and towns that in some cases are larger than those of some early Old World civilizations (such as the Minoan and Harappan civilizations, for example). Further, geographers and archaeologists have shown that parts of the landscape in the Amazon floodplains and the rich-soil interfluves are covered with the middens and abandoned earthworks of this occupation (Denevan 1966; Erickson 1980; Porras 1987; Smith 1980; Sternberg 1960).

Even some of the earlier prehistoric settlements appear to have been larger than those of the present indigenous occupation. The numerous early pottery-age shell mounds of the lower Amazon sometimes reach 10–20 meters in height and 5–20 hectares in area. They are so extensive, in fact, that they have been used as commercial lime mines, providing fertilizer and road-building material for more than 200 years (Roosevelt 1990b). The occupation sites of the late prehistoric complex societies are even larger. On Marajo Island at the mouth of the Amazon, there are several cases of 10–20 km^2 areas with clusters of from 20 to 40 artificial mounds containing numerous cemeteries, superimposed earthen house foundations, adobe cooking facilities, and large garbage dumps (Roosevelt 1991a). In the Santarém area between Manaus and Belém, late prehistoric stratified midden sites of several meters' thickness stretch for miles above the floodplains (Hartt 1883, 1885; Nimuendaju 1949; Roosevelt 1990b; Smith 1879). At an upland site in the Ecuadorian Amazon, earthworks for ceremonies and habitations cluster in an area of more than 12 km^2 (Porras 1987), and complexes of densely packed agricultural earthworks, causeways, and large habitation mounds cover thousands of hectares in the Bolivian Amazon (Denevan 1966; Erickson 1980). The Bolivian earthworks are large enough to be clearly visible from aircraft, and the ancient causeways still serve as roadbeds. The late prehistoric archaeological midden sites themselves have been an important soil resource for commercial agriculture in the Brazilian Amazon since the inception of large-scale plantation agriculture in the mid nineteenth century (Smith 1879; Smith 1980; Sternberg 1960).

Implications for Amazonian Ethnology

The new findings from prehistory have unavoidable implications for our understanding of living Amazonian Indians. Although their lifeways have often been interpreted as ancient adaptations to tropical lowland environments, the archaeological sequence includes a much wider variety of social and ecological adaptations than is found among living Amazonians, and comparisons of prehistoric and ethnographic cultures and populations reveal some striking contrasts among them.

The lifeways of some peoples in late prehistoric times are significantly different from those of native Amazonians today, who characteristically rely on swidden horticulture and foraging, and live in small and shifting settlements with primarily perishable material culture. Very few groups still rely on the seed crops that were staple foods in many areas before the European conquest, and there are no longer any functioning chiefdom polities in Amazonia, although some groups maintain oral traditions of ranked organization. Seen in the context of the long trajectory of indigenous Amazonian cultures, the lifeways of present-day ethnographic village societies appear to be a cultural pattern that was to a large extent displaced from the floodplains and more fertile interfluves of Amazonia 2,000 years ago by more complex, populous, and sedentary groups. The village lifeway seems to have expanded in Amazonia again since the complex societies were disrupted by the European invasion. In some cases, the conquest's demographic disruptions appear to have led some people who earlier emphasized maize or manioc cultivation to place a greater emphasis on a hunting-and-gathering way of life (Roosevelt 1993a; this idea was first proposed by the archaeologist Donald Lathrap [1968]). Thus the present-day Indians' cultural and ecological patterns cannot be explained as simply adaptations to the environment. Their changing interactions with other societies must also be taken into account.

The Ethnohistorical Transition

Recent historical research on the impact of the European conquest provides ample evidence that convulsive changes wrought by contact and conquest transformed the lifeways of Indians in many areas, and it reveals something of the process of the development of some of the cultural and biological adaptations seen today (Moreira Neto 1988; Rodrigues de Oliveira 1988; Whitehead 1988). Historical studies in the floodplains show that the European conquest effected the transition from the ancient chiefdoms to indigenous village societies or peasant communities through a long process involving military defeat, decimation, forced migration, enslavement, miscegenation, and acculturation. These processes of transformation are examined by Porro, Whitehead, de Oliveira, and Nelly Arvelo-Jiménez and Horacio Biord in Part I of this book.

In response to the European invasion, the areas that held the majority of the massive late prehistoric occupations of Amazonia were rapidly emptied of Indians, who now persist in a mosaic with non-Indian communities, mostly at the margins of the basin. Although the traditional concept of the "ethnographic present" often leads anthropologists to depict Indians as living undisturbed in their ancestral territories, postconquest processes led to extensive dislocations. These processes are documented by many historical accounts and by rapid changes in the character of the archaeological record in the hinterlands of the basin, such as Wüst describes in Chapter 12. As de Oliveira shows in Chapter 5, few Indian groups have lived as majorities in their homelands since 1850, and Indians' access to resources and their security from outside interference have been seriously compromised as a result (Moreira Neto 1988; Schmink and Wood, eds. 1984). Physical anthropological comparisons between prehistoric and ethnohistorical-period skeletal remains suggest that a rapid deterioration in native health occurred in the floodplains after the conquest due to the adverse impact of geographic, political, economic, and ecological marginalization on the Indians' conditions of life (Alvim n.d.; Greene 1986; Roosevelt 1989, 1991a).

Despite the turmoil, many groups have managed to adjust to the changed conditions while at the same time retaining their traditional culture by retreating to isolated areas, avoiding permanent settlement, or collecting or making materials for exchange or sale to non-Indians. Although perhaps not as satisfactory to scholars from urban industrial nations as the image of the primeval Indian isolated in the forest, the Amazonian Indians' actual way of life is much more interesting when it is recognized as a complex indigenous adaptations to conquest and nationalization as well as to Amazonian environments. The fact that many groups have managed to survive and develop new patterns of culture and behavior is a testament to their creativity and resilience in the face of great difficulties. Further, their adaptation to change is a continuing process, as is shown in Parts III and V in the chapters by Nancy Flowers, Darrel Posey, and Jean Jackson.

It is clear that the destabilization of native polities during the conquest and the deculturation and decimation that occurred during missionization greatly changed native cultures and population patterns. Some new complex societies, described by Whitehead in Chapter 2, arose in response to trading and military opportunities engendered by the conquest. The conquest also limited some groups' access to resources by sequestering Indians in marginal territories or confining them to subordinate socioeconomic and political classes. In addition, the widespread coercive employment of Indians on plantations and in extractive industries in the nineteenth century caused substantial changes in subsistence, demography, disease levels, social organization, and gender relations, and concomitantly in the characteristics of households and dwellings. This process was hypothesized in early analyses (e.g., Steward and Murphy 1956), but concrete information about what the specific changes were in particular cases is being revealed only through actual research on the periods involved.

Amazonian Indians apparently responded to different contact situations in a wide variety of ways. In areas of commercial forest extraction, some groups began to de-emphasize agriculture and abandoned the traditional communal households for nuclear family households. In the floodplains of the Bolivian Amazon and the middle Orinoco in Venezuela, where before the conquest there had been sedentary agricultural chiefdoms that relied on maize, Europeans soon established ranches, and those who chose to maintain indigenous lifeways were reduced to marginal, nomadic hunting and gathering and/or forced labor as porters or ranch hands. Others in those areas became Christianized and acculturated to European ways, and joined people of European origin in the peasant rancher population. In the Peruvian and Ecuadorian Amazon, where maize had also been an important staple in late prehistoric times, many Indians have now turned to manioc-based subsistence in the face of population loss and the entry of a cash economy. Some Ucayali Basin Indians, like the Shipibo, eat manioc, bananas, or plantains species but produce maize and introduced seed crops, such as rice, for sale in the nearby urban centers.

In the lower Amazon floodplains, the period of missionization had created a new ethnic group by the eighteenth century: the Tapuyas, or generic Indians. Indian cultures per se were almost completely eliminated there by 1850, and plantations and cattle ranches were established by European settlers with the help of the forced labor of a culturally and biologically mixed population. In the Guianas, Indians were displaced from the coastal plains, and the European settlers established large commercial plantations of rice and other crops there.

Nevertheless, traditional ethnographies customarily explain the present configurations and adaptations of Amazonian Indians without reference to the many marked changes that have taken place in indigenous lifeways and their political, economic, and social context in the last 500 years. Although anthropologists customarily record changes in Amazonian Indians' social and political organization, economy, and demography, the ethnographic patterns are still tacitly assumed to be generally representative of preconquest times, and evidence of the impact of conquest on Indian lifeways is not usually taken into consideration in explaining present patterns. In order to gain a clearer understanding of the reasons for the patterns of native lifeways in specific regions today, it is important to evaluate the specific impact of the European conquest. Here lies the strategic importance of the ethnohistoric period for future research in the region: it documents the process of transition from prehistory to ethnology. By studying the historical and ethnographic periods in an interdisciplinary manner and by subjecting them to archaeological research, we can gain valid comparative information to use in clarifying the nature of the transition.

Cultural and Biological Evolution in Amazonia

The complex changes in native lifeways revealed by the prehistoric and historical records raise questions about the nature of causality in long-term

cultural and biological change in Amazonia. The historical relationships of
social and political forms to each other and to subsistence systems and craft
economies in Amazonian environments need to be investigated to gain
knowledge of their causal interaction through time. We need to explore the
history of exploitive technology and economic policies in relation to demography and the latter's relationship, in turn, to changing patterns of diet and
health. The total cultural developmental sequence of Amazonia can be a
rich source of information about the evolutionary relationship of organizational, technological, and demographic change to people's access to resources and overall quality of life.

To learn about the impact of changes in economy, organization, and ideology on people's health, ethnographic research must integrate a broad range
of bioanthropological studies and make them analytically contiguous with
the data from prehistory. For this purpose it is important to augment standard
medical anthropological methods with those that can effect meaningful comparisons of living populations with archaeological populations. For example,
to understand better the significance of prehistoric human osteological patterns and thus the state of human health over the long term, the bone pathology of living people of known diet, health, and physiological status needs to
be recorded. In addition, to understand the regional interaction and migrations of Amazonian Indian populations, we need to know how people compare with one another genetically over time and space and how such patterning is related to other factors, such as ecological adaptation, migration,
propinquity, war and alliance, and language. Genetic traits such as dental
morphology, which are easily observable for both living and skeletal populations, need to be studied to uncover the nature of biological change through
time. If collected and analyzed at a regional level, such data can provide
important evidence about the movements and geographic origins of both
living and extinct populations. Anthropologists have speculated freely about
prehistoric and historical migrations on the basis of cultural and linguistic
distributions (Lathrap 1970; Meggers and Evans 1983), but their ideas have
never been tested with prehistoric human biological information even
though current linguistic and cultural patterning fails to predict living populations' genetic patterning (Black et al. 1983). The integration of physical
anthropological information from the prehistoric, ethnohistorical, and
ethnographic populations has never been attempted in Amazonia, although
the results would be very significant theoretically. Many methods are available to gain comparative longitudinal information so that the ecological
adaptation of living and prehistoric people can be systematically compared.
The most important first step in such research is for anthropologists in the

different specialities to communicate with one another about their interests and findings.

Small-scale preliminary research has already had important results, some of which are presented and discussed in Part II of this book. As mentioned earlier, comparisons of the osteological traits of living and prehistoric Amazonians suggest appreciable genetic continuity within the basin and a lack of substantial prehistoric intrusions into the gene pool from the Andes, contrary to some migration hypotheses (Greene 1986; Roosevelt 1991a). Also as mentioned above, biological remains have already produced evidence of profound changes in subsistence adaptation during prehistoric and historical times (Roosevelt 1980, 1989, 1990c; van der Merwe et al. 1981). Most modern Amazonian Indians are swidden horticulturalists, getting their calories from the cultivation of starchy crops such as manioc or plantains and their protein from fish and game, as described by Dufour and Beckerman in Chapters 7 and 8 of this book. In contrast, as explained above, for the millennium before the conquest, most prehistoric Amazonian groups studied so far subsisted on various seed crops supplemented with fish, game, and gathered plants. Much of their dietary protein, as indicated by studies of their bone collagen, came from plants, with a much smaller proportion coming from fauna, in contrast to living Indians. Earlier prehistoric peoples, such as the early foragers and early pottery-age people, got the majority of their protein from fauna, like today's Indians. Appropriate to their greater population densities, the late prehistoric Indians' diet was at a lower trophic level than that of both earlier and later Indians, who lived much less densely on the land. Thus the changes in native demography that occurred both before and after conquest seem to coordinate temporally with changes in ecological adaptation, though the causal relationships are not unidirectional. Both population growth and political change preceded the rise of maize cultivation, which in turn fostered population concentration. After conquest, the decimation and dislocation of tribes is associated with the emphasis on manioc as a staple.

Over and above the possible mutual causal effects of changing subsistence, demography, and social organization, we need to consider the impact of changing ecological adaptation and social and political organization on the quality of native people's lives. There is evidence that some living Amazonians' low socioeconomic and political status has adversely affected their health and nutrition compared to that of preconquest people. In addition, behavioral gender dichotomies characteristic of some present-day Amazonian Indian groups (see, e.g., Da Matta 1982; Kelekna 1981 and this vol.) seem to be associated with the poorer physiological status of women and children relative to men. In Chapter 10, Kelekna characterizes the gender dichotomies of the Achuar and discusses the possible causes of such cultural patterns, among them warfare. In turn, a gender and age bias in socioeconomic organization may be very important in shaping overall health and demographic patterns in a population because most individuals may end up experiencing chronic poor physiological status, which is a general condition for children and their mothers.

Anthropologists often describe Amazonian Indians as healthy and well-nourished, but the health status of Indian groups is commonly inferred from visual assessments of adult men's health, which is usually comparatively favorable because of their preferential access to resources and greater tolerance for nutritional inadequacies than is the case with young children and pregnant or lactating women. However, as Hern and Dufour show in Chapters 6 and 7, the average stature of Amazonians today tends to be relatively low (160 cm or less for men), the physiological status of children is often poor, and many children manifest depressed growth curves. The pattern of low stature and flat growth curves among Amazonian Indians is commonly assumed to be a genetic adaptation to the exigencies of millennia of life in the tropical forest (Roosevelt 1991b). However, these patterns are also common among Brazilian mixed-race rural and urban underclasses living in the Amazon and elsewhere. In these groups, the anthropometric patterns have an obvious relationship to poor socioeconomic status and consequent poor access to resources, health-care, and education, because genetic hybrid vigor due to miscegenation would be expected to have increased people's stature. Thus, comparable aspects of Amazonian Indians' development and physique may well be physiological adaptations to their present ecological and economic marginality rather than genetically determined adaptations to their environment. Support for this interpretation lies in the fact that most measurable individuals in prehistoric skeletal populations are of relatively high stature, with an average height of 172 cm for males, similar to the present-day U.S. average and that of the Brazilian landowning, educated class. Although we do not yet have data on the osteological pathology rates of living Amazonians, the pathology rates of the tall prehistoric individuals are significantly less than those found in the skeletons of short-statured nineteenth-century Indians (Greene 1986; Roosevelt 1991a), a contrast that suggests a postconquest deterioration in the Indians' conditions of life. Some living Amazonians (Flowers, this vol.), however, have average stature more in line with prehistoric Indians, apparently because they have avoided the direct impacts of contact more effectively than other groups. The Xavante discussed by Flowers in Chapter 11 seem to be such a group.

To help understand the causality of such ecological and physical patterns in Amazonian Indian populations, research strategies will need to produce comparable biological information for ancient, historical, and modern populations in Amazonia. In the past, important changes in human biology have gone unrecognized because of a lack of problem-oriented collaboration among the subfields of Amazonian anthropology.

Ideology and Social Organization

Academic barriers within anthropology especially hinder any attempt to explain the patterns of ideology and organization in indigenous societies in Amazonia, a topic explored by Descola in Chapter 9, Kelekna in Chapter 10, and Brown in Chapter 13. Social structures, symbols, concepts, and people's interactions have traditionally been described and interpreted without reference to their historical and ecological contexts, with the result that explanations have tended to be either circular or superficial. Similarly, in the study of social organization and ideology, native explanations of concepts and organization have often been accepted at face value rather than being analyzed empirically, and the opinions of a few individuals, often acculturated males no longer living in the society, have been presented as the norms of the group (as in Reichel-Dolmatoff 1971). Traditional social organization and ideology have usually been interpreted functionally as benign and integrative, and as appropriate, traditional adaptations to the environment and the exigencies of group life. Their unfavorable effects on some people's liberty and health status go unrecognized because specialists in medical anthropology seldom compare their data with that of scholars of social organization.

We need to become more aware of the differential participation of different groups in societal norms and the relationship of social ideology to social practice and access to resources. Amazonian social anthropologists have suggested some of the ways in which these factors interact but have not done systematic research to test the suggestions. Although many researchers have taken the role of participant observer, they have usually focused on the dominant group's point of view and have not sufficiently investigated the attitudes and situation of subdominant groups in native societies. As Kelekna shows in Chapter 10 (and in Kelekna 1981), women's experiences in Amazonian societies can be quite different from men's and ought to be considered for a fuller picture of social interaction. More active participation of Indians themselves in research would also be expected to enrich our hypotheses and lead to new directions for investigation, as exemplified in Darrell Posey's essay in this volume, as well as in Dorothea and Norman Whitten's studies (Whitten 1976; Whitten and Whitten 1988). Also, the common anthropological synchronic,

structural-functional explanatory approach, which lies behind many informative ethnographies, does not deal satisfactorily with evidence that social
organization and ideology changed during the prehistoric-ethnographic transition (Roosevelt 1987, 1989, 1991a: 403–20). Prehistoric Amazonian cosmology has been interpreted primarily with reference to the precepts of current Amazonian cosmology (Roe 1982; Roosevelt 1991a) despite the fact
that some prehistoric ritual and symbolic complexes are sometimes quite
different from those of living Amazonians in scale, content, organization,
and the participation of different social and political groups. Especially striking are changes through time in the representation of animals, men, and
women, suggesting that there have been important changes in attitudes toward culture, nature, and gender that correlate closely with changes through
time in the nature of the economy, political integration, and social organization in Amazonia and cannot be understood without reference to these factors. Therefore, cosmology, ritual, and symbolism in Amazonian groups need
to be evaluated systematically in the context of cultural change in the long
term. In Chapter 13, Brown makes a convincing case that millenarian religious movements have their origins in preconquest native political concepts
of paramount chiefship, an institution that has disappeared since the conquest
due to suppression of independent native military and political movements.
Visual archaeological parallels to the sun-centered chief-shaman symbolic
complex that Brown defines ethnographically can be found in the sun-ray
headdresses of the large terra cotta statues of rattle-shaking men from the late
prehistoric Santarém culture (Palmatary 1960). Of special interest for understanding the changing interaction of art and politics is the process of adaptation of traditional symbol systems to indigenist political movements, a subject that Jean Jackson explores in Chapter 17.

    Another important question for future research concerns the relationship
of native religion and ideology to material culture and the economy and
organization of societies. Of special interest for explanatory purposes is the
particular ecological, social, and political content of cosmologies (C. Hugh-
Jones 1979; S. Hugh-Jones 1979). Amazonian Indians seem to synthesize
cosmology both from both social ideology and their expert knowledge of the
natural environment. Anthropologists tend to specialize either in ideologi-
cal/social studies or in ecological/economic studies, but valid interpretation
of the cosmological systems seems to require a knowledge of both. Also,
although anthropologists have made the patterning of mental symbols a research priority, following the influence of Claude Lévi-Strauss, the changing
nature of systems of *visual* symbols and of material culture through time and
space needs to be studied as a key aspect of the interaction of ideology and

ritual with social organization and political economy. Including the visual material aspects seems logical, considering the fact that Amazonians do not seem to value idea symbols any more than visual ones, and it gives us the advantage of being able to compare symbols over the archaeological-historical-ethnographic continuum.

Language

In the future, linguistic studies in particular can play a much larger role in comprehensive explanations of Amazonian lifeways, the topic covered in Part IV of this book. As Klein describes in Chapter 15, the traditional explanatory function of linguistic studies of Amazonia has been as distributional evidence for ancient migrations and diffusion. The linguistic diffusionists have argued that specific styles of archaeological art, such as Barrancoid or Saladoid, can be directly associated with the language families found in the vicinity of the styles today, but from the same archaeological and linguistic patterns the different scholars have come up with diametrically opposed hypotheses (Lathrap 1970; Meggers 1975). These contradictory diffusionary explanations for the geographic patterning of languages in Amazonia need to be reevaluated in the face of abundant ethnohistorical evidence for extensive postconquest population movements that suggests that the distribution of languages today may be very different from the distribution before the European conquest and thus is not secure evidence for prehistoric patterns. Further, studies of the associations among language, culture, and migration in Amazonia suggest that language family and specific patterns of material culture are not tied to one another over the long term (e.g., Black et al. 1979). Even the long-assumed historical linguistics theory that language families begin as unitary phenomena and then develop through diversification needs to be reconsidered. As with other aspects of culture, it seems likely that there may have been as great a linguistic diversity long ago as there is today. In any case, the possibilities need to be tested to the extent that we can. Early research on language distributions suffered from inadequate empirical evidence. The existing records of ancient Amazonian languages in conquest-period archives of missionaries and colonial administrators need to be studied for concrete evidence of past distributions, and the processes of both diversification and convergence in languages need to be re-examined in regions that have series of written or taped records.

Going beyond the question of language and migration to historical ecology, Balée and Moore show the value of linguistic analysis for reconstructions of the history of plant cultivation and landscape management. Another fruitful direction would be to analyze the relationship of language to a range of social and political interactions and to develop lexical evidence of past patterns of organization. Further, there should be an important role for linguistics in the enrichment of studies of art and ritual. The ancient art of Amazonia reveals the existence in visual symbolism of some of the rhetorical devices and elements that occur in Amazonian languages today and also others that are absent from present languages (Roosevelt 1991a). Coordinated longitudinal studies of visual and verbal symbols in relation to social, ecological, and ritual systems since the conquest could furnish significant evidence of the participation of symbols in these systems. Through the collaboration of linguists with other anthropologists, significant areas for comparative research can be identified.

Research Methods and Data Collection

Overall, Amazonian studies would benefit from more examination of epistemology: the question of how we know things. On the one hand, some of us tend to test theory through logical analyses instead of relating it critically to empirical evidence. Others who are more interested in particular regional data, on the other hand, tend to ignore the theoretical significance of their subject. The majority have tended to specialize theoretically, methodologically, and geographically and do not take advantage of the interpretive value of a high-quality, comprehensive knowledge of cross-regional and temporal variation. Up-to-date regional syntheses of data for explanatory purposes hardly exist, and much theorizing is carried out without considering what empirical knowledge exists. Even when evolutionary synthesis has been attempted, as in the *Handbook of South American Indians* (Steward, ed. 1946–50), a lack of awareness of data about systematic change through time in Amazonian cultures and lifeways has marred the interpretation of regional patterning.

Amazonia nonetheless possesses extraordinarily rich sources of information relevant to theoretical problems in many areas of study, and improvements in research technology are making some of the data accessible for the first time. Systematic study of such research data has the potential to clarify some of the major interpretive problems in Amazonian anthropology. The most valuable research resources are the numerous indigenous peoples that are still around to study. Another important resource is the archaeological record, composed of countless archaeological sites full of artifacts, structures, and biological and geological remains. Few areas of the world have both a rich archaeological record and such an extensive indigenous population. This rare combination of anthropological sources cries out for more comprehensive and critical ethnoarchaeological research.

To obtain a better explanation of the similarities and differences between living and prehistoric Amazonian Indians' lifeways, the evidence of archaeology needs to be compared systematically with evidence from ethnography through the methods of ethnoarchaeology. Ethnology has traditionally provided an important baseline of data for the interpretation of archaeology, but archaeology can also provide an important test for ethnographic interpretations, as discussed above. The material patterning produced by the activities of contemporary Amazonian Indian communities could provide comparative information for interpreting the remains of the ancient communities if we had more specific information about the material consequences of ethnographic lifeways and about the spatial patterns of archaeological sites. For example, if households are patrilocal rather than matrilocal, what are the patterns produced in the material record in the nature, use, and arrangement of facilities and the creation and disposition of material objects? As another example, we need to find out what is the body chemistry and bone pathology of people of known diet and activity patterns so that we can better interpret the archaeological patterns and their significance in relation to ethnographic patterns. Comprehensive ethnoarchaeological research in such areas will require the use of specialized methods such as random sample video, computerized record keeping and analysis, and electronic homing and mapping devices in order to keep track of the abundant data in both space and time. Comparative medical anthropological studies of living and prehistoric people will require the use of automated noninvasive measurement and analytical techniques, such as those developed for clinical studies of bone density, pathology, and tissue chemistry. Thus the reorientation of anthropological research toward interdisciplinary comparative studies will require the adoption of appropriate methods of data collection, storage, and analysis.

In addition to the information to be found in existing archaeological sites and living communities, more than two centuries of research have produced large collections of anthropological and historical material that is stored in museums and libraries. Preliminary study of the extensive biological collections has resulted in new information about environmental, genetic, and physiological changes during the long human occupation (Roosevelt 1989, 1991a, 1992a). Museums across the world also contain large collections of utilitarian and ritual paraphernalia with extensive documentation, collections that span the important ethnohistoric-ethnographic transition in Amazonian cultures. Through the study of such collections, the changing form and content of culture through time can inform us about the interrelationships

Figure 1.1. Indian groups in lowland South America.

1. Achagua	27. Karipuna	53. Siona-Secoya
2. Aché	28. Kayapó (Cayapó)	54. Solimões
3. Achuar	29. Krahô	55. Tapajó
4. Aguaruna	30. Locono (coastal)	56. Tarumã
5. Aisauri	31. Makú (Macú)	57. Tembé
6. Araweté	32. Makuna	58. Ticuna
7. Arua (Aruan)	33. Manao (Manoa)	59. Trio
8. Asháninka	34. Matses	60. Tukanoans (Tucanoans)
9. Asurini	35. Mayes	61. Tucunyapé
10. Baktiari	36. Mekranotí	62. Tupinambá
11. Baniwa	37. Mundurucú	63. Uanano
12. Bará	38. Mura	64. Waiãpi
13. Barí	39. Mura-Pirajã	65. Waimiri-Atroari
14. Bororo	40. Nambicuara	66. Waorani (Auca)
15. Carib	41. Omagua (downstream)	67. Wai-Wai
16. Cayapa	42. Omagua (upstream)	68. Wajana
17. Cocama	43. Palicur	69. Wapishana
18. Cocamilla	44. Parakanã	70. Warao
19. Colorado	45. Pemon	71. Xavante
20. Conduri	46. Piapocos	72. Xerente (Sherente)
21. Guajibo (Hiwi)	47. Piaroa	73. Yagua
22. Ka'apor	48. Pumé (Yaruro)	74. Yanomamo (Yanomama, Yanomami, Yanoama)
23. Kanela	49. Runa	
24. Kapon	50. San Carlos	75. Yao
25. Karajá (Caraja)	51. Sharanahua	76. Ye'kuana
26. Karíña	52. Shipibo	

TRINIDAD

VENEZUELA

GUYANA
SURINAM

FRENCH
GUIANA

COLOMBIA

SAN
FERNANDO
DE APURE

PARMANA

CIUDAD
BOLIVAR

MACAPÁ

MANAUS

SANTARÉM

BELÉM

ECUADOR

P E R U

B R A Z I L

C H I L E

BOLIVIA

PARAGUAY

A R G E N T I N A

URUGUAY

among ideology, ecological adaptation, and socioeconomic and political integration. Developing better-quality research based on all these irreplaceable human, cultural, and environmental resources can also help in the effort to preserve them by showing their value as information.

Few Amazonian scholars have recognized either the broad range of empirical evidence available for study or its interpretive significance. Much research is still carried out without considering basic cross-regional and historical information about indigenous Amazonia. Many fields of research in the area have made crucial discoveries and obtained important insights that could have a significant impact on the conclusions of other subfields, but these have not been incorporated into the other fields because of a lack of communication, comprehension, and study by scholars of the substance of each other's research. We act as if other fields are incomprehensible, but clearly they need not be. In the same way that professors explain their fields to students, researchers can make their work intelligible to colleagues in other fields. The current narrow subfield specialization is related more to the sociology of scholarship than to the epistemological needs of research. People seem to oppose other approaches and specialties as a form of professional competition, and disciplinary boundaries that are mere conveniences for organizing professional training are touted as inherent in the data. There is resistance to the integration of theory and data between subfields as inappropriate or threatening, and members of different paradigms express opposition to each other's work. In various ways, then, the professional organization of Amazonian research has been hindering the investigation of crucial theoretical problems of the area. One of the roles of the Wenner-Gren Foundation for Anthropological Research has been the solution of research problems through scholarly exchange and debate. Accordingly, Lita Osmundsen and Sydel Silverman encouraged me to organize an international conference to consider Amazonian anthropology from an integrated point of view, and this book is the product of that conference.

Toward a New Synthesis

The Wenner-Gren International Conference "Amazonian Synthesis" brought together some of the innovative scholars who are at the forward edge of the movement to reinterpret and document the anthropology of Amazonia. The purpose of the conference was to discuss a research strategy for Amazonia that would integrate the four fields of anthropology in the study of native Amazonian peoples and cultures. In the favorable setting provided by Wenner-Gren at Rosas dos Ventos, near Petropolis, Brazil, the conferees summarized theoretically significant information and outlined new research approaches.

By developing empirical and theoretical links that relate findings in various fields to the conclusions of others, the papers that resulted from the Amazonian conference can help stimulate needed interdisciplinary interchange in the future. Collaboration and discussion among different kinds of specialists encouraged them to take into consideration the results of each other's work and to discuss how to develop better-quality and more comparable information. As I have outlined in the Preface, the presentations of the conferees highlighted some of the exciting possibilities that such a strategy could open up in the search for a better understanding of the nature and history of the indigenous occupation of Amazonia. The 17 essays in this book mark a first effort at tracing that trajectory up to the present (fig. 1.1). Without a clearer understanding of the dynamic relationship of Amazonian peoples with their habitats and with their neighbors, we have little hope of aiding their survival into the future.

REFERENCES

Allen, W. L.
1968   A ceramic sequence from the Alto Pachitea, Peru: Some implications for the development of tropical forest culture in South America. Ph.D. diss., University of Illinois.
Athens, J. S.
1989   Pumpuentsa and the Pastaza phase in southeastern Ecuador. *Nawpa Pacha* 24:1–19.
Barse, W.
1990   Preceramic occupations in the Orinoco River Valley. *Science* 250:1388–90.
Betendorf, João Felipe
1910   Chronica de missao dos Padres da Companhia de Jesus no Estado de
[1698]   Maranhao, *Revista do Instituto Histórico e Geográfico Brasileiro* (Rio de Janeiro) 72 (1): 1–697.
Black, F. L., F. M. Salzano, L. L. Berman, Y. Gabbay, T. A. Weimer, M.H.L.P. Franco, and J. P. Panday
1983   Failure of linguistic relationships to predict genetic distances between the Waiapi and other tribes in lower Amazonia. *American Journal of Physical Anthropology* 60: 327–35.
Boomert, A.
1980   The Sipaliwini archaeological complex of Surinam: A summary. *Nieuw West-Indische Gids* 54 (2): 94–107.

1983   The Saladoid occupation of Wonotobo Falls, Western Surinam. *Proceedings of the Ninth International Congress of the Study of the Pre-Columbian Cultures of the Lesser Antilles*, 97–120. Montreal.

Brochado, J.
1980   The social ecology of the Marajoara culture. M.A. thesis, Department of Anthropology, University of Illinois, Urbana.

Bryan, A. L.
1983   South America. In *Early man in the New World*, edited by R. Shutler, 137–46. Beverly Hills: Sage Publications.

Bush, M. B, D. R. Piperno, and C. Colinvaux
1989   A 6,000 year history of Amazonian maize cultivation. *Nature* 340: 303–5.

Campbell, K. E., and C. D. Frailey
1984   Holocene flooding and species diversity in southwestern Amazonia. *Quaternary Research* 21:369–75.

Campbell, K. E, C. D. Frailey, and J. Arellano L.
1985   The geology of the Rio Beni: Further evidence for Holocene flooding in Amazonia. *Contributions in Science* 364, 1–18. Los Angeles: Natural History Museum of Los Angeles County.

Carvajal, Gaspar de
1934   *The discovery of the Amazon according to the account of Friar Gaspar de Carvajal and other documents*. New York: American Geographical Society.

Colinvaux, P., K.-B. Liu, M. Steinitz-Kannan, M. B. Bush, M. C. Miller, and D. R. Piperno
1990   Climatic and vegetational change in Late Pleistocene and Early Holocene Amazonia. Paper presented at conference, Amazonia: A dynamic habitat; Past, present, and future, organized by A. C. Roosevelt, at Washington, D.C., American Association for the Advancement of Science.

Cruxent, J. M., and I. Rouse
1958–59   *An archaeological chronology of Venezuela*. 2 vols. Pan American Union Social Science Monographs, No. 6. Washington, D.C.: Pan American Union.

Da Matta, R.
1982   *A divided world: Apinaye social structure*. Cambridge, Mass.: Harvard University Press.

Denevan, W.
1966   *An aboriginal cultural geography of the Llanos de Mojos of Bolivia*. Ibero-Americana No. 48. Berkeley: University of California Press.
1976   The aboriginal population of Amazonia. In *The native population of the Americas in 1492*, edited by W. Denevan, 205–34. Madison: University of Wisconsin Press.

Erickson, C.
1980   Sistemas agricolas prehispanicos en los Llanos de Mojos. *America Indigena* 40:731–55.
Evans, C., and B. J. Meggers
1960   Archaeological investigations in British Guiana. *Bulletin of the Bureau of American Ethnology* 177. Washington, D.C.: Smithsonian Institution.
1968   Archaeological investigations on the Río Napo. *Smithsonian Contributions to Anthropology* No. 6.
Franzinelli, E., and E. Latrubesse
1992   *Geologia quaternario de Amazonia: Conferencia international; Resumos.* Manaus: Universidade Federal de Amazonas.
Greene, D.
1986   Assessment of the state of preservation of human skeletal remains from Marajo Island, Para, and potential for Marajoara cemetery excavation. Unpublished report submitted to the National Science Foundation.
Hames, R., and W. Vickers, editors
1983   *Adaptive responses of native Amazonians.* New York: Academic Press.
Hartt, C. F.
1871   Brazilian rock inscriptions. *American Naturalist* 5 (3): 139–47.
1883   Contributions to the ethnology of the River of the Amazons. Manuscript, Archives, Peabody Museum, Harvard University.
1885   Contribucoes para a ethnologia do valle do Amazonas. *Archivos do Museu Nacional* 6:1–174. Rio de Janeiro.
Hilbert, P. P.
1955   *A ceramica arqueologica da regiao de Orixim.* Instituto de Antropologia e Ethnologia do Para, Publication No. 1. Belém: Museu Paraense Emilio Goeldi.
1959   *Achados arqueologicos num sambaqui do Baixo Amazonas.* Instituto de Antropologia e Etnologia do Para, Publication No. 10. Belém: Museu Paraense Emilio Goeldi.
Jennings, J. D.
1964   *Prehistoric man in the New World.* Chicago: University of Chicago Press.
Junk, W. J.
1970   Investigations on the ecology and production-biology of the "floating meadows" (*Paspalo-Echinochloetum*) on the middle Amazon. *Amazoniana* 2:449–95.
1973   Investigations on the ecology and production biology of the "floating meadows" (*Paspalo-Echinocloetum*) on the middle Amazon. *Amazoniana* 4:9–102.
Kelekna, P.
1981   *Sex assymetry in Jivaroan Achuara society: A cultural mechanism promoting belligerence.* Ph.D. diss., Department of Anthropology, University of New Mexico, Albuquerque.

Lathrap, D.
1968   The "hunting" economies of the tropical forest zone of South America:
            An attempt at historical perspective. In *Man the hunter,* edited by R. B.
            Lee and I. Devore, 23–29. Chicago: Aldine.
1970   *The upper Amazon.* New York: Praeger.
Lopes Frois, D., and M. Imazio da Silveira
n.d.   Caverna da Gaviao. Manuscript submitted for publication.
Magalis, J. H.
1975   A seriation of some Marajoara painted anthropomorphic urns. Ph.D.
            diss., Department of Anthropology, University of Illinois, Urbana-
            Champaign.
Maybury-Lewis, D., editor
1979   *Dialectical societies.* Cambridge, Mass.: Harvard University Press.
Meggers, B. J.
1971   *Amazonia: Man and nature in a counterfeit paradise.* Chicago: Aldine.
1975   Application of the biological model of diversification to cultural distribu-
            tions in tropical lowland South America. *Biotropia* 7:483–96.
1977   Vegetational fluctuation and prehistoric cultural adaptation in
            Amazonia: Some tentative correlations. *World Archaeology* 8 (3): 287–
            303.
1985   Aboriginal cultural adaptation to Amazonia. In *Key environments:
            Amazonia,* edited by G. T. Prance and T. E. Lovejoy, 307–27. Oxford:
            Pergamon Press.
Meggers, B. J., and C. Evans
1957   Archaeological investigations at the mouth of the Amazon. *Bulletin of
            the Bureau of American Ethnology* 167. Washington, D.C.: Smithsonian
            Institution.
1983   Lowland South America and the Antilles. In *Ancient South Americans,*
            edited by J. E. Jennings, 286–335. San Francisco: W. H. Freeman.
Miller, E. T.
1987   Pesquisas arqueologicas paleoindigenas no Brasil Ocidental. In *Investi-
            gaciones paleoindias al sur de la linea ecuatorial,* edited by L. Nunez and
            B. J. Meggers, 37–61. Estudios Atacamenos No. 8. San Pedro de
            Atacama, Chile: Instituto de Investigaciones Arqueologicas, Univer-
            sidad del Norte.
Moreira Neto, C. de Araujo
1988   *Indios de Amazonia, De maioria a minoria (1750–1850).* Petropolis,
            Brazil: Editora Vozes.
Murphy, R., and J. Steward
1956   Tappers and trappers: Parallel processes in acculturation. *Economic
            Development and Culture Change* 4:335–55.
Nimuendaju, C. U.
1949   Os Tapajo. *Boletim do Museu Paraense Emilio Goeldi* 10:93–106.

Oliveira, A. G. de

1988   Amazonia: Modificacioes sociais e culturais decorrentes do processo de ocupacao humana (sec. XVII ao XX). *Boletim do Museu Paraense Emilio Goeldi, Serie Antropologica* 41 (1): 65–116.

Porras, P.

1987   *Investigaciones arqueologicas a las faldas de Sangay, Provincia Morona Santiago, Tradición Upano.* Quito: Artes Gráficas Senal, Impresenal Cia.

Porro, A.

1981   Os Omagua del alto Amazonas: Demografia e padroes de povoamento no saeculo XVII. In *Contribuicoes a antropologia em homenagem ao Professor Egon Schaden,* 207–31. Museu Paulista Serie Ensaios No. 4 São Paulo: Universidade de São Paulo.

1983–84   Os Solimões ou Jurimaguas: Territorio, migraciones e comercio intertribal. *Revista do Museu Paulista* 29:23–38.

1987   O antigo comercio indigena na Amazonia. *D. O. Leitura* 5:56.

Projeto Radambrasil

1976   *Mapa geologico.* Folha SA.21. Levantamento de Recursos Naturais, vol. 10. Departamento de Producão Mineral, Brasil.

Roe, P.

1982   *The cosmic zygote: Cosmology in the Amazon Basin.* New Brunswick, N.J.: Rutgers University Press.

Reichel-Dolmatoff, G.

1971   *Amazonian cosmos: The sexual and religious symbolism of the Tukano Indians.* Chicago: University of Chicago Press.

Roosevelt, A. C.

1978   La Gruta: An early tropical forest community of the middle Orinoco. In *Ensayos antropologicos en homenaje a José M. Cruxent,* edited by E. Wagner and A. Zucchi, 173–201. Caracas: Centro de Estudios Avancados/Instituto Venezolano de Investigaciones Cientificas.

1980   *Parmana: Prehistoric maize and manioc subsistence along the Amazon and Orinoco.* New York: Academic Press.

1987   Chiefdoms in the Amazon and Orinoco. In *Chiefdoms in the Americas,* edited by R. Drennan and C. Uribe, 153–85. Lanham, Md.: University Press of America.

1989   Natural resource management in Amazonia before the conquest: Beyond ethnographic projection. In *Natural resource management by folk and indigenous societies in Amazonia,* edited by D. Posey and W. Balée, 30–62. Advances in Economic Botany No. 7. New York: New York Botanical Garden.

1990a   The historical perspective on resource use in Latin America. In *Economic catalysts to ecological change: Working papers in tropical conservation and development,* 30–64. Gainesville: University of Florida, Center for Latin American Studies.

1990b   The developmental sequence at Santarém on the lower Amazon, Brazil.
           Report to the National Endowment for the Humanities.
1991a   *Moundbuilders of the Amazon: Geophysical archaeology on Marajo Island,
           Brazil.* Studies in Archaeology. New York: Academic Press.
1991b   Determinismo ecologico na interpretacão do desenvolvimento social
           indígena da Amazonia. In *Origens, adaptacões, e diversidade biológica do
           homen nativo da Amazonia,* edited by W. Neves, 103–41. Belém: Museu
           Paraense Emílio Goeldi.
1992a   Arqueologia Amazonica. In *Historia dos Indios no Brazil,* edited by
           Manuela Carneiro da Cunha, 53–86. São Paulo: Companhia das Letras/
           Secretaria Municipal de Cultura.
1992b   Secrets of the forest: An archaeologist looks at the past—and future—of
           Amazonia. *The Sciences* 32 (6): 22–28. New York: New York Academy
           of Sciences.
1993a   Ancient and modern hunter-gatherers in Lowland South America: An
           evolutionary problem. *Program and abstracts of the annual meeting of the
           American Association for the Advancement of Science.* Boston.
1993b   The rise and fall of the Amazon chiefdoms. *L'Homme* 126–28, 33 (2–4):
           255–83.
n.d.   *The excavations at Corozal: Stratigraphy and ceramic seriation.* Yale Univer-
           sity Publications in Anthropology No. 82. In press.
Roosevelt, A. C., M. Imazio, S. Maranca, and R. Johnson
1991   Eighth millennium pottery from a shell midden in the Brazilian
           Amazon. *Science* 254:1621–24.
Roosevelt, A. C., C. Lopes Machado, M. Imazio, and M. Lima Costa
n.d.   Late Pleistocene cave dwellers in the Amazon twelve thousand years
           ago. Manuscript. In preparation for *Science.*
Schmink, M., and C. H. Woods, editors
1984   *Frontier expansion in Amazonia.* Gainesville: University of Florida
           Press.
Schmitz, I.
1987   Cacadores antigos no sudoeste de Goias. In *Investigaciones paleoindias al
           sur de la línea ecuatorial,* edited by L. Nunez and B. J. Meggers, 16–35.
           Estudios Atacamenos No. 8. San Pedro de Atacama, Chile: Universidad
           del Norte, Instituto de Investigaciones Arqueologicas.
1990   Prehistoric hunters and gatherers of Brazil. *Journal of World Prehistory*
           1:53–126.
Schmitz, I., A. Sales Barboso, and M. Barberi Ribeiro, editors
1978–80   *Annuario de divulgacao cientifica.* No. 5. Goiania, Brazil: Universidade
           Catolica de Goias.
1981–84   *Annuario de divigulcacao cientifica.* No. 10. Goiania, Brazil: Universidade
           Catolica de Goias.

Simoes, M.

1976 Nota sobre duas pontas-de-projetil da Bacia do Tapajo (Para). *Boletim do Museu Paraense Emilio Goeldi*, new ser., 62:1–14. Belém.

1981 Coletores-pescadores ceramistas do litoral do Salgado (Para): Nota preliminar. *Boletim do Museu Paraense Emilio Goeldi*, new ser., 78:1–26. Belém.

Simoes, M., D. F. Lopes, M. Imazio da Silveira, and M. P. Magalhaes

1985 Current Research: Brazil. *American Antiquity* 50:175.

Smith, H.

1879 *Brazil: The Amazons and the coast.* New York: Charles Scribner's Sons.

Smith, N.

1980 Anthrosols and human carrying capacity in Amazonia. *Annals of the Association of American Geographers* 70:553–66.

Spencer, C., and E. Redmond

1991 Investigating prehistoric chiefdoms in the Venezuelan Llanos. *World Archaeology* 24 (1): 134–57.

Sternberg, H. O'R.

1960 Radiocarbon dating as applied to a problem of Amazonian morphology. *Comptes rendus du XVIIIe Congrès International de Géographie*, 2:399–424. Rio de Janeiro: Universidade do Brasil, Centro de Pesquisas de Geografia do Brasil.

Steward, J., editor

1946–50 *Handbook of South American Indians.* Bureau of American Ethnology Bulletin 163. 6 volumes. Washington, D.C.: Smithsonian Institution.

van der Merwe, N., A. C. Roosevelt, and J. C. Vogel

1981 Isotopic evidence for prehistoric subsistence change at Parmana, Venezuela. *Nature* 292:536–38.

Vargas, I.

1981 *Investigaciones arqueologicas en Parmana: Los sitios de La Gruta y Ronquin, Estado Guarico, Venezuela.* Caracas: Biblioteca de la Academia Nacional de la Historia.

Whitehead, N. L.

1988 *Lords of the tiger spirit: The history of the Caribs in colonial Venezeula and Guyana, 1498–1820.* Dordrecht, Holland: Foris Publications.

Whitten, N. E., Jr.

1976 *Sacha Runa: Ethnicity and adaptation of Ecuadorian jungle Quichua.* Urbana: University of Illinois Press.

Whitten, D. S., and N. E. Whitten, Jr.

1988 *From myth to creation.* Urbana: University of Illinois Press.

PART I   FIRST TRANSFORMATIONS

2

The Ancient Amerindian Polities of the Amazon, the Orinoco, and the Atlantic Coast

A Preliminary Analysis of Their Passage from Antiquity to Extinction

NEIL LANCELOT WHITEHEAD

This chapter is concerned to establish a preliminary framework for understanding the historical change that Amazonian societies have undergone since the arrival of the Europeans and Africans. As will become evident, there has been a deep alteration in both the scale and complexity of those societies, such that modern Amerindian groups are an uncertain guide as to how Amazonian peoples may have lived in the past. Because the subject of general social change is so vast, it is approached here through a specific examination of the transformation of indigenous political and economic systems in the colonial and modern eras. However, since our understanding of the Amazonian past has also been impeded by inappropriate anthropological models of language use, ecology, and political economy, it is necessary to reconceptualize basic social and historical processes in this region, rather than just to add "new data" to "old theory" (see Whitehead 1993a). To this end, a critique of past approaches, as well as suggestions as to new directions that might be taken, is offered here.

The Uses of Linguistic Distribution and Ceramic Series

It is common in the anthropological literature on Amazonia and Orinoquia to find attempts to describe an archaic or historically obscure "society" which use linguistic attributes as virtually the only criterion for making sociological distinctions among groups. While it is certainly true that linguistic exclusiveness has become a paramount factor in the ethnic consciousness of Amerindian groups, this was not always the case, so the ordering of the historical and archaeological data on such a basis should be considered at best premature and at worst misleading despite some of the conceptual advantages that are evident in doing so (Renfrew 1987, 99–120). As Sorensen realized in his analysis of multilingualism in northwest Amazonia, "A linguistic theory limited to one language / one group situations is inadequate to explain . . . [the] actual linguistic competence of the people of the Northwest Amazon" (1972, 91), a point Colson strongly reiterated in regard to groups in northeast Amazonia (1983–84a, 11; 1983–84b).

For modern scholars, just as for the first Europeans, language has offered a source of apparently objective features through which the ethnicity of others can be defined and understood. However, the actual practice of Amerindian multilingualism suggests that it was only one among many factors, such as genealogical calculation and response to the European presence, that underlay observed ethnic affiliations (Whitehead 1992a). Given this lack of appreciation of the historical variation in language use, it is not surprising that prevailing linguistically based models of contemporary Amerindian society and culture are uncritically projected back into the past, as in Hemming 1978 and 1987. Obviously it should be our historical understanding of the last half-millennium of interaction between Europe and America that conditions our analysis of the modern ethnic groups, not the other way round.

In view of this, and in view of the formative stage at which the search for general principles of historical understanding still remains, attempts to reconstruct the history of particular ethnic or linguistic groups are rejected here in favor of analyzing a few critical relationships of special relevance to the synthesis across disciplines that the original symposium proposed; though, as I demonstrate elsewhere (1988), such an exercise in the history of an ethnic formation is appropriate for different purposes. Nevertheless, failure to perceive the past regional scale and supra-ethnic character of Amerindian social organization has undoubtedly impeded our understanding of its history (see Chap. 5, this vol., and Whitehead 1992a).

In the same way that it is thought that linguistic distribution might be used to map ethnic and political identities, it has also been argued (Lathrap 1970, 113–27) that the distribution of ceramic types can be related to the past migrations of linguistic communities. It seems unlikely that this procedure is really valid either, but this does not mean that the data on ceramic distribution are not useful; indeed, they provide prima facie evidence of zones of economic exchange and social interaction. The relation of language or ethnicity to preferred pottery types and styles and the way that pottery entered regional exchange systems are thus questions that need to be answered before further use can be made of this data for the purpose of cultural reconstruction (Arnold 1985, 1–3). Nonetheless, as Meggers and Evans (1957, 35) have shown in the case of the river Araguari (Amapá, Brazil), the limits of the distribution of a pottery type may sometimes coincide with a cultural boundary that is known from the historical record, as is also perhaps the case for the eastward extension of the Barrancoid series (Keymis 1596, 8). Accordingly, Amerindian social formations are discussed here as they are revealed in the historical sources, not simply as constructs derived from ceramic or linguistic distributions. Such distributions are certainly of initial value in codifying and classifying the data, but their utility as indicators of past ethnic boundaries relies on questionable assumptions about the role of linguistic competence and ceramic usage in ethnic ascription.

Ancient Amerindia

There is a profound contrast between ancient and modern Amerindia. This is most evident in the extent to which "societies" were formerly variable in their ethnic and linguistic composition, regional in their economic operation, and politically sophisticated to the extent that they might encompass tens of thousands of individuals. Such inferences are based on calculations of the aboriginal populations in the floodplain areas and the reported extent of the political allegiance of Amerindian kings, lords, and captains (for a sample analysis of the Orinoco data, see Whitehead 1988, 32–41, 61). Indeed, the general message of the early and unpublished documentation must be that the social and economic poverty of "Tropical Forest Society," especially away from the major floodplains, as annunciated by Meggers and Evans (1957, 17–32; see also Evans and Meggers 1960, 346–47; Meggers 1971, 120), is simply not attested to, and is derived mainly from their general distrust and ignorance of these early sources. Thus Meggers and Evans used inaccurate secondary sources to make a general assessment of the historical material relating to the mouth of the Amazon (1957, 556–89). This procedure led to serious errors of interpretation and an unwarranted generalization as to the poverty of the archival material, as in the citation of an extremely defective edition of Acuña's *Nuevo descubrimiento* to justify an extremely limited search of the historical records (Meggers and Evans 1957, 556). As far as more recent archaeological data is concerned, the work of Roosevelt (1980, 1991), for example, underlines the point that the historical evidence is far more accurate and extensive than Meggers and Evans's earlier work had allowed.

On systematic investigation, testimony from the early documents continually stresses the great abundance of both floral and faunal resources, as well as the intensity with which they could be exploited (Acuña 1859, 61, 67–73; Aguado 1951, 413; Carvajal 1934, 180, 209; Oviedo 1959, 397–98; Ralegh 1848, 51). Further evidence of this abundance, as well as the great productivity of Amerindian agricultural techniques, is clearly given by the chroniclers (Aguado 1951, 492–96; Carvajal 1934, 175, 192–93, 230, 232; Harcourt 1906, 378; Oviedo 1959, 392, 397; Simon 1861, 60–61) and sometimes can be directly quantified by studying the exchange of foodstuffs and trade goods between Amerindians and Europeans (Whitehead 1988, 151–70). As the Oyapock River colonist John Wilson (1906, 346–47) bluntly expressed it, "we lived very good [and] cheap."

The fact that some Amerindian economies were geared to producing such food surpluses in antiquity is also demonstrated by the existence of indigenous markets and exchange systems in fish meal and manioc flour, as well as the large-scale "ranching" of turtles and iguanas (Acuña 1859, 68; Carvajal 1934, 192, 207, 211; *Lettres* 1781, 8:360; Simon 1861, 97, 104). Moreover, the use of seed and tuber crops, other than manioc, was far more common than modern ethnographic experience might suggest (Roosevelt 1980; Whitehead 1988, 48–49) even in those areas, such as the Atlantic coast, which have been previously thought to be agriculturally unproductive (Espinosa 1969, 204; Harcourt 1906, 361, 381; Leigh 1906, 314, 319). The archaeological evidence also suggests that intensive cultivators once occupied this region using mounding and irrigation techniques to control flooding (Versteeg 1985; Whitehead 1992b), as on the Orinoco (Zucchi and Denevan 1979; Whitehead 1988, 42) and the Amazon (Roosevelt 1991, 204).

In light of the long and inconclusive debate on the significance of "protein capture" in Amazonia (see Ferguson 1989), it may be noted also that neither "famine" nor a specific "meat hunger" (other than in the special case of anthropophagy) was a prevalent cultural theme, as has sometimes been reported ethnographically. In any case, such cultural attitudes would not of themselves be evidence as to protein availability because a differential access to dietary resources was one aspect of the social differentiation that was once a common feature of Amerindian social organization (Roosevelt 1991, 58, and see below). Moreover, the early accounts repeatedly stress the ready availability of faunal resources, especially deer, "poultry," and fish, which all featured strongly in the Amerindian diet. Any assessment of the original productivity of Amerindian hunting made on the basis of current ethnographic data

(Hames and Vickers 1983, 139–325) must therefore also take account of the impact of Old World species on New World flora and fauna. A particular example of the importance of this event was the rapid way in which wild cattle, pigs, and goats may have directly degraded the grassland-savannas making them less favorable to the indigenous species (Butzer 1992; Whitehead 1988, 30–32).

The production of Amerindian economies, though highly specialized in certain areas, was not necessarily regionally centralized but was instead usually performed by the domestic household, which consisted of an extended family (*parentela*). There were important exceptions to this general pattern, as in the production of a number of elite items such as pottery, gold, and lapidary items (Boomert 1987; de Goeje 1931–32; Whitehead 1990c). As a result, many key economic relationships were of necessity interethnic and intervillage, since a resource-based specialization of domestic production underlay the highly developed Amerindian specialist craft technologies in wood, stone, clay, metals, and animal and plant products. It must thus be remembered that craft specialization need not have entailed any particular degree of physical or social centralization of the producers, since the distribution of natural resources was generally directly related to the different product groups produced, as it is today (Colson 1973).

For these same reasons, ethnic boundaries did not necessarily coincide with particular economic, political, or linguistic systems but could instead be founded on a craft technique or specialization that was sustained by being part of a wider system of exchange (Colson 1983–84b; 1985). At a certain level of ethnic naming, therefore, groups that shared ethnicity were apparently known by reference to an economic specialization in the production and/or exchange of particular items. Thus, the Arawaks (Lokono), who were the principal traders to the Spanish of flour known as *aru/yaruma* in the Lokono and Warao languages, were contemptuously referred to as *aru-ak* (Brinton 1871, 1; Ralegh 1848, 49n). Similarly, an archaic name for the Warao was Tivetive, being the Lokono term for the species of water snail that featured strongly in the Warao diet. The name Warao itself means "canoe maker" or "canoe owner" and reflects the antiquity of their proficiency in this art (Wilbert 1977, 303–4). An analogous "economic" interpretation of group naming perhaps might also be feasible for a wide range of recorded names, such as Panare (traders), Yumaguaris (miners), Naboresa/Maku (laborers), Kaikussiana (dog breeders).

Just as modern anthropologists have emphasized the importance of external relations in sustaining group identity and viability, so in the past the greater complexity and historical depth of such relationships locked very widely dispersed groups into patterns of mutually sustaining exchange. Of particular note in the area under discussion was the exchange of worked jade (*takua*) from the lower Amazon for goldwork (*calcuri*) from the lower Orinoco and circum-Roraima region (Acuña 1859, 128; Ralegh 1848, 27–29), as well as the use of money along the Guayana coast and Orinoco, well into historical times (Keymis 1596, 39, 42). Such "exchange" should be also understood to include warfare and raiding because the control of human labor, or its products, defined the dynamics of political power within which Amerindian leaders operated. It is in this context that apparently intractable feuding relationships, such as that of the Arawak and Carib, might be better understood and used to identify indigenous organization at the regional level.

It should be emphasized that advanced economic systems were *not* necessarily physically coextensive only with the most agriculturally viable areas, such as floodplains, but actually united fluvial and interfluvial areas. This allowed access to the economic benefits of the major waterways to those who lived in supposedly "marginal" environments, such as the Guayana highlands, where highly valuable economic items—such as poisons, metals and jewels—were nonetheless produced and exchanged (Acuña 1859, 119–20; Carvajal 1934, 212, 217–20; Keymis 1596, 14, 17; Ralegh 1848, 52, 56–57; Harcourt 1906, 387).

For these reasons, chieftaincy developed as much in the interfluvial as in the floodplain areas, with political power being exercised at a geographical distance via lines of economic interaction. These arteries of power, which generated variant forms of political complexity, have recently been redescribed as the "routes of knowledge" for the spread of prophetic cults (Colson 1985). The past political complexity of the uplands is well illustrated by the history of the Lokono chieftains (*aruaki*), who, until the eighteenth century, constituted a powerful polity that straddled the Amazon and Orinoco drainage basins in the area of the Sierra Acarai / Tumuc Humuc, linking the Corentyn and Berbice with the Paru and Trombetas rivers (Anon. 1906, 409–13; Carvajal 1934, 205–10; *CDI* 21:221–28; Ojer 1966, 161–233).

Similarly, the Manoan chieftains to the west and Karipuna to the southeast formed zones of political dominance based on their preeminence as regional traders. Following Edmundson (1906), de Goeje (1931–32) and Rivet (1923), this Manoan polity was closely identified with information gathered in Guayana concerning the possible sources of worked gold (Whitehead 1990c). The Karipuna—traders of weapons, jewels, and esoteric carvings along the Amazon and the Guayana coast (Boomert 1987; Acuña 1859, 107; de Goeje 1931–32)—were closely related culturally to the Lokono and are sometimes not explicitly distinguished from "Arawaks" in the early sources (Carvajal 1934, 223). This conflation of ethnic groups, along with other "inconsistencies" in the early documents, actually raises fundamental questions as to the validity of linguistically based schema of historical and ethnological classification in both the Amazon and Caribbean regions, and should not be taken as a simple token of European cultural confusion (Whitehead 1994).

The modes of leadership that were erected upon these networks of exchange and production linking the domestic producing units might be broadly defined as trading-military or theocratic-genealogical. It was by means of these ideological and cosmological frameworks that significant political followings, which could be an effective force in extravillage political life, were generated. The intensity of this process of ethnogenesis was greatly increased by the challenge to traditional political patterns that the Europeans constituted (Whitehead 1990b). Amerindian political action was therefore directed toward building personal followings through the manipulation of genealogy, the successful conduct of martial enterprises, or the display of esoteric knowledge, such as prophesy, the use of poisons, or the creation of sacred rattles. However, the minimum size of such a following, its threshold for political effectiveness, was in turn defined by conditions external to any given group (such as the presence of extant polities competing for the same human resources or the preexisting rules of political succession) and itself varied over time. This can be seen in the way that the introduction of guns suddenly allowed relatively small and marginal social groups to become politically very significant (see Whitehead 1990a, 1990b, 1992a).

The Caribs may be cited as an example of the postcontact dominance of a trading-military polity, and the Lokono as an example of the persistence of genealogical power bases well into historical times. The dynamics of political power in these circumstances are thus directly susceptible to study from the history of their contact with the Europeans. The Carib (Kari'ña) case has been thoroughly described elsewhere (Whitehead 1988, 1990a, 1990b, 1992a), while we may note the reports of both segmentary lineage and matriclan organization, as among the Lokono and Palikur, as well as the principle of hereditary succession to leadership, as among the Guayano, whose individual leaders constituted an elite that was closely related genealogically (Ralegh 1848, 38, 86; Keymis 1596, 15–18).

If a "feudal" control of persons therefore formed a dynamic element in Amerindian leadership (and we may note that this concept has been used to establish significant distinctions among contemporary Amerindian groups

[Rivière 1985, 101–9]), then it was through the process of an ethnic and political aggrandizement or in the defense of established ethnic boundaries that
particular chieftaincies would seek political acceptance and successive polities
would be created, only to disintegrate again if their contingent "ethnicity" was
not transmitted to subsequent generations. As Ralegh (1848, 94) remarked
of these ancient elites, "the Lords of [these] countries desire many children
of their owne bodies, for in those consist their greatest trust and strength."

The reality of the power exercised by these elites is also evident from their
ability to order executions or floggings (Harcourt 1906, 372, 376–77), as well
as the differential burial and marriage customs that they practiced (Ralegh
1848, 109–10). So too the use of elite dialects (Grenand and Grenand 1987;
Taylor and Hoff 1980) and evidence of panethnic theocratic groups (Léry
1927, 225–33) and of megalithic sites (Hurault and Frenay 1963; Linne
1928) are strong indications that such elites may have achieved considerable
transgenerational stability by the sixteenth century.

The political organizations that these genealogical elites created and operated are highly reminiscent of "feudal" formations. The control of people
rather than the redistribution or expropriation of specific economic resources
was, as has already been mentioned, the ultimate expression of political
dominance. Indeed, analogies between the political structures of medieval
Europe and those of sixteenth century Amerindia were made by Amerindians
and Europeans alike. As a result, descriptive terms passed in both directions,
most notably in the case of *capitán* and *cacique*.

Specific detail as to the regional organization of these elites is seen in the
example of the Guayano. The *acarawena* (king) of the Guayanos, Topiawari,
was feasted by Ralegh in 1595, and he described the political geography of
Guayana for his host (1848, 75–104). A close reading of Ralegh's account of
this discourse, in addition to a survey of the toponymic evidence, strongly
suggests that the basic political and spatial entities of this kingdom beyond
the village level were constituted as follows: (1) a group of villages sharing a
section of river, called a "countrey" by Ralegh (indicated by the linguistic element "cai" in native terms); (2) a number of such "countreys," which went to
form a "province" (also indicated in Spanish sources by the name of the principal cacique); (3) a maximal "lordship" or "kingdom," comprising a number
of river systems (as in Topiawari's dominance of the Orinoco's south bank).

Political authority was held at all levels by hereditary chieftains belonging
to Topiawari's immediate family (i.e., a son or a nephew). A similar macro-
political structure may be inferred for the Yao settled at the mouth of the
Oyapock in the early seventeenth century (Harcourt 1906, 368–73), or even

from much later Lokono accounts (Stæhelin 1913, II-2:173–77). The accuracy of these inferences is supported by the fact that the Spanish explicitly followed such rules of succession when attempting to usurp Topiawari's accession to the kingship of the Guayanos following the Spaniards' execution of the previous king, Morequito, who had been Topiawari's nephew. To this end, the Spanish promoted the candidacy of the deceased king's nephew, having first baptized him "Don Juan" (Ralegh 1848, 38).

An unequal distribution of resources may well have been an eventual consequence of the survival of these ruling families through a number of generations. But it was the management of this political inheritance of the past, rather than the management of an ecological balance between culture and environment, that persistently conditioned Amerindian leadership. Therefore it could be argued that the intensification of agricultural production can initially take place under these polities but that political expansion to control this intensifying production in other settlements/polities takes place through ethnic absorption of these groups either in the form of "slave labor" or through a political redefinition of ethnic boundaries. At the household level, this process is reflected in the endogamous polygamy of the chiefs, priests, and warriors and/or the nobility and divinity of their ancestry. The Lokono lords had one word for those who lay outside of their ancient polity: *faletti* (i.e., barbarians; see Whitehead 1992a).

In contrast, the warrior and trading elites, such as the Caribs or Manoa, seem to have been characterized by exogamous polygamy that favored rapid and varied ethnic recruitment. In addition, these elites extended the use of particular affinal categories, such as the Cariban term *poito*, to give it meanings as various as "son-in-law," "partner," "client," "servant," or "slave." In this way they could achieve the political incorporation of their politically and economically subject populations within existing kinship systems. However, the political and economic dominance that these particular groups exercised in the colonial period was arguably itself a direct product of the European presence. Like the Asante and Iroquois (Wesler 1983), they manifestly based part of their political authority on the redistribution of European manufactures (Whitehead 1988, 1990b, 1992a). It is therefore important to recall that it was partly because these new ethnic formations challenged the power of the ancient ruling elites that they have become represented to us in the historical record as intractably rebellious and warlike. In short, they were as *caribe* (wild, fierce) for the ancient elites as they were for the Europeans. It is to a consideration of how the Europeans interacted with the Amerindian polities, both ancient and modern, that we now turn.

European Contact and the Extinction of Amerindia

Sociopolitical interaction between Europeans and Amerindians was uneven
and sporadic throughout the area under discussion, which was largely unaffected by the great pandemics that hit coastal Brazil, the Caribbean, and
Andean regions in the sixteenth century (Whitehead 1988, 23). The aboriginal polities that were initially encountered did not survive unchanged, but
the relative autonomy of the Amerindian political economy persisted until
the mid seventeenth century, when both Iberian missionary effort and the
development of Dutch and Portuguese plantations combined to alter the
demographic position of the native population dramatically.

Accordingly, the study of ethnic formation and disintegration in this area
is of special value to an understanding of historical process, since the European documentation portrays a situation in which Amerindian cultures persisted for over two centuries alongside those of European colonialism. In
particular, close historical investigation of Carib origins strongly suggests
that the regional dominance achieved by their chieftains by the mid seventeenth century, a key moment in the creation of modern Carib ethnicity, was
based, in economic terms, on their redistribution of European goods in the
Orinoco Basin and the Guayana uplands. In their incessant struggle for
ethnic aggrandizement, often simplistically interpreted as "slave trading" by
hostile Spanish commentators (Whitehead 1988, 184–89), they well exemplify that process of ethnogenesis that so strongly characterizes Amerindian
history over the last half millennium.

In contrast to this situation of ethnogenesis, both from our own analytical
point of view and apparently within indigenous political categories as well,
were ranged the extant elites. It was with these elites that the Spanish made
their initial alliances and from whom they received their first "education" in
the politics of the region. Accordingly, the Spanish absorbed some of the
political priorities and prejudices of these individuals, and subsequent European policy toward the Amerindians sometimes represented the unconscious
application of these acquired indigenous categories. Nowhere is this more
clearly shown than in the special treatment accorded *caribe* groups by the
Spanish who had adopted the viewpoint of the Hispaniolan caciques and
Lokono lords (*adumasi*) that groups which were *caribe* were also evidently
barbarians (Whitehead 1988, 172–75; Whitehead 1992a).

The fact that the Spanish adopted the cultural viewpoint of the ruling
elites did not mean, however, that they accorded them any special consideration; indeed, many were imprisoned or executed in unsuccessful attempts to

master the indigenous population. This policy, in turn, only strengthened native opposition and encouraged such groups as the Carib (Kari'ña) along the Orinoco or the Aruan at the mouth of the Amazon to expand into the power vacuum left by the destruction of the old order. Nonetheless, in the eyes of some Europeans, ancient Amerindian political and cultural life was of a level of sophistication that rivaled or even exceeded that of their homelands.

Accordingly, the Dutch, French, and English, despite their cultural chauvinism, saw nothing incongruous in striking a series of alliances with the chieftains of the Atlantic coast that required the formal signing of treaties, the exchange of hostages, and the receipt of Amerindian women as "wives" (Whitehead 1990b, 1993c).

The overriding factor in the eventual European domination of this area, however, was undoubtedly the susceptibility of the Amerindians to introduced diseases. In short, the basic demographic trajectory was downward, with accelerating effect in the eighteenth century as European settlements and their associated black slave populations, previously negligible in number and size, expanded rapidly (Whitehead 1988, 9–42, 131–51). This is not to suggest that contacts prior to this time had not resulted in localized epidemics or that the Europeans had not had profound effects on the distribution of power in Amerindian societies, only that the Amerindian political economy was still dominant over the European one in this region. Hence the need, even where the aboriginal population remained intact, to import slave labor: Amerindian labor power was still under the control of indigenous leaders.

In the context of ferocious epidemics, however, as human resources drained away, the system of human and material exchanges that had sustained these sophisticated polities collapsed. This led in turn to the disintegration of some ethnic formations and the amalgamation of others, as well as to a general deterioration in the productivity and scale of Amerindian subsistence practices (Denevan 1992). The initial instability of the newer ethnic formations and the challenge they represented to established ones seem to be key reasons why periodic efforts were made to revitalize and affirm Amerindian ethnicity in the face of a rapid disintegration in extravillage relationships (Brown and Fernández 1992; Colson 1985; Thomas 1982, 146). Sometimes this even led to internecine conflict. In the case of the Carib, for example, there was a division into Spanish and Dutch factions, and in the case of the Pemón and Kapon, the assassination cult of *kanaima* (jaguar-men) emerged in the nineteenth century (Whitehead 1990a). It is out of this process of the radical transformation of ethnic boundaries that modern ethnographic distributions emerged and modern Amerindian cultures were created.

European Trade and Amerindian Ethnogenesis

It is easy enough to appreciate that the great value that came to be placed on European manufactures and the fact that they were unattainable with Amerindian technologies posed intractable problems for the traditional leadership of both the coastal and inland polities. Thus, although the Europeans were keen, as in Mexico and Peru, to use the ruling elites as a means of establishing their own authority, under the conditions of intercolonial conflict that applied along the whole Atlantic coast, they were not able to establish direct alliances with the upland polities that controlled both the trade in precious metals and other trans-Guayana commerce (Whitehead 1993c). As a result, the Europeans were forced to accept trading proxies who managed the interior trade for them, the European enclaves then acting also as foci for this intensifying trade (Keymis 1596, 39–43; Wilson 1906, 344).

In this way, European trading practices came to favor local coastal leaders over inland regional ones and provided the material base for the emergence of new ethnic formations, because the coastal chieftains now found that the terms of indigenous trade had altered to their advantage. As European colonial techniques themselves became more sophisticated, overt policies of preferential trading and the covert or unconscious assumption of an ethnic ranking among the local Amerindian groups gradually undermined the political and economic autonomy of even the most influential Amerindian traders. Coupled with changing colonial priorities in the eighteenth century and the demographic impact of the rapid expansion of non-Amerindian populations, it was the colonial, not the indigenous economy which finally came to dominate the region and which provided the missionaries with a material base for the evangelization of the heathens.

In consequence, new social priorities also came to the fore among the Amerindians, most notably in the emphasis on the immediate locality as the only safe sphere of social interaction and in the nature of gender relations, which now heavily favored male dominance. In both spheres the underlying causes seem to have been the facilitation of traditional male activities by the use of European manufactures, a consequent emphasis on the management of trade relations with the Europeans, and new patterns of warfare and raiding, which were themselves directly related to the advent of this trade (Whitehead 1988, 49–51; Whitehead 1990a; Whitehead 1990b).

As the European colonial economy gained further stability in the region — notably through the trade between the Dutch and the Spanish on the Orinoco and the definitive establishment of the Portuguese on the Amazon, as well as the expansion of the plantation system throughout this area — so the political and economic significance of trade with Amerindian groups declined and they came to be viewed almost solely as a potential source of labor to be harvested directly by the slavers and missionaries.

The Amerindian response to these new conditions was to adopt the alternative tactics of retreat or assimilation, a pattern of response to colonialism that has been found globally (Ferguson and Whitehead 1992, 251–55). In the specific area under consideration, the trading polities of the Manoa, Karipuna, Lokono, and Carib that had evolved in the fifteenth and sixteenth centuries disintegrated in the eighteenth century as the flow of European goods was restricted to customary payments for services within the colonies. At the same time, the advance of the missionaries in both the Portuguese and Spanish territories brought repeated epidemics to even isolated villages. The Carib and Manoan traders were then challenged directly by the missionaries, who offered trade goods or threatened military reprisal to induce many of their client groups to resettle. In essence, the missionaries and the dominant ethnic chieftains were competing for the same scarce resource: people.

By the close of the eighteenth century, Amerindia had been utterly destroyed. The Spanish and Portuguese effectively inhibited regional trade and controlled the main waterways of the Amazon and Orinoco. Certainly in the highlands themselves, especially following the famous revolt of the Ye'cuana in 1751, an indigenous economy still existed, but ultimately it was integrated with the local economies of both Santo Tomé and Essequibo. So also, just as the Caribs had done in the seventeenth and early eighteenth centuries, the Ye'cuana used their monopoly of steel tools and guns to hold a relatively dominant position in this trading system right up to modern times (Arvelo-Jiménez 1971; Hamilton-Rice 1921, 321–44).

The coastal and floodplain groups whose ethnicity survived the demographic collapse of the mid eighteenth century existed largely as a labor pool for the national economies of the region, often practicing a mode of life barely distinguishable from that of the criollos. Certainly, as the first ethnographers began to collect their reports, there was little to suggest that such groups ever again achieved the level of sophistication that they had had at contact, and this was undoubtedly one of the central reasons why subsequent attitudes to the historical record have been so naïve.

Equally important is the fact that, as mentioned above, European colonial policy itself created and sustained new ethnic formations where it did not actually force the amalgamation of disparate groups through demographic collapse (Whitehead 1992a). Good examples of this latter process were the absorption of the Taruma by the Wai-Wai (Rivière 1966) and the Mayes by the Palikur (Grenand and Grenand 1987). Modern ethnographic groupings may thus be of very recent origin, and it is for this reason also that their current linguistic profile is a very poor tool for historical or archaeological analysis (Whitehead 1993a).

Conclusion

As I mentioned in the introduction, the polities described in the foregoing pages, as well as the analysis of their historical trajectories, are a direct construct of the documentary record. However, the use of this record has yet to be properly developed, for it is an unfortunate feature of both historical and anthropological writing that, even where attempts are made to use the rich data that exists (e.g., Hemming 1978, 1987; Taussig 1987), the general lack of any consistent methodology in the analysis of historical sources, or an explicit theoretical posture as to the purpose of historical explanation, means that such attempts remain imprisoned within outmoded paradigms. Nor are the consequences of this failing limited merely to inhibiting progress in the historical understanding of the Amerindian, because many assumptions about the social and cultural potential of Amazonian societies, and hence about the meaning of sociocultural practice as it is found by the ethnographer, have been directly derived from a very negative and incomplete reading of the historical literature.

Historical anthropology in Amazonia has yet to establish its methodological bases (Whitehead 1993a, 1993b). All too often little attention is paid to such basic rules of historiographical procedure as the need to understand the origin of a documentary series or an individual document, or how to correctly reference such documents. Moreover, there is scant regard for evaluating sources in their own historical context or understanding why it is vital to examine a very wide range of documentation in its original language and in its original version. Clearly such research is time-consuming, but this only underlines the point that such work cannot be undertaken as an adjunct to some other field project but is a substantive field project in its own right.

This is not to suggest that no useful analogies can be made between the existing archaeological record and an analysis based on the documentary record. In certain techniques of spatial analysis, hypotheses concerning the structure of ancient trade and evidence from ceramic and petroglyph studies are all immediately revealing when combined with the historical data. For example, Renfrew's work on the spatial recognition of ancient polities from the archaeological data (Renfrew 1984) is paralleled by the techniques used here to identify such polities from the documentary record, while spatial analysis has already had manifest benefits for the study of Mesoamerican archaeology (Blanton 1981; Fox 1987). In the historian's case, such tasks can often be greatly facilitated by the type of information contained in the documentary data.

Accordingly, Renfrew's notion of predicting polities from "central places" is extremely suggestive for the historical material reviewed here. The list of such sites in Amazonia is extensive; it includes market towns, stone circles and alignments, ritual centers, burial mounds, earthworks, and "urban" centers. With the addition of toponymic and ethnographic evidence, a further stage of micro-analysis is possible, such as has been described in this chapter for the mouth of the Orinoco, and would probably be feasible for the entire Guayana coast as far as the mouth of the Amazon.

Similarly, when considering the processes that underlie the formation and decay of ethnic formations and their associated polities, if, as I suggested in the introduction, we are to move beyond models of direct mass migration or conquest (important though these phenomena may be) as explanations of observed linguistic and ceramic distributions, then other mechanisms must be identified. However, as Renfrew (1987, 126–31) indicates, many physical distributions could easily have been achieved without anyone moving farther than a few kilometers from their natal home. It is thus possible that some of the better-documented long-distance migrations—such as those of the Tupinambá, Wayapi, Wapishana, and Karipuna—were not just part of an ancient migratory pattern of Amerindian culture but were directly stimulated by the European presence, notwithstanding the prophetic tradition of the Tupi, which certainly continued to animate population movements after 1500 (Clastres 1975; Whitehead 1994).

By such means we might also explain the combined and uneven economic development of different ethnic formations and provide a model for the development of multi-ethnic economic systems. Following such a model, political forms such as the chiefdom and state, regardless of how these may be delineated genealogically or ecologically, would be a product of the political management of "households." In short, although the "household," or *maloca*, is an analytical constant in ethnography, such social forms do not necessarily represent adequate analytical categories for diachronic research (Meillassoux 1981; Rivière 1977; Rivière 1985, 107). Therefore it is the study of the structure and process of "household" interaction through time which is critical to advancing our analysis of past and present ethnic formations. This may be especially relevant when deciding whether these polities were in fact "states," since developed exchange systems can inhibit or make redundant the organization of such "states" (Blanton 1981, 234).

Equally suggestive in this regard is Renfrew's analysis of modes of trade and their spatial implications (1984, 120, fig. 10). All of these trade relationships, from simple reciprocity to full colonial enclaves and ports of trade, can be recognized for the area under discussion, which implies that we are dealing with civilizations of considerable complexity, possibly even protostates. This observation has already been forcefully made by Roosevelt (1980, 1987), while Denevan and Schwerin (1978), Tarble (1985), Whitehead (1988), and Zucchi (1985) have already applied ecological and spatial models to the analysis of ceramic and population distributions for the Orinoco Basin.

Clearly then, the benefits of surveys or excavations informed by analysis of the early European records are considerable (e.g., Whitehead 1992b) and certain sites, such as the native town of Hittia on the Berbice River or the town of Arowacai at the mouth of the Orinoco, would naturally to suggest themselves as relevant to these research aims.

Among the principal benefits of such an exercise would be the coordination of the data from archaeological, ethnographic, and historical investigation, which at present tend to relate to dissimilar objects of analysis, as well as the focusing of attention on the regional integration of Amerindian populations that, as it has been the intention of this paper to show, is the first and fundamental step toward a new understanding of the civilization of Amerindia. For, as Father Acuña (1859, 61) wrote, "if the Ganges irrigates all India, . . . if the Nile irrigates and fertilizes a great part of Africa: the river of the Amazons waters more extensive regions, fertilizes more plains, supports more people, and augments by its floods a mightier ocean: it only wants, in order to surpass them in felicity, that its source should be in Paradise."

REFERENCES

Acuña, C. de
1859   A new discovery of the great river of the Amazons. In *Expeditions into the valley of the Amazons,* edited by C. R. Markham, 44–142. London: Hakluyt Society.

Aguado, P. de
1951   *Recopilación historial de Venezuela.* Caracas: Academia Nacional de la Historia.

Anonymous
1906   A relation of Marwin River. In *Hakluytus posthumus,* edited by S. Purchas, 16:403–13. Glasgow: Hakluyt Society.

Arnold, D. E.
1985   *Ceramic theory and cultural process.* Cambridge: Cambridge University Press.

Arvelo-Jiménez, N.
1971 *Political relations in a tribal society: A study of the Ye'cuana Indians of Venezuela.* Cornell Dissertation Series. Ithaca, N.Y.: Cornell University.

Blanton, R., R. Kowalewski, J. Appel, and G. Feinman
1981 *Ancient Meso-America.* Cambridge: Cambridge University Press.

Boomert, A.
1987 Gifts of the Amazons: "Green stone" pendants and beads as items of ceremonial exchange in Amazonia and the Caribbean. *Antropologica* 67:33–54.

Brinton, D. G.
1871 The Arawack language of Guiana. *Transactions of the American Philosophical Society* 14:427–44.

Brown, M., and E. Fernández.
1992 Tribe and state in a frontier mosaic: The Asháninka of eastern Peru. In *War in the tribal zone: Expanding states and indigenous warfare,* edited by R. B. Ferguson and N. L. Whitehead, 175–98. Santa Fe: School of American Research Press with the University of Washington Press.

Butzer, K. W., editor
1992 The Americas before and after 1492: Current geographical research. *Annals of the Association of American Geographers* 82:346–568.

Carvajal, G. de
1934 Discovery of the Orellana River. In *The discovery of the Amazon according to the account of Friar Gaspar de Carvajal and other documents,* edited by J. T. Medina, translated by B. T. Lee, 167–235. New York: American Geographical Society.

Clastres, H.
1975 *La terre sans mal: Le prophétisme Tupi-Guarani.* Paris: Éditions du Seuil.

CDI
1864–84 *Collección de documentos inéditos de Indias: América y Oceania.* 42 vols. Madrid.

Colson, A.
1973 Inter-tribal trade in the Guiana highlands. *Antropologica* 34:5–69.
1983–84a A comparative survey of contributions. *Antropologica* 59/62:9–38.
1983–84b The spatial component in the political structure of Carib speakers (Guiana Highlands). *Antropologica* 59/62:73–124.
1985 Routes of knowledge: An aspect of regional integration in the circum-Roraima area of the Guiana Highlands. *Antropologica* 63/64:103–49.

Goeje, C. H. de
1931–32 Oudheden uit Suriname: Op zoek naar de Amazonen. *West-Indische Gids* 13:449–82, 497–530.

Denevan, W.
1992 The pristine myth: The landscape of the Americas in 1492. *Annals of the Association of American Geographers* 82:369–85.

Denevan, W., and K. H. Schwerin.
1978   Adaptive strategies in Karinya subsistence, Venezuelan llanos. *Antropo-logica* 50:3–91.
Edmundson, G.
1906   Early relations of the Manoas with the Dutch, 1606–1732. *English Historical Review* 21:229–53.
Espinosa, A. Vasquez de
1969   *Compendio y descripción de las Indias Occidentales.* Madrid: Biblioteca Autores Españoles.
Evans, C., and B. J. Meggers.
1960   *Archaeological investigations in British Guiana.* Bureau of American Ethnology, Bulletin 177. Washington, D.C.: Smithsonian Institution.
Ferguson, R. B.
1989   Game wars? Ecology and conflict in Amazonia. *Journal of Anthropological Research* 45:179–206.
Ferguson, R. B., and N. L. Whitehead, editors
1992   *War in the tribal zone: Expanding states and indigenous warfare.* Santa Fe: School of American Research Press, with the University of Washington Press.
Fritz, S.
1922   *Journal of the travels and labours of Father Samuel Fritz in the river of the Amazons between 1686 and 1723.* Edited by G. Edmundson. London: Hakluyt Society.
Grenand, F., and P. Grenand
1987   La côte d'Amapa, de la bouche de l'Amazone a la baie d'Oyapock, à travers la tradition orale Palikur. *Boletín Museo Emilio Goeldi, ser. Antropologia* 3:1–77.
Hames, R. B., and W. T. Vickers, editors
1983   *Adaptive responses of native Amazonians.* New York: Academic Press.
Hamilton-Rice, A.
1921   The Rio Negro, the Casaquiare Canal and the upper Orinoco, September 1919–April 1920. *Geographical Journal* 58:321–44.
Harcourt, R.
1906   A relation of a voyage to Guiana. In *Hakluytus posthumus*, edited by S. Purchas, 16:358–403. Glasgow: Hakluyt Society.
Hemming, J.
1978   *Red gold: The conquest of the Brazilian Indians, 1500–1760.* Cambridge, Mass.: Harvard University Press.
1987   *Amazon frontier: The defeat of the Brazilian Indians.* London: Macmillan.
Hurault, J., and P. Frenay
1963   Pétroglyphes et assemblages de pierres dans le sud-est de la Guyane Française. *Journal de la Société des Américanistes* 52:159–66.

Keymis, L.
1596   A relation of a second voyage to Guiana. London.
Lathrap, D.
1970   The upper Amazon. London: Thames and Hudson.
Leigh, C.
1906   Voyage to Guiana, and plantation there. In Hakluytus posthumus, edited
            by S. Purchas, 16:309–23. Glasgow: Hakluyt Society.
Léry, J. de
1927   Histoire d'un voyage fait en la terre du Brésil, autrement dite Amérique.
            Edited by C. Clerc. Paris: Payot.
Lettres
1781   Lettres édifiantes et curieuses. Vol. 8. Paris.
Linne, S.
1928   Les recherches archéologiques de Nimuendajú au Brésil. Journal de la
            Société des Américanistes 20:71–92.
Meggers, B. J.
1971   Amazonia: Man and culture in a counterfeit paradise. Chicago: Aldine.
Meggers, B. J., and C. Evans.
1957   Archaeological investigations at the mouth of the Amazon. Bureau of
            American Ethnology, Bulletin 167. Washington, D.C.: Smithsonian
            Institution.
Meillassoux, C.
1981   Maidens, meal and money. Cambridge: Cambridge University Press.
Ojer, P.
1966   La formación del Oriente Venezolano. Caracas: Universidad Católica
            Andres Bello.
Oviedo y Valdes, G. F.
1959   Historia general y natural de las Indias. Madrid.
Ralegh, W.
1848   The discoverie of the large, rich and bewtiful empire of Guiana. Edited by
            R. Schomburgk. London: Hakluyt Society.
Renfrew, C.
1984   Approaches to social archaeology. Edinburgh: Edinburgh University Press.
1987   Archaeology and language. London: Jonathan Cape.
Rivet, P.
1923   L'orefèverie précolombienne des Antilles, des Guyanes et du Vénézuéla.
            Journal de la Société des Américanistes 15:182–213.
Rivière, P. G.
1966   Some ethnographic problems of southern Guyana. Folk 8/9:302–12.
1977   Some problems in the comparative study of Carib societies. In Carib-
            speaking Indians, edited by E. Basso, 39–42. Tucson: University of
            Arizona Press.

1985   *Individual and society in Guiana.* Cambridge: Cambridge University Press.
Roosevelt, A. C.
1980   *Parmana: Prehistoric maize and manioc subsistence along the Amazon and Orinoco.* New York: Academic Press.
1987   Chiefdoms in the Amazon and Orinoco. In *Chiefdoms in the Americas,* edited by R. Drennan and C. Uribe, 153–86. Lanham, Md.: University Press of America.
1991   *Moundbuilders of the Amazon: Geophysical archaeology on Marajo Island, Brazil.* New York: Academic Press.
Simon, P.
1861   *Sixth historical notice of the conquest of tierra firme.* Edited by C. R. Markham. London: Hakluyt Society.
Sorensen, A. P.
1972   Multilingualism in the northwest Amazon. In *Sociolinguistics,* edited by J. Pride and J. Holmes, 78–93. Harmondsworth, Eng.: Penguin Books.
Stæhelin, F., editor
1913–19   *Die Mission der Brüdergemeine in Suriname und Berbice im achtzehnten Jahrhundert.* Paramaribo: Hernhutt.
Steward, J., editor
1946–50   *Handbook of South American Indians.* Bureau of American Ethnology, Bulletin 143. Washington, D.C.: Smithsonian Institution.
Tarble, K.
1985   Un nuevo modelo de expansión Caribe para la epoca prehispánica. *Antropologica* 63/64:45–81.
Taylor, D., and B. Hoff
1980   The linguistic repertory of the Islan-Carib in the seventeenth century: The men's language—a Carib pidgin. *International Journal of American Linguistics* 46:301–12.
Thomas, D. J.
1982   *Order without government: The society of the Pemon Indians of Venezuela.* Urbana: University of Illinois Press.
Versteeg, A. H.
1985   The prehistory of the young coastal plain of west Suriname. *Berichten van de Rilksdienst Oudheidkundig Bodemonderzoek* 35:653–750.
Wesler, K. W.
1983   Trade politics and native polities in Iroquoia and Asante. *Comparative Studies in Society and History* 25:641–60.
Whitehead, N. L.
1988   *Lords of the tiger spirit: A history of the Caribs in colonial Venezuela and Guayana, 1498–1820.* Royal Institute for Linguistics and Anthropology, Caribbean Studies Series, no. 10. Dordrecht and Providence, R.I.: Foris Publications.

1990a   The snake warriors: Sons of the tiger's teeth; A descriptive analysis of Carib warfare, 1500–1820. In *The Anthropology of War,* edited by J. Haas, 146–70. Cambridge: Cambridge University Press.

1990b   Carib ethnic soldiering in Venezuela, the Guianas and Antilles, 1492–1820. *Ethnohistory* 37:357–85.

1990c   The Mazaruni pectoral: A golden artifact discovered in Guyana and the historical sources concerning native metallurgy in the Caribbean, Orinoco and Northern Amazonia. *Archaeology and Anthropology* 7:19–38.

1992a   Tribes make states and states make tribes: Warfare and the creation of colonial tribe and state in northeastern South America, 1492–1820. In Ferguson and Whitehead 1992, 127–50.

1992b   The mound complexes at Fort Nassau, Berbice River (Guyana). Memorandum on file at the Walter Roth Museum of Anthropology, Georgetown, Guyana.

1993a   Ethnic transformation and historical discontinuity in native Amazonia and Guayana, 1500–1900. *L'Homme* 126/128:289–309.

1993b   Recent research on the native history of Amazonia and Guayana. *L'Homme* 126/128:499–510.

1993c   Native American cultures along the Atlantic littoral of South America, 1499–1650. In *The meeting of two worlds: Europe and the Americas, 1492–1650,* edited by W. Bray, 197–231. Oxford: Oxford University Press/ British Academy.

1994   Ethnic plurality in the native Caribbean: Remarks and uncertainties as to data and theory. In *Wolves from the sea: Readings in the anthropology of the Native Caribbean,* edited by N. L. Whitehead, 60–79. Leiden: KITLV Press.

Wilbert, J.

1977   To become a maker of canoes: An essay in Warao enculturation. In *Enculturation in Latin America: An Anthology,* edited by J. Wilbert, 303–58. UCLA Latin American Center Publications. Los Angeles.

Wilson, J.

1906   The relation of Master John Wilson . . . into England from Wiapoco in Guiana 1606. In *Hakluytus posthumus,* edited by S. Purchas, 16:338–51. Glasgow: Hakluyt Society.

Zucchi, A.

1985   Evidencias arqueologicas sobre grupos de posible lengua Caribe. *Antropologica* 63/64:23–44.

Zucchi, A., and W. M. Denevan

1979   *Campos elevados e historia cultural prehispánica en los llanos occidentales de Venezuela.* Caracas: Universidad Católica Andres Bello.

3

The Impact of Conquest on Contemporary Indigenous Peoples of the Guiana Shield

The System of Orinoco Regional Interdependence

NELLY ARVELO-JIMÉNEZ AND HORACIO BIORD

The concept of "culture" as a static inventory of traits, implicitly assumed by diverse anthropological orientations, has prevented an understanding of the cultural history of Orinoco societies throughout the postconquest centuries of its evolution. Additionally, the aboriginal Orinoco cultures belong to a cultural matrix created and recreated over the course of several millennia by the ethnic groups of the Orinoco River Basin, yet comprehension of the relationship between the broader regional cultural context—the Orinoco matrix—and the local cultures has lacked an explanatory model. Thus we decided to look at our subject through an heuristic model that focuses on interethnic levels of sociocultural integration, that is, recurrent conjunctions and alliances among autonomous polities.

The anthropological literature of the Orinoco Basin, in giving special privilege to the study of local cultures, has perpetuated and reinforced the European perception of a world marked by cultural divisions and composed of fragmented social institutions. Moreover, in focusing on certain sociocultural characteristics (such as self-sufficient economies and the segmentary organization of social formations), previous work in this field has emphasized ethnic differentiation. In doing so, it depresses the discussion of phenomena which, though most clearly manifested and observed on a local or ethnic level, have their locus on the regional or interethnic level. Contrary to these current postures, which characterize the Orinoco ethnic groups as self-contained polities and which conceive of the interethnic interactions as strictly commercial or warlike, we propose to interpret the convergence of interethnic relationships not as isolated or casual facts but as evidence of the existence of levels of sociocultural integration different from the purely ethnic. We visualize it as a system of regional interdependence within the Orinoco Basin and refer to it as the System of Orinoco Regional Interdependence. Our proposal is that the ethnic components of this system created a complex regional web of interethnic relations that served to integrate them in a horizontal and differentiated manner. This type of integration did not signify a loss of local political autonomy nor of cultural or linguistic diversity among its various ethnic components (Arvelo-Jiménez 1980, 1984; Biord-Castillo 1985; Morales [Méndez] and Arvelo-Jiménez 1981). Furthermore, we assume that interactive processes such as commerce, the prestation of ritual services, marriage alliances, political pacts, raids, and warfare may have been articulatory mechanisms whose functioning entailed the existence of interethnic levels of integration. On the other hand, we assume that beyond any differences in substance and detail, the cultural development of Orinoco has a structural continuity manifested in the persistence and transformation of certain structural elements, a hypothesis we have begun to test with data from the sixteenth century to the present day.

Our assumption has benefited from the theory of "cultural control" (Bonfil Batalla 1986), which states that the ability of an ethnic group to define itself depends on the significant control it maintains over the nucleus of its own (autochthonous) culture, or culture proper (*cultura propia*). This cultural control refers to the system of relationships by which a group exercises its social decision making about its material, organizational, cognitive, symbolic, emotive, and other cultural resources. In each moment of its history, an ethnic group manages its own and foreign cultural resources according to the political dynamics of interethnic relations in which is it immersed. If the ethnic group possesses the social capacity to make decisions about its own cultural elements, it displays a nucleus of autonomous culture (*cultura autónoma*); if it is able to decide about the integration of foreign cultural resources, it also maintains a sphere of appropriated culture (*cultura apropiada*). Conversely, if its relations with respect to its own resources result from foreign decisions (that is to say, from other ethnic groups participating in the interethnic system), it can be said to have a sphere of alienated culture (*cultura enajenada*). Moreover, if both the cultural resources utilized and the decisions taken with respect to them are externally derived, it has a sphere of imposed culture (*cultura impuesta*). The control that an ethnic group maintains over its basic nucleus of cultural resources defines its existence as either a differentiated polity or a differentiated sociocultural segment within a multi-ethnic state. The disappearance of such control would be the logical outcome of the spheres of alienated and imposed culture growing to the point of enveloping and extinguishing the nucleus of autochthonous cultural resources. This theory is underlined by a concept of "culture" which is defined by reference to interethnic processes, not according to a static inventory of traits. It thus permits an understanding of the dynamics that interrelate diachronically as well as synchronically, the Colbacchini with the structural, change with stasis.

We proceed to make a partial reconstruction of the System of Orinoco Regional Interdependence by identifying the environmental and sociological characteristics that have structural significance and conducting a diachronic study of the interethnic levels of sociocultural integration achieved by some of the system's group components from the sixteenth to the nineteenth centuries.

We identify three principal biomes that make up the Orinoco Basin: (a) the humid tropical forest of the Guiana interfluvial zone; (b) the savanna, and (c) the floodplain. In the first two, the faunal and floral resources display an even but dispersed distribution, and the availability of some raw materials is limited—for example, clay for ceramics, stones for making grating boards, the specific type of bamboo used to fabricate the inner tubes of blowguns, etc. However, although the ethnographic record corroborates the circulation of elaborate products made from the limited raw materials (Fried 1983), there is no evidence of a true economic specialization by the societies with direct access to the scarce raw materials.

The economics of these societies have been characterized by the simple reproduction of the conditions necessary to produce the energy consumed by the producers, which is then reinvested into the productive process. Consequently, the distribution of the modest surpluses derived from these economies was oriented toward neither accumulation nor economic specialization but rather to the creation or reinforcement of political ties with other, structurally similar societies.

Such surpluses, in being modest, were not the result of a specialized production by ethnic groups, nor did they obey a territorial division determined by the presence or absence of raw materials. Some of the surplus items that could have become significant exchange "markers" (for instance fish, curare, and *quiripa*)[1] never were produced exclusively by a single group, nor was their circulation due to a lack of knowledge on the part of the receptor societies about how to manufacture them. We believe that this restricted exchange was in reality a deliberate cultural strategy developed by Orinoco polities to induce interaction between ethnic or local groups. This strategy was reinforced by the practice of establishing fixed trading partners for deferred, successive transactions based on contracts that are impossible to break without provoking dangerous supernatural sanctions.

In addition, the same ethnographic record informs us of the existence of small, dispersed, politically decentralized societies and contains no evidence that either proves or suggests the existence of polities of greater social complexity than those reported by the chroniclers for the interfluvial and savanna zones.

The Orinoco polities of the savanna and interfluvial zones did not develop formal military institutions (i.e., no standing armies) as a means of defending their material and cultural resources or their territorial boundaries. More informal punitive actions (or threats of action) did exist, such as hostile offensives into neighboring communities, armed hunting parties in marginal zones, or threats of black sorcery (see Ross 1980). But the defense of the frontiers of their peripheral lands, which by nature were highly flexible and transitory, was effected by designing strategies that were distinct from purely military actions.

Nevertheless, the border between trade and warfare was always precarious. When a commercial relationship in the territory of another group soured and turned hostile, the victorious group was accustomed to taking prisoners of war. Hence there is evidence from the archaeological and ethnographic records that some of the innovations incorporated into the system were a result of hostile intervention. The prisoners of war were incorporated into the respective domestic groups of the victorious warriors, and eventually a fair percentage of them acquired total affiliation in their captor's group through interethnic marriage. Alliances brought about through interethnic marriage did have more than just sociopolitical consequences; they also fomented intercultural learning and borrowing, as well as multilingualism. By taking into account this form of cultural communication, the wide diffusion of techniques, styles, modes, and religious beliefs throughout the length and breadth of the Orinoco Basin is made more intelligible.

The prestation of religious services among the diverse ethnic groups served to sanction on the ideological level the participation of each ethnic group in the system.

The overall outcome was the creation of recurrent mechanisms of conjunctions and alliances, that is, networks of social, economic, and religious prestations and counterprestations that we have conceptualized as the System of Orinoco Regional Interdependence, within which no ethnic group achieved the political or economic supremacy to control the cultural decisions and resources of the others.

The scale of the Orinoco is much smaller than the vast Amazon flood-plains. However, compared to the interfluvial and savanna biomes, the Ori-noco floodplains offer a wider variety of resources, including major concentra-tion of animal protein and alluvial soils. There is still a lot to be learned about the social complexity of the Orinoco floodplain polities and their inter-action with those of the interfluvial and savanna zones. The archaeological data is slim, though there are a few illuminating clues, such as: (a) Roosevelt's demographic data for a site in the middle Orinoco floodplain, which point to a significant increase in population density from A.D. 100 to 1500 (Roosevelt 1980, 15–18); (b) the social complexity that we infer was inherent in the polities that belonged to the Osoid Series of the middle Orinoco llanos (230 B.C.–A.D. 1200) (Zucchi 1968);[2] (c) the settlement hierarchy reported by Garson (1980) for Hato la Calzada. These data, when complemented by further research on regional demographic patterns and political organization, may throw light on the existence and variety of complex social formations and how they were related to the interfluvial and savanna polities.

The interpretation of the complex networks of interethnic relations that existed among the societies occupying the northeastern sector of the South American mainland—the middle and lower Orinoco, and contemporary Ven-ezuelan Guiana during the sixteenth and seventeenth centuries (see fig. 3.1)—provided the initial stimulation for proposing a new analytical model. Our ethnohistorical reconstruction of the Kari'ña, or Carib,[3] society made evident that it was methodologically and historically misleading to attempt to understand the Kari'ña as if they were a self-contained polity. This recon-struction brought out the necessity of examining the relationships between the Kari'ña and neighboring ethnic groups or those groups residing in terri-tories peripheral to their own (for example, the peoples of the llanos of the Orinoco). A rereading of the existing data led us to consider the llanos as part of the System of Orinoco Regional Interdependence, with Kari'ña soci-ety being the center of this system during the seventeenth century (Morales [Méndez] and Arvelo-Jiménez, 1981).

Ethnohistorical analyses of the llanos and Orinoco polities also made it possible to infer the existence of interethnic levels of integration. This is a different interpretation of the body of data used by the Moreys (Morey 1975; Morey and Morey 1975). They characterized the interactions between the llanos groups and those inhabiting the middle Orinoco as a commercial rela-tion, among whose main expressions were the fairs celebrated annually on the shores of the great river. Following this same line of reasoning, several eth-nographic descriptions refer to trade circuits existing in the twentieth cen-tury among the Carib-speaking Ye'cuana, Pemon, Makushi, Akawaio, and

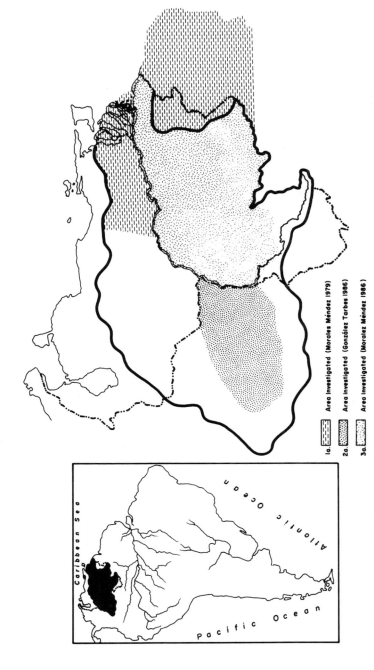

Figure 3.1. The System of Orinoco Regional Interdependence, or the Orinoco Interethnic System.

1a. Area investigated (Morales Méndez 1979)

2a. Area investigated (González Tarbes 1986)

3a. Area investigated (Morales Méndez 1986)

Caribbean Sea

Atlantic Ocean

Pacific Ocean

Patamona of the interfluvial zone of the Guiana shield but make no attempt to explain what connection said circuits have to the trade and other multiplex linkages that connected Orinoco societies in former centuries. In contrast, we have begun to rethink Orinoco history. To characterize as purely commercial the multiple articulatory mechanisms of the Orinoco societies is to overemphasize and decontextualize the significance of commerce. A rereading of the ethnographic material concerning these societies enables us to discern interethnic levels of integration that indicate the proper role and place of commercial relations within the System of Orinoco Regional Interdependence.

Our insight into the complexity of the System of Orinoco Regional Interdependence has been equally enriched by the ethnohistorical reconstructions completed for the Guajibo of the Meta River llanos and for the Kari'ña of the eighteenth century (González Tarbes 1986). These studies provide data that expand our knowledge of the geographical extension of the Orinoco interethnic levels of integration (see fig. 3.1, areas 1 and 2).

From the Guajibo case we can apprehend the structure and functioning of interethnic relations in this section of the Orinoco llanos. Given the great variety of micro-environments, the Guajibo and their neighbors (mainly the Achagua) created mechanisms of cooperation and reciprocity that permitted them to exploit jointly those micro-environments with other culturally different groups. In this manner they were able to overcome the problem of competing for scarce resources despite their lack of membership in a larger, and unified polity. The study of the Guajibo also informs us about the modalities of participation in the networks of interethnic relations by those societies that did not occupy the areas adjacent to the banks of the Orinoco, that is, participation through intermediaries. Additionally, we are able to understand some of the interlacing that took place between the traditional indigenous institutions of the Orinoco llanos societies and the new phenomena that resulted from the imposition of colonial economic and political policies (González Tarbes, 1986).

The Kari'ña, in the face of the militarization and fortification of the lower and middle Orinoco in the eighteenth century (carried out under the leadership of military governors and Spanish missionaries), resorted to the use of alternate routes transecting the interfluvial zones to carry out their commercial operations and other activities associated with them. These passages (see figs. 3.3 through 3.6 and the Appendix)—though they bypassed the principal routes, which had become virtually expropriated by the colonial powers— still managed to provide an effective connection between the strategically dispersed populations inhabiting this vast zone. We believe that the Orinoco was the axis of the System of Orinoco Regional Interdependence and that

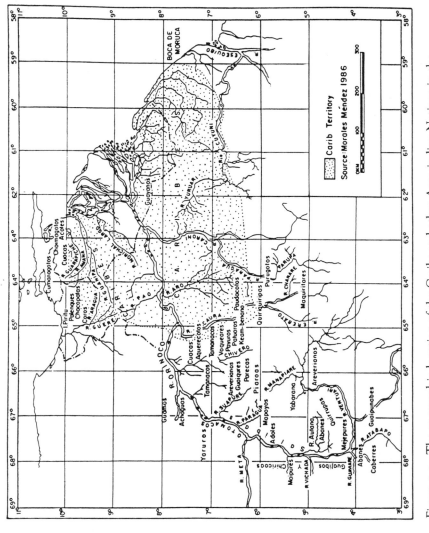

Figure 3.2. The geographic location of the Caribs and other Amerindian Nations in the eighteenth century.

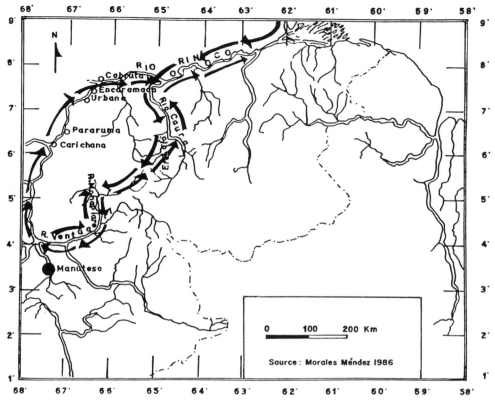

Figure 3.3. The Carib Caura–Ventuari route in the eighteenth century.

the passages reported by the eighteenth-century chroniclers may have functioned as secondary or complementary routes of interaction. Around the
1850s, after the foundation of several colonial towns in the western section of
what is today Venezuela's Amazonas state and the eastern Colombian llanos,
mainly the Kari'ña but also other indigenous groups began to seek safety in
using the alternative routes to perpetuate their multiplex interethnic relationships. They could thus avoid the many traps (including military harass-
ment) set up by the colonial system. The majority of the colonial towns were
located along the Orinoco floodplain and the Atabapo-Negro river system.
These fluvial-based outposts of settlement helped the Spanish to secure the
expropriation of the Orinoco River, which up to then had served as the central axis of the regional System of Orinoco Regional Interdependence, which
was controlled by Indians. Today these complementary routes still provide the

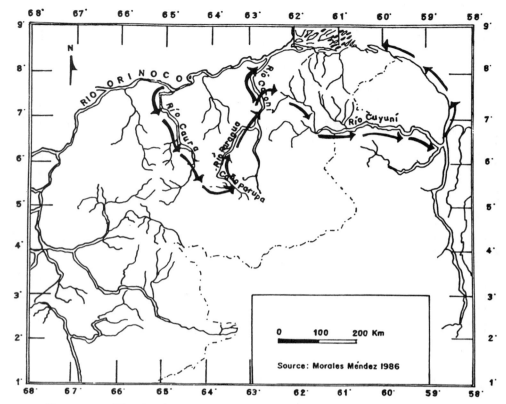

Figure 3.4. The Carib Caura–Caroní–Cuyuní route in the eighteenth century.

logistical bases for the interethnic networks among the Orinoco societies located in the interfluvial zone of the Guiana shield.

The foundation of about ten major river towns along the Orinoco, Atabapo, and Negro rivers resulted in the nucleation of close to 20 percent of the
Indian population (Primov 1981) and in the emergence of several new economic strategies. Additionally, in the nineteenth century, further colonial
expansion impaired the regional system, and this situation eventually gave
rise to a "reduced" (pacified) indigenous population inserted in the lowest
rung of the Spanish and neo-colonial regimes. In turn, the autonomous Indian population living in the interfluvial zone still had a scattered settlement
pattern, with small and politically independent villages linked to colonial or
neocolonial towns and markets via the trading system. Until the eighteenth
century, floodplain peoples and the interfluvial settlements were linked by a
horizontal flow of goods and services. Since then they have continued to be

linked but by a vertical flow defined by the superior value placed on colonial or neocolonial goods and services compared to those of the Indian people.

Data from the nineteenth century are critical for understanding further structural transformations of the System of Orinoco Regional Interdependence as a result of colonial frontier expansion toward the area south of the Orinoco River. However, until now we have had data only on colonial and neo-colonial trade for that century.[4] Trade functioned as an articulatory mechanism between two emerging social segments within the "national society," that is, (a) reduced or pacified Indian populations, and (b) autonomous Indian populations. The former provided the labor force exploited by the *criollos*,[5] who upon independence from colonial rule replaced the missionaries and colonial officials in the subjugation of the reduced Indian segment of the

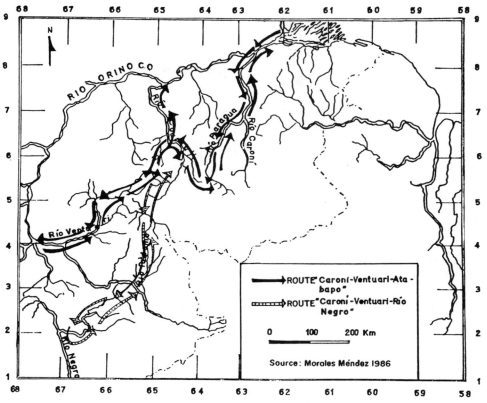

Figure 3.5. The Carib Caroní–Ventuari–Atabapo and Caroní–Ventuari–Río Negro routes in the eighteenth century.

population, simultaneously serving in business as merchants and in politics as government administrators. The autonomous Indian populations located in the interfluvial zone were linked to the reduced Indians through trade. It is likely that these culturally autonomous peoples continued to be the main keepers and innovators of the structural principles of the System of Orinoco Regional Interdependence. This statement finds some support in data provided by nineteenth-century sources written by explorers, including news as to how reduced Indians, settled around criollo towns, also received goods via interfluvial routes known and used exclusively by the Indians. We believe that these routes in the interfluvial zone are the same as or are related to those mentioned in the eighteenth-century chronicles. We may conclude that these routes were not only the vehicles for the circulation of trade goods; they also functioned as channels to link the indigenous world by, among other things, the flow of information.

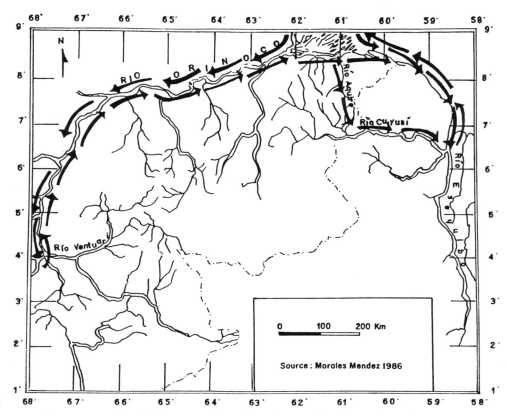

Figure 3.6. The Carib routes "Esequibo–Orinoco" in the eighteenth century.

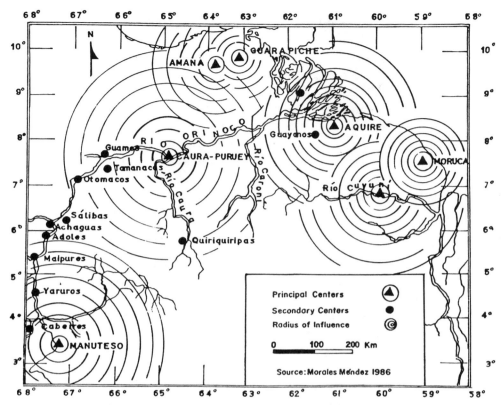

Figure 3.7. Centers of Carib exchange in the eighteenth century.

Our hypothesis that the System of Orinoco Regional Interdependence, though necessarily modified, was still in operation in the interfluvial zone in the nineteenth century is also supported by the localization of the colonial and neo-colonial towns. These centers marked the actual frontiers of the politicoeconomic control exercised by the expanding "national society." The Indian goods to be exported to Manaus or Angostura flowed into the above-mentioned towns, which continued to be located along the main fluvial axis.

For each century we have been able to isolate several of the most important mechanisms that contributed to the insertion of indigenous peoples into the colonial and neocolonial systems of socioeconomic stratification, that is, the differential terms of trade and the links among debt/peonage (*aviamiento/endeude*), alcoholism, and the exploitation of Indian labor.

The practice of debt/peonage, which implies receiving goods in advance as a form of payment or a loan, became widespread. Criollo merchants or traders maximized their profits by setting high prices for their goods while at the same time devaluing the prices they paid for indigenous goods. This differential rate of exchange made Indian debts unpayable. The institution of debt/peonage gradually deepened its roots in the trading system between criollos and Indians and eventually gave way to the institution of debt inheritance, by which the relatives of the Indian debtor entered the chain of-debt by being held accountable the debt of a dead relative. Debt/peonage also brought about the buying and selling of debts, in which the debts of an Indian were bought by any criollo merchant interested in his labor. The practice amounted to de facto slave labor. We infer that the Indians did not initially resist the institution of debt/peonage because they wrongly perceived its nature. They entered willingly into the practice without knowing that the rationale of the capitalist economy responsible for creating peonage was radically different from the traditional Indian system of deferred exchange.

The flow of goods in the nineteenth century, which is summarized in table 3.1, suggests a continuity in the Indian production of goods compared with previous centuries. It also clearly points out the extant social division of labor for that century: the criollos were in control of politics, trade, and transportation, and the Indians produced food and crafts and collected raw materials.

As payment for their marketable goods, the Indians often received adulterated alcohol (i.e., alcohol spiked with additives), which was a main item of commercial speculation in the trade between criollo merchants and Indians (Michelena y Rojas 1867, 234–36, 263–64, 339; Codazzi in Michelena y Rojas 1867, 331; Spruce 1970, 1:377–78). The unfortunate combination of debt/peonage and induced alcoholic dependence became a notoriously efficient mechanism for subjugating the Indians. Following a trend initiated in the eighteenth century, commercial flows went from floodplains to interfluvial zones and back again. However, the differential rate of exchange increasingly deepened social stratification and the economic subordination of Indian peoples, for whom, nevertheless, this exchange was the only way they had to gain access to coveted and by now much-needed European goods.

Indian wage labor—whose origins can be traced to the eighteenth century, when Indians were hired as house servants and trail guides (baqueanos)—was frequently obtained by force (Bueno 1933, 105, 113–15, 132; Humboldt 1956 3:232, 4:76). In fact, in order to procure an adequate labor force, the practice of the entrada[6] became widespread. Corporal punishment was also common, and house service was inflicted upon children under the pretext that they had to help pay previously accrued debts (Bueno 1933, 106, 108, 115, 116, 130, 136, 140; Humboldt 1956, 3:252, 298, 303, 4:127–8). The

Table 3.1. Main Goods and Services Traded During the Nineteenth Century

Animals	Processed Vegetables and Animal Products	Manufactured Goods	Cash Crops	News	Services
squirrels, turtles, cattle (horses, pork, etc.), monkeys	cassava bread, chica, karaña,[a] quiripa, ñopo, skins, lard, vegetable oil, cotton, alcohol, cheeses, sweets, turtle oil, salted meat, tiger skins, turtle eggs, fresh meat, chichiqui,[b] Brazil nuts, cayman meat	clothing, beads, steel tools (axes, machetes, knives, nails, fishhooks), shotguns, hammocks, arrows	corn, beans, yams, sweet potatoes, rice, cocao, coffee, sugar cane, melon, watermelon, tobacco, manioc, plantains	news about potential warfare	domestic servants for missionaries, work for wages, slave labor (Indians and Negroes)

SOURCES: Bueno 1933:6, 13, 50–51, 71–74, 86–87, 96–97, 115–16, 129–32, 152; Humboldt 1956:232, 242, 260, 272, 288, 293–94, 298; IV: 49, 126–28; Cortés de Madariaga 1964:515, 519, passim; Michelena y Rojas 1867:234–36, 262, 264, 276–81, 325, 334, 342, 344, 359; Tavera Acosta 1954 [1907]:19–22, 57, 59, 209, 211, 233; Spruce 1970:344, 363, 377–79.

[a] A scented resin used for body paint.
[b] A fiber used for making brooms, brushes, etc.

exploitation of the Indian labor force can also be inferred from the lack of a fixed rate of pay for their labor they carried out and from the custom of paying them in kind (by *trueque*)[7] (Codazzi in Michelena y Rojas 1867, 263–64, 325, 329, 322–332, 339).

In addition to going through this process of economic insertion and political subjugation, indigenous peoples also lost their capacity to make decisions about how to handle their cultural resources. For example, the indigenous people had created and kept the technology for collecting and processing turtle eggs, which were abundant along the Orinoco's sandbanks. Although they continued to gather and trade turtle eggs, by the nineteenth century these important commercial centers along the Orinoco sandbanks were administered by officers from the expanding national society.

Our partial reconstruction of the System of Orinoco Regional Interdependence has been carried out in the form of a dialogue between the past and the present in which we have been able to discern continuities, ruptures, and transformations in the structural elements that have connected the ethnic groups, the components of the system. The underlying assumption is that the contemporary Indian groups living in the Orinoco Basin, even if they are not now understood to be culturally differentiated segments of their major encompassing Venezuelan and Colombian societies, have been able to maintain control over some of their own cultural resources. It is understood that external as well as endogenous changes have not only transformed these cultures but have also enriched them with the addition of appropriated cultural resources. As a part of the System of Orinoco Regional Interdependence, each ethnic group handled the nucleus of cultura propia and in turn a sphere of alien resources that would gradually be incorporated into its own culture proper as well. After the European colonial encounter, when different European parties and capitalist premises were fed into the system, the horizontal relations among the ethnic groups were broken. In addition, colonial conditions stimulated both the suppression of many of the Indians' own cultural and the introduction of alien cultural resources. We can thus understand how and why the control and decisions about its own resources were gradually modified for each ethnic group. One can also visualize the aggregated impact on the whole System of Orinoco Regional Interdependence. Nevertheless, it is important to remember that it is not the presence or absence of an extant corpus of cultural traits that supports the existence of a group or an interethnic system. The Orinoco polities, in responding to the colonial situation of imposed cultural changes via political, military, or ideological mechanisms, dropped resources, which affected the autonomous nuclei of each of their cultures. But at the same time, many of these societies incorporated alien cultural resources and in the process redefined both their own and others' into a new synthesis.

Since our initial conceptualization of the System of Orinoco Regional Interdependence, when we reconstructed data from the indigenous societies of northeastern Venezuela relating to their participation in the fairs located in the middle and lower Orinoco, there has been an enlargement of the empirical base that supports our understanding of the system:

(a) Ethnographic evidence illustrating interethnic relations between the Guajibo and Achagua of the western part of the Orinoco llanos, and more specifically the political strategies developed to allow for joint exploitation of natural resources from the various micro-environments;

(b) The interpretation of the role of the interfluvial routes as complementary passages connecting the different ethnic groups of the Guiana shield; and also how the Kari'ña of the eighteenth century came to rely on them to maintain the system. In spite of the fact that indigenous peoples lost control over the Orinoco floodplain (in the middle and lower river zones) and consequently of the resources contained therein, those alternative routes allowed the system to continue;

(c) The retreat into the interfluvial zone as the privileged arena for interethnic relations[8] allowed us to understand how the Orinoco societies were able to maintain the system despite suffering considerable demographic disruption and increasing external suppression of their material, symbolic, and organizational resources (i.e., alterations in settlement patterns and in economic and political relations). It is not surprising, therefore, to rediscover minicircuits of trade in full operation in the twentieth century, particularly in the interfluvial zone (Butt Colson 1973; Coppens 1972; Koch-Grünberg 1979, 1981, 1982; Thomas 1972);

(d) Our interpretation about the genesis of the debt/peonage system allows us to understand the connection between the indigenous institutions of deferred exchange and the neocolonial mechanism of debt/peonage. The indigenous groups, upon entering into trade relations with the Europeans, accepted advance payments (which trapped them irreversibly in debt) because they erroneously perceived it as equivalent to deferred exchange. Thus it is understood why the integration of the Orinoco societies into the colonial market system was not totally forced. The Europeans, in penetrating the System of Orinoco Regional Interdependence, introduced not only new products (e.g., steel tools and firearms) but also new economic premises, such as terms of differential exchange, debt/peonage system, and the nucleation of population as requirements for gaining access to those products. The new rules (of economic dealing) were imposed with the help of ideological mechanisms and military operations, which together facilitated the implantation of politico-economic domination.

Despite the changes recounted here, cultural and linguistic heterogeneity has not been eradicated during the last two centuries of domination. Ethnic groups continued and continue to redefine their nuclei of cultural autonomy, although their unequal relation with the dominant encompassing society has resulted in the growth of spheres of alienated and imposed culture.

The exercise of rethinking the history of the Orinoco peoples has enabled us to propose the existence of a System of Orinoco Regional Interdependence that is opposed to the current vision of Orinoco history and to illustrate why the Indian groups of the tropical lowlands are not societies bounded by environmental conditions that make the disintegration of their institutions inevitable. Indeed, a model like the System of Orinoco Regional Interdependence could be of help to discern how the Orinoco societies achieved multiple relationships of regional solidarity or levels of integration above the strictly local or ethnic.

APPENDIX

The main interfluvial routes were:

(a) Through the upper Caura River up to the Mura Rapids, the Kari'ña entered the Nichare River; after several days of navigation, they arrived at the Chamacu Mountains, where they left their canoes; they continued their trip on foot through the plains of the Manapire River Valley; they walked for two to four days until they reached the Manapire river, where they used canoes to reach the Ventuari River, which flows into the Orinoco River; after reaching the latter, they could arrive at the Guaviare and Cimite Rivers, where the port of Manuteso fair was held every year. The return trip was through the same route, that is, the Ventuari-Caura Rivers. Sometimes the Kari'ña followed a route along the left bank of the Orinoco River since there were no human settlements (Vega 1974; Gilij 1965; Gumilla 1963; Caulín 1966).

(b) In order to get in touch with the people of the Paragua River, the Kari'ña went down the Caura River. Beginning in the Mura rapids and navigating five days downstream, they reached the Pará waterfalls, where they had to take an overland route due to a series of rocks located in the river, which make navigation impossible. They followed this overland route until they reached the headwaters of the Caura River, and in less than a quarter of a league they arrived at the stream called Parupa. They followed the river downstream until they arrived at the Caroní (Caulín 1966 [1782]; Humboldt 1956).

(c) One alternative route to the Caura River route was that of the Caroní River. Across the Parupa, the Kari'ña entered the Chanaro River and through the Erebato [the upper Caura River] they reached the valley of the Manapiare [which flows into the Ventuari]. Navigating the latter downstream, they reached the Atabapo River [which flows into the Orinoco]. But sometimes the Kari'ña went from the Ventuari to the Padamo River and from the latter to the upper Orinoco and the Río Negro (Humboldt 1956).

(d) In order to reach the Cuyuní River, the Kari'ña used the Yuruari River, whose headwaters are very close to the Caroní River (Caulín 1966).

NOTES

1. *Quiripa*, a species of shellfish, was utilized as a unit of exchange value upon which trading accounts were made.

2. The present-day political delimitation between Venezuela and Colombia has resulted in the literature referring to the western llanos of Venezuela, to the eastern llanos of Colombia, and to the Orinoco region as if they were three geographically distinct units. González-Tarbes's (1986) global denomination of "Orinoco llanos" to refer to the Orinoquia of Colombia and the western, central, and eastern llanos of Venezuela seems to be a more accurate designation. Also, according to altitudinal levels, see Fermín-Gómez, 1965).

3. This study is based on the chronicles of the era and on the incorporation of ethnographic data from other ethnic groups with which the Kari'ña interacted (Morales-Méndez 1979).

4. For the nineteenth century we have been able to work only with published sources, which focus on trade relations. This serious shortcoming must be overcome in the near future with research in archives and with data coming from the oral history of the Orinoco ethnic groups.

5. The term *criollo* is used here to refer to neo-colonial, neo-Venezuelan and neo-Colombian populations, usually composed of mixed racial types (i.e., *mestizo*) and carriers of hybrid cultures.

6. The entrada was the practice of employing soldiers or armed civilian personnel to compel Indians to work for criollo enterprises.

7. Trueque in the postcolonial period is not exactly equivalent to the notion of barter. The latter involves a negotiation by both parties on a more or less equal footing for the exchange of goods and/or services. *Trueque*, on the other hand, as it is discussed here, involved an unfair advantage on the part of one of the parties such that the disadvantaged counterpart was left cheated by the exchange. In this case the Criollo commanded a knowledge of numbers, their addition and subtraction, and the real value of trade goods, which the Indian did not have.

8. Future research will have to determine whether there were different and complementary functions in the articulatory mechanism of the floodplains and of the

interfluvial zone prior to colonial encounter, whether the minicircuits reported in the ethnography from the twentieth century are the result of the use to which the interfluvial routes were put after the mid eighteenth century, or whether in pre-Hispanic times there existed a whole range of trade centers that made the interethnic connections even more intimate and intricate than we have visualized.

REFERENCES

Abbad, I.
1967   Visita de Fray Iñngo Abbad a las provincias de Nueva Barcelona y
            Guayana en 1773. In *Las Misiones de Píritu* (1773), edited by L. Gómez
            Canedo, 122–57. Fuentes para la historia colonial de Venezuela, vol.
            84, pt. 2. Caracas: Biblioteca de la Academia Nacional de la Historia.
Arvelo-Jiménez, N.
1980   Una perspectiva analítica: La antropología en el caso Nuevas Tribus.
            Manuscript at the IVIC, Department of Anthropology, Caracas,
            Venezuela.
1983a   Recursos humanos o el juego de las fuerzas en la región amazónica. In *El
            universo amazónico y la integración Latino Americana*, 103–15. Caracas:
            Universidad Simón Bolívar, Instituto de Altos Estudios de América
            Latina.
1983b   Introduction. In *Sistemas ambientales venezolanos*, vol. 1: *La organización
            social política y económica de las principales etnias del Territorio Federal
            Amazonas*, 184–206. Proyecto VEN/19/001. Región Guayana Territorio
            Federal Amazonas. Caracas: Ministerio del Ambiente y de los Recursos
            Naturales Renovables and UNESCO. Mimeographed.
1984   The political feasibility of tribal autonomy in Amazonia. Manuscript in
            the IVIC, Department of Anthropology, Caracas, Venezuela.
Binford, L. R.
1972   *An archaeological perspective*. New York: Seminar Press.
Biord-Castillo, H.
1985   El contexto multilingüe del sistema de interdependencia regional del
            Orinoco. *Antropológica* 63–64:83–101.
Blanton, R. E., S. A. Kowalewski, G. Frenman, and J. Appel
1981   *Ancient Mesoamerica*. New York: Cambridge University Press.
Bonfil Batalla, G.
1983   Lo propio y lo ajeno, una aproximación al control cultural. *Anuario
            Antropológico* 86:13–56.
1986   La teoría del control cultural en el estudio de procesos etnicos. Caracas:
            Tipografía Americana.
Butt Colson, A.
1973   Intertribal trade in the Guiana Highlands. *Antropológica* 34:1–70.

Caulín, A. (1782)
1966   *Historia de la Nueva Andalucía.* Fuentes para la Historia Colonial de
[1782]   Venezuela, 81–82. Caracas: Biblioteca de la Academia Nacional de la
            Historia.

Coppens, W.
1972   Las relaciones comerciales de los Ye'kuana del Caura-Paragua. *An-*
            tropológica 30:28–59.

Cortés de Madariaga, J.
1964   Diario y observaciones del presbítero doctor José Cortés de Madariaga
[1811]   en su regreso de Santa Fe a Caracas. . . . In *Relaciones geográficas de*
            Venezuela, edited by A. Arellano Moreno, 495–532. Fuentes para la
            Historia Colonial de Venezuela, vol. 70. Caracas: Biblioteca de la
            Academia Nacional de la Historia.

de Alcala, D. A.
1967   Escritura de concordia por la cual los misiones capuchinos, franciscanos
            y jesuítas delimitan sus respectivas zonas de apostolado en el Orinoco y
            Guayana. . . . In *Las Misiones de Píritu* (1773), edited by L. Gómez
            Canedo, 39–42. Fuentes para la Historia Colonial de Venezuela, vol.
            84, pt. 2. Caracas: Biblioteca de la Academia Nacional de la Historia.

de Carabantes, J.
1968   El P. José de Carabantes da cuenta al Consejo de Indias de la misión de
[1660]   Cumaná. Caracas: Biblioteca de la Academia Nacional de la Historia.

de Chaves y Mendoza, L.
1968   Visita del oidor de la Audiencia de Santo Domingo, D. Luis de Chaves
[1783]   y Mendoza a los pueblos de doctrina y misión de los capuchinos en la
            provincia de Cumaná, 1783. In *Misión de los capuchinos en Cumaná,*
            edited by B. de Carrocera, 474–510. Fuentes para la Historia Colonial
            de Venezuela, vol. 90, pt. 3. Caracas: Biblioteca de la Academia
            Nacional de la Historia.

de Humboldt, A.
1956   *Viaje a las regiones equinocciales del nuevo continente Hecho en 1799, 1800,*
            1802, 1803 y 1804. Biblioteca Venezolana de Cultura, Viajes y
            Naturaleza collection, 2d ed. Caracas: Ministerio de Educación.

de Vega, A.
1974   Noticia del principio y progresos del establecimiento de las misiones de
[1744]   gentiles en el río Orinoco por la Compañía de Jesús. . . . In *Documentos*
            Jesuíticos para la historia de la Compañía de Jesús en Venezuela, 3–149.
            Fuentes para la Historia Colonial de Venezuela, vol. 118, pt. 3. Caracas:
            Biblioteca de la Academia Nacional de la Historia.

Diguja Villagómez, J.
1761   Testimonio de la vista hecha por el Señor Dn. Joseph Diguja Villagómez,
            Coronel de los Reales Ejércitos en las Provincias de la Nueva Andalucía,

Nueva Barcelone y Guayana en el año de 1761. Archivo General de la Nación (Caracas), Visitas Públicas, vol. 3, folios 242–99 vto.

Fermín-Gomez, M.
1965   The Orinoco Basin: A geographical unit. Ph.D. diss., Boston University.

Fried, N. E.
1983   Notes on Guianan Indian beliefs and their effect on intergroup relations. Student paper, Department of Anthropology, Columbia University.

Garriga, B. de la, J. A. de Cervera, and R. de Mataro.
1775   Relaciones del estado actual de las misiones de los padres capuchinos catalanes de Guyana. . . . Archivo General de la Nación (Caracas), Misiones, vol. 5.

Garson, A. G.
1980   Prehistory, settlement and food production in the Savanna region of La Calzadade Páes, Venezuela. Ph.D. diss., Yale University.

Gilij, J.
1963   Ensayo de historia Americana. Fuentes para la Historia Colonial de
[1741]   Venezuela, 71–73. Caracas: Biblioteca de la Academia Nacional de la Historia.

González Tarbes, M. de la G.
1986   Ocupación y uso de la tierra y relaciones interétnicas: Los Guajibo de los llanos del Meta (Siglos XVI al XVIII). Master's thesis. Centro de Estudios Avanzados. Caracas: Instituto Venezolano de Investigaciones Científicas.

Gumilla, J.
1963   El Orinoco ilustrado y defendido. Fuentes para la Historia Colonial de
[1741]   Venezuela, 68. Caracas: Biblioteca de la Academia Nacional de la Historia.

Koch-Grünberg, T.
1979–81   Del Roraima al Orinoco, 3 vols. Caracas: Banco Central de Venezuela.
[1917–24]

Machado, J. V.
1845   Memoria que a la Honorable Diputación de Guayana dirige el Gover-nador de la Provincia en 1845. Archivo Histórico de Guayana (Ciudad Bolívar), Sección Gobernación de Guayana.

Michelena y Rojas, F.
1867   Exploración oficial por la primera vez desde el norte de la América del Sur . . . Brussels: A. Lacroix, Verboeckhoven and Company.

Mintz, S. W.
1959   Internal market systems as mechanisms of social articulation. In Inter-mediate societies: Social mobility and communication, edited by V. F. Ray, 20–30. Proceedings of the 1959 Annual Spring Meeting of the Ameri-can Ethnological Society. Seattle: University of Washington Press.

Morales Méndez, F.
1979   Reconstrucción etnohistórica de los Kari'ña de los siglos XVI y XVII.
            Master's thesis. Centro de Estudios Avanzados. Caracas: Instituto
            Venezolano de Investigaciones Científicas.
Morales [Méndez], F., and N. Arvelo-Jiménez
1981   Hacia un modelo de estructura social caribe. *América Indígena* 41:
            602–26.
Morales Méndez, F., M. Capriles de Prada, and H. Biord-Castillo
1987   Historia Kari'ña de los siglos XVI y XVII. *Boletín de la Academia Nacional
            de la Historia* 277 (70): 79–99.
Morey, N.
1975   Ethnohistory of the Colombian and Venezuelan llanos. Ph.D. diss.,
            University of Utah.
Morey, R. V., and N. Morey
1975   Relaciones comerciales en el pasado en los llanos de Colombia y
            Venezuela. *Montalbán* 4:533–64. Caracas: Universidad Católica Andrés
            Bello.
Murra, J. V.
1975   El control vertical de un máximo de pisos ecológicos en la economía de
            las sociedades andinas. In *Formaciones económicas y políticas del mundo
            andino,* 59–115. *Historia Andina,* vol. 3. Lima: Instituto de Estudios
            Peruanos.
Pelleprat, P.
1965   *Relato de las misiones de los padres de la Compañía de Jesús en las Islas y en
[1655]   Tierra Firme de América Meridional.* Fuentes para la Historia Colonial de
            Venezuela, 77. Caracas: Bibloteca de la Academia Nacional de la
            Historia.
Primov, F.
1981   Descriptive outline of the post-Columbian history of the Territorio
            Federal Amazonas until 1879. Manuscript. IVIC, Department of Anthro-
            pology, Caracas, Venezuela.
Roosevelt, A. C.
1980   *Parmana: Prehistoric maize and manioc subsistence along the Amazon and
            Orinoco.* New York: Academic Press.
Ross, J. B.
1980   Ecology and the problem of tribe: A critique of the Hobbesian model of
            preindustrial warfare. In *Beyond the myths of culture,* edited by E. B. Ross,
            33–60. New York: Academic Press.
Sahlins, M.
1972   *Stone Age economics.* Chicago: Aldine.
Spruce, R.
1970   *Notes of a botanist in the Amazon.* 2 vols. New York: Johnson Reprint
            Corporation.

Tavera Acosta, B.
1954   *Río Négro. Reseña etnográfica, histórica y geográfica del Territorio*
[1907]   *Amazonas.* Caracas.
Thomas, D. J.
1972   The indigenous trade system of Southeast Estado Bolívar, Venezuela.
            Antropológica 33:3–37.
Torrelosnegros, S. M.
1968   Resumen del estado de la misión de Cumaná, hecho por el P. Prefecto
[1780]   Simón María de Torrelosnegros, en el quese recogen importantes datos
            sobre las poblaciones misionales y doctrinas así como las estadísticas de
            ellas. . . . In *Misión de los Capuchinos de Cumaná*, edited by B. de
            Carrocera, 448–55. Fuentes para la Historia Colonial de Venezuela, vol.
            88–90, pt. 3. Caracas: Biblioteca de la Academia Nacional de la
            Historia.
Zucchi, A.
1967   La Betania: Un yacimiento arqueológico del Occidente de Venezuela.
            Ph.D. diss., Facultad de Ciencias Económicas y Sociales. Caracas:
            Universidad Central de Venezuela.

4

Social Organization and Political Power in the Amazon Floodplain

The Ethnohistorical Sources

ANTONIO PORRO

. . . that provinces so large yet with so few people, so distant from one another, with no police, nor reason, no government, without principal chiefs nor obedience to anybody.

—Laureano de la Cruz, 1653, on the Omagua

They are governed by Principales in the villages; and in the middle of this province, which is very large, there is a Principal, or their King, whom they all obey with great subjection, and they call him Tururucari, that means their God; and he considers himself so.

—Mauricio de Heriarte, 1662, on the Omagua

At first glance, the ethnohistorical sources concerning the sociopolitical organization of the Amazon floodplain in the sixteenth and seventeenth centuries pose more questions than answers. The writings of explorers, missionaries, and administrative officers who dealt with the matter are not only brief but contradictory in the picture they give us of the level of social and political integration of the so-called provinces of the Amazon River. Problems such as territoriality, population, size and appearance of the villages, the stratified or egalitarian character of societies, and the nature of political power are frequently treated in completely different ways, of which the excerpts quoted above are good examples. Because of the sources' scarcity and ambiguity, modern authors have approached these questions in different ways depending on the sources used and even on some selectivity in their analysis.

Scholars have felt the need for a revision of our understanding of these problems in recent years due to archaeological advances in the Amazon region.

There is now a consensus that during the thousand years that preceded Euro-pean occupation, several Amazonian populations reached a more complex degree of social development than the one observed by ethnographers since the nineteenth century. The discovery of archaeological sites of unusual ex-tension and artificial mounds with evidence of dwelling as well as funeral functions (the latter including elements suggesting differential access to ma-terial goods), has led archaeologists to assume the existence of political sys-tems similar to the circum-Caribbean chiefdoms. Although archaeological sequences do not point very clearly to the synchrony of this cultural horizon with the beginning of European conquest, several archaeologists have hoped that the early chronicles would record a way of life in accordance with the archaeological evidence and with the presumed political organization.

Unfortunately, modern models of pre-Columbian ethnic boundaries and political units have shown frequent misuse of historical data, haphazard treat-ment of sources (including the use of secondary instead of available primary sources), and misconceptions about social, cultural, and demographic change brought by early colonial contact. Examples include Métraux's (1948, 704–6) undue distinction between the Yoriman or Soliman of Acuña and Heriarte, and the Yurimagua of Samuel Fritz; and Meggers's (1971, 122–30) merging of Carvajal's and Acuña's Omagua instead of linking the latter to Carvajal's Aparia.

Amazonian hinterland settlement in the last thirty years has shown the rapid disintegration of Indian populations that had remained in partial or total isolation from neo-Brazilian society. There is conclusive evidence that the same process has been occurring along the Amazon River since the mid sixteenth century. European colonists explored the floodplain in two distinct periods separated by a gap that lasted, in the upper and middle Amazon, for three to four generations. The first period occurred in the mid sixteenth century with the Orellana and Ursúa-Aguirre expeditions. The second one started with the lay Franciscans Brieva and Toledo (1636) and continued with Pedro Teixeira (1637–1639), Laureano de la Cruz (1647–1650), and Samuel Fritz (1686–1724). On the Brazilian side, expeditions did not show this gap. They began about 1600 with the foundation of Belém (Pará) and reached the present-day Brazilian frontier on the upper Amazon a century later. Teixeira's expedition, although organized by Portuguese authorities, was recorded by the Spanish-speaking chronicler Acuña.

The two periods of Amazonian exploration left a reasonable ethnographic documentation that discloses very different situations with regard to demog-raphy, social organization, political power, and religious institutions. The sixteenth-century chronicles describe the unmodified Indian way of life, but information is almost always scanty and shallow because of the dangers and hazardous conditions endured by the travelers, which did not allow for accurate observation. On the other hand, Portuguese and Spanish chronicles of the second period were written under safer conditions, and in some cases after lengthy stays of missionaries and officers among populations already in the process of acculturation.

The population decline that accompanied and frequently preceded the foreigners can be evaluated, although not quantified, by comparing Carvajal's, Vásquez's and Altamirano's reports with those of Acuña, Cruz, and Heriarte a century later. The first epidemic recorded in the Brazilian upper Amazon was witnessed by Laureano de la Cruz in 1648 among the Omagua. When smallpox reached the village where the friar lived, a third of the population died within three months, and the villages' population was already much smaller than it had been in the mid sixteenth century. The massive expedition of Ursúa and Aguirre, with 370 solders and more than 500 Peruvian Indians, surely carrying the new diseases, had taken nine months to descend the Amazon, with predictable results on the health conditions of the riverine populations. It should not be a matter of surprise, therefore, that population numbers of the seventeenth century chronicles are much lower than those of the previous century, a circumstance that has led some historians to consider them as fanciful and to discard the first reports. The aggravation of demographic catastrophe by the persistence of institutions like contraceptive practices, abortion, and infanticide, whose function was to restrain population increase in precontact times, has been observed in modern ethnography and is also recorded among the Omagua (de la Cruz 1900) and other tribes (de Souza Ferreira 1894) during the seventeenth century.

What follows is an outline of the natives' social and political organization. It is not a systematic inventory, which would certainly be uncertain due to the poverty of the sources, but is instead a selection of data relevant to anthropological theory concerning some of the principal tribes of the upper and middle Amazon.

Tribal Territories and Settlement Patterns

Aparia and the Omagua

The sixteenth-century sources comment on the powerful chiefdom or "province" of Aparia, also called Carari and Manicuri, which extended from the lower Napo down to the region of São Paulo de Olivena, between the mouths of the Javari and Ia rivers in the Brazilian Amazon. Along more than 700 kilometers there were some twenty riverine villages with a total of fifty to sixty great houses. The principal village, Great Aparia (or "of Aparia, the Great"), was located some distance upriver from the present-day Brazilian-Colombian frontier. Francisco Vásquez (1561) says that in Carari and Manicuri,

> they are all the same people and dress and language, and the same arms, houses, and clothing. All these Indians are friends and confederate so that it looks like a single province instead of two, because the settlement is continuous, with no division. . . . All the villages are situated on the riverbanks, with no other settlements in the backlands; most are small and are some ten to fifteen leagues distant from one another. According to a good evaluation, the people from that province are not many, because in the villages we have seen there must be seven or eight thousand Indian inhabitants, or a maximum of ten thousand. (Vásquez 1909, 430–31)

This evaluation is consistent with those of other sources of the time but is much inferior to that of Altamirano, for whom in the first village found below the Napo mouth,

> there came to receive us in the middle of the river more than 300 canoes, and the one that had the fewest people carried ten, and the other, twelve Indians . . . and thus they gave the governor, Pedro de Ursua, a great gift of more than fifty canoes of fish, corn, peanuts, and yams . . . ; the village [was] very large, with more than 8,000 Indians. . . . There was in this province food for the troops, enough for more than six months, as along the riverbanks, more than four leagues upward and downward [from the village, there were] gardens of corn and sweet manioc, being a land of excellent climate, and the river never flooded. (de Espinosa 1948 [1629], 383–84)

Cultural and even linguistic evidence allows us to associate the Aparia of the sixteenth century with the Omagua of the following century (Porro 1981), although the upstream Omagua migration assumed by Lathrap (1972) seems to have been inverted in this late state of independent Omagua. In the mid seventeenth century the Omagua still occupied a territory comparable to the one of 1542–1561, although it was removed some 300 kilometers downstream from the mouth of the Atacuary (the present-day Peruvian-Colombian frontier on the left bank of the Amazon) down to the region of Foz do Mamoriá between the mouths of the Jutaí and the Juruá. As in the previous century, the Omagua villages succeeded one another "so frequently that as soon as one was lost to the eye, another appeared. [The Omagua's land's] width is, it seems, small as is not larger than the river" (de Acuña 1874 [1641], 109).

East and west of this territory, long stretches of the floodplain were kept uninhabited by periodic Omagua raids against the neighboring tribes. In

1691, Samuel Fritz located and mapped twenty-four Omagua villages, almost all on islands and some fifteen to thirty kilometers distant from one another (Noticias auténticas, 30:222–23). There are no concrete references on the subject of Omagua villages on the riverbanks. The population decline of the Omagua villages over the course of a hundred years had been dramatic; the six villages described by de la Cruz in 1647 (before the epidemic) had from eight to twenty-eight houses and a population of from 70 to 330 (de la Cruz 1900 [1653], 80–88). Compared to sixteenth-century estimates, this amounted to a drop of almost 70 percent.

Machifaro and the Aisuari

In the mid sixteenth century the right bank of the Amazon from Tefé to Coari (about 200 kilometers) was occupied by the province of Machifaro or Machiparo, a name which disappeared in subsequent chronicles. Carvajal (1934, 198) wrote that

> in the opinion of all, [it] extended for more than eighty leagues [some 320 kilometers, but 60 leagues in Oviedo's version of Carvajal], for it was all of one tongue, these [eighty leagues] being all inhabited, for there was not from village to village [in most cases] a crossbow shot, and one which was farthest [removed from the next] was not half a league away, and there was one settlement that stretched for five leagues without there intervening any space from house to house; . . . from its resources and its appearance it must be the most populous that has been seen.

A chronicler from the Ursúa expedition, on the other hand, mentions twenty-five to thirty villages, "not as good as those of the first province" (de Zúñiga 1865 [c. 1561], 228), with what would correspond to an average distance of seven kilometers between villages. The westernmost of these villages, near the lake of Tefé, was a sort of stronghold for the constant wars against the Omagua from Aparia. In 1538 Diogo Nunes would have found some five to six thousand warriors there (Drumond 1950, 99); Carvajal mentions more than 2,000, and Altamirano, whose estimates are usually quite high, gives numbers similar to those of Nunes. An Orellana officer managed to land with twenty-five men,

> and made a foray for a distance of half a league [two to three kilometers, perhaps less, due to Carvajal's short leagues] out through the village . . . ; and when the aforesaid Lieutenant had perceived the great extent of the settlement and of its population, he decided not to go farther . . . [because] a squadron of more than five hundred Indians was in the square. (Carvajal 1934, 192, 194)

In 1560, when Ursúa arrived in this place, he found some 300 to 400 armed men, besides women, children, and other "nonfighting Indians" (Vásquez 1909 [1561], 431). These two references, where estimates of the number of enemies seem more casual than previous overall evaluations, can be considered more reliable. Assuming a 1:4 ration for the warriors' numbers in relation to the overall population, the latter figure would be from 1,500 to 2,000 people.

Eighty years later, Acuña called the region's inhabitants Curuzirari, and from Laureano de la Cruz (1651) on, they were known as Aisuari. By this time, perhaps as a result of the first Portuguese raids in the middle Amazon and of the weakening of Omagua power upstream, they had occupied part of the buffer zone separating the two provinces. Their westernmost site, Teixeira's and Acuña's Village of the Gold, was situated ninety kilometers above Tefé. From there downriver, villages were so frequent that "no more than four hours after [having seen one], new ones were found, and sometimes, during all of half a day, we could see their hamlets" (de Acuña 1874 [1641], 114).

Though the Aisuari also depended on river resources, unlike the Omagua they were strongly entwined with the floodplain ecosystem and with the mainland populations and economy. Diogo Nunes wrote that "in each village [there were] many houses full of dry fish that they went to sell on the back lands, and they have trade with other Indians. The paths are wide and well beaten because many people use them" (Drumond 1950, 100). Altamirano describes these paths in detail, with shelters or trading places every three leagues, in the middle of gardens of manioc and corn "for sustenance and supply of travellers and merchants that went to and from the provinces of the back lands, to trade with the people of the Machifaro province and neighboring ones, the trading being of pottery and fish, that was excellent in the province of Machifaro, for gold sheets and trinkets, and other things of estimation of the land" (de Espinosa 1948 [1629], 386). Gold sheets and trinkets came to the Aisuari of Machifaro from the Caquetá and the Uaupés through the upper Rio Negro, as later reported by Acuña and Fritz (Porro 1985). The upper part of this trade route was still active at the beginning of the nineteenth century (de Souza 1848, 198).

The Solimões or Yurimaguas

In 1542, Carvajal described the province situated immediately east of Machifaro: It began two leagues upstream from the Lake Coari, with "a village on the model of a garrison, not very large, on an elevated spot overlooking the river. . . . This village was fortified. . . . There were many roads here that entered into the interior of the land, very fine highways" ("muchos caminos que entraban la tierra adentro muy reales"). Below the Coari there were "numerous and very large settlements and very pretty country and very fruitful land . . . and because the villages were so numerous and so large and because there were so many inhabitants the Captain did not wish to make port, and so all that day we passed through settled country."

In the region of Codajás, on a high bank, rose the principal village of the province, which the Spaniards called the Village of Pottery, because of the many beautiful polychrome ceramics made there. "It looked so nice that it seemed as if it might be a recreation place of some overlords of the inland . . . [as it was approached by] many roads and fine highways" (Carvajal 1934, 201–2).

It seems that Vásquez (1561) is speaking of the Village of Pottery when he finds in this same region

> another Indian village bigger than any other found up to now, as it was more than two leagues in length; the houses stood one beside the other along the riverside, and the Indians had run away from the village, leaving us the houses with an endless supply of corn . . . ; their houses are square and small, covered with cane [with palm trees, in another manuscript (see also Vásquez 1909)]. Behind this village, one crossbow shot from the riverbank, there is a lagoon or channel, beside which the village runs so as to appear like a long, narrow island. (Vásquez 1909, 443)

Altamirano adds that the great village "flooded every now and then when the river overflowed the land for more than 200 leagues, and for these times they had other houses, made as palafittes on the trees, with all things necessary for living" (quoted in de Espinosa 1948 [1629], 387–88).

The name Carvajal gave this province, Oníguayal or Omagua, has bewildered historians and anthropologists. Since the seventeenth century it has been called Culiman (by Rojas), Yoriman (by Acuña), Sorimões (by Heriarte), and Yurimagua (by Fritz). It must not be confused, therefore, with the historical Omagua of the lower Napo and upper Amazon, called Aparia by Carvajal. In 1639, as in the previous century, the province extended almost 250 kilometers along both banks of the river from the Coari down to a point a little above the Purus (Porro 1983–84, 26). Yoriman, according to Acuña, was

> the best-known and most belligerent nation of all the Amazon, which frightened the Portuguese fleet in its first entrance [Teixeira's travel upstream]; it is a land so full of people that nowhere did we see together more barbarians than on it. . . . [The region of Cipotuba and Codajás was] where was

concentrated its greatest strength [and it had] the biggest village found in all
the river, its houses occupying an extension of more than half a league; . . .
[the houses kept] four, five, and sometimes more families. (de Acuña 1874,
118–19)

Ten years later, Laureano de la Cruz, who found the region already deva-
stated by epidemics and by the first Portuguese raids, said that the Yoriman
villages had some twenty to twenty-four houses each (1900, 109). Putting
together both reports and allowing five people per nuclear family, five families
per house, and twenty-two houses per village, we have an average of 550
inhabitants per village. Some villages must have been larger, like the one
with an extension of half a league in which Pedro Teixeira managed to collect, in five days, some 280 hectolitres of manioc flour, "which gave us food
for all the rest of the voyage" (de Acuña 1874, 119).

Chieftainship

Settlement patterns in the upper Amazon, which we exemplified through
the Omagua, Aisuari, and Yurimagua data, leave no doubt about the demographic density of the floodplain as a whole and the great size of many villages. Although this type of settlement is usually associated with relatively
complex forms of social organization and political power, modern researchers
have been extremely cautious in this regard, and much data has not been exploited. Writing on chieftainship, Métraux merely suggested that "the statement that the Omagua chief (*zana*) had more authority than in most tribes
of the area may mean that he controlled not merely the household, but the
village" (1948, 697–98).

Ethnohistorical data on the extension of political power in the Amazon
floodplain vary with the period and place, and show a predictable parallelism
with the historical process of the depopulation and disarticulation of Indian
societies. The fifteenth-century chronicles, especially Carvajal, speak clearly
of provinces whose extension was coincident with their lords' jurisdiction.
Oviedo noted that once

we went off to find a settlement called Aparia, which [name] is [likewise that
of] a preeminent overlord of that [settlement] and the province to which it
belongs, and it [i.e., the province] is situated on both sides of the river . . . ;
we pushed on along the shores and through the country belonging to the
settlements owned by this chief, and that was a long distance owing to the
fact that his is an extensive dominion. (Oviedo, quoted in Carvajal 1934,
411–12)

As Carvajal described it,

> we arrived in the province belonging to Machiparo, who is a very great over-
> lord and one having many people under him, and is a neighbor of another
> overlord just as great, named Omaga, and they are friends who join together
> to make war on other overlords who are [located] inland, for they [i.e., the
> latter] come each day to drive them from their homes. This Machiparo has
> his headquarters quite near the river upon a small hill, and holds sway over
> many settlements and very large ones. (Carvajal 1934, 190).

Were Carvajal the only source, we should accept him with reservation, because in his account it is often difficult to separate the real from the imagined.
Also, in the style of the period, he has a tendency to personify political
power in the figure of the king. In the case of Machiparo, contrary to Aparia,
the *great overlord*, it seems, was not even seen by Orellana's companions. But
the seventeenth-century chronicles, as long as they are.discussing societies
still relatively integrated, corroborate the idea of centralized power. According to Acuña, the Omagua "are so much subjected to their principal *Cabanagem* that [they] do not need more than one word to have their orders instantly
obeyed" (de Acuña 1874 [1641], 109).

Heriarte, who wrote in 1662 but who had been familiar with the Amazon
since 1637, when he joined Teixeira's expedition, says that the Omagua "are
governed by Principals in the villages; and in the middle of this province,
which is very large, there is a Principal, or their King, whom they all obey
with great subjection, and they call him Tururucari, which means their God;
and he considers himself so" (1975 [1662], 185). He says also that the Aruak
of the lower Rio Negro "have a Principal in the mouth [of the river], which
is situated [on the] Amazon, considered as King, by the name of Tabapari. He
keeps under his rule many villages of different nations and is obeyed by them
most respectfully" (1975 [1662], 182). On the Tapajos, he declares that
"these Indians are governed by Principals, one in each hamlet ["rancho"]
with twenty or thirty couples [or "houses"?], and all are governed by a great
Principal, who is very much obeyed" (1975, 180).

The disappearance of the political units that the first chroniclers called
provinces could have been one of the first social consequences of depopulation, forced migrations, and missionarization. Laureano de la Cruz witnessed
the beginnings of this process among the Omagua only ten years after Acuña
had admired their good order and "police." At the end of the seventeenth
century, Samuel Fritz, paraphrased by Maroni, would say that in spite of the
state of decadence they lived in, "the Omagua were proud of having had

always, even before they became Christians, a type of police and government, living most of them a life in society, showing great subjection and
obedience to their principal *curacas*" (*Noticias auténticas*, 30:195).

Hierarchical Groups

Besides having external relationships of domination and subordination, several peoples of the Amazon floodplain were internally ranked. Unfortunately,
in few cases are the sources sufficiently clear to allow a description in precise
sociological terms. While early chronicles let us suppose the existence of eth-
nically homogeneous provinces with centralized political power, the few more
detailed descriptions show a more complex pattern of relationship, with varying degrees of power and prestige. An example of this is the Irurí (Irurizes),
one of the five nations related to one another that in the second half of the
seventeenth century, occupied the right bank of the lower Madeira between
the Aripuanã and the island of Tupinambarana. According to Betendorf,

> the Irurizes are divided into five villages, each one with its principal; they
> say they descend from a woman who became pregnant from heaven and gave
> birth to five sons, of which the first is called Iruri, the second Unicor, the
> third Aripuana, the fourth Surury, and the fifth Para-Parichara. . . . The
> Irurizes' villages are governed by elective principals so that the most capable
> among them succeeds after the death of their principal; and in the villages,
> only those who are related ["parentes"] can have a separate house, as the
> vassals live in gardens ["roças"] belonging to those who govern them, so the
> villages comprise nothing but principals, who elect above them a chieftain
> ["cabo"], which is like the headman of all. There were . . . five great villages
> of this same nation; the first of Irurizes, the second of Paraparixanas, the
> third of Aripuanas, the fourth of Onicores, and the fifth of Tororizes, besides
> some small villages of little consideration; those five, though, comprised
> more than twenty villages, as each garden of those principals was a good
> village of vassals. . . . [During a visit paid by the Paraparixanas to the Irurizes
> villages, the visitors] had in their hands some staff wands split open at the
> end, showing that they had vassals and were noble among their own. Each
> one of them had some lads in front . . . and there they remained some four
> or five days, never entering the houses of that village, even though they have
> close relatives there on account of being married one to the other. . . . The
> principals are buried in some great hollow trunks like great barrels, and there
> they also bury alive his dearest mistress and his handsomest boy. (Betendorf
> 1910, 355, 464–67)

Thus Iruri was both the collective name of five groups that claimed to have
a common mythic female ancestor and also the specific denomination of one

of these groups. Each one of them occupied a territory or "great village," which comprised a bigger village, where only members of the group lived and four or five "roças," or small hamlets, where "vassals," perhaps from a different ethnic group, lived. As they were superior to their subjects, the inhabitants of the five bigger villages came to be overall chiefs or principals. It is also possible that the subjects were not a subordinated people but rather that a single tribe had a hierarchically superior lineage, all of whose members lived in the biggest village. Each of the five groups or principal lineages, apparently exogamous, had an elective chief, but there is no word of a supreme chiefdom common to the five groups. On the other hand, the elective chiefs commanded great influence and prestige, as they had several wives or concubines and young male companions who were buried alive with the dead chief.

Chantre y Herrera, who based his writings on Jesuit reports of the seventeenth and eighteenth centuries, says that among the Omagua, Peva, Tucuna, and Cauachis of the upper Amazon, there were "some families recognized by the others as distinctive and superior, which we might call nobility, as they maintain a lordly air that gives them more regard and honor. It will be difficult for a young boy or girl of this superior class to marry beneath him or herself, as none of the elders who arrange these marriages between nobles would agree to it" (Chantre y Herrera 1901 [1767], 83).

Chantre y Herrera also describes the ceremony or rite of passage with which the Omagua proclaimed the "nobility" of boys and girls. The children were carried to the principal house in litters preceded by a retinue of women and musicians. There, men and women seated on benches and mats, respectively, waited for them. The village chief (zana) then proceeded to the children's ritual hair cutting and presented them to the adults, saying, "Aiquiana ene zana," which means, This is thy Lord (Chantre y Herrera 1901 [1767], 84). In the continuation of this hierarchy of lineages, a woman retained her husband's status:

> Because, with the *cacique, principal,* or captain dead, the younger brother, to whom the honor belongs, comes forward, and he marries his brother's widow, whose children, if any, will be adopted as his own, although it becomes necessary to leave his own wife and children. . . . (Chantre y Herrera 1901 [1767], 73)

> . . . as they thought that there was a kind of reason or convenience in which the second brother would succeed the first in office and in which the *capitana* could not be lowered in the dignity that was hers during her husband's life. (Chantre y Herrera 1901 [1767], 115)

Beneath the levels of this lineage stratification, the Omagua had slaves—prisoners of war or individuals purchased from other tribes. Each family had one or two for home and agricultural services, and, Chantre y Herrera noted, "they treat their servants with much affection, as they would their children, they clothe them, eat from the same plate, and sleep with them under the same awning" (*Noticias auténticas*, 30:194).

The coexistence of social stratification with institutions that have a tendency to neutralize it is also found among other tribes of the Amazon floodplain. In the words of Heriarte, the Tupinambarana of the middle Amazon

> are predominant and subjugate other nations such as the Aratús, Apcuitáras, Yaras, Goduis, and Cariatos. They use them as vassals and receive tribute from them. They say that . . . they arrived at this site . . . and conquered the natives subjugating them, and with time they intermarried and became related, but the natives never failed to recognize the superiority of the Tupinambaranas. . . . They have seven or eight wives. To those under their domination they give their daughters in marriage. . . . (de Heriarte 1975 [1662], 181)

Problems and Research Directions

Studies of settlement patterns, demography, tribal territories, social organization, and political structure in the Amazon floodplain are just beginning. The preceding pages present a synthesis of some of these problems based on half a score of published sources of uneven value. Few Spanish, Portuguese and Latin American civil and religious archives have been studied with regard to the problems, and except for some work done in the Peruvian Amazon, there is no meaningful archaeological data for the late Precolumbian period. Consequently, when we give the matter something more than a merely descriptive treatment, there are still many more questions than answers. Nevertheless, some relevant points can already be resolved, and some hypotheses can be suggested.

Tribal Territories in the Floodplain and in the Mainland

Due to the geography of Spanish and Portuguese exploration, most of the historical data concern the Amazon shoreline, mainly the *várzea*, or floodplain, where larger populations and more complex social and political organizations were possible than in the *terra firma*, or mainland (Meggers 1971; Denevan 1977; Moran 1990). What is left to know is whether, as some sources suggest, the riparian provinces also extended throughout the mainland, and to what extent. In this case, and gainsaying recent ethnographic evidence, did the mainland also display, at least in some cases, the demographic, social, and political patterns of the floodplain? And should the "tropical forest culture" of some modern mainland tribes be considered as a "regressive" result of a recent (300- to 400-year) adaptation to this ecosystem?

Social Stratification and Political Power

The theoretical framework I suggest that we apply in the Amazon floodplain consists of Service's (1962) and Fried's (1967) evolutionary stages of political organization. The matter in question is whether we are faced with egalitarian, ranked, or stratified societies. Setting aside occasional (and apparently careless) references to Amazonian states or kingdoms (Lathrap 1972, 17–18), the matter to be discussed is whether they were tribes or chiefdoms. Several sources suggest that the provinces were territorially defined and socially stratified units in which a centralized political power was superimposed over several local groups. Pointing in this direction are several references to high-status lineage and nobility attributes among the Omagua (Chantre y Herrera) and the Iruris and Tapajos (Betendorf), as well as to "major *principales*" or "kings" among the Omagua (Carvajal, Heriarte, Fritz), on the lower Rio Negro tribes (Heriarte), and also among the Conduris and Tapajos (Carvajal, Heriarte).

Intertribal Domination

The discussion of evidence of institutionalized relations of domination and subordination among different tribes or chiefdoms must start by defining the nature of the social units mentioned by the sources (local groups, lineages, tribes, chiefdoms?). Did Betendorf's description of the Iruris' *principal* and vassals concern different lineages of the same tribe or different tribes? The Tupinambarana were considered superior by the middle Amazon tribes among which they established themselves in the mid sixteenth century, but as time went by "they intermarried and became related" (Heriarte 1975, 181; see also Acuña 1874); how did they keep up that "superiority" for more than a hundred years? And how did those hierarchical relations stem from the known egalitarian organization of the eastern Brazilian Tupinambá? Were the Nhamundá and Trombetas Conduris really submissive to some hinterland group that Carvajal idealized as the "amazons"? These and other similar questions must be answered if we want to understand the stage of social evolution achieved by the floodplain's societies. Some clues in this direction may be suggested by evidence of specialized production and distribution of specific raw materials and artifacts like vegetable ash salt (salt obtained from vegetal ashes), stone axes, wood carvings, and small gold pendants (Porro 1985).

Religion and Power

Last but not least is the problem of the status and social role of the religious specialists. Are we dealing with medicine men or shamans (as in the typical tropical forest cultures) or with the holders of a functional apparatus of idols and a formal cult analogous to that of the formative stages of ancient civilizations? The latter hypothesis seems to be supported by personages (men-gods?) like the Guaricaya of the Yurimagua and Aisuari (Fritz), by the Carabayanas' "priests of idols" (Heriarte), and by the cult of deified ancestors of the Tapajos (Betendorf).

There is a long way to go before most of these questions will be answered. Fifty years ago Julian Steward brought American anthropology to a significance advance when he demonstrated the basic unity of what he called "tropical forest cultures." Today we have much less certainty than in his time, but the simple fact that we are posing these questions and can suggest directions for their solution indicates that there has been substantial progress in our understanding of the ancient peoples of Amazonia.

REFERENCES

Except for Carvajal 1934, all translations are the author's.

Altimarano. *See* de Espinosa 1948.
Betendorf, João Felipe
1910   Chronica da missao dos Padres da Companhia de Jesus no Estado do
[1698]   Maranhao, *Revista do Instituto Histórico e Geográfico Brasileiro* (Rio de
              Janeiro) 72 (1): 1–697.
Chantrey Herrera, J.
1901   *Historia de las misiones de la Campañía de Jesus en el Marañon Español.*
[1767]   Madrid: A. Avrial.
de Acuña, C.
1874   Nuevo descubrimiento del gran rio de las Amazonas. Transcription of
[1641]   1st ed. in *Memórias para a história do extincto Estado do Maranhao*, 2:58–
              143. Rio de Janeiro: Hildebrandt.
de Carvajal, G.
1934   *The discovery of the Amazon.* Edited by H. C. Heaton. American Geo-
[1542]   graphical Society, Special Publication No. 17. New York.
de Espinosa, A. V.
1948   *Compendio y descripción de las Indias Occidentales.* Smithsonian Institu-
[1629]   tion, Miscellaneous Collections, 108. Washington, D.C.

de Heriarte, M.
1975   Descrição do estado do Maranhão, Pará, Corupá e Rio das Amazonas.
[1662]   In *História Geral do Brasil*, edited by F. A. de Varnhagen, 8th ed., 3:171–
            90. São Paulo: Melhoramentos.
de la Cruz, L.
1900   *Nuevo descubrimiento del Rio de Marañon llamado de las Amazonas.*
[1653]   Madrid: La Irradiación.
Denevan, W. M.
1977   The aboriginal population of Amazonia. In *The native population of South
            America in 1492*, edited by W. M. Denevan, 205–34. Madison: Univer-
            sity of Wisconsin Press.
de Souza, A. F.
1848   Notícias geográficas da Capitania de São José do Rio Negro. . . . *Revis-
            tado Instituto Histórico e Geográfico Brasileiro* (Rio de Janeiro) 10:411–
            504.
de Souza Ferreira, J.
1894   América abreviada, suas noticias e de seus naturaes, . . . *Revista do
            Instituto Histórico e Geográfico Brasileiro* (Rio de Janeiro) 57 (1): 5–
            153.
de Zúñiga, G.
1865   Relación muy verdadera de . . . Rio Marañon. In *Colección de*
[c. 1561]   *Documentos Inéditos . . . de América y Ocenia*, 4:215–82. Madrid:
            Archivo de Indias.
Drumond, C.
1950   A carta de Diogo Nunes e a migração dos Tupí-Guaraní para o Peru.
            Revista de História (São Paulo) 1:95–102.
Fried, M.
1967   *The evolution of political society.* New York: Random House.
Lathrap, D. W.
1972   Alternative models of population movements in the tropical lowlands of
            South America. In *XXXIX Congreso Internacional de Americanistas: Actas
            y Memorias*, 4:13–23. Lima.
Maroni, P. See *Noticias auténticas.*
Meggers, B. J.
1971   *Amazonia: Man and culture in a counterfeit paradise.* Chicago: Aldine.
Métraux, A.
1948   Tribes of the middle and upper Amazon River. *Handbook of South Amer-
            ican Indians.* Vol. 3. Bureau of American Ethnology Bulletin no. 143.
            687–712. Washington, D.C.: Smithsonian Institution.
Morán, E.
1990   A ecologia humana das populações da Amazônia. Petrópolis, Brazil:
            Vozes.

Myers, T. P.

1973   Toward the reconstruction of prehistoric community patterns in the
            Amazon Basin. In *Variation in anthropology*, edited by D. Lathrap and
            J. Douglas, 233–52. Urbana: Illinois Archaeological Survey.

Noticias auténticas del famoso rio. Marañon (Presumed author: Pablo Maroni), edited
            by M. J. de la Espada. *Boletín de la Sociedad Geográfica de Madrid* 26–33
            (1889–92). Includes Samuel Fritz's *Diary* and other Jesuit sources.

Nunes, D. [1553?] *See* Drumond 1950.

Porro, A.

1981   Os Omagua do alto Amazonas: Demografia e padrões de povoamento no
            século XVII. In *Contribuições á antropologia em homenagem ao Professor
            Egon Schaden*, 207–31. São Paulo: Museu Paulista, Série Ensaios, no. 4.
            São Paulo.

1983–84   Os Solimões ou Jurimaguas: Território, migrações e comércio intertribal.
            Revista do Museu Paulista (São Paulo), new ser., 29:23–28.

1985   Mercadoria e rotas de comércio intertribal ne Amazônia. *Revista do
            Museu Paulista*, new ser., 30:7–12.

Roosevelt, A. C.

1991   *Moundbuilders of the Amazon*. San Diego: Academic Press.

Service, E. R.

1962   *Primitive social organization*. New York: Random House.

Vásquez, Francisco

1909   Relación verdadera de todo lo que sucedió en la jornada de Omagua y
[1561]   Dorado. . . . In *Historiadores de Indias*, edited by M. Serrano y Sanz,
            2:423–84. Madrid.

5

The Evidence for the Nature of the Process of Indigenous Deculturation and Destabilization in the Brazilian Amazon in the Last Three Hundred Years

Preliminary Data

ADÉLIA ENGRÁCIA DE OLIVEIRA

The objective of this chapter is to review the history of the cultural and social transformations—deculturation and destabilization—that indigenous groups in Brazilian Amazonia have undergone since first contact. Initially, factors such as warfare, the demand for slaves for diverse kinds of work, and missionary action were essential to the deculturation process. More recently, beginning principally in the 1970s, the accelerated process of the occupation of the Amazon has contributed to Indians becoming conscious of the problems they confront and to a consequent movement toward ethnic self-affirmation. These transformations, however, did not occur simultaneously in all of Amazonia because of its cultural and historical diversity and its size.

Research presented here is still in the preliminary phase and treats only the basic bibliographic references on the history of the region, including the voyages of Orellana, Rojas, and Pedro Teixeira; it does not include consultations of archives outside Brazil. Two products of this research that treat the problem of deculturation have already been published (de Oliveira, 1983, 1988), and the present chapter is a summary of the factors that have led to the deculturation and decimation of Amazonian Indians in Brazil.

Decimation and Deculturation of Large Indian Populations

From the moment Spanish and Portuguese colonizers arrived in the Amazon region in the sixteenth century the history of their relationship with the Indian population has been one of subjugation of the indigenous peoples, invasion of their lands, introduction of disease, and misuse of their natural resources. This exploitation resulted in the deculturation and depopulation of the Indians and led many groups to physical and cultural extinction.[1]

When Francisco de Orellana made the first voyage on the Amazon River in 1541, descending from the headwaters near the Pacific to the Atlantic, he not only discovered the greatest river on earth, in terms of volume of water, but also described the very large and densely populated villages that were then on its banks. According to Friar Gaspar de Carvajal (de Carvajal, de Rojas, and de Acuña 1941), the chronicler of the voyage, these villages possessed broad paths, with landing places along the river, and an abundance of food. The expedition of Pedro de Ursúa and Lope de Aguirre (1560 to 1561),[2] larger and more aggressive than that of Orellana, descended the Amazon approximately twenty years later in search of riches and the mythical "Province of Omágua" but ended in tragedy. The record of this expedition also notes villages, the abundance of food, and a technology of environmental exploitation. This chronicle also speaks of roads that were probably commercial routes and of densely populated areas.

Almost one century after the voyage of Orellana, in 1639, Father Cristobal de Acuña reported the voyage of Pedro Teixeira returning to Belém from Quito on the same river navigated by Orellana. He also told of extensive and densely populated villages, providing more details than Carvajal on the cultural characteristics of the Indians, and citing the names of tribal groups and affirms that "all this new world . . . is inhabited by barbarians of distinct provinces and nations. . . . There are over a hundred and fifty, all with different languages, as large and densely populated as those that we saw on all this route" (my translation, de Carvajal, de Rojas, and de Acuña 1941, 199).

Rojas, during this same period, also writes that the river of the Amazons, the islands, and the lands "hinter" were so heavily populated "that if you threw a needle up in the air, it would fall on the head of an Indian and not on the ground" (my translation, de Carvajal, de Rojas, and de Acuña 1941, 107–8). In spite of the evident exaggeration contained in this statement, it provides, in an impressionistic way, an idea of the density of settlement and the impact that the size and continuity of the village had on the first travelers.

In relation to the evidence that groups in this area traded among themselves, there is the work of Porro (1984), who shows that intertribal commerce was a systematic economic activity, there being no doubt that there existed "local specialization in the production and distribution of goods" (Porro 1984, 4). The goods must have circulated by traditional trade routes, such as the (rivers) Negro-Japurá, and commerce was also carried out at long distances[3] with people of the Andean highlands.

In addition to the data from the early chroniclers, there seems to be evidence of more extensive settlement from archaeological research.[4] Even though the research carried out in Amazonia is modest so far, preceramic and ceramic sites have been found in Marajó, Santarém, along the Atlantic coast in the state of Pará, the lower Amazon, Amapá, Rondônia, Mato Grosso, Serra dos Carajás, Northern Maranhão, the Xingu/Tocantins interfluvial region, and along the Solimões, Negro, Japurá, Purus, Guaporé, Mamoré, Madeira, Juruena, Aripuanã, Uatumã, Jatapu, Urubu and Nhamundá-Trombetas Rivers in the Brazilian Amazon. Many sites have also been found in the other countries with Amazon territories.

The oldest dates determined by carbon 14 indicate that hunter-gatherers occupied the area between about 12,000 and 1,000 B.C., including some populations that specialized in gathering shellfish and in fishing that produced shell mounds along the Atlantic coast and the margins of some rivers. The latter initiated ceramic activities around 3,200 B.C. (Simões 1981, 17–18, and 1983, 7).

The archaeological data collected indicate a variety of adaptations related to the cultivation of manioc and maize spreading throughout the Amazon Basin from the end of the second millennium B.C. onward.

In summary, Amazonia was occupied in diverse directions by Indian groups of different origins and different cultural patterns before the arrival of Europeans. However, whatever the route they traveled to arrive in this region, it is certain that humans were already present in the area approximately 11,000 years ago (personal communication from Anna C. Roosevelt), and since that moment occupied different types of environments: the Atlantic coast, the valleys of large and small rivers, lakes and settlements built in *várzeas, terra firme* and in the interior of the forest, or in open areas.

Recent research, undertaken by archaeologists of the Museu Goeldi (Belém, Pará) in the region of Cachoeira Porteira, in Porto Trombetas (Rio Trombetas, Pa.) in a stretch of the margins of the rivers Amazonas and Trombetas (just below Porto Trombetas), on the river Xingu in the region of the Projeto Carajás (rivers Itacaiúnas and Parauapebas-Pa.) provides evidence of continuous occupation of various sizes. According to Dirse Kern[5] a fairly significant density of sites was found in the region of Cachoeira Porteira. In thirty days of fieldwork, forty-three archaeological sites were located, not very far from one another, and of different sizes. One of them was approximately 500 m by 300 m. Klaus Hilbert, who conducted research on the margins of the Amazonas and Trombetas among other places, affirms that this area is covered with sites, all belonging to the "Konduri" complex (the phases have not yet been defined). He located three sites each day during fifteen days' fieldwork, giving a total of nearly forty-five sites. On the Iriri, a tributary of the Xingu, according to data provided by Fernando Marques, a site of approximately 130,000 m^2 was located, with ceramic and lithic material discovered up to 80 cm depth. In the region of Projeto Carajás, according to data furnished by Daniel Lopes and Maura Silveira, the sites are continuous, of varied sizes, and there are places where they appear on both margins. The distances between one site and another alternate between 500 m and 5,000 m, and their sizes vary from 40,000 m^2 to 22,000 m^2 to only 300 m^2.

Present research of Anna Roosevelt in Marajó indicates that "the overall population of the Marajoara society would have been at least 100,000, and probably more" (1989b, 78).

Evidently, there are several possible hypotheses to explain the density of archaeological sites in certain areas, such as: (a) the great density of sites reflects a high demographic density; or (b) the density reflects the occupation of the same group, in different localities, forming various sites in the same space of time; or (c) certain groups utilized more than one settlement, moving from one place to another now and again.

Dirse Kern, who is a soils specialist, would discard this last hypothesis, taking into consideration the density of the occupational refuse principally in sites with archaeological black soil, where the soils are highly modified. She suggests that this would require either a very long period of settlement, or a high population density.

Moreover, as Smith says,

> it is difficult to estimate how large a population inhabited each black earth locality. Native buildings were, and still are made from wood and palm fronds that soon disintegrate. Another problem is that aboriginal cultures in the region use different village plans, ranging from a large communal house to a circle of dwellings. The large riverine *terra preta* sites may have been occupied for various periods by different groups, each time deepening and possibly extending the area of stained earth. But the entire area of even the largest sites may have been settled at one time; the 80 ha. Manacapuru site[6] could have been occupied by as many as 18,000 Indians. (1980, 563–564)

Without doubt, the reconstruction of the prehistoric past presents difficulties. Among these obstacles to knowledge are lack of research, since there are few researchers and the area to be investigated is large; the density of the vegetation, which makes the localization of archaeological vestiges difficult; the rarity of instruments of resistant material, such as stone; and the climate, which is not favorable for the preservation of materials such as wood, fiber, bones, and so on, from which the majority of such articles were made. However, using technical resources such as flotation, and the analysis of the chemical composition of the soil, evidence of large amounts of organic material can be detected.

Despite *very scarce data* on Amazonian prehistory for *such a vast territory,* it is important to note that whatever the direction taken by the original migrations, human groups occupied diverse forms of environment, as we have already emphasized. The vestiges of their passage include *sambaquis* (shell mounds), caves, the remains of houses built on stilts, rock inscriptions and paintings, mounds, and *hypogea,* or artificial wells.

Though we must read with care the information of the early writers, mainly because of probable European ethnocentric fantasies and distortions, it is important to verify that when the tribal groups of Amazonia suffered the impact of first contact with individuals of another ethnic group, it seems that they lived in very large, well laid-out villages and had more than adequate food supplies. Although the information of these early writers may contain exaggerations about the size of the villages, the number of inhabitants, and the abundance of food, what is important is that recent research in archaeology is demonstrating not only a great density of sites in certain areas, which has deeply impressed some researchers, but also that the flood plains and *terras firmes* (uplands) of the river Amazonas and its tributaries could have been densely populated (one of the hypotheses) by individuals who took from nature sufficient nourishment and materials to survive. Collecting, agriculture, hunting, fishing, and, it seems, also animal rearing were the basis of their subsistence.

Data provided by Friar Bartolomé de Las Casas (1984) shows a dense and continuous population for Spanish America, demonstrating that the situation before or at the very beginning of European contact must have been similar throughout much of the Amazonian region. As we have already mentioned, there is evidence that the groups in all this area traded among themselves.

When the Europeans arrived in Brazilian Amazonia, the most densely populated indigenous villages were, above all, concentrated on the margins of rivers. These Indians lived in a rather simple way compared with the Aztec and the Maya groups of the Central American region, and the Pre-Incas and

Incas of the Andean area, which were the most complex civilizations that they encountered.

However, a more detailed analysis of the evidence left in archaeological remains of ceramics in Brazilian Amazonia would verify that, even in this region, some societies reached a reasonable degree of complexity, such as those represented by the Marajoara phase (the area of open plains in the east-central part of the Island of Marajó) and by the Guarita subtradition (the ceramic complex of greatest geographical distribution in the Amazon Basin, occurring in the stretch between the mouth of the river Tefé and the middle and lower courses of the rivers Negro and Madeira). If the great development of ceramic industry is considered, the Santarém culture should be mentioned.[7] This culture, according to some specialists, is correlated to groups that existed in various parts of Central America and is found in the basin of the river Tapajós (Nimuendajú 1949, 93–106). Up to now, however, systematic studies with the aim of understanding the origin and development of this culture are just beginning.

Despite the fact that the present state of archaeological research in Amazonia does not allow many inferences to be made about the patterns of occupation of the epoch, it can be supposed, by the quantity of the sites found in this area and the quality of some ceramics that occur in them, that the size of the villages and the forms of social and political organization differed partly from present-day patterns. This is corroborated by information given by the early writers of the region.

Before the arrival in 1616 of Francisco Caldeira Castelo Branco in the Bay of Guajará, where Belém is situated today, the region had already been traveled over not only by Orellana and the others who came after him, but also, after 1580, by English, Dutch, Irish, and French individuals who established settlements between the Oiapoque and the vicinity of the river Tapajós, maintaining contact with the Indians, with whom they traded.

Since these Europeans intended to create colonies in Amazonia, the Portuguese, commanded by Castelo Branco, headed towards this area, which was the extreme edge of the dominion of the Crown of Portugal, with the intention of expelling them and occupying this piece of the Brazilian coast. This was done at the expense of the tribal territories; this occupation took on three closely interrelated aspects:[8]

1. That of defense and occupation of the territory through military encounters, construction of fortifications and river journeys like that of Pedro Teixeira.

2. The economic, which, in the beginning, had its activities directed towards the planting of sugar-cane and extraction of the so-called *drogas do sertão* (cacao, sarsaparilla, urucu (annatto), cloves, cinnamon, anil, seeds, puxuri, vanilla) and, later was followed by an agricultural experiment and the introduction of cattle-raising. For the collection of the drogas do sertão, with which Portugal aimed to substitute the spices, the Indian was an essential labor force because of his knowledge of the river, the forest, and the products sought. For this activity they were brought down from their villages and enslaved to serve as guides, rowers, and collectors.

3. The religious, or better, missionary activity, which aimed to make the Indian a Christian, bringing him down from his villages to the centers of catechism and "civilization." In these centers the Indian lost his own ways of thinking, feeling, and acting in consequence of the impositions of the missionaries. Thus, the many small and large towns of Amazonia sprang up.

The missionary work in Amazonia, as well as the military occupation, was carried out by Portugal. In its religious agents Portugal really had very strong support for its political action in this region. Although the missionaries partially "saved" the Indians physically from the greed of the colonists, they were the people principally responsible for the Indians' cultural extinction. The missionaries helped the Portuguese colonists and soldiers to open up Amazonia, expanding the territory but deculturing its first inhabitants, leading a great part of these to extinction. In exercising the role of educator with exclusiveness, among the indigenous communities in settlements as well as among the colonists in the early centers, the missionaries, at the same time that they taught reading, writing, arithmetic, and religion also propagated the ideology of Portuguese colonialism. They thus collaborated in the consolidation of colonialism in Amazonia.

In this phase of Portuguese expansion there were a lot of Indians in Amazonia and few non-Indians. A large part of the contingent that formed the troops that opened up this region was made up of Indians. They were enslaved not only to work in public and domestic services, in the construction of churches and houses, in the salting of fish, in the confection of turtle butter, in fields, and in the collection of drogas do sertão, but also to serve as soldiers and rowers in the troops of conquest.

The enslavement of Indians was permitted when they were *resgatado*[9] (rescued) from death at the hands of enemies or when they were imprisoned in *guerra justa*[10] (just war). In both cases the law made it easy to cheat, while justifying the attitude of the colonizer. Although the missionaries often quarreled with the colonists because of the *resgates* and *guerras justas* they also indirectly enslaved Indians through the *descimentos*.[11] Thus the descimentos and the resgates and the guerras justas played a fundamental part in the physical extinction of the Indian of Amazonia and in the loss of his particular ways of life.

Another factor of fundamental importance in the depopulation of Indians was the diseases brought by the Europeans such as smallpox, influenza, and others.

With the advance over their lands, the Indians started to revolt against the Portuguese domination and to rebel against enslavement. However, the Luso-Brazilians had superiority of arms and lethal diseases. The Indians were brutally reduced from seemingly large numbers until today, when they are only approximately 160,000, in various stages of contact. The first skirmishes fought in the villages of Cumã, Caju, Mortigura (Conde) Iguape, Guamá were followed by massacres of Indians along the Tocantins and Pacajá. During this phase of Portuguese expansion, battles that led entire groups to extinction occurred in the Tapajós, Madeira, Xingu, Negro, and several other places. The chronicle records, for example, that one governor of the Captaincy of Pará, Bento Maciel Parente, entrusted by the governor-general of Brazil with the War of the Tupinambás, in 1619 wiped out the Indians from Taputapera in Maranhão to the mouth of the Amazon. These Tupinambás were the same Indians who had peacefully made contact with Francisco Caldeira de Castelo Branco and occasionally revolted against the tyranny of the colonists, but, above all, they were the people who had actively collaborated in implanting Portuguese rule in the Amazonian world. With their knowledge of the environment they helped the Portuguese and Brazilians to survive in this region. With the aid of their labor, the colonists became established in the area.

While the Luso-Brazilians expanded more and more in Amazonia, widening their frontiers, the Indians continued to die from epidemics of smallpox, influenza, measles, tuberculosis, and other diseases, and were slaughtered in war,[12] decultured by the missionary and Pombaline action, and were losing their lands. Some groups remained safe from this contact, while others were able to flee, going further into the forest, seeking the headwaters of the rivers. The Pombaline policy[13] was consolidated by Francisco Xavier de Mendonça Furtado, brother of the marques de Pombal, and the first governor of the state of Grão Pará and Maranhão, created on 31 July 1751 to succeed the state of Maranhão and Grão Pará. He based his actions on measures such as:

1. The creation of the Captaincy of São Jose do Rio Negro (3 March 1755) to guarantee the Portuguese possession of the interior of Amazonia.

2. Miscegenation between Indians and Portuguese (4 April 1755), in order to "civilize" the Indians and populate the region. For this purpose, the colonist or soldier who married an Indian woman received rewards in lands, work instruments, money, arms, and other things, as well as avoiding any disapprobation.

3. A law about the freedom of the Indians of Pará and Maranhão (6 June 1755), which really only existed on paper.

4. Resolutions in order that the settlements and villages would receive Portuguese denominations and were raised in category (6 June 1755). The first villages to be raised to "vilas" were Mortigura (present day Conde) and Sumaúma (Beja). When Mendona Furtado arrived in Grão-Pará in 1751 there were two large towns (Belém and São Luís) and four vilas (Mocha and Tapuitapera in Maranhão, Vigia and Cametá in Pará), as well as a large number of villages. When he left the government (1759), he had converted forty villages into "vilas" and twenty-three into hamlets, besides creating four more "vilas" in Macapá, Rio Negro, Rio Javari and Rio da Madeira (de Mendonça 1963, 3:1201, 1202, 1227).

5. The permit that established the Companhia Geral do Comércio do Grão Pará e Maranhão (7 June 1755), with which it was intended to introduce black slaves into Amazonia and that, from the beginning, suffered opposition from the Jesuits. Despite the prosperity obtained by the creation of this company (which went out of business in 1778) having been ephemeral, agricultural experiments were financed, cattle-raising increased, and ships were constructed during its existence. In addition, the Colony was supplied with African labor,[14] which also entered Amazonia by other ways. This did not stop the colonists and directors of settlements from evading the existing laws and continuing to enslave Indians.

6. A law that took from the missionaries the secular government of the villages (7 June 1755).

The Companhia ended up controlling commerce in the backlands, villages, "vilas," and towns of Belém and São Luís, as well as monopolizing the indigenous labor and showing reluctance to obey the orders from Portugal.

When the temporal government of the villages was taken from the missionaries, the Diretório dos Indios was created in May 1757. For each village that was transformed into a *vila*, or hamlet with a Portuguese name, there were, in addition to the *principal* (chief of the Indians), a lay director, judges, and aldermen. The Indians were divided into two groups: one was for the defense of the state and other necessities of the royal service; the other was divided among the colonists for various duties such as canoe crews and agricultural work, through a salary that had to be previously deposited with the director. *Língua geral*[15] was prohibited (although it continues to exist up to the present day), and the teaching of Portuguese language was compulsory in the schools that were maintained by the Indians.

The directors also had to promote the development of agriculture and commerce, stimulating the Indians not only to work, but also to live the "civilized life," developing in them a love for property and wealth, aiming to eliminate the habit of nudity, stimulating their participation in catechism and other things. The settlements were to have at least 150 people, and the descimentos were to be promoted under the inspection of the director in order that the settlements increased in population.

Whites, who had previously been prohibited from living in Indian settlements, could live in them on the condition that they were well behaved and obtained authorization from the governor. In fact, some were compelled to live in Indian settlements. Marriages between whites and Indians were encouraged. While the Indians remained in "barbaric rusticity," the directors would be their tutors. The director controlled everything, and it is easy to imagine the abuses that they committed. They not only possessed great power but subscribed to many stereotypes about the Indians.

These observations show that the policy of deculturating, "civilizing," and enslaving the Indian continued in a form at least as violent as the one in effect when the missionaries governed the villages, leading to the extinction of many groups and to a situation in which those who escaped fled to the headwaters of the rivers.

During this period black slaves had arrived in Amazonia, and Portugal had a policy sufficiently open to permit the entry of those who collaborated with its colonialist action. Although the non-Indian element was increasing more and more, the great majority of the population continued to be Indian despite the fact that by the end of the eighteenth century, groups such as the Tupinambá, Aruã, Tapajó, and Omagua were extinct. The Mura, after suffering yearly attacks by the Tropas Auxiliares da Capitania and various punitive expeditions, as well as the effects of epidemics such as smallpox and measles, were finally conquered between 1784 and 1786. From then on, they suffered the process of depopulation and deculturation.

Indigenous groups of diverse origins on the margins of the rivers were persecuted and enslaved at the end of the eighteenth century and disappeared. The Diretório, which had been planned to deal with a situation created by the false freedom of the Indians, ended up becoming an instrument of slavery for the Indian. Troops—no longer for resgate but for descimentos organized not only by the governors but also by justices of the peace and administrators of agriculture and commerce—penetrated the backlands and headwaters of the rivers looking for tribal groups, which were taken to the settlements of whites and mestizos. As the Indians were pacified new vilas sprang up. In addition to their customary occupations as rowers, fishermen, and so on, they were used in the expeditions undertaken to demarcate the limits of the colony, and many of them were compelled to row to Mato Grosso to bring correspondence. Finally, on 12 May 1798, by Royal Charter, the Diretório was abolished. Those Indians who could, abandoned the settlements and fled up the river and hid in the forests.

The persecutions and enslavement of indigenous groups occurred in various places of the state of Grão Pará and Rio Negro (equivalent to Brazilian Amazonia today) at the end of the eighteenth century. For example, beginning in 1794 the Portuguese depopulated the coast of the Amazon River in the direction of the Oiapoque River to thwart the Indians and blacks being received by the French.

Around 1820, 78 percent of the population of this area (akin to today's Amazon) was composed of Indians ranging from those who had not been contacted to those who had direct relations with the surrounding colonial society (Moreira Neto 1988, 37).

Although at this time the population of the Amazon was predominantly indigenous, a rural class made up in general of acculturated Indians, often mestizo, with a strong nationalistic feeling had already formed in the region. Soon after the proclamation of independence in September of 1822, the Portuguese attempted to retain the state of Grão Pará and Rio Negro under their rule, which was in part facilitated by the fact that this region, besides being inhabited mostly by Indians or their descendants, also constituted an important Portuguese stronghold. Thus, the established authorities headquartered here continued to maintain their loyalty to the Portuguese Crown, and this area was the only one in Brazil that maintained political connections with the metropolis (Lisbon). However, on 11 August 1823, when the ship *Maranhão*, of the fleet of Admiral Cochrane and under the orders of John Grenfell, was at anchor in Belém, independence was proclaimed. The date of 15 August was chosen by governmental commission for the celebration of joining in the proclamation of independence. Because it took so long for news to travel to Rio Negro, it was only in November that the state fully adopted independence.

In 1835 Cabanos, participants in a native movement known as Cabanagem,[16] began a revolt in the Grão Pará against the Portuguese, who occupied the positions of power both in politics and in the economy. Around this time, the population of the area did not exceed a hundred thousand people, excluding the Indians who were not integrated into the regional population. By the end of this conflict, more than thirty thousand individuals had been killed, many Indian settlements were almost entirely wiped out, such as the Mura Indians of the Autazes lakes (AM); agriculture and the raising of cattle on Marajó and the lower Amazon were quite ruined and the population destroyed. It had been proven, however, that the rural mass had already reached a degree of regional identity, but the Cabanos ended up defeated by troops loyal to the empire.

Agricultural and pastoral production having declined, intensification of extractive activities was necessary. This was facilitated by the industrial use of rubber, which was initially used by the Cambebas or Omaguas Indians of the valley of the rivers Solimões-Marañon as a way of waterproofing textiles and plait work. Between approximately 1840 and 1910 the Amazon entered a phase of expanded production of gummiferous plant materials, attracting to the area a great number of migrants from the northeast, as well as foreign immigrants. In this phase rubber absorbed practically all the economic activity of the area; even after production began to decline, rubber continued to be one of the lesser commercial products of the area.

With the growing demand for rubber in the world market, especially after the discovery of the vulcanization process, governmental measures encouraged the populating of the Amazon with the introduction of the steamboat in the region and the creation of the Province of the Amazon (1850), among others. The estimated total population (among Indians, caboclos, and Portuguese) was around 137,000 people in 1820; it grew to 323,000 in 1870, to 695,000 in 1890, and to 1,217,000 people in 1910. Between 1872 and 1910, it is presumed that more than 300,000 immigrants entered the Amazon from the Brazilian northeast. But, while the so-called civilized population grew, the Indian population contracted with the diminution of their lands.

As the demand for rubber in the international market increased, there was more pressure on the Indians to help discover more rubber trees, due to their knowledge of water courses used to bring rubber to the point of departure for its distribution. The cooperation of the men in the search for new trees was ensured by sequestering the women and the children, a technique that contributed to the extinction of groups more exposed to contact.

Consequently, depopulation and deculturation continued during the rubber boom[17] in the nineteenth century, when the reduction of Indian territories and the compulsory engagement of Indians in latex extraction increased.

Many of them were forced to leave their traditional lands that they had occupied from time immemorial, when they were not killed outright by groups of armed *civilizados*. Xingu Indians such as the Tucunyapé were brought to extinction. In the area between the rivers Juruá and Purus, inhabited by tribal groups who spoke Pano, Aruak, and Katukina languages, there were no whites at the beginning of the occupation by rubber-tappers. Ten years later, when it became the principal region for the production of rubber, most of these groups had physically or culturally disappeared, whereas the number of civilizados was above fifty thousand. Another region profoundly altered by the penetration of whites was the Madeira-Guaporé-Mamoré, with the construction of the railroad. Without any assistance from official organizations the Indians land in this region were subjected to continued depredations by construction companies and land invaders. Moreover, the white occupation of the north of Mato Grosso on the Amazon side affected several groups who occupied the valleys of the rivers Madeira, Tapajós, and Araguaia-Tocantins. In this latter area, the Karajás, Xavante, and Xerente were involved, and, on the frontiers of Maranhão the groups most affected were the Timbira, principally the Krahô.

Extractive operations, which in this period focused on Brazil nuts, copaiba oil, and other products, as well as rubber, narrowed and diminished the lands of various indigenous groups, leading to a disorganization of their lives on the economic, social, and religious level, in addition to very serious depopulation.

During this period, considered the golden age for Amazonia, its immigrant population increased while its first inhabitants were disappearing. In 1911–14 the almost total Brazilian monopoly of rubber ended with the entrance into the market of production by rationalized planting in the Orient, starting from the seeds of rubber trees collected in the Amazon by the Englishman Henry Wickham and transplanted to Ceylon (now Sri Lanka). At the end of the First World War, accordingly, an inverse demographic process occurred with the out-migration of a great part of the immigrants that had arrived in the region. This population decrease was followed by various losses, such as the bankruptcy of large import-export houses, the closing of rubber tree plantations, and so on. Some of the great merchants, however, redirected their extractive activities to the chestnut and to timber, keeping the supply system (known as "aviemento") functioning. The raising of prices for these products created employment possibilities.

As in previous centuries, when many changes occurred during a period of rubber extraction, problems for Indians were caused by the occupation of the land by settlers and the commerce of products existing there. The way objectives were achieved, the intensity of the activities, and the political strategies used by the state varied. The basic effect at this time was that the Amazon began to lose its essentially native face.

With the economic importance that the Amazon had assumed due to the production and exportation of rubber, President Afonso Pena decided to take the area out of isolation by extending telegraph lines from Cuiabá to Amazonas-Acre. For this he nominated General Candido Mariano da Silva Rondon, chief of the Commission of the Construction of Telegraphic Lines of Mato Grosso to Amazonas. And, from 1907 to 1917, the commission, according to Ribeiro (1959), built 2,270 kilometers of telegraphic lines, the great majority of them cutting through regions that were not inhabited before, having installed twenty-eight stations that would become populated. He proceeded with various surveys. Many tribal groups lived in all the area that he visited, and instead of exterminating them as most pioneers had done until then, he put them under the protection of his troops, pacified them, and got his soldiers to respect his positive philosophy, which was best expressed in one phrase that became famous: "To die if necessary, to kill never." His actions, together with those of other Indianists and intellectuals, resulted in the creation, in 1910, of the Service for the Protection of the Indians (SPI). In 1967, having deviated from the objectives with which it was created, the SPI was replaced by the National Indian Foundation (FUNAI).

After 1920, the region of Marabá in the middle of the Tocantins River (PA) became the center for the production of Brazil nuts in the Amazon. And in this same area around 1939–40, mainly in the area between Marabá and Jacundá, diamond mining began to replace Brazil nut production; plantations were abandoned because of the withdrawal of the international buyers. In this period cattle breeding also developed in this region, but between 1920 and 1940 its major concentration was on Marajó Island where cattle raising had begun on the banks of the Arari at the end of the seventeenth century.

During the two periods of government of Getulio Vargas (1930–1945 and 1951–1954) programs for the development of Amazonia were formulated. It was looked upon as a region where one of the greatest problems the national administration would ever face was concentrated. The goals were to end the backwardness in which its inhabitants lived and in this manner benefit the "national whole." In 1942 Getulio Vargas signed the "Washington Treaties" with the North American government. As a part of these agreements the procedures to be taken to increase rubber production in order to address the requirements of the allied forces, and the sum to be paid for the exported product, were fixed. But, besides providing for the return of the rubber plantations and the rubber cycle, which the federal government understood to be a

great opportunity for the development of the Amazon economy, the agreement included clauses intended in the long run to develop not only rubber
production but also the financing of transportation programs, of research by
the Agronomical Institute of the North in Belém, created in 1941, and of
public health programs.

Such negotiations, although they should have permitted the creation of
an infrastructure that would later serve as the base for the development of
mechanisms for regional integration, were instead responsible for the "Battle
for Rubber" (see Dean 1987, 87–107) that sent to death by disease and
poverty around forty thousand "soldiers for rubber," who were, in general,
northeastern peoples who had moved to the Amazon between 1942 and 1945
in answer to government pleas. With the failure of the "Battle for Rubber"
and worried by these failures and the international ambition over Amazonia
at the end of World War II, the constituents of 1946 accepted the proposal
for a Plan for the Economic Valorization of Amazonia (PVEA) that ended up
causing the creation of the Superintendency for the Plan of Economic Valorization of Amazonia (SPVEA), replaced by the Superintendency for the Development of Amazonia (SUDAM) in 1966.

Later, with the development policies for Amazonia that were inaugurated
in the 1960s, the strongest onslaught of internal expansion in the Amazon
region started, led by large business groups. Without entering into details
about these policies,[18] I will summarize the principal factors that have led not
only to tribal and regional disorganization, but also to profound effects on
Amazonian ecosystems.

In the 1960s, in addition to the construction of the Belém-Brasília highway, which linked the north of Brazil to the central south, the power of
regional coordination of development projects was increased with the modification, transference, or creation of public agencies. For example, the SPVEA
was transformed into SUDAM, the Banco de Crédito da Amazônia acquired
more powers and resources when it became the Banco da Amazônia, and the
Zona Franca was created in Manaus and supervised by the Superintendency
of the Zona Franca of Manaus (SUFRAMA), with the aim of developing western Amazonia. The military command of Amazonia was also transferred,
from Belém to Manaus, with the objective of placing the center of military
power of the region in the back country. There was, in addition, an increase
from 50 to 75 percent in the participation of fiscal incentives over the total
cost of the project, these being extended to foreign companies.

During the 1970s there was an attempt to integrate the east and west in
Amazonia with planning for two highways: the Transamazônica (BR-230) with
the branch Cuiabá-Santarém (BR-165) and the Perimetral Norte situated to

the north of the river Amazonas. The plan was intended to solidify the river-highway system of Amazonia through three transverse east-west routes: the river Amazonas would join the Perimetral Norte and Transamazônica highways, which would cut other diagonal, longitudinal, and radial routes to form a network of navigable rivers and terrestrial highways. There was an attempt to create a union between less and more developed areas, of the north and the south, bringing qualified labor from the northeast to utilize and occupy the lands and other natural resources of Amazonia and the Central Tablelands. During this period Project RADAM made maps of Amazonia from aerial photography, remote sensing, and complementary studies so as to obtain an inventory of the minerals, soils, and vegetation of the Amazonian region. The objective, from an integrationist perspective of the nation, was to improve the conditions for the expansion of capital and to minimize the crisis of unemployment in the northeast and central south, settling migrants from both these areas in Amazonian colonizing projects. However, the objective did not work out as planned, and what was really achieved was the spread of diseases.

In 1973 as the colonization projects began to fail, large companies assumed the task of "developing" the Amazonian area. With this, the penetration of cattle ranching and large landed estates, which were occupied by both legitimate and illegitimate means, increased. With this encroachment, the situation of the indigenous groups and the small family property holders became more and more precarious, and conflicts for possession of the land increased.

When the II Plano Nacional de Desenvolvimento, 1975–79, was inaugurated during the Geisel government, Amazonia was no longer seen as a "problem area" but was looked upon as a "resource frontier." This fact favored a stronger and stronger expansion of capitalism in the region, and its "development" became directed by large private companies. Among the programs inaugurated were:

1. The Programs of Agriculture–Cattle-Raising and Agriculture–Mining Poles of Amazonia (POLAMAZONIA), whose objective was to increase the exploitation of the natural resources of the region and with these to open new fronts of conquest of external markets, thereby strengthening the alliance between the state and the private company, both national and foreign, in leading the process of occupying and "developing" the empty spaces of the Amazonian area.
2. The Integrated Program of Development of the Northwest of Brazil (POLONOROESTE), which includes the zone of influence of the Cuiabá–

Porto Velho highway, that is, the west and northwest of the state of Mato Grosso and the state of Rondônia.

In this region there has been the greatest migration flux of the country, which has been directed, principally, to the agricultural sector. The III Plano Nacional de Desenvolvimento, 1980–85, mentions the necessity to "promote the rational and nonpredatory exploitation of new areas, such as, for example, Amazonia." However, the implementation of programmed activities by these development policies led to a great wave of migrants moving to the region, accompanied by new technology, which is putting the balance of nature at risk, as is happening in areas undergoing deforestation. Large national and multinational companies established themselves in Amazonia where, due to tax incentives, they have been turning over the soil in search of minerals, deforesting huge areas for cattle-raising and industrial projects, dedicating their activities to lumbering, and flooding areas where Indians and regional populations live and where there are special flora and fauna — without any real concern for the well-being of the regional inhabitants. The ecological, economic, and technological experience of the native acquired through centuries of daily familiarity with Amazonia has been ignored. Thus, with the building of great highways, which was the first step towards development in the Amazon, followed by the incentives for colonization and by the installation of cattle-raising projects, mining companies, placer mining, timber companies, and hydroelectric plants, both the Indian and the regional inhabitant as well as a most exotic and complex region of humid tropical forest are being affected by the predatory activities of humans from the outside. The objective — the settlement and development of the area — is not being achieved in a planned way, since very few permanent jobs have been created, the problem of the agrarian crisis of the northeast and central south has not been solved, and *well-being* of the regional populations has not been realized.

The rhetoric of "national development" was present, too, in the project I Plano de Desenvolvimento da Amazônia da Nova Rebública, 1986–1989 (First Development Plan for Amazonia of the New Republic, 1986–1989), which basically had in view the development of the back country. Among the planned actions was the "projeto Calha Norte." Despite the fact that this IPDA of the New Republic talked of ecological defense, one can foresee that the impact of these programs will not only continue to be reflected in damage to the environment, affecting the natural resources, but will also impact adversely on the economic welfare of the inhabitants of the region. As these areas were being affected environmentally and economically by factors of transformation, the internal organization of the local human communities were equally affected by the impact of these factors.

The Development Plan for Amazonia, 1992–1995, puts aside the rhetoric of development at any cost and speaks of the "promotion of the social and economic development supported and compatible with the conditions of the Amazonian ecosystems," which, actually, has been a global preoccupation. After being used as a reserve of natural resources for emerging industrialization and as a frontier of occupation of the national territory, the aim now is the alliance of scientific and technological advances with the rational utilization of self-sustaining natural resources of Amazonia in order to end the misery and to generate well-being in the region. To explore the practicability of such aims, seven interlinked priority programs have been created.

In speaking about the tribal groups affected by this development action since the 1960s, we may take the examples of the Parakanã Indians (Pa), who were faced with such problems as the construction of the Transamazon Highway and the hydroelectric plant of Tucuruí; the Waimiri-Atroari (AM and RR), with the construction of the hydroelectric plant of Balbina; the Yanomami (AM and RR) and the Waiãpi (Ap.), with the invasion by miners and mining projects within their lands; the Kayapó (Pa.), first, with the presence of ranches in the limits of their territory and now, with the threat of construction of the hydroelectric plants of the Xingu; and the Nambikwara (Valley of the Guaporé), who had problems both with cattle-raising companies and with the course of the BR-364 highway (POLONOROESTE), as well as other Indian groups. The population of the Nambikwara, who at the beginning of this century were estimated to be about ten thousand individuals, did not surpass eight hundred individuals in 1980. Thus, the harmful impact of Amazon development on Indians has been enormous.

In addition to the Grandes Projetos, other activities, such as those of the rubber extraction industry and of various economic groups (the paulistas) affect, for example, the life of the Indians and rubber-gatherers of the Juruá-Purus region, while the Mura-Pirahã[19] of the rivers Maici and Marmelos (tributaries of the Madeira) suffer the influence of itinerant traders who invade their lands to collect Brazil nuts, latex, copaiba oil, and other products. Indians are also sought as a labor force for these undertakings and were recruited to work on the Transamazon Highway. Small landowners who, with false papers, allege among other things that the area is legally registered, have invaded the lands of the Mura of the Lakes of Autazes (AM). The cattle-breeders of the region are also a constant threat to the Muras' land. What we can see is that the search for natural products and, in some cases, indigenous labor continues to be a direct factor in the invasion of their territories with consequent depopulation, social disintegration, and deculturation.

In Amazonia there are also several religious orders that work with the Indians and the general population. After long practice full of prejudice and intolerance, with the goal of Europeanizing Indians, certain religious orders are undergoing a radical change of attitude toward tribal groups. This change of attitude toward Indian cultures, traditions, survival as distinct ethnic groups, and command of their own destiny is evident principally among the Catholics (although orders such as the Salesians, for example, still resist the changes), especially the Native Missionary Council (CIMI). The orders also act together with the government, to guarantee the Indians the possession of their tribal territory, which is also being assisted by several groups that support the Indians in Brazil.

Indian support groups joined with Indian leadership to achieve great advances in the Federal Constitution of 1988, not only with respect to ethnic differences but also to the territorial rights of the Indians, giving a deadline of 5 October 1993 for the Indian lands to be delimited.

Basic Social and Cultural Change for Indian Groups and the Occupation of Amazonia

As I have tried to show in the foregoing discussion, the great problems that the Indians of Amazonia (and of Brazil in general) have always faced were the takeover of the land that they inhabited for its natural resources, and the utilization of their labor so that the colonizer could both establish himself in the region and obtain desired capital. The colonizers sought the drogas do sertão, which were cacao, sarsaparillas, urucu (annatto), cloves, cinnamon, anil, oleaginous seeds, aromatic roots, puxuri, and vanilla. They extracted timber, realized experiments in agriculture, raised cattle, collected latex and Brazil nuts, and sought diamonds and gold. More recently, the lands and natural resources have been sought to execute colonization projects, highways, mining, cattle-raising projects, the construction of hydroelectric plants, the commercialization of timbering, and other ends.

In this process many indigenous groups were cut down by wars, diseases, and hunger, while others suffered deculturation through missionary action, enslavement by the tropas de resgate and guerras justas, and compulsory labor in the extraction of latex and various agents. Yet others were safe from this economic exploitation because of the difficult access to their territory. Some sought refuge at the headwaters of the rivers, in little explored areas, surviving up to the present day. Whatever their initial number was, nowadays there are about 220 tribal groups, with a total of approximately 200,000 individuals living in Brazilian Amazonia (CEDI/PETI 1990). Their situations range from relative isolation, where they preserve their original languages and cultures, to the position of groups that no longer maintain the cultural elements that differentiate them from other Indians and from the national society but continue to identify themselves as Indians.

If we accept as a working hypothesis—indicated by the documents of the early travelers, the writers of the sixteenth and seventeenth centuries, as well as the most recent data of archaeological research—that dense and continuous populations, some with differentiated social classes, occupying diverse ecosystems, and using diverse technology in adapting to the environment in which they were localized, inhabited Brazilian Amazonia, then we can say that the basic changes[20] that have occurred there under the pressure of the colonizer, the latex extractor, and others, as well as the present-day projects were:

1. The organization of a new physical space, with the loss of tribal territories and with the expansion of Europeans.
2. Detribalization and deculturation, in many cases the emergence of a new social category, detribalized[21] and deculturated Indians.
3. The demographic decline, causing alterations in the social, political, economic, and religious systems of indigenous groups. Often, as Porro (1983, 6) affirms, this fall resulted in an "irreversible process of sociocultural disintegration. Marriage norms could not be observed because of a lack of available partners; important ceremonies to maintain group solidarity could not be carried out because of an insufficient number of individuals apt to play specific roles; techniques of birth-control, formerly efficient to maintain demographic balance became perverse in as far as they held up the return of population increase."
4. Substitution of tribal rule by secular and religious and later, civil rule, resulting from the Jesuit-Pombal conflict.
5. At present, and with specific reference to Indians, what can be seen is that a little more than three centuries after the beginning of the Portuguese expansion and occupation of Amazonia, the human, social, and cultural aspects of the region have radically changed. For example, the role of the native labor force or as a matrix for the biological reproduction of the species has been taken over in some areas by colonists who arrived in Amazonia through the forced colonization projects or by other means; in other areas, such as those where metal extraction occurs, fundamental change has taken place because present-day economic processes require greater specialization than earlier methods.

Today there is no longer demand to change specific Indian groups into generic Indians because the Federal Constitution of 1988 broke with the earlier tradition of Indian assimilation espoused by previous constitutions by recognizing Indians and their right to be different and to retain the lands that they occupy. The constitution gave a deadline of 5 October 1993 to delimit the Indian lands and to increase the competence of the legislative and judiciary powers when referring to the rights of Indians. It was an advancement in the Indian questions obtained through the joint effort of the Indian movement and the movement to support the Indians. These movements organized the initiatives that referred to Indian rights in the constitution of this country, advising the Congress in the elaboration of the proposals and constitutional amendments; in addition, they tried to mobilize public opinion in favor of Indian rights. This effort had a fundamental role in the approval of the eight articles (about Indians) of Chapter 8 in the federal constitution. Indians and the organizations that support them are working so that the rights obtained can be consolidated and so that they will not be altered in the constitutional revision to be done in the second semester of 1993.

NOTES

1. On the process of depopulation and deculturation during the period 1750–1850, see Moreira Neto (1988).

2. Although we have not yet had direct access to the data from this expedition we know of it from the work of Sweet (1974, 17–34).

3. For details of this form of commerce see also Myers 1971, 19–30.

4. For Amazonian Archaeology see Hilbert (1968); Lathrap (1970); Meggers and Evans (1957); Myers (1973); Roosevelt (1989a, 1991, 1992); and Simões (1981 and 1983).

5. Personal communication with the author.

6. This site, localized by Peter Hilbert in 1960, is 2 km long, on the banks of the River Solimões, by 400 m wide (Hilbert 1968, 123).

7. See Correa 1965, 3–5.

8. See Reis 1956.

9. *Resgates* (rescues) were practices that legitimized the enslavement of Indians by means of "rescuing" Indians who had been captured by other Indians and were being held to be eaten as prisoners of war. Because this was a rescue from death it was held to be beneficial and redeeming to the prisoner, who afterward became a slave of the colonist.

10. Wars on Indians were considered *guerras justas* (just wars) when Indians had attacked or robbed a colonist, when they refused to aid the Portuguese in disputes

with other tribal groups or to defend their lives and properties, when they resisted Christianization, and when they allied themselves with the Dutch, English, or French, considered enemies of the crown.

11. *Descimentos* (literally "coming down") was the practice, in colonial times, of transferring Indians from their communities in the interior to Portuguese villages along rivers and the coast. Some were required to work for colonists as paddlers in canoes sent out to obtain valuable "plants from the backlands" (drogas do sertão) or in the cultivation of sugar, tobacco, cotton, and other agricultural products, while the rest worked for the states in defense and public works. Indians of different cultural traditions were resettled together. To make them "come down" they were attracted with promises and presents or coerced by force and fear. About *resgate, guerra justa,* and *descimentos,* see de Azevedo 1930, 166; and Guajará 1968, 121–22.

12. Among the wars we may take the example of that which wiped out the Manáos Indians (1723 to 1727), who lived between the Rio Negro and the Rio Branco and who had been led in a rebellion by the chief Ajuricaba.

13. This policy, which aimed to "Portuguese" Amazonia, tried, in short, to end the missionary force (above all, that of the Jesuits) and to keep the frontiers that had already been conquered, consolidating the Portuguese power in the area and attempting to link the extreme north to the rest of the country through Mato Grosso.

14. Concerning blacks, see Figueiredo 1977; Salles 1971; and Vergolino e Silva 1968.

15. Língua Geral Amazônica was a lingua franca based on Tupinambá, the Tupian language of the eastern coast of Brazil. It was described by Jesuit missionaries during colonial times and widely adopted by whites, mestizos, and Indians in Amazonia.

16. On the Cabanagem, see di Paolo 1985 and Moreira Neto 1988.

17. Concerning this period see Dean 1987; Moreira Neto 1971; Oliveira 1983; Ribeiro 1970; and Santos 1977.

18. See de Oliveira 1983 and 1988.

19. Data collected in the field (1976) by the author.

20. See de Oliveira 1988.

21. The *detribalized,* the Tapuio, has been defined and analyzed by Moreira Neto (1988).

REFERENCES

CEDI/PETI
1990   *Terras indígenas no Brasil.* São Paulo: CEDI.
Correa, C. G.
1965   *Estatuetas de scerâmica na cultura Santarém.* Publicações Avulzas do museu Paráense Emílio Goeldi, vol. 4.
de Azevedo, J. L.
1930   *Os Jesuítas no Grão-Pará, suas missões e a colonização.* Coimbra: Imprensa da Universidade.

de Carvajal, G., A. de Rojas, and C. de Acuña
1941   *Descobrimento do rio Amazonas.* Serio Brasiliana, 203. São Paulo: Nacional.

de Las Casas, B.
1984   *O paraíso destruído: A sangrenta história da conquista da América espanhola.* Série Visao dos Vencidos. Porto Alegre: L & PM / História.

de Mendonça, M. C.
1963   *A Amazônianao era pombalina: Correspondência inédita do governador e capitão-general do estado do Grão-Pará e Maranhão Francisco Xavier de Mendona Furtado 1761–1769.* Rio de Janeiro: IHGB.

de Oliveira, A. E.
1983   Ocupaçao humana. In *Amazônia desenvolvimento, integracao, ecologia,* by E. Salati et al., 144–327. São Paulo: Brasiliense.
1988   Amazônia: Modificações sociais e culturais decorrentes do processo de ocupação humana (século XVII ao II). *Boletim do Museu Paraense Emílio Goeldi—Antropologia,* 4 (1): 65–115.

Dean, Warren
1987   *Brazil and the struggle for rubber—a study in environmental history.* Cambridge: Cambridge University Press.

di Paolo, R.
1985   *Cabanagem; a revolução popular de Amazônia.* Belém: Conselho de Cultura. Coleção História do Pará, Serie Arthur Vianna.

Figueiredo, N.
1977   *Amazônia: Tempo e gente.* Belém: Prefeitura Municipal de Belém. (Prêmio Carlos Nascimento)

Guajará, D.A.R.
1968   Catechese de Indios no Pará. *Annaes da Bibliotheca e Archivo Público do Pará* (Belém) 2:117–83.

Hilbert, P. P.
1968   *Archaeologische Untersuchungen am mittleren Amazonas.* Marburger Studien zur Volkerkunde, No. 1. Berlin: Dietrich Reimer Verlag.

Lathrap, D. W.
1970   *The upper Amazon.* New York: Praeger.

Meggers, B. J.
1971   *Amazonia: Man and culture in a counterfeit paradise.* Chicago: Aldine.

Meggers, B. J., and C. Evans
1957   *Archaeological investigations at the mouth of the Amazon.* Bureau of American Ethnology Bulletin 167. Washington, D.C.: Smithsonian Institution.

Moreira Neto, C. de A.
1971   *A política indigenista durante o sécula XIX°.* Rio Claro. Ms. Tese: Doutorado.

1988   Indios da Amazônia: De Maioria a Minoria (1750–1850). Petrópolis:
            Vozes.
Myers, T. P.
1971   Aboriginal trade networks in Amazonia. In Networks of the past: Regional
            interaction in archaeology, edited by P. D. Francis, F. J. Kense, and P. G.
            Duke, 19–30. Archaeological Association, University of Calgary.
1973   Toward the reconstruction of prehistoric community patterns in the
            Amazon Basin. In Variation in anthropology, edited by D. Lathrap and
            J. Douglas, 233–51. Urbana: Illinois Archaeological Survey.
Nimuendaju, C.
1949   Os Tapajó. Boletim do Museu Paraense Emílio Goeldi, 10:93–106.
Porro, A.
1983   Amazônia, os Indios antes do massacre. Leitura (São Paulo), 2 (18):
            6–7.
1984   Mercadorias e rotas de comércio intertribal na Amazônia. ANPOCS 89
            Encontro Anual.
Reis, A.C.F.
1956   A Amazônia que os Portuqueses revelaram. Coleção Vida Brasileira. Rio
            de Janeiro: MEC.
Ribeiro, D.
1959   A obra indigenista de Rondon. América Indígena 19 (2).
1970   Os Indios e a civilização: A integracão das populacões—indígenas no Brasil
            moderno. Coleção Retrato do Brasil, 77. Rio de Janeiro: Civilazação
            Brasileira.
Roosevelt, A. C.
1989a   Resource management in Amazonia before the conquest. In Natural
            Resource Management by Indigenous and Folk Societies in Amazonia, edited
            by William Bale and Darrell Posey, 30–61. New York: New York Botani-
            cal Garden.
1989b   Lost civilizations of the lower Amazon. Natural History 74–83.
Salles, V.
1971   O Negro no Pará: Sob o regime da escravidão. Coleção Amazônica, Série
            José Veríssimo. Rio de Janeiro: FGV.
Santos, R. A. de O.
1980   História econômica da Amazônia (1800–1920). 2 vols. São Paulo: T. A.
            Queiroz (T.A.Q.).
Simões, M. F.
1981   Coletores: Pescadores ceramistas do litoral do Salgado (Pará); Nota prelimi-
            nar. Boletim do Museu Paraense Emílio Goeldi, new ser., Antropologia,
            78.
1983   A Pré-história da bacia Amazônica. Uma tentativa de reconstituição. In
            Cultura Indígena, 5–12. Belém: Museu Paraense Emílio Goeldi.

Smith, N.J.H.

1980   Anthrosols and human carrying capacity in Amazonia. *Annals of the Association of American Geographers* 70 (4): 553–66.

Sweet, D. G.

1974   *A rich realm of nature destroyed: The middle Amazon valley, 1640–1750.* Ph.D. diss., University of Wisconsin.

Vergolino e Silva, A.

1968   *Alguns elementos novos para o estudo do negro na Amazônia.* Publicacões avulsas do Museu Paraense Emílio Goeldi, No. 8. Belém.

PART   II   HABITAT AND HUMAN BIOLOGY
              IN PERSPECTIVE

6

Health and Demography of Native Amazonians

Historical Perspective and Current Status

WARREN M. HERN

On a recent excursion to Chapada dos Guimarães to photograph Brazilian wildlife, I had the good fortune to encounter a young Bororo man who was then living near the town of that name. He offered to show me a special waterfall near his home. We descended through the brush to a beautiful scene. The falls cascaded some ten meters to a shallow pool. The young man slipped off his shorts and plunged under the waterfall. He whooped and called me to join him, so I did. I imitated his joyful Bororo whoop, and we both roared with laughter. The water in that pristine place was cool and wonderful. It was a precious moment.

My new friend is only one generation from a tribal life in the bush. He now lives a marginal existence as an artist and day laborer with his pleasant wife, a *branca* (white woman), who was pregnant and about to deliver their first child. The waterfall he loves and shared with me is in a pathetically small patch of undisturbed forest surrounded by the devastation of an advancing "civilization." The natural forest and wildlife are being replaced by cultivated crops. Pesticides and fertilizers now flow into the Brazilian Pantanal, the greatest wetland wildlife refuge in the Americas.

We sat by my friend's house after a dinner of vegetables and sipped maté as we watched the moon rise. The evening air was filled with the smoke of great fires on the plains below. "Estão matando o pulmão do mundo (They are killing the great lung of the Earth)," he said. "First they kill us, and then they kill the earth." The government would not let him return to his village, he said. He had lived away too long. His family was gone, but he wanted to be with his friends, to speak Bororo, to take part in rituals. His tribe, he said, is dying. They will soon be gone, he said.

This was a moving personal experience for me, but more than that, it seems to capture a little bit of the fate of the Amazonian Indians.

To speak of the health and biology of native Amazonians, one must first see that they are victims of two massive historical assaults, one at the time of conquest and the other, even more inexorable, in the twentieth century. Many of them have been in highly isolated enclaves until the past few decades, but they have gone from contact to displacement and decimation in a generation. The ultimate enemies of the native Amazonians are the loss of their pristine environment and the loss of their unique cultures.

Historical Perspective

The first people to enter the South American tropical lowlands probably arrived around 10,000 years ago, according to Martin (1973). Carneiro (1974) agrees with this estimate. Lathrap (1977) estimates that intensive cultivation of bitter manioc in alluvial flood plains began 6,000 to 7,000 years ago, but Roosevelt (1980, 1989) suggests a date of 4000–5000 BP. Lathrap (1968, 1970), especially, thinks that riverine populations were relatively dense by the time of conquest. Both Lathrap and Roosevelt agree with other authors— Denevan (1976), Dobyns (1966), Lipschutz (1966), Myers (1988), and Thornton (1987)—that indigenous populations collapsed following the conquest.

Dobyns (1966) estimated a 20:1 loss of population among indigenous groups following the conquest due to the introduction of European disease, slave trading, and intertribal warfare, although Denevan (1976, 212) states that a 35:1 ratio may be more accurate. It is not unlikely that depopulation ratios reached 50:1, on the basis of reports cited by Dobyns. Meggers (1971, 151) states that a smallpox epidemic occurred in the lower Amazon in 1621 and reached the upper Amazon in 1651. Meggers also states that yellow fever and malaria were introduced to the South American continent following the importation of slaves from Africa. Steward and Métraux (1948) note that smallpox epidemics also occurred in 1670–80, following Western contact, and decimated native populations in the upper Amazon Basin. Myers (1988) estimates a reduction of as much as 99.5 percent of the Omagua, Cocama, and indigenous populations of the lower Huallaga in the 150 years following European contact.

Wagley (1974a) and Chagnon and Melancon (1983, 1984) have described the catastrophic effects of depopulation on native tribes, including the loss of many cultural traditions.

In studying two Brazilian tribes, the Tenetehara and Tapirapé, Wagley (1974b) noted that they had two quite different approaches to controlling fertility and natality. The Tapirapé, valuing small families with no more than three children and no more than two of the same sex, sanctioned infanticide to maintain this norm. The Tapirapé also practiced postpartum sexual abstinence. Among the Tenetehara, infanticide was permitted only occasionally. Both tribes were encouraged by missionaries to have as many children as possible. Their success in dealing with the loss of population as the result of Western contact was quite different. Wagley reported that the Tenetehara were growing in numbers and that the Tapirapé culture was disintegrating. Among other things, the Tapirapé social organization is much more vulnerable to disruption by population loss.

In addition to severe population loss in the time after European contact, native Amazonians have been subjected to unprecedented destruction of their environment since World War II with the construction of numerous highways across the Andes and across the Brazilian Amazon (Moran 1983; Saffirio and Hames 1983; Wagley 1973). This has been accompanied by widespread colonization and deforestation (CNPq/CIPA 1984 Hecht 1983; Lisansky 1990; Moran 1989; Stearman 1983). Various countries, including Brazil, Bolivia, Ecuador, and Peru, have sponsored colonization of the Amazon as the partial result of population growth in other parts of those countries (Bedoya 1981; Fearnside 1986, 7; Moran 1981, 75; Stearman 1983, 52; Whitten 1981, 5). In 1987 alone, 47 million acres were burned in Brazil, of which 40 percent was primary rain forest (Brown et al. 1989, 4; Simons 1988). Other development projects such as hydroelectric dams have destroyed or threaten to obliterate colossal areas of native Amazonian environments (Smith 1982; Treece 1987). Aside from the abundantly documented fact that these projects have had catastrophic effects for native populations (Ramos and Taylor 1979), the long-term implications for biodiversity and for regional and global climate change are extremely ominous (Gómez-Pompa et al. 1972; Shukla et al. 1990; Tans et al. 1990).

Demographic Studies of Native Amazonians

Denevan (1976, 291) estimates that 8,500,000 indigenous people lived in Amazonia at the time of conquest, although Myers (1988) estimates that there may have been as many as 10,000,000 in parts of the upper Peruvian

Amazon. Denevan estimates that, following a reduction of the Indian population to approximately 250,000, it has increased now to around 500,000. Population nadirs probably occurred at around the end of the nineteenth century. Gunter Tessman, for example, estimated that the Shipibo numbered approximately 3,000 in 1920, whereas the Shipibo-Conibo population now numbers between 25,000 and 40,000 (Bergman 1981; Hern 1988). Many tribes have become extinct; others have flourished or have absorbed others.

Contemporary demographic studies

Thorough contemporary demographic studies of Amazon Indian societies are uncommon. Studies of the Xavante (Neel et al. 1964), Caingang (Salzano 1961), Yanomamo (Chagnon 1977), and Shipibo (Hern 1971, 1977, 1988, 1992a, 1992b), appear to be among the main demographic reports available until recently, but they are often not comparable. Black et al. (1978) studied eight unacculturated tribes in northeast Amazonia. Flowers (1990) gives a report of repeated observations of the postcontact demography of the Xavante. An exceptionally thorough report of the Mucajai Yanomama by Early and Peters (1990) provides one of the only longitudinal demographic studies of a single group. There are no integrating studies that give overall demographic information about all Amazonian tribes.

A principal difficulty in obtaining accurate demographic information, of course, is that Amazon tribes have not had written languages until recently, and in any case, systems of counting are often lacking. Categories of time are general and do not allow precise interpretations. The Shipibo word for *yesterday*, for example (*vakish*), is the same as the word for *tomorrow*. *Moatian* means "a long time ago" and serves for most reckonings of over a year. Even having birth "documents" are not certain guides to birth dates. Birth certificates are sometimes not sought immediately after a birth. Reports of dates to recording officials are approximate and may be misunderstood or recorded improperly. Owners may cheerfully change documented birth dates in order to attain certain objectives, such as military induction. Stillbirths may not be counted as term births, thereby complicating the calculations of birth interval length or reproductive span. Children who have died or been killed may be forgotten or ignored. Requests for estimates for time or dates are sometimes interpreted as entertaining opportunities for the creative imagination, not to be taken seriously. As a result, the only way it is possible to obtain some accurate demographic data is to live permanently with a group and observe every vital event. This, obviously, is not practical for most observers.

Data collected by Maybury-Lewis, Salzano, Chagnon, Neel, and Peters in

connection with ethnographic and genetic studies are among the most detailed demographic reports.

Neel and Salzano (1970) found that one group of Xavante had a mean
completed fertility of 5.7 and speculated that the Xavante practiced postpartum sexual abstinence in order to control fertility. Neel and Chagnon (1968)
found an overall mean completed fertility for the Xavante of 3.6 and 3.2 for
the Yanomama. They described these numbers as "unbelievably low" and
suspected that births resulting in infanticide are not reported as live births.
The result is one live birth every 4.4 years for the Xavante and one every 6.6
years for the Yanomamo. Both the Xavante and Yanomamo (Chagnon 1977)
practice sororal polygyny, with a 50 percent polygyny rate among Yanomamo
males. Mean age for the Xavante is 18; mean age for the Yanomamo is 22.
Infant mortality is 18 percent for the Yanomamo. Neel and Chagnon reported that the proportions of the populations under the age of 15 for the
Xavante and Yanomama was 39 percent and 32 percent, respectively. The
authors judged that both birth rates and infant-child mortality rates were
lower for the Yanomama than for the Xavante. Salzano, Neel, and Maybury-
Lewis (1967) also found that 39 percent of the Xavante population was under
15 years of age. Flowers (1983) found that a comparable Xavante group was
younger in 1977, with 48.6 percent under the age of 15. Mean birth intervals
were 20.9 months, although for women whose babies had died, intervals
were only 16.6 months. In a 1988 follow-up study, Flowers (1990) showed
that, after an initial postcontact decline, fertility increased markedly among
the São Domingos Xavante. I have found exceedingly high fertility rates
among the Shipibo (Hern 1977, 1988, 1992a, 1992b) that appear to have
been partially the result of disruption of traditional cultural patterns such as
polygyny, which dampened fertility (table 6.1).

Neel and Weiss (1975) calculated a general fertility rate of .250 for the
Yanomama with a net reproduction rate of 1.25. Yanomama women complete
a pregnancy every 3–4 years, with 85 percent of the births resulting in a live
birth. The authors estimated annual population growth rates at between 0.5
and 1.0 percent. Fifty percent of the women who reach age 15 die before
menopause. Childhood mortality rates have dropped considerably, but overall, combined infant and child mortality, including infanticide, stood at
about 50 percent at the time of the report.

Early and Peters (1990, 20) show an increase in mortality among the
Mucajai Yanomama in the two years immediately preceding contact compared with lower mortality in the two years before that, with general diminution of death rates and population increase in postcontact years. Even with

Table 6.1. Polygyny

Authors	Yr	Tribe	< 15 (%)	rate (%)	EFR	GFR
Salzano	61	Caingang	35.7	—	—	—
Hern	77	Shipibo	54.7	7.1	130.0	0.305
Hern	88	Shipibo	49.3	13.0	93.2	0.278
Neel	78	Yanomama				
N & C	68	Yanomama	32.0			
N & C	68	Xavante	39.0			
N & W	75	Yanomama				0.250
J & K	69	Cashinahua	—	27.0	113.5	
SN & M	67	Xavante	38.9	40.2		
A & S	72	Cayapo	48.4			
S & C	80	Wapishana	39.0			
SC & N	79	Ticuna	41.0			
Salzano	85	Macushi	51.0			
NS et al.	64	Xavante	39.3			
Buck	68	Mestizo	54.1			
Flowers	83	Xavante	48.6			

KEY
A & S   Ayres and Salzano 1972
J & K   Johnston and Kensinger 1969
N & C   Neel and Chagnon 1968
N & W   Neel and Weiss 1975
NS et al.   Neel, Salzano, et al. 1964
S & C   Salzano and Callegari-Jacques
SC & N   Salzano, Callegari-Jacques, and Neel
SN & M   Salzano, Neel, and Maybury-Lewis 1967

DEMOGRAPHIC INDICES:
EFR (Effective Fertility Rate): $\frac{\text{number of children} > 5 \text{ y/o}}{\text{number of females } 15-49}$
(a.k.a. Child-woman ratio)
GFR (General Fertility Rate): $\frac{\text{number of live births}}{\text{number of females } 15-49}$
TFR (Total Fertility Rate): Sum of age-specific birth rates
GRR (Gross Reproduction Rate): Sum of age-specific female birth rates
NRR (Net Reproduction Rate): Sum of age-specific female survival rates
MCF (Mean Completed Fertility): average number of live births among women of completed fertility age 50 +
RONI (Rate of Natural Increase): Crude Birth Rate minus Crude Death Rate

TFR	GRR	NRR (%)	RONI (%)	MCF
—				6.6
9.9	4.9	—	4.89	9.3
8.5	4.4	3.7	7.6	
	7.0			8.2
		1.25	0.5	
				5.7

data from twenty-eight years of observation by Peters, the authors could not reach firm conclusions concerning changes in longevity following contact (Early and Peters, 1990, 73, Table 7.2).

In a study of the health status of Cayapó Indians, Ayres and Salzano (1972) found that 48.4 percent of the population was under 15 years of age. In an earlier study of the Caingang, Salzano (1961) found that 35.7 percent of the population was under 15, whereas 54.5 percent of a mestizo population was under 15.

Neel (1970) reports a 15 to 20 percent infanticide rate for primitive tribes in the Amazon, with weaning at three years for Yanomamo. Polygyny provides an important device for natural selection, according to Neel. Polygyny is common throughout South American tropical forest societies (Siskind 1973), although its effects on fertility are not well documented.

Goldman (1979) observed among Cubeo that women are not eager to bear children. Cubeo women had knowledge of abortifacients and acknowledge performing infanticide. An unwanted child is buried alive on the spot where it is born. Childbirth is considered a dangerous period. Sexual abstinence is practiced by both parents for one year.

Infanticide is practiced among the Mundurucú in the cases of twins and congenital birth defects (Murphy and Murphy 1974, 166).

Larrick et al. (1979) reports a high incidence of infanticide and stillbirth among the Waorani of Ecuador, who otherwise appear to be quite healthy.

Devereux (1955) reported use of *imi rau* among "Kashinaia" [Cashinahua] as a contraceptive and as an abortifacient. The Jivaro of Ecuador used *sacha mangue*. The words *imi rau* as reported by Devereux are virtually identical to the Shipibo words *jimi*, "blood," and *rao*, "medicine."

Johnston et al. (1969) and Johnston and Kensinger (1971) found a 27 percent polygyny rate among the Cashinahua, a Panoan tribe, and noted that the medicine man proscribed the use of either modern or herbal contraceptives. A conscious decision to cease using abortifacients has contributed to a high fertility rate. Also, the practice of infanticide is not observed to the same degree as before. This tribal "population policy" was reported to have been a response to a declining population viewed as the result of Western contact and an epidemic in 1951. The effective fertility ratio for the Cashinahua was 113.5 compared to 96.3 for the Hutterites (Eaton and Mayer 1953).

Siskind (1973) observes that the Sharanahua, also a Panoan group, have abortions in order to have three-year birth intervals. The Sharanahua have three ways of making women scarce: through limited sexual access, polygyny, and female infanticide.

Bugos and MacCarthy (1984) cite the example of the Ayoreo of southwestern Bolivia, who practice infanticide. The Ayoreo total fertility rate is 6.185; infanticide lowered it to 4.02. The strength of the authors' conclusions are diminished by the fact that women who did not practice infanticide were excluded from the sample.

Early and Peters (1990, 76) report that both induced abortion and infanticide are practiced among the Mucajai Yanomamo, and infanticide may account for as much as 44 percent of all infant deaths.

Holmberg (1985) reports that Siriono women observe a one-month period of postpartum sexual abstinence.

A comparison of various demographic indices in different tribes is shown in table 6.1.

One interpretation of table 6.1 is to note that earlier studies of tribal groups showed lower proportions of individuals under 15 years of age, whereas later studies (Flowers 1983; Salzano 1985) shower higher proportions of approximately 50 percent. The earlier studies, with the 0–15 age group under 40 percent, may be correlated with higher rates of polygyny (compare Salzano, Neel, and Maybury-Lewis 1967, with Hern 1977). Although these studies are not strictly comparable, it appears that acculturation (or deculturation, as the case might be), is associated with higher fertility and a younger population.

Generalizing from these sparse data is hazardous, but it seems that following a catastrophic depopulation in the first four hundred years following Western contact, at least some Amazonian populations are experiencing high fertility and rapid population growth, whereas others have become extinct or nearly so. It remains to be seen whether those experiencing rapid population growth can maintain their traditional cultures in any respect.

In many ways, native Amazonians have experienced a reversal of the "epidemiologic transition" described by Omran (1971). Whereas Omran's theory begins with an "Age of Pestilence and Famine," proceeds to an "Age of Receding Pandemics," and thence to an "Age of Degenerative and Manmade Disease," the Amazon Indians have had a mirror image of this experience since European contact. Roosevelt (1989) and Greene (1986) describe few except chronic diseases in Marajo skeletons that predated European contact (Neel 1977; Salzano 1988). The pandemics began when the Europeans arrived. Coimbra (1989), in describing the health effects of disruptions of social networks and subsistence patterns among the Surui, shows that the group is experiencing all three phases of the "epidemiologic transition" at once.

Health Status of Native Amazonians

Our information about the health status of early Amazonians is almost non-existent except for some skeletal remains found at Marajo (Greene 1986). There is evidence that tuberculosis, hookworm, *trypanosoma cruzi*, and treponemal diseases were present in prehistoric South American populations (Allison 1973; Allison et al. 1974; Baker and Armelagos 1988; Cockburn, 1961a, 1961b; Coimbra 1988; Hackett 1963). However, most of the evidence for these diseases comes from west coast archaeological remains, and we do not know the extent to which these diseases affected those in the lowlands. These afflictions are not reported in the Marajo individuals. In the rest of the Amazon, paleopathological evidence is lacking due to the unsuitable conditions for the preservation of human remains (Coimbra 1988). We must surmise a fundamentally vigorous and ingenious aboriginal population, however, that survived in an exceedingly complex and hostile environment by identifying a wide variety of food, technical, and medicinal resources (Behrens 1981; Berlin and Berlin 1978; Dufour 1987; Hern 1976; Milton 1984; Pollock 1988; Posey 1983; Ross 1978; Tournon 1984). The simple fact is that Amazon societies, however vigorous and complex, were overwhelmed by the introduction of Old World diseases and European aggression. Black (1975) asserts that the severe impact of epidemic disease introduced from the Old World was due both to social disruption and to genetic isolation.

Introduced Diseases

MEASLES (RUBEOLA). Black et al. (1982) state that the measles virus probably did not exist at the time the Western Hemisphere was populated by migration across the Bering land bridge, and probably did not even exist at the time of European contact. Their basis for this assertion is that Amazonian tribes having first contact typically display no evidence of exposure to the measles antigen, nor do they have antibodies to many other common viral disease agents. The antibody response of Amerindians to measles vaccination is essentially the same, if somewhat more symptomatic, as that of other populations, indicating no genetic immunodeficiency in this regard (Black et al. 1982; Black et al. 1970; Black et al. 1974; Neel, Centerwall, et al. 1970).

SMALLPOX (VARIOLA MAJOR). Smallpox has been a great killer in Amazonia since the time of conquest. From the time of the first reported epidemic of smallpox in 1621 (Meggers 1971) until the last in 1964 (personal observation), smallpox probably killed millions of native Amazonians. Working as a medical student in the upper Peruvian Amazon in 1964, I encountered numerous cases of smallpox in what was the last epidemic in the Western Hemisphere. Most of the several hundred Shipibo and mestizos whom I vaccinated had never previously been vaccinated. Throughout the region, almost 100 percent of the populations of whole native villages were afflicted with high mortality rates (R. Eichenberger, personal communication). Thornton et al. (1991) have shown that Native American populations may have had variable recovery rates following decimation by epidemics such as smallpox.

TUBERCULOSIS. Tuberculosis has been endemic in the Americas since prehistoric times, and there is a high incidence of the disease among contemporary Amerindian populations (Clark et al. 1987). The introduction of tuberculosis into the Amazon is fairly recent (Black 1975), but it is the main health problem in many native Amazonian groups today (Flowers 1983; Black et al. 1974). Clark speculates that the current epidemic may stem from either exposure to more virulent strains of *Mycobacterium tuberculosis* or environmental change leading to a loss of exposure to natural vaccination, presumably when Amazonians were separated from their hemispheric ancestors. The widespread Amazonian practice of communal eating and drinking has unquestionably contributed to the epidemic spread of tuberculosis. In the Peruvian Amazon, in particular, the preparation of *masato* from masticated manioc is a popular and probably deadly custom in this regard.

MALARIA. Malaria is also a recent arrival in the Amazon (Black 1975), and its spread has been perpetuated by deforestation and urbanization. Deforestation, in particular, is a contributing factor to the development of hyperendemic *vivax* malaria in the Peruvian Amazon (Sulzer et al. 1975). The vector for *Falciparum* malaria, *Anopheles gambiae*, was discovered in Brazil in 1930 and eradicated by 1941, according to Cockburn (1961b), but I have heard anecdotal accounts from other physicians who have reported cases of *Falciparum* in the Amazon.

YELLOW FEVER. Cockburn (1971) stated that the principal vector of yellow fever, *Aedes aegypti*, has probably been in South America for only four hundred years. Black found high frequencies of antibodies to arboviruses, including yellow fever, among three Carib and four Cayapó Indian villages (Black et al. 1974), indicating prolonged exposure to these agents.

CHAGA'S DISEASE AND LEISHMANIASIS. *Cutaneous* and *mucocutaneous leishmaniasis* is widespread throughout the upper Peruvian Amazon Basin (personal observation), but documentation of the distribution of these diseases in Amazonia is sparse. Coimbra (1988) notes that *Trypanosoma cruzi* are found in Chilean mummies dating from 470 B.C. and that both the organism and its vector, the triatomine insect, are found throughout the Amazon Basin. In spite of this long history in the Americas and wide distribution in the Amazon Basin, according to Coimbra, the number of autochthonous parasitic infections is small among native Amazonians by comparison with other populations. Coimbra attributes the low Chaga's disease infection rate to the high human mobility and small settlement size of Amazon Indians. Chaga's disease is a serious potential threat to native Amazonian populations, however, since development and urbanization permits the domiciliation of triatomines.

In Coimbra's view, mobility is of adaptive value among preindustrial Amazon populations and minimizes contamination of surroundings with pathogens. Also, he notes that animal domestication was not generally practiced until recently.

ONCHOCERCIASIS. Microfilaria are found in various Amazon Indian groups (Beaver et al. 1976; Lawrence et al. 1979; Lawrence, Erdtmann, et al. 1980), and exposure to onchocerciasis has been found in Ecuador (Guderian et al. 1987) and Brazil (Morães et al. 1974). Although clinical manifestations of the disease have not yet become widespread (Salzano and Neel 1976), it is only a matter of time before this severely debilitating disease affects large numbers of native Amazonians.

SCHISTOSOMIASIS. Schistosomiasis has become widespread throughout the hemisphere but has not yet become endemic in the Amazon. It is endemic in northeastern Brazil (Lee 1985a, 69), and it threatens to become a major health problem for Amazonians. The Amazon habitat is highly suitable for the spread of schistosomiasis, especially if large dams are constructed in the region (Lee 1985b).

HELMINTHIASIS. Infection with multiple species of intestinal parasites is the rule in relatively undisturbed Amerindian tribes, according to Lawrence (Lawrence, Neel, et al. 1980). When native Amazonians become sedentary, however, they may be at higher risk of clinically important parasite burdens. Chernela and Thatcher (1989) found that the nomadic Maku had ascaris infection rates as low as 34 percent, whereas 75 to 100 percent of the sedentary Tukano were infected. Schwaner and Dixon (1974) found that hookworm egg counts were six times higher in a sedentary unacculturated Tucuna Indians than among a mixed Tucuna-mestizo population living in a more urbanized settlement.

Chronic Diseases

The incidence of cardiovascular diseases has not been found to be high in native Amazonian populations. Weinstein, Neel, and Salzano found that chronic and degenerative diseases were rare in a population of Xavante Indians and that blood pressures were generally low (1967), a result replicated by Ayres and Salzano in the Cayapó (1972). Both Oliver et al. (1975) and Larrick et al. (1979) found that blood pressures did not increase with age among the Yanomama and Waorani, respectively. Both groups of investigators attributed the low blood pressure levels to low dietary salt levels. Glanville and Geerdink made the same observation earlier in the Trio and Wajana tribes (1970). Lowenstein (1961) found that unacculturated Carajas Indians had lower blood pressures than sedentary Mundurucús, and that the Mundurucús experienced blood pressure increases with age. Tenbrinck (1964) found lower blood pressures among Peruvian Amazon Indians of different tribes than among mestizos from the same region. Nowaczynski et al. (1985), studying relationships between blood pressure and serum aldosterone levels, determined that the salt-free diet of the Yanomama gave them higher aldosterone and lower blood pressure levels by comparison with the more acculturated Guaymi Indians of Panama. Fleming-Moran and Coimbra (1990) found that the lifestyles of lowland South American Indians include many protective factors against hypertension, but these conditions are rapidly changing and native Amazonians are being exposed to more stress.

Obesity is uncommon in native Amazonians; Glanville and Geerdink found that skinfold thickness among the Trio and Wajana tribes remains constant throughout life (Glanville and Geerdink 1970).

Diabetes is virtually unknown among native Amazonians. In their study of two tribes in Brazil, the Yanomama and Marubo, Spielmann et al. found that the less acculturated group, the Yanomama, showed no significant rise in one-hour blood glucose levels characteristic of glucose-intolerant North American control subjects (1982).

Donnelly et al. (1977) found that dental deterioration was positively associated with exposure to Western culture.

Violent and Accidental Death

In their study of the Waorani, Larrick et al. (1979) found that 4 percent of all deaths were due to snakebite. Although I have not calculated cause-specific death rates among the Shipibo, since 1964 I have observed an increasing proportion of deaths due to accidental gunshot wounds, homicide, and vehicular accidents. Reports of children drowning and dying from falls are common among the Shipibo. Intervillage and intertribal warfare has been an important cause of mortality for Amazonian tribes in the past, and Chagnon (1988) reports that 30 percent of all adult male deaths among the Yanomama are due to violence.

Infanticide is still practiced in some Amazonian tribes, but its significance as a major cause of death appears to have diminished, especially in the past century.

Current Health Status

In their general assessment of health and physical status of the Xavante, Weinstein, Neel, and Salzano recorded their impression of "exuberant health and vitality" among the children and adult males, but *premature aging in the women* (emphasis added). Larrick et al. made the same observations concerning the Waorani (1979). Black found the nutritional status of Brazilian Cayapó Indians to be generally good (Black et al. 1977). Cayapó infants were small but gained in size and weight with age. Moran notes that no survey has ever recorded signs of protein deficiency among autochthonous South Americans in their native habitats (Moran 1981, 207) In fact, protein intake is frequently higher than minimum daily requirements. Bergman observed that the Shipibo consume up to seventy-five grams of protein per day (Bergman 1980). Chagnon and Hames (1979) found that the Yanomamo consume approximately the same amount of protein per day.

Flowers (1983) observed that the Xavante people she studied in 1977 were in generally good health, although tuberculosis was a major health problem. She recorded a 27 percent mortality rate up to the age of two, with most deaths occurring as the result of respiratory diseases.

In a study of the nutritional status of Indian children in the Alto Xingu region, Fagundes-Neto et al. found that 96 percent of the children were well nourished and only 3 percent were malnourished (1981). Height was normal for 84.8 percent. By contrast, 54 percent of the children in low-income urban families were malnourished. In tribal life, food was available and equally distributed, fertility control was practiced, and there was an absence of socioeconomic unevenness. This was offset by the presence of endemic malaria.

Hodge and Dufour (1991) found that high infant mortality rates and growth retardation among Shipibo children may be the result of an interaction of suboptimal nutrition and infectious diseases.

While nutrition assessment is critical to evaluation of general health, an extended discussion of the nutritional status of native Amazonians is not included in this chapter since it is thoroughly reviewed by Darna Dufour elsewhere in this volume.

In my own studies of the Shipibo, I have found them to be in excellent health but extremely vulnerable to tuberculosis and the acute infectious diseases of childhood (Hern 1971). The infant mortality rate of 97.5 per 1,000 live births that I reported in 1977 is minimal (Hern 1977), since subsequent studies have shown infant mortality rates up to 50 percent (Hern 1988). The vast majority of Shipibo infant and child deaths are due to acute gastrointestinal and respiratory diseases. Infant and child gastrointestinal diseases are facilitated by the ubiquitous fecal contamination of water and food in spite of almost obsessive Shipibo cleanliness. Neonatal tetanus is a major cause of neonatal death for Shipibo and other Amazonian tribes, which generally have no immunologic experience with the tetanus antigen (Black et al. 1974).

A major cause of death for Shipibo women is cervical cancer, owing, I think, to a combination of high fertility, lack of male circumcision, and the desperate use of caustic substances for contraception (Hern 1976). Women also experience significant mortality associated with childbirth, although actual rates of maternal mortality have not been established for native Amazonian women. The early onset of childbearing and high fertility over a prolonged period undoubtedly contributes to the "premature aging" of women noted by Weinstein and others. The discouragement of polygyny by missionaries has resulted in shorter birth intervals and higher individual fertility for Indian women (Hern 1988, 1992a, 1992b). The consequences are inimical to the health of both women and their children.

Conclusion

In the future, the health and welfare of native Amazonians will be affected by numerous external factors over which they have little or no control. Among the most important of these, aside from the lack of access to the same level of health care afforded to other national populations, will be the environmental policies of national governments. Salzano (1990) points out that these include the construction of colossal dams for hydroelectric energy, as in Brazil, that destroy the environments necessary for the survival of indigenous groups. Another policy is the seemingly inexorable highway construction, colonization, and deforestation that accompanies the expansion of other populations.

Pucallpa, which was an aboriginal Shipibo settlement, had no more than 3,000 inhabitants in 1943. These had arrived at about the time the first trans-

Andes highway in Peru was pushed through to the Ucayali River. By 1964, when I made my first trip to the Peruvian Amazon, Pucallpa's population was estimated at 25,000. There were dirt streets and Saturday night gunfights. The Shipibo were displaced and treated as subhumans. By 1984, the population of Pucallpa was estimated at between 125,000 and 200,000. That is at least a 5,000 percent increase in forty years. Mestizo fishermen from Pucallpa now regularly exploit Ucayali waters some two hundred kilometers from Pucallpa in areas previously fished exclusively by Shipibo and a few local mestizos. Aramburú estimates that the annual population growth rate of the upper Peruvian Amazon Basin has been between 4 and 5 percent per year between 1940 and 1981 (Aramburú 1982, 16), and it may be as much as 10 percent including immigration (Aramburú, personal communication).

The aboriginal environment of the native Amazonians is shrinking rapidly and under great pressure from outside sources of development and exploitation. A significant factor in this is that the populations of nearly all Amazon Basin countries are growing at rates from 3 to 4 percent per year (World Resources Institute 1987). By the year 2000, the Amazon Basin countries will add *at least* the following numbers to their populations (from 1990):

Brazil	28.0 million
Bolivia	2.0 million
Colombia	5.5 million
Ecuador	3.0 million
Guyana	0.9 million
Peru	5.0 million
Suriname	0.1 million
Venezuela	4.0 million
TOTAL	48.5 million

The countries that ring the Amazon Basin will add the equivalent of half the current population of Mexico or roughly twice the current population of Canada over the next ten years (Zachariah and Vu 1988). Population pressure from outside is likely to have an enormous destructive effect on the Amazon environment and its native inhabitants. Combined with accelerating deforestation and urbanization (Merrick 1986, 25), population pressure means that much of the Amazon will have been transformed within a hundred years from a sparsely settled wilderness rain forest with tiny, isolated settlements of indigenous inhabitants to a scrub desert interrupted by rapidly growing cities.

There is nothing in the history of the human species to prepare us or our native Amazonian friends for this experience.

REFERENCES

Allison, M. J., D. Mendoza, and K. A. Pezie
1973   Documentation of a case of tuberculosis in Pre-Columbian America.
            American Review of Respiratory Disease 107:985–91.
Allison, M. J., A. Pezzia, I. Hasegawa, and E. Gerszten
1974   A case of hookworm infestation in a Precolumbian American. American
            Journal of Physical Anthropology 41:103–6.
Aramburú, C. E.
1982   Expansión de la frontera agraria y demográfica de la selva alta Peruana.
            In Colonización en la Amazonía, by C. E. Aramburú, E. Bedoya G., and
            J. Recharte B., 1–39. Lima: Ediciones CIPA.
Ayres, M., and F. M. Salzano
1972   Health status of the Brazilian Cayapo Indians. Tropical and Geographical
            Medicine 24:178–85.
Baker, B. J., and G. J. Armelagos
1988   The origin and antiquity of syphilis. Current Anthropology 29 (5):
            703–37.
Beaver P. C., J. V. Neel, and T. C. Orihel
1976   Dipetalonema perstans and Mansonella ozzardi in Indians of southern
            Venezuela. American Journal of Tropical Medicine and Hygiene 25 (2):
            263–65.
Bedoya, E.
1981   La destrucción del equilibrio ecológico en las cooperativas del Alto
            Huallaga. Lima: Centro de Investigación y Promoción Amazonica, Serie
            Documento 1.
Behrens, C.
1981   Time allocation and meat procurement among the Shipibo Indians of
            Eastern Peru. Human Ecology 9:189–220.
Bergman, R.
1980   Amazon economics: The simplicity of Shipibo Indian wealth. Ann Arbor:
            University Microfilms International.
Berlin, B., and E. Berlin
1978   Etnobiología, Subsisténcia, y Nutrición en una sociedad de la selva trop-
            ical: los Aguaruna (Jíbaro). In Salud y nutrición en sociedades nativas,
            edited by A. Chirif, 13–47. Lima: Centro de Investigatión y Promoción
            Amazónica.
Black F. L.
1975   Infectious diseases in primitive societies. Science 187:515–18.
Black, F. L., W. H. Hierholzer, F. P. Pinheiro, A. S. Evans, J. P. Woodall,
    E. M. Opton, B. S. West, G. Edsall, W. G. Downs, and G. D. Wallace
1974   Evidence for persistence of infectious agents in isolated human popula-
            tions. American Journal of Epidemiology 100:230–50.

Black, F. L., W. J. Hierholzer, D. P. Black, S. H. Lamm, and L. Lucas
1977   Nutritional status of Brazilian Kayapo Indians. *Human Biology* 49 (2):
            139–54.
Black, F. L., W. J. Hierholzer, J. F. Lian-Chen, L. L. Berman, Y. Gabbay, and
  F. P. Pinheiro
1982   Genetic correlates of enhanced measles susceptibility in Amazon
            Indians. *Medical Anthropology* 6 (1): 37–46.
Black, F. L., F. P. Pinheiro, O. Oliva, W. J. Hierholzer, R. V. Lee, J. Briller, and
  V. A. Richards
1978   Birth and survival patterns in numerically unstable proto agricultural
            societies in the Brazilian Amazon. *Medical Anthropology* 2 (3): 95–127.
Black, F. L., J. P. Woodall, A. S. Evans, H. Liebhaber, and G. Henle
1970   Prevalence of antibody against viruses in the Tiriyo, an isolated Amazon
            tribe. *American Journal of Epidemiology* 91:430–38.
Brown, L. R., C. Flavin, and S. Postel
1989   A world at risk. In *State of the world*, 1989, edited by L. R. Brown et al.,
            4. New York: W. W. Norton for The Worldwatch Institute.
Buck A. A., T. T. Sasaki, and R. I. Anderson
1968   *Health and disease in four Peruvian villages*. Baltimore: Johns Hopkins
            Press.
Bugos, P. E., and L. M. McCarthy
1984   Ayoreo infanticide: a case study. In *Infanticide: Comparative and evolu-
            tionary perspectives*, edited by G. Hausfater and S. B. Hrdy, 503–20. New
            York: Aldine.
Carneiro, R. A.
1974   The transition from hunting to horticulture in the Amazon Basin. In
            Man in adaptation: The cultural present. 2d ed. Edited by Y. A. Cohen.
            Chicago: Aldine.
Chagnon, N. A.
1974   *Studying the Yanomamo*. New York: Holt, Rinehart, and Winston.
1977   *Yanomamo: The fierce people*. 2d ed. New York: Holt, Rinehart, and
            Winston.
1983   *Yanomamo: The fierce people*. 3d. ed. New York: Holt, Rinehart, and
            Winston.
1988   Life histories, blood revenge, and warfare in a tribal population. *Science*
            239:985–92.
Chagnon, N. A., and R. B. Hames
1979   Protein deficiency and tribal warfare in Amazonia: new data. *Science*
            203:910–13.
Chagnon N. A., and T. F. Melancon
1983   Epidemics in a tribal population. *The Impact of Contact: Two Yanomamo
            Case Studies*. Working Papers on South American Indians #6/Cultural
            Survival Occasional Paper #11.

1984   Reproduction, numbers of kin and epidemics in tribal populations: A case study. In *Population and biology: A bridge between disciplines*, edited by N. Keyfitz, 147–67. Liege, Belgium: Ordina Editions.

Chernela, J. M., and V. E. Thatcher

1989   Comparison of parasite burdens in two native Amazonian populations. *Medical Anthropology* 10:279–85.

Clark, G. A., M. A. Kelley, J. M. Grange, and M. C. Hill

1987   The evolution of mycobacterial disease in human populations: A reevaluation. *Current Anthropology* 28 (1): 45–62.

Cockburn, T. A.

1961a   Eradication of infectious diseases. *Science* 133:1050–58.

1961b   The origin of treponematoses. *Bulletin of the World Health Organization* 24:221–28.

1971   Infectious diseases in ancient populations. *Current Anthropology* 12: 45–62.

Coimbra, C.E.A., Jr.

1988   Human settlements, demographic pattern, and epidemiology in lowland Amazonia: The case of Chaga's disease. *American Anthropologist* 90 (1): 82–97.

1989   From shifting cultivation to coffee farming: The impact of change on the health and energy of the Surui Indians in the Brazilian Amazon. Ph.D. diss., Indiana University.

CNPq/CIPA.

1984   Población y colonización en la alta Amazonía Peruana. Lima: Consejo Nacional de Población/Centro de Investigación y Promoción Amazónica.

Denevan, W. M.

1976   Epilogue. In *The native population of the Americas in 1492*, edited by William M. Denevan, 289–92; Table 00.1, p. 291. Madison: University of Wisconsin Press.

Devereux, G.

1955   *A study of abortion in primitive societies*. New York: Julian.

Dobyns, H. F.

1966   Estimating aboriginal American population: An appraisal of techniques with a new hemispheric estimate. *Current Anthropology* 7:395–416.

Donnelly, C. J., L. A. Thomson, H. M. Stiles, C. Brewer, J. V. Neel, and J. A. Brunelle

1977   Plaque, caries, periodontal diseases, and acculturation among Yanomamo Indians, Venezuela. *Commmunity Dental and Oral Epidemiology* 5:30–39.

Dufour, D. L.

1987   Insects as food: A case study from the Northwest Amazon. *American Anthropologist* 89 (2): 383–97.

Early, J. D., and J. F. Peters
1990   *The population dynamics of the Mucajai Yanomama.* New York: Academic
            Press.

Eaton, J. W., and A. J. Mayer
1953   The social biology of high fertility among the Hutterites. *Human Biology*
            25:206–64.

Fearnside, P. M.
1986   *Human carrying capacity of the Brazilian rainforest.* New York: Columbia
            University Press.

Fleming-Moran, M., and C.E.A. Coimbra
1990   Blood pressure studies among Amazonian native populations: A review
            from an epidemiological perspective. *Social Science and Medicine* 31
            (5):593–601.

Flowers, N. M.
1983   Seasonal factors in subsistence, nutrition, and child growth in a Central
            Brazilian Indian community. In *Adaptive responses of native Amazonians,*
            edited by Raymond B. Hames and William T. Vickers, 357–90. New
            York: Academic Press.
1990   Contact and demographic change: The Xavante case. Paper presented
            at the 59th Annual Meeting of the American Association of Physical
            Anthropologists, 4–7 April, Miami, Florida.

Glanville, E., and R. Geerdink
1970   Skinfold thickness, body measurements and age changes in Trio and
            Wajana Indians of Surinam. *American Journal of Physical Anthropology*
            32:455–61.
1972   Blood pressure of Amerindians from Surinam. *American Journal of Phys-
            ical Athropology* 37:251–54.

Goldman, I.
1979   *The Cubeo: Indians of the Northwest Amazon.* 2d ed. Urbana: University
            of Illinois Press.

Gómez-Pompa, A., C. Vázquez-Yanes, and S. Guevara
1972   The tropical rain forest: A nonrenewable resource. *Science* 177 (4051):
            762–65.

Greene, D.
1986   *Assessment of the state of preservation of human skeletal remains from Marajó
            Island, Pará, Brazil, and the potential for Marajoara cemetery excavation.*
            Report submitted to the National Science Foundation.

Guderian, R. H., C. D. Mackenzie, and J. R. Proaño
1987   Onchocerciasis in Ecuador: absence of microfilaraemia. *Journal of Tropi-
            cal Medicine and Hygiene* 90:213–14.

Hackett, C. J.
1963   On the origin of the human treponematoses. *Bulletin of the World Health
            Organization* 29:7–41.

Hames, R. B., and W. T. Vickers
1983   *Adaptive responses of native Amazonians.* New York: Academic Press.
Hecht, S.
1983   Cattle ranching in the Eastern Amazon: Environmental and social
            implications. In *The dilemma of Amazonian development,* edited by E. F.
            Moran, 155–88. Boulder, Colo.: Westview Press.
Hern, W. M.
1971   Community health, fertility trends, and ecocultural change in a Peru-
            vian Amazon Indian village: 1964–1969. Master's of Public Health
            thesis, University of North Carolina School of Public Health.
1976   Knowledge and use of herbal contraceptives in a Peruvian Amazon
            village. *Human Organization* 35:9–19.
1977   High fertility in a Peruvian Amazon Indian village. *Human Ecology* 5
            (4): 355–67.
1988   Polygyny and fertility among the Shipibo: An epidemiologic test of an
            ethnographic hypothesis. Ph.D. diss., University of North Carolina
            School of Public Health.
1992a   Polygyny and fertility among the Shipibo of the Peruvian Amazon. *Popu-
            lation Studies* 46:53–64.
1992b   Shipibo polygyny and patrilocality. *American Ethnologist* 19 (3): 501–22.
Hodge, L., and D. Dufour
1991   Cross-sectional growth of young Shipibo Indian children in eastern
            Peru. *American Journal of Physical Anthropology* 84:35–41.
Holmberg, A. R.
1985   *Nomads of the long bow: The Siriono of eastern Bolivia.* [1969] Prospect
            Heights, Ill.: Waveland Press
Johnston, F. E., and K. M. Kensinger
1971   Fertility and mortality differentials and their implications for micro-
            evolutionary change among the Cashinahua. *Human Biology* 43:
            356–64.
Johnston F. E., K. M. Kensinger, R. L. Jantz, and G. F. Walker
1969   The population structure of the Peruvian cashinahua: Demographic,
            genetic and cultural interrelationships. *Human Biology* 41:29–41.
Larrick, J., J. Yost, J. Kaplan, G. King, and J. Mayhall
1979   Patterns of health and disease among the Waorani Indians of eastern
            Ecuador. *Medical Anthropology* 3 (2): 147–89.
Lathrap, D. W.
1968   The "hunting" economies of the Tropical Rain Forest Zone of South
            America: An attempt at historical perspective. In *Man the hunter,* edited
            by R. B. Lee and I. DeVore, 23–29. Chicago: Aldine.
1970   *The upper Amazon.* New York: Praeger.
1977   Our father the cayman, our mother the gourd. In *The origins of agricul-
            ture,* edited by C. A. Reed, 713–51. The Hague: Mouton.

Lawrence, D. N, B. Erdtmann, J. W. Pest, J. A. Nunes de Mello, G. R. Heply,
    J. V. Neel, and F. M. Salzano
1980   Estudos epidemiolôgicos entre populacoes indigenas da Amazonia. II.
            Prevalencias de microfilaremia de *Mansonella ozzardi*: comparacao de
            dois metodos de diagnostico. *Acta Amazonica* 10 (4): 763–69.
Lawrence, D. N., R. R. Flacklam, F. O. Sottneck, G. A. Hancock, J. V. Neel, and
    F. M. Salzano
1979   Epidemiologic studies among Amerindian populations of Amazonia. II.
            Prevalence of *Mansonella ozzardi*. *American Journal of Tropical Medicine
            and Hygiene* 28 (6): 991–96.
Lawrence, D. N., J. V. Neel, S. H. Abadie, L. L. Moore, L. J. Adams, G. R. Healy,
    and I. G. Kagan
1980   Epidemiologic studies among Amerindian populations of Amazonia. III.
            Intestinal parasitoses in newly contacted and acculturating villages.
            American Journal of Tropical Medicine and Hygiene 29 (4): 530–37.
Lee, J. A.
1985a   Economic development and pollution control. Chap. 2 in *The envi-
            ronment, public health, and human ecology: Considerations for economic
            development*, 19–53. Baltimore: Johns Hopkins Press, for The World
            Bank.
1985b   Health considerations for economic development. Chap. 3 in *The envi-
            ronment, public health, and human ecology: Considerations for economic
            development*, 54–87.
Lipschutz, A.
1966   La despoblación de las Indias despues de la conquista. *America Indigena*
            26:229–47.
Lisansky, J.
1990   *Migrants to Amazonia: Spontaneous colonization in the Brazilian frontier.*
            Boulder, Colo.: Westview Press.
Lowenstein, F. W.
1961   Blood pressure in relation to age and sex in the tropics and subtropics.
            Lancet 1:389–92.
Lyon, P. J.
1985   *Native South Americans: Ethnology of the least known continent.* Prospect
            Heights, Ill.: Waveland Press.
Martin, P. S.
1973   The discovery of America. *Science* 197:969–74.
Meggers, B. J.
1971   *Amazonia: Man and culture in a counterfeit paradise.* Arlington Heights,
            Ill: AMH Publishing Corporation.
Merrick, T. W.
1986   Population pressures in Latin America. *Population Bulletin* 14 (3): 1–50.

Milton, K.
1984   Protein and carbohydrate resources of the Maku Indians of Northwest
            Amazonia. *American Anthropologist* 86 (1): 7–27.
Morães, M.A.P, and G. M. Chaves
1974   Onchocerciasis in Brazil: New findings among the Yanomama Indians.
            Bulletin of the Pan American Health Organization 8:95–99.
Moran, E.
1981   *Developing the Amazon.* Bloomington: Indiana University Press.
1989   Adaptation and maladaptation in newly settled areas. In *The human ecol-
            ogy of tropical land settlement in Latin America,* edited by D. A. Schumann
            and W. L. Partridge, 20–39. Boulder, Colo.: Westview Press.
Moran, E., editor
1983   *The dilemma of Amazonian development.* Boulder, Colo.: Westview Press.
Morse, D.
1961   Prehistoric tuberculosis in America. *American Review of Respiratory
            Disease* 83:489–504.
Murphy, Y., and R. F. Murphy
1974   *Women of the forest.* New York: Columbia University Press.
Myers, T. P.
1988   El efecto de pestilencia sobre las poblaciones de la Amazonia superior.
            Amazonia Peruana 8:61–81.
Neel, J. V.
1970   Lessons from a "primitive" people. *Science* 1970:815–22.
1977   Health and disease in unacculturated Amerindian populations. In
            Health and disease in tribal societies, edited by K. Elliott and J. Whelan,
            155–77. Ciba Foundation Symposium 49. Amsterdam: Elsevier.
1978   The population structure of an Amerindian tribe, the Yanomama.
            Annual Review of Genetics 12:365–413.
1982   Infectious disease among Amerindians. *Medical Anthropology* 6 (1):
            47–55.
Neel J. V., W. R. Centerwall, N. A. Chagnon, and H. L. Casey
1970   Notes on the effect of measles and measles vaccine in a virgin-soil popu-
            lation of South American Indians. *American Journal of Epidemiology* 91
            (4): 418–29.
Neel, J. V., and N. A. Chagnon
1968   The demography of two tribes of primitive, relatively unacculturated
            American Indians. *Proceedings of the National Academy of Sciences* 59 (3):
            680–89.
Neel, J. V., and F. M. Salzano
1970   Further studies on the Xavante Indians. 10. Some hypotheses-generaliza-
            tions resulting from these studies. *American Journal of Human Genetics*
            19:554–74.

Neel, J. V., F. M. Salzano, P. C. Junqueira, F. Keiter, and D. Maybury-Lewis
1964   Studies on the Xavante Indians of the Brazilian Mato Grosso. *Human
            Genetics* 16 (1): 52–140.
Neel, J. V., and K. M. Weiss
1975   The genetic structure of a tribal population, the Yanomama Indians. 12.
            Biodemographic studies. *American Journal of Physical Anthropology*
            42:25–52.
Nowaczynski, W., W. J. Oliver, and J. V. Neel
1985   Serum Aldosterone and protein-binding variables in Yanomama Indians:
            A "no-salt" culture as compared to partially acculturated Guaymi
            Indians. *Clinical Physiology and Biochemistry* 3:289–306.
Oliver, W. J., E. L. Cohen, and J. V. Neel
1975   Blood pressure, sodium intake, and sodium related hormones in the
            Yanomamo Indians, a "no-salt" culture. *Circulation* 52:146–51.
Omran, A. R.
1971   The epidemiologic transition. *Milbank Memorial Fund Quarterly* 49:
            509–38.
Pollock, D. K.
1988   Health care among the Culina, western Amazonia. *Cultural Survival
            Quarterly* 12 (1): 28–32
Posey, D. A.
1983   Indigenous ecological knowledge and development of the Amazon. In
            The dilemmas of Amazonian development, edited by E. F. Moran, 225–57.
            Boulder, Colo.: Westview Press.
Ramos, A. R., and K. I. Taylor
1979   *The Yanoama in Brazil, 1979.* IWGIA Document 37. Copenhagen: ARC/
            IWGIA/Survival International.
Roosevelt, A. C.
1980   *Parmana: Prehistoric maize and manioc subsistence along the Amazon and
            Orinoco.* New York: Academic Press.
1989   Natural resource management in Amazonia before the conquest: Beyond
            ethnographic projection. In *Natural resource management by folk and
            indigenous societies in Amazonia*, edited by D. Posey and W. Balée, 30–62.
            Advances in Economic Botany No. 7. New York: New York Botanical
            Garden.
Ross, E. B.
1978   Food taboos, diet, and hunting strategy: The adaptation to animals in
            Amazon cultural ecology. *Current Anthropology* 19 (1): 1–36.
Saffirio, J., and R. Hames
1983   The forest and the highway. In *The impact of contact: Two Yanomamo case
            studies.* Working Papers on South American Indians #6/Cultural Survi-
            val Occasional Paper #11.

Salzano F. M.

1961   Demography of the Caingang Indians. *Human Biology* 33:110–30.

1985   Changing patterns of disease among South American Indians. In *Diseases of complex etiology in small populations: Ethnic differences and research approaches,* edited by F. M. Salzano, 301–23. New York: Alan R. Liss.

1990   Parasitic load in South American tribal populations. In *Disease in populations in transition: Anthropological and epidemiological perspectives,* edited by A. C. Swedlund and G. J. Armelagos, 201–21. New York: Bergin and Garvey.

Salzano F. M., and S. M. Callegari-Jacques

1980   Demographic and genetic relationships among Brazilian Wapishana Indians. *Annals of Human Biology* 7 (2): 129–38.

1988   Disease patterns. In *South American Indians: A case study in evolution,* edited by F. M. Salzano and S. M. Callegari-Jacques, 87–113. Oxford: Clarendon.

Salzano F. M., S. M. Callegari-Jacques, and J. V. Neel

1979   Demografia genetica dos indios Ticuna da Amazonia. *Acta Amazonica* 9 (3): 517–27.

Salzano F. M., and J. V. Neel

1976   New data on the vision of South American Indians. *Bulletin of the Pan American Health Organization* 10 (1): 1–8.

Salzano F. M., J. V. Neel, and D. Maybury-Lewis

1967   Further studies on the Xavante Indians. 1. Demographic data on two additional villages: genetic structure of the tribe. *American Journal of Human Genetics* 19 (4): 463–89.

Schwaner, T. D., and C. F. Dixon

1974   Helminthiasis as a measure of cultural change in the Amazon Basin. *Biotropica* 6 (1): 32–37.

Shukla, J., C. Nobre, and P. Sellers

1990   Amazon deforestation and climate change. *Science* 247:1322–25.

Siskind, J.

1973   Tropical forest hunters and the economy of sex. In *Peoples and Cultures of Native South America,* edited by D. R. Gross, 226–40. Garden City, N.Y.: Natural History Press.

Simons, M.

1988   Amazon settlers turn forests to ash in name of progress. *New York Times,* 11 October.

Smith, R. C.

1982   The dialectics of domination in Peru: Native communities and the myth of the vast Amazonian emptiness. *Cultural Survival Occasional Paper No. 8.* Cambridge: Cultural Survival.

Spielman R. S., S. S. Fajans, J. V. Neel, S. Pek, J. C. Floyd, and W. J. Oliver
1982   Glucose tolerance in two unacculturated Indian tribes of Brazil.
            Diabetologia 23:90–93.
Stearman, A. M.
1983   Forest to pasture: frontier settlement in the Bolivian lowlands. In *The
            dilemma of Amazonian development,* edited by E. F. Moran, 51–63. Boul-
            der, Colo.: Westview Press.
Steward, J. H.
1949   The native population of South America. In *The comparative ethnology
            of South American Indians.* Vol. 5, *Handbook of South American Indians,*
            edited by J. H. Steward, 655–68, 698–710. *Bureau of American Ethnol-
            ogy Bulletin* no. 143. Washington, D.C.: U.S. Government Printing
            Office.
Steward, J. H., and A. Métraux
1948   Tribes of the Peruvian and Ecuadorian Montaña. In *The tropical forest
            tribes.* Vol. 3, *Handbook of South American Indians,* edited by J. H.
            Steward, 555–95. Bureau of American Ethnology Bulletin no. 143.
            Washington, D.C.: U.S. Government Printing Office.
Sulzer, A. J., R. Cantella, A. Colichon, N. N. Gleason, and K. W. Walls
1975   A focus of hyperendemic *Plasmodium malariae*–*P. vivax* with no *P. falci-
            parum* in a primitive population in the Peruvian Amazon jungle. *Bulletin
            of the World Health Organization* 52:273–78.
Tans, P. P., I. Y. Fung, and T. Takahashi
1990   Observational constraints on the global atmospheric CO_2 budget.
            Science 247:1431–38.
Tenbrink, M. S.
1964   Blood pressure comparisons in tropical Africans and Peruvians. *New York
            State Journal of Medicine* 64:2584–87.
Tessman, G.
1928   *Menschen ohne Gott: Ein Besuch bei den Indianern des Ucayali.* Stuttgart:
            Strecker and Schroder.
Thornton, R.
1987   *American Indian holocaust and survival: A population history since 1492.*
            Norman: University of Oklahoma Press.
Thornton, R., T. Miller, and J. Warren
1991   American Indian population recovery following smallpox epidemics.
            American Anthropologist 93:28–45.
Tournon, J.
1984   Investigaciones sobre las plantas medicinales de los Shipibo-Conibo del
            Ucayali. *Amazonia Peruana* 5 (10): 91–118.
Treece, D.
1987   *Bound in misery and iron: The impact of the grande carajas programme on the
            Indians of Brazil.* London: Survival International.

Wagley, C.

1974a   The effects of depopulation upon social organization as illustrated by the Tapirapé Indians. In *Native South Americans: Ethnology of the least known continent,* edited by P. J. Lyon, 373–76. Prospect Heights, Ill.: Waveland Press.

1974b   Cultural influences on population: A comparison of two Tupi tribes. In *Native South Americans: Ethnology of the least known continent,* edited by P. J. Lyon, 377–84. Prospect Heights, Ill.: Waveland Press.

1977   *Welcome of tears: The Tapirapé Indians of Brazil.* Prospect Heights, Ill.: Waveland Press.

Wagley, C., editor

1973   *Man in the Amazon.* Gainesville: University of Florida Press.

Weinstein, E. D., J. V. Neel, and F. M. Salzano

1967   Further studies on the Xavante Indians. 6. The physical status of the Xavantes of Simões Lopes. *American Journal of Human Genetics* 19 (4): 532–42.

Whitten, N. E.

1981   Introduction. In *Cultural transformations and ethnicity in modern Ecuador,* edited by N. E. Whitten, 1–41. Urbana: University of Illinois Press.

World Resources Institute

1987   *World Resources 1987.* New York: Basic Books.

Zachariah, K. C., and M. T. Vu

1988   *World population projections, 1987–88 edition: Short- and long-term estimates.* Baltimore: Johns Hopkins Press (World Bank).

7

wwww

Diet and Nutritional Status
of Amazonian Peoples

DARNA L. DUFOUR

The purposes of this chapter are to review and evaluate the available data on
diet and nutritional status of ethnographically known indigenous populations
in Amazonia, to examine the nutritional problems characteristic of the area,
and to examine the changes in diet and nutritional status that accompany
acculturation. Ideally we would like to be able to define nutritional problems
of Amazonia in terms of ecological variables, subsistence practices, exposure
to disease, and so on. Much of what has been written about diet in Amazonia,
however, is anecdotal, or at best, qualitative. This kind of data is useful in
providing a general description of the diet but provides little information on
the adequacy of the diet or on potential nutritional problems.

Guidelines in Assessing Diet and Nutritional Status

Diet refers to food energy and nutrients actually consumed by the organism.
Nutritional status refers to the biological state of the organism with regard to
the balance between the supply of energy and nutrients and the organism's
needs (McLaren 1976). Indicators of nutritional status are a set of variables
that provide a measure of this state of balance. The most commonly used
indicators are dietary intake, on the intake side of the equation, and anthro-

pometric measurements and clinical signs, on the biological status side.

Dietary intake is a very indirect measure of nutritional status. It is based on the assumption that "adequate" intake results in satisfactory nutritional status. Adequacy is defined in relation to need, or indirectly in relationship to some standard, such as "recommended allowance." The most useful measurements of dietary intake are those of the "usual" intake of individuals of known sex, body weight, and activity level carried out over a number of days during the seasonal cycle. The dietary intake of household groups is hard to interpret because of variations in age-sex composition and intrahousehold patterns of food distribution. Data on the yield of subsistence systems is even more difficult to interpret because it provides information on food availability, not on food intake.

Anthropometry is considered to be the most useful and practical tool for the assessment of nutritional status in children (WHO 1986). Although a number of different anthropometric measurements have been used, the most useful appear to be weight-for-height and height-for-age (WHO 1986). Weight-for-height is considered an indication of present nutritional status (Waterlow et al. 1977). Deficits in weight-for-height are referred to as "wasting," and are taken to indicate acute dietary deficiency. Height-for-age is an indication of the rate of growth over time. Low height-for-age is referred to as "stunting." It develops slowly, and is considered indicative of long-term nutritional inadequacy or generally poor environmental conditions, especially ones in which chronic or repeated infections are prevalent (WHO 1986). In this sense stunting is a nonspecific indicator of the overall quality of life, rather than a specific indicator of dietary deficiency.

For adults, the classic anthropometric indicator of nutritional status has been weight-for-height. James et al. (1988) have recently proposed that the body mass index (BMI), defined as weight/height^2, could be used to identify chronic energy deficiency (CED).

Clinical signs are observable pathological conditions that are suggestive of particular nutrient deficiencies and those that accompany moderate to severe protein-energy malnutrition (PEM). Their usefulness in assessing nutritional status is limited, however, because they are difficult to define objectively and are quite variable in occurrence (Jelliffe 1966).

Interpretation of Nutritional Status Indicators

The interpretation of all indicators of nutritional status is dependent on reference values or standards with which they can be compared. For anthropometric characteristics the United States National Center for Health Statistics

(NCHS) standards have been recommended for international use (WHO 1986). In this chapter however, "standard" refers to the Harvard growth standards published in Jelliffe (1966) unless otherwise indicated. These have been widely used and will be used here to facilitate comparison of the data available. The means of the Harvard standards are very similar to the fiftieth percentile values of the NCHS data and the WHO growth curves data (Stephenson, Latham, and Jansen 1983).

The question of whether all children throughout the world have the same potential for growth is still unresolved. However, the working assumption is that ethnic differences are much less important than other factors such as poor food intakes and disease as causes of growth failure in children (Eveleth and Tanner 1976; Habicht et al. 1974; Waterlow et al. 1977). Weight-for-height is nearly independent of age between 1 and 10 years, and is thought to also be relatively independent of ethnic group between ages 1 and 5 (Habicht et al. 1974; Waterlow et al. 1977, 491; and Wray 1975).

For weight-for-height the cutoff between normal and low is usually set at $< 80\%$ of the standard, and for weight-for-age $< 90\%$ of the standard. The biological significance of these cutoff points is still unclear. For BMI the cutoff has been set at 18.5 because functional impairment is likely at lower levels (James et al. 1988).

Clinical signs are rated as either present or absent. Presence in $> 10\%$ of the population is considered high. For dietary intake current FAO/WHO/UNU (1985) recommendations are probably the most appropriate since they attempt to take into consideration the types of environmental conditions and disease loads found in the tropics.

Diet and Nutritional Status of Ethnographic Groups

For descriptive purposes it is useful to divide Amazonia into three regions: northern, western, and southern peripheral Amazonia. These distinctions conform to Fittkau's ecological subregions (Herrera et al. 1978). The ethnographic groups for which there is some information on diet or nutritional status are shown on figure 7.1. Almost all have subsistence systems based on swidden horticulture, hunting, fishing, and gathering, and except for the Xavante inhabit tropical forest environments.

Northern Peripheral Amazonia

There is data available for the Trio and Wajana in the Guianas, several groups from Venezuela including the Yanomami, and Tukanoans in Colombia. All of these groups were swidden horticulturalists when studied.

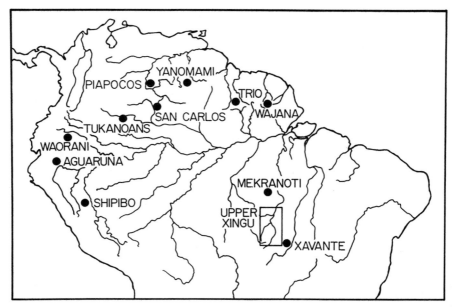

Figure 7.1. The approximate location of indigenous groups discussed in this
chapter.

TRIO AND WAJANA. The Trio and Wajana inhabited river margins in low-
lying forested areas of the Guianas (Gillin 1948). Rainfall in the area is
about 2,000 mm/yr (Salati et al. 1978), and there is a short (3–4 month) dry
season (Prance 1978). There is little information on diet except that it was
based on bitter manioc (also cassava, *Manihot esculenta* Crantz), prepared as
casabe (manioc bread), and fish (Gillin 1948, 829). The first missions were
established in both groups in 1961. Their nutritional status was evaluated
shortly afterwards (1967–68), when they were still living in small, temporary
villages and self-sufficient in food. Glanville and Geerdink (1970) examined
737 individuals, and reported that "on the whole the people give the impression of being fit, well nurtured and in good health." They found no cases of
edema, and none of goiter. Severe anemia was rare. Malaria was endemic,
but acute episodes were rare.

Dietary protein intake was estimated (from the ratio of urinary nitrogen to
creatine) to be not less than 60 gm/day for adults, and not less than 2 gm/kg
body weight/day for children under 12 years. These levels of intake are above
the FAO/WHO/UNU (1985) safe level.

In young children (3–4 years) average height-for-age was > 90% of the standard for boys, but < 90% for girls. Average weight-for-height was within the normal range for both boys and girls. School children were below the NCHS fifth percentile for height, but within the normal range (< 80% of standard) for weight-for-height. Adults were short (see figure 7.2), but average weight-for-height was 95 to 105% of standard.

PIAPOCOS, PIAROAS, GUAHIBOS, AND CUIBAS. Boza and Baumgartner (1962) investigated the food habits and nutritional status of indigenous

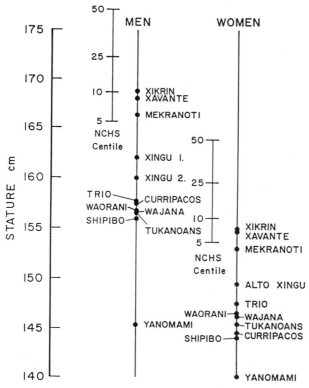

Figure 7.2. The mean stature of Amazonian adults compared to NCHS percentiles. Data are from Niswander et al. 1967 (Xavante); Black et al. 1977 (Xikrin and Mekanoti); Hugh-Jones 1972 (Xingu 1); Eveleth 1974 (Xingu 2); Glanville and Geerdink 1970 (Trio and Wajana); Dufour ms (Tukanoans); Behrens 1984 (Shipibo); Holmes 1985 (Curripaco and Yanomami); Larrick et al. 1979 (Waorani).

groups living along the upper Orinoco and Ventuari Rivers in southern Venezuela in 1952. This is an area of tropical savanna with gallery forests along
the rivers. Rainfall is between 1,000 and 1,500 mm/yr. Most of the groups
they encountered were Piapocos, Piaroas, and Guahibos living in villages
along the river margins and practicing swidden horticulture. Casabe made
from bitter manioc was the most frequently consumed food, followed in rank
order by fish, *yucuta* (a beverage of manioc meal and water), meat, fruits (all
types), and maize. They noted that of the fruits, palm fruits were particularly
important in the diet. In addition to game animals, they also reported the
use of a variety of small fauna including frogs, snakes, bats, and insects. They
also encountered a small number of Cuibas, whom they described as nomadic
hunters and gatherers inhabiting gallery forest and savannas, but did not
describe their diet in any detail. Most other observers have reported the
Cuiba as having some agriculture.

In clinical examinations of some 452 individuals Boza and Baumgartner
did not find any evidence of frank malnutrition or goiter. The most common
clinical signs were spongy, bleeding gums (23%), a sign suggestive of vitamin
C deficiency, and xerosis of the skin (17%). The latter can be due to environmental causes or to dietary deficiency of essential fatty acids (Jelliffe 1966).
They did not report data on the condition of hair. Nor did they report anthropometric data by age and sex.

YANOMAMI. The Yanomami inhabit interior mountainous rain-forest regions of southern Venezuela away from the major rivers. Lizot's (1977) data
for the Central Yanomami indicate that plantains and bananas are the dietary
staples, and game is the principal source of animal protein (see table 7.1).
His data also indicate a heavier reliance on nondomesticated plant foods
than is evident for other groups in the area.

Holmes (1985) reported nutritional status for two Central Yanomami villages in the Parima Mountains. She noted that the young adults gave the
impression of being fit and healthy, but that "these populations as a whole,
including young children and older adults do not show community-wide good
nutritional status" (Holmes 1985, 251). She found that most children between 1 and 12 years of age were thin, and many would be considered moderately to severely malnourished (see table 7.2). Teenagers, by contrast, were
well proportioned. Adults were short, males averaging 145.3 cm and females
136.2 cm. Indeed, they are the shortest people in Amazonia.

SAN CARLOS DE RIO NEGRO: CURRIPACOS. The diet and nutritional status
of native Amazonians living in San Carlos de Rio Negro, a town of about six

Table 7.1. Composition of Amerindian Diets in Terms of the Percent of Total Energy (E) and Protein (P) Contributed by Different Foods

Foods	Yanomami[a] %E	%P	Tukanoans[b] %E	%P	Shipibo[c] %E	%P	Aguaruna[d] %E	%P	Siona-Secoya[e] %E	%P
Manioc	—	83	21	11	2	61	12	33	6	—
Plantain/banana	76	14	—	76	28	16	6	20	4	—
Fruits	—	—	?	?	6	7	—	—	—	—
Other cultigens	—	5	4	2	2	—	19	6	—	—
Wild plants	7	6	1	1	—	—	<1	<1	—	—
Fish	2	7	8	58	6	40	10	55	9	44
Game	15	69	1	8	4	20	4	17	11	36
Animals, various	1	4	2	5	—	—	<1	<1	—	—
Pork & chicken	—	—	2	8	—	—	—	—	—	—
Miscellaneous	—	—	—	3	3	7	3	—	—	—

[a]Data for two villages collected over a 42-day period (Lizot 1977). "Animal, various" includes insects and crustaceans.

[b]Data from Dufour 1983 for four households observed over a 3-day period. "Animals, various" includes insects.

[c]Calculated from Behrens 1986. Figures are for means for 17 households visited on 25 different days. "Other cultigens" include rice, potatoes, squash and beans. Values do not include fruits or gathered food, which was estimated to be less than 1% of the total weight of all foods consumed.

[d]Data from Berlin and Berlin 1977. "Miscellaneous" foods include roots and tubers, seeds and other plant parts, crustaceans, frogs, and insects. Approximately a third of the energy derived from manioc is in the form of manioc beer or masato.

[e]Data for Siona-Secoya at Shushufindi from Vickers 1989 for 3-day weighed records for four adults and one child. Cultigens included peach palm (16% of total food energy), papaya, and sugarcane; "other" included rice and sugar.

Table 7.2. Anthropometric Indices of Nutritional Status in Preschool Children (Except as Indicated), Sexes Combined

Group (Date)[b]	Age, yrs	N	Percent of Sample Within Each Decile of Standard[a]				
			≥ 100	90–99	80–89	70–79	< 70
WEIGHT FOR HEIGHT							
Aguaruna (1972–75)[c]	1–5.0	35	?	33	32	29	6
Bakairi[d]	1–5.0	37	65	27	8	0	0
Curripaco (1980–83)[e]	0–5.9	34	38	29	3	0	0
Shipibo[f]	< 10.0	43	?	63	23	12	2
Tukanoans (1976–87)[g]	2–5.9	120	?	93	7	0	0
Yanomami (1982)[h]	?	93	30	53	16	1	0
Xingu Tribes (1974–76)[i]	0–5.0	175	66	30	3	<1	0
HEIGHT FOR AGE							
Curripaco (1980–83)[e]	0–5.9	31	10	58	26	6	0
Kayapó (1970–76)[j]	0–5.9	87	18	66	16	0	0
Tukanoans (1976–78)[g]	2–5.9	120	?	43	50	3	3

[a] Harvard standards as quoted by Jelliffe (1966). Height for age to 60 months, weight for height to 108 cm. Age grouped as recommended by Waterlow et al. 1977 when possible.

[b] Date of study.

[c] Berlin and Markell 1977. Data reported as ≥ 90%.

[d] Picchi 1982.

[e] Holmes 1981. Includes children from San Carlos de Rio Negro and surrounding villages (Venezuela).

[f] Behrens (1984). Data reported as ≥90%.

[g] Dufour, n.d. Includes groups living in Vaupés region on rivers Cuduyari, Quereri, Alto Papuri, Paca. Groups included Cubeo, Tukano, Tatuyo, Carapana, Barasana, and Desana (Colombia).

[h] Holmes 1985. Data read from figure 4 (Holmes 1985, 250) for girls and boys 52 to 108 cm. Ages not available. Data is considered preliminary since number of observations read from graph is greater than sample size reported.

[i] Fagundes-Neto et al. 1981. Groups from the Alto Xingu, including Camaiuras, Auetis, Uaura, Iualapitis, Meinacos, Cuicuro, Calapalo, Matipu-Nafugua, and Trumais (Brazil).

[j] Black et al. 1977. Includes Xikrin and Mekranoti (Brazil). Data read from published growth charts.

hundred persons, and three surrounding villages was studied by Holmes (1981, 1985) in 1980. Ecologically, the area is rain forest drained by black-water rivers. Rainfall is high, 3,600 mm/yr, and not less than 100 mm in any month (Hill and Moran 1983). The traditional diet was based on fish or meat soups with added starch from mañoco (manioc meal) or casabe. The usual beverage was yucuta. Fish was the principal source of animal protein. Household protein intakes in San Carlos and one of the outlying villages were estimated to be above FAO/WHO (1973) safe levels.

In clinical examinations Holmes (1985) found signs of sparse and/or dyspigmented hair in 25 to 50% of young children (n = 35) and "moon-face" in 12%. These are signs suggestive of undernutrition (Jelliffe 1966). In general, the children were short for their age, but normal in weight-for-height (see table 7.2). Most schoolchildren and adolescents were normal weight-for-height (table 7.3), but in terms of weight-for-age, 80% were below the tenth percentile of the Venezuelan standard. Adults were small, but normal weight-for-height.

TUKANOANS. The diet and nutritional status of Tukanoan Indians in the Colombian Vaupés region was studied by Dufour (1983, n.d.) and Ortiz (1981). Ecologically, the Vaupés area is similar to that of the Rio Negro Basin. The Tukanoan diet is based on bitter cassava, prepared as casabe, and fish.

Dietary intake was assessed for household groups in 1977 (see table 7.1.). Total household energy and protein intakes compared favorably with FAO/WHO (1973) recommendations based on age, body weight, and activity level (Dufour 1983). Ortiz (1981) reported similar results for a sample of 40 households in 1979.

Weighed food records were also kept for Yapu adults in 1977–78. Mean energy intakes were 100% or more of the FAO/WHO (1973) recommendations for moderately active adults of corresponding body weight (Dufour 1984a) (see table 7.4). The energy intakes also appeared adequate in comparison to estimates of energy expenditure (Dufour 1984b). Mean protein intakes were above the FAO/WHO (1973) safe level for both men and women.

Seasonal differences in energy intake were not great, but protein intake varied considerably. It was higher in the November-January period, the driest time of the year, when fishing is usually very good, and lower in May-June, the height of the rainy season, when fishing is usually poor. Gathered foods, including insects, were most important in the diet in the May-June period. Men had higher total intakes of animal protein, but when animal protein intake is considered as a percent of total energy intake, the sex difference disappears.

Table 7.3. Weight-for-Height in School Children and Adults

Group (Date)[b]	Age in yrs., Sex	N	Percent of Sample Within Each Decile of Standard[a]				
			≥ 100	90–99	80–89	70–79	< 70
SCHOOL CHILDREN							
Aguaruna (1972–75)[c]	6–19	32	59	29	6	6	
Bakairi[d]	4–19M	47	96	2	0	0	0
	F	52	94	4	2	0	0
Curripaco (1980–83)[e]	6–17	52	94	6	0	0	
Tukanoans (1976–87)[f]	6–19M	249	98	1	< 1	1	
	F	222	98	1	< 1	< 1	
Yanomami (1982)[g]	M	60	67	23	8	2	0
	F	42	71	21	7	0	0
ADULTS							
Aguaruna (1972–75)[c]	20 + M	50	54	36	6	4	
Bakairi[d]	20 + M	56	66	23	9	2	
	F	68	78	18	1	3	0
Curripaco (1980–83)[e]	18 +	47	94	4	0	0	
Tukanoans (1976–87)[f]	20 + M	205	94	6	0	0	
	F	188	92	8	0	0	

[a]Harvard standards as quoted by Jelliffe (1966).

[b]Date of study.

[c]Berlin and Markell 1977. Data reported as ≥ 90%.

[d]Picchi 1982, 153–56.

[e]Data from Holmes 1981, 113. Includes children and adults from San Carlos de Rio Negro and surrounding villages (Venezuela). Data reported as ≥ 90%.

[f]Dufour, n.d. Includes groups living in Vaupés region on rivers Cuduyari, Quereri, Alto Papuri, and Paca. Groups included Cubeo, Tukano, Tatuyo, Carapana, Barasana, and Desana (Colombia). Data tabulated as ≥ 90%.

[g]Holmes 1985. Data read from figure 4 (Holmes 1985, 250) for girls 110–62 cm and boys 112–70 cm. Ages not available.

In terms of a yearly average, approximately 81% of all dietary energy was derived from carbohydrate, 11% from protein (8% from animal protein), and 8% from fat. This level of protein calories is not unusual in self-selected diets (FAO/WHO 1973, 22); the level of energy derived from fat, however, is very low. The diet, therefore, has a very low energy density, and the sheer volume of food required to meet energy needs is a potential constraint, especially for children.

The nutritional status of children and adults in Yapu was similar to that found in other groups of Tukanoans (Dufour n.d.). Almost all young children were normal weight-for-height, but about half were small for their age, < 90% standard weight-for-age (see table 7.2). School children exhibited a similar pattern. Almost all had weight-for-heights within the normal range, but they were small for their age (below NCHS third percentile). Values for arm-muscle circumference were close to the U.S. fiftieth percentile (Frisancho 1981) for both males and females, indicating that body protein stores were well maintained.

The nutritional status of Tukanoan adults was generally good. They were short in stature (fig. 7.2), but mean weight-for-height was 95% of the standard for males and 100% of the standard for females. Levels of subcutaneous fat were low by U.S. standards (Frisancho 1981), but arm muscle areas were at about the U.S. twenty-fifth percentile for males and seventy-fifth for females, indicating that skeletal musculature was well maintained and suggesting that

Table 7.4. Mean Energy and Protein Intakes of Tukanoan Adults and Percent FAO/WHO (1973) Recommendations by Season and Sex (Protein from Animal Sources Is in Parentheses)

Season[a]	Sex	N	Energy			Protein	
			Intake kcal	% FAO	Expenditure kcal	Intake g	% FAO
Nov.–Jan.	M	9	3,335	113	2,806	96 (70)	218
Nov.–Jan.	F	10	2,413	106	2,133	80 (65)	200
May–June	M	10	3,017	100	2,956	70 (49)	152
May–June	F	13	2,396	123	2,051	65 (39)	176

[a]Records were kept for 3 days in Nov.–Jan. and 1 day in May–June. Adequacy of protein intakes is based on the assumption that the Yapu diet has a protein quality of at least 70% relative to milk or eggs.

energy and protein requirements were being met.

Ortiz (1981) reported clinical signs of undernutrition (hair lacking in luster, sparse, or dyspigmented) and iron deficiency anemia (pale conjunctiva) in about half of 61 children examined.

Western Peripheral Amazonia

For western peripheral Amazonia there is information on four groups: Waorani, Siona-Secoya, Jivaro, and Shipibo. They inhabit rain forests on the lower slopes of the Andes, or *montaña,* and in the adjacent lowlands. Rainfall is high in the areas they occupy, and there is no real dry season (Behrens 1984, 72; Berlin and Markell 1977; Prance 1978). All of the groups are swidden horticulturalists and share a similar diet based on plantains and sweet manioc.

WAORANI. The Waorani inhabit tropical forests in eastern Ecuador at elevations of 250–425 m. When studied in the 1970s their diet was based on sweet manioc, much of which was consumed as a premasticated drink, and plantains. Most of their animal protein was derived from game. Peach palm (*Bactris gasipaes*) was seasonally important in the diet. (Larrick et al. 1979; Yost and Kelly 1983). Larrick et al. (1979) reported that with few exceptions (< 5% of the 293 individuals examined), the Waorani appeared to be in excellent health and without evidence of malnutrition. They did not report growth data for children, but the adults are short (fig. 7.2).

SIONA-SECOYA. The Siona-Secoya studied by Vickers (1989) in the early 1970s lived in rain forest environments in northeastern Ecuador. Their diet was based on manioc and plantains, with most of the animal protein coming from game animals. Data from 1986 reported by Benefice and Barral (1991) suggests a diet more reliant on plantains and an increased use of purchased foods like sugar, rice, and oil. Benefice and Barral (1991) found that a large proportion (30%) of the preschool-aged children had height-for-age deficits (z-scores of −2 or greater) when compared to the NCHS growth data, but most had height-for-weight values in the normal range. Body mass indices of adult males and females were in the normal range, 25.9 and 24.8 kg/m^2, respectively. They also found that more than 25% of all children < 7 years of age presented symptoms of infection, and a high percentage of the children (75%) had stool specimens positive for at least one parasite.

AGUARUNA JIVARO. The Aguaruna Jivaro occupy a region of dense tropical rain forest at elevations of 200–1600 m in the Peruvian montaña (Ross 1976, 22). Berlin and Markell (1977) reported diet intake of five households (26 persons) for a twenty-day period (in 1974) when fishing was good. They found that sweet manioc and plantains provided 75% of the total energy intake, and fish was the major source of animal protein (table 7.1). The Aguaruna also used game animals, crabs, birds, snails, shrimp, and frogs, but domestic animals (chicken, pigs) were not important in their diet. Cassava was prepared by boiling, by roasting, and as beer. The plantains were boiled or roasted, and the bananas were usually prepared as a gruel.

Household energy and protein intakes were well above FAO/WHO (1973) recommendations based on age, sex, and body weight. Mean per capita intakes of calcium, phosphorus, iron, vitamin A, thiamine, riboflavin, niacin, and vitamin C were also above recommended levels. The diet was similar to that reported by Ross (1976) for the Achuara Jivaro both in terms of composition and per capita intake.

Anthropometric data for the Aguaruna (Berlin and Markell 1977) indicates that 35% of the young children were wasted (< 80% reference weight-for-height) (table 7.2). Mortality in this group was estimated at 32%. School children were healthier, only 12% of whom were < 80% of the standard weight-for-height. In adults, 10% had weight-for-heights < 80% of the standard. No data on adult stature were reported.

Berlin and Markell (1977) reported clinical signs of malnutrition in all age-sex groups. The most common signs were sparse or dyspigmented hair in young children (26% and 52%), and spongy, bleeding gums in school children (52%) and adults (60%). The latter is indicative of vitamin C deficiency, but dietary intake appeared adequate. One case of classical kwashiorkor was found. Clinical signs of iron-deficiency anemia (pale conjunctiva) were common in all age-sex groups, but anemia was not confirmed by hemoglobin determinations.

SHIPIBO. Behrens (1986) reported food intake data for 17 Shipibo households in one village in the headwaters of the Pisqui River in 1981. Plantains/bananas provided 76% of the total energy intake, sweet manioc, 11%, and fish, game, and domestic animals, 12% (table 7.1). Bergman (1974) described a similar diet for the Shipibo on the alluvial floodplain of the Ucayali River.

Southern Peripheral Amazonia

For the region south of the Amazon there are data available for the Mekranoti and Xikrin (Kayapó), the tribes of the upper Xingu and the Xavante.

MEKRANOTI. The Mekranoti habitat is continuous evergreen forest (Werner 1983), with approximately 2,000 mm/yr of rainfall (Salati et al. 1978), and a 3–4 month dry season (Prance 1978). There is no detailed information on their diet, but Black et al. (1977) reported that their food staples were sweet potatoes, bitter manioc, plantain, and maize, in that order, and that meat, from a variety of game animals, was the principal source of animal protein. The Mekranoti studied by Werner (1983) in 1976–77 trekked several months of the year, but the only nondomesticated vegetable food they consumed was Brazil nuts (*Bertholetia excelsia*).

Black et al. (1977) examined the nutritional status of a mixed age-sex sample of 219 Mekranoti and Xikrin between 1970 and 1976. They found that children under 2 years were short for their age in comparison to the Harvard standard, but then seemed to grow faster during the next 4 years. After age 5 the height of most children was on or above the Harvard median. Sample sizes, however, were very small, 25 for boys and 19 for girls. In terms of weight-for-height, children under 2 years of age were thin, but after two years weight-for-height ratios were close to U.S. values. Adult heights were similar to those reported earlier by da Rocha and Salzano (1972). The Mekranoti are among the tallest and heaviest of all Amerindians (fig. 7.2). Arm-muscle circumference of adults was at or above the U.S. median. Serum albumin values for children were moderately high, and those of adults were comparable to U.S. values. In summary, these findings indicate relatively good nutritional status. Black et al. (1977) did, however, note that a few individuals stood out as less well nourished.

ALTO XINGU TRIBES. The Alto Xingu area is home to a number of tribal groups, such as the Bakiri, Kalapalo, Kuikuro, Matipuhy-Nafuqua, Meinacu, Waura Iaualapiti, Aueti, Juruna, Kamaiura, Suia, Trumai and Txikaõ. Ecologically, the Alto Xingu is a transitional zone between Amazonian forest and herbaceous and brush plants characteristic of central Brazil (Eveleth 1974), and it includes a combination of rain forest, gallery forest and savanna. Rainfall is about 2,000 mm/yr, and there is a 3–4 month dry season. Amerindians inhabit the tropical rain forest environments along the Xingu and its affluents.

All of the groups are swidden horticulturalists. There is no detailed information on diet, but according to Fagundes-Neto et al. (1981) the staple foods are bitter manioc, prepared as *beiju* (casabe), and fish. Game is not important in the diet, with hunting restricted to a few small animals like monkeys and some birds. They reported the use of a variety of nondomesticated fruits, honey, turtle eggs, and "piqui" (*Caryocar* sp.), which ranks high in the diet. This description of diet agrees with that of other observations made between 1953 and 1975 (Carneiro 1961, 1983; Hugh-Jones et al. 1972). Carneiro

(1983) reports that manioc used is "bitter." Food appears to be plentiful (Carneiro 1961; Hugh-Jones et al. 1972).

Nutritional status was examined by Fagundes-Neto et al. (1981) in a series of 336 physical examinations of children over a three-year period (1974–76). They found no clinical signs of "severe protein-calorie malnutrition." Over 99% of all children were within the normal range for weight-for-height (see table 7.2.). Ages were not determined, but on the basis of an indirect analysis of growth rates, they did not find evidence of what they considered "severe stunting." It is unclear, however, exactly what "severe" means. Adult stature is intermediate for Amazonian Indians but low in comparison to the NCHS percentiles (fig. 7.2).

XAVANTE. The Xavante inhabit an area of *cerrado* vegetation on the Central Brazilian Plateau. Gross et al. (1979) describe cerrado as an open, semideciduous tree-and-scrub woodland with strips of evergreen gallery forest along streams. Rainfall averages 1100–1600 mm/yr, and there is a 3–4 month dry season, during which there is virtually no rain (Flowers 1983). Maybury-Lewis reported that in 1955–58 the Xavante were living in the cerrado and swiddening in the gallery forest. They trekked all year except for about three weeks, which they devoted to horticulture. Their diet was based on nondomesticated roots, *palmito*, nondomesticated nuts, fruits, and game (Maybury-Lewis 1974, 43–44). The roots functioned as the carbohydrate staple. In the swiddens they grew maize, beans, and pumpkins, and these foods were important in the diet right after their harvest.

Growth data for children and adolescents from the 1940s reported by Eveleth et al. (1974) indicates that most girls 5 to 10 years of age and most boys 5 to 14 years of age were within the third and ninety-seventh percentiles of the British growth standards for stature, and a number are above the fiftieth percentile. After that, however, growth in length leveled off, and most of the individuals measured were below the British third percentile.

The nutritional status of the Xavante at Post Simões Lopes was studied in the early 1960s by Weinstein et al. (1967). They reported that "as a rule individuals of both sexes and all ages were well developed and apparently well nourished, muscular with little adiposity. . . . [The] general impression was of exuberant health and vitality in the children and adults, but premature aging in the women. . . . Adult males show evidence of great stamina" (Weinstein et al. 1967, 532, 539). Neel et al. (1964) described the Xavante at Post Pimentel Barbosa in 1962 in similar terms.

The most common clinical sign among the Post Simões Lopes Xavante was goiter (10% of adult males and 41% of adult females) (Weinstein et al.

1967). The goiters were of moderate size, but there was no evidence of hyper-
or hypothyroidism, and investigators concluded that the iodine deficiency
was not very great (Neel et al. 1968).

Niswander et al. (1967) plotted the stature of Xavante children, 4 to 12
years of age, on the Harvard growth charts. Most of the mean values were on
or about the Harvard tenth percentile. Sample size, however, was very small,
15 girls and 30 boys. Aging was considered "reasonably accurate." Adult
stature was intermediate between that of the Xikrin and Mekranoti, which
makes the Xavante among the tallest of the Amazonian Indians.

The more recent work (1976–77) of Flowers (1983) with the Xavante at
Pimentel Barbosa indicated that they have adopted upland rice as a dietary
staple and were trekking only about two weeks of the year. They collected
nondomesticated roots only occasionally, but did collect large quantities of
palmito, palm nuts, and other fruits. Palmito was eaten fresh, or dried and
pounded into a flour that was boiled into a thick soup. Game was more
important in the diet than fish. Flowers (1983) reported that they sold some
of their rice but included few purchased foods in the diet.

Flowers (1983) plotted a small sample of children (30 boys and 15 girls)
on the Harvard growth charts and found that the results were similar to those
reported by Niswander et al. (1967). Weight-for-age of children < 1 year of
age was 95–99% of the WHO standard, and of children 1–2 years of age was
between 82 and 90% of the standard (total $n = 26$). In the latter Flowers
(1983) found a seasonal pattern of weight gain that was related to the agricultural cycle. Her data on the weight of food consumed by households shows
evidence of seasonal differences in total food intake.

Adequacy of Amerindian Diets

The reported composition of the diets of Amerindian groups living in rain-
forest environments is summarized in table 7.1. In most diets over 76% of the
energy is derived from two staples, manioc and plantains/bananas, and over
68% of the protein is from animal sources. The animals used include a variety
of wild fauna, but fish is typically the most important. The protein quality of
the diet is high, because of the high percentage of total protein coming from
animal sources. Nondomesticated plant foods do not appear to be particularly
important sources of energy, except in the traditional Xavante diet, where
nondomesticated roots were the staple.

Seasonality in energy and protein intake does not appear to be an important constraint. The dietary staples are harvested continuously, except in the
case of the Xavante rice-based diet. The intake of nondomesticated vegetable

and animal foods does vary seasonally, but there are no indications of seasonal inadequacies in the data available.

In the manioc-based diets there is a clear distinction between groups in western peripheral Amazonia, where manioc is consumed boiled, baked, and as a drink, and the rest of Amazonia, where it is consumed primarily as bread. From a nutritional point of view the diets based on boiled or baked roots and beer are higher in bulk and lower in energy density. On such diets the volume of food young children must consume to meet their energy and nutrient needs is a potential constraint. The very low fat content ($<$ 9% of calories) of Amerindian diets, suggested by the Tukanoan data, is also a potential constraint for children. It is generally assumed that diets in which fat contributes $<$ 15% of the calories are not concentrated enough for a child (Wheeler 1980).

Dietary energy intake in Aguaruna and Tukanoan household groups and adults appears to be adequate. Protein intakes for Aguaruna, Curripacos, Tukanoans, Trio, and Wajana also appear adequate.

Anthropometric indices of nutritional status in young children are summarized in table 7.2. In terms of weight-for-height, most of the children are in the normal range, but children in two groups in western Amazonia, Shipibo and Aguaruna, show high prevalences of thinness or wasting. In terms of height-for-age the children are generally small. In all, 16% of Kayapó, 26% of San Carlos area, and 50% of Tukanoan children, and the mean values of Wajana and Trio girls, are $<$ 90% of the standard.

Anthropometric indices of nutritional status in school-age children and adolescents show a similar pattern. Most children are within the normal range in terms of weight-for-height. This includes the Mekranoti and Xikrin as well as the groups listed in table 7.3. Again, the Aguaruna children are the thinnest, 12% of whom were $<$ 80% of standard. In terms of height-for-age, Tukanoan, Trio, Wajana, and San Carlos children are very small. Xavante children are somewhat taller for their age, but still short in comparison to the Harvard standard. Means for the Xingu children are on, or above the Harvard fiftieth percentile from 6 to 9 years, but after that, below the tenth percentile. Mekranoti and Xikrin children are the tallest and are on, or above, the Harvard fiftieth percentile.

On the basis of the evidence of stunting in children, it is no surprise that adults are generally short. Means for both males and females are below the NCHS tenth percentiles except for the Xikrin and Xavante (fig. 7.2). Short stature in adults is not, in itself, indicative of poor nutritional status. In terms of weight-for-height indices and measures of body composition, the nutritional status of adults is generally good. Most adults are in the normal range for weight-for-height (table 7.3). BMIs for the populations listed in figure 7.2, calculated from mean height and weight, range from 22.2 to 25.0. These values, as well as those of the Siona-Secoya, are above the proposed cut-off of 18.5 for CED. For the Aguaruna, weight and height data are not available, but it is likely that the 10% of the adults with height-for-weight values < 70% of the standard have BMIs of 18.5 or less. There is no body weight data available for the Yanomami.

The clinical signs of undernutrition reported in Aguaruna, Tukanoan, and San Carlos children were primarily those related to the condition of the hair. These signs can also be due to environmental agents (Jelliffe 1966, 43), but their presence is consistent with the anthropometric indicators of undernutrition. The number of cases of what investigators have called "malnutrition" is very low: 3 cases in 184 Kayapó subjects (Ayres and Salzano 1972); < 5% of 293 Waorani (Larrick et al. 1979); 1 case for 112 Aguaruna (Berlin and Markell 1977). More common in the literature are descriptions of the excellent health of Amazonians, but these are invariably with reference to adults, and usually males.

There is little evidence of specific nutrient deficiencies. Pale conjunctiva, a sign suggestive of iron-deficiency anemia, was noted in Tukanoan children and Aguaruna children and adults, but in the Aguaruna there was no biochemical evidence of iron deficiency. Spongy, bleeding gums, a sign suggestive of vitamin C deficiency, were fairly common among Aguaruna, and the groups examined by Boza and Baumgartner (1962). Werner (1983) also reported one case of scurvy among the Mekranoti. The only goiter noted was among the Xavante, although iodine deficiency without goiter has been reported for the Yanomami (Reviere et al. 1968). It is of considerable interest that goiter has not been reported for any native Amazonians on manioc-based diets since the cyanide in manioc is a known goitrogen (Delange et al. 1982).

In addition to goiter, the cyanide in manioc-based diets has also been associated with neurological problems (tropical ataxic and epidemic spastic paraparesis) in Africa, but these problems have not been reported in Amazonia. It appears that although some groups prefer high-cyanide varieties of manioc (Dufour 1988), the traditional processing systems used for casabe and related products are very effective at reducing the cyanide content of foods (Dufour 1989).

The high prevalence of stunting in Amerindian children and the consequent short stature of adults is not easy to interpret. The possibility that genetic factors may be limiting growth cannot be ignored (Davies 1988), but given the degree of stunting and other indicators of undernutrition in children, it is likely that environmental factors are more important than genetic ones (Martorell 1985). Body size is a reflection of heredity as well as of all previous life experiences, including infection, inattention, and neglect, as well as nutrition (Calloway 1982). Stunting is really a nonspecific indicator of health status, and since there is no dietary intake data for children, it is impossible to estimate the extent to which nutritional variables are responsible for the delays in growth. The high-bulk, low-caloric density of Amazonian diets may make it difficult for young children to meet their dietary needs when food is available, or to catch up after a period of deficit. Further, the possibility of chronic or recurrent food deficits in children's diets resulting from fluctuations in household food supplies, or inequitable food distribution within the household cannot be ruled out.

Disease is very likely contributing to the slow growth and thinness seen. Holmes (1984) demonstrated the negative impact of measles on nutritional status in the San Carlos area and pointed out that full recovery took six months to a year. For the other groups discussed here there is ample evidence of chronic infection. Malaria is endemic among the Alto Xingu groups (Fagundes-Neto et al. 1981), Kayapó (Ayres and Salzano 1972), and Trio and Wajana (Glanville and Geerdink 1970), and malarial infections have been associated with faltering growth (McGregor 1982). Intestinal parasitism is prevalent (Berlin and Markell 1977; Chernela and Thatcher 1989; Holmes 1984; Larrick et al. 1979), but its impact on nutritional status is not entirely clear. Holmes (1984) found no relationship between weight-for-height and worm burden, but other studies, such as that of Gupta et al. (1977), have shown that deworming enhances linear growth. There are also a number of reports of mild, but probably chronic infections, such as eye disease among the Trio and Wajana (Glanville and Geerdink 1970) and skin diseases that could depress growth in childhood among the Kayapó (Ayres and Salzano 1972) and the groups studied by Boza and Baumgartner (1962).

Changes in Diet and Nutritional Status with Acculturation

Although it is generally assumed that the health of native Amazonians deteriorates with acculturation, only two studies have specifically examined the effects of acculturation on diet and nutritional status. Dricot-D'ans and Dricot (1978) looked at adult male Machiguenga Indians and found a significant deterioration in the nutritional status in the more acculturated of three villages. Holmes (1985) studied four sites in the San Carlos area showing a clear acculturation gradient. At the most acculturated site, San Carlos de Rio Negro (a town of six hundred), the diet was similar to the traditional diet but included meat of domesticated animals, and food costs were subsidized by the government. The other sites were smaller, more traditional villages, largely dependent on subsistence horticulture, hunting, and fishing. In comparing these four sites she did not find any significant correlation between degree of acculturation and nutritional status.

Summary and Conclusion

The diets of ethnographically known native Amazonians in tropical forest environments are based on manioc and plantains/bananas, with high-quality protein coming from wild fauna. Nondomesticated plant foods do not appear to be very important in the diets of most groups, but their role in the diet has not been well studied and may be underestimated. The composition of these diets is known for only a few groups. It appears adequate in protein and other nutrients, but the diets are high in bulk and low in caloric density. Dietary intake of household groups and adults appears adequate, and the nutritional status of adults is generally good. Children, however, are small for their age, and in some groups many would be classified as undernourished on the basis of weight-for-height or clinical signs of undernutrition. It is likely that diet in combination with disease stress is responsible for the delayed growth and relatively poor nutritional status seen in some children.

REFERENCES

Ayres, M., and F. M. Salzano
1972   Health status of Brazilian Cayapo Indians. *Tropical and Geographical Medicine* 24 (2): 178–85.
Behrens, C. A.
1984   Shipibo ecology and economy: A mathematical approach to understanding human adaptation. Ph.D. diss., University of California, Los Angeles.
1986   The cultural ecology of dietary change accompanying changing activity pattern among the Shipibo. *Human Evolution* 14:362–96.
Benefice, E., and Barral, H.
1991   Differences in life style and nutritional status between settlers and Siona-Secoya Indians living in the same Amazonian milieu. *Ecology of Food and Nutrition* 25:307–22.
Bergman, R. W.
1974   Shipibo subsistence in the upper Amazon rainforest. Ph.D. diss., University of Wisconsin, Madison.

Berlin, E. A., and E. K. Markell
1977   An assessment of the nutritional and health status of an Aguaruna Jivaro community, Amazonas, Peru. *Ecology of Food and Nutrition* 6:69–81.
Berlin, O. B., and E. A. Berlin
1977   Etnobiologia, subsistencia, y nutrición en una sociedad de la selva tropical: Los Aguaruna Jivaro. Berkeley, Calif.: University of California Language Behavior Research Laboratory.
Black, F. L., W. J. Hierholzer, D. P. Black, S. H. Lamm, and L. Lucas
1977   Nutritional status of Brazilian Kayapó Indians. *Human Biology* 49 (2): 139–53.
Boza, F. V., and J. Baumgartner
1962   Estudio general, clínico y nutritional en tribus indigenas del Territorio Federal Amazonas de Venezuela. *Archivos Venezolanos* 2:144–225.
Calloway, D. H.
1982   Functional consequences of malnutrition. *Reviews of Infectious Diseases* 4 (4): 736–45.
Carneiro, R. L.
1961   Slash-and-burn cultivation among the Kuikuru and its implications for cultural development in the Amazon Basin. In *The evolution of horticultural systems in native South America: Causes and consequences,* edited by J. Wilbert, 47–67. Caracas: Sociedad de Ciencias Naturales La Salle.
1983   The cultivation of manioc among the Kuikuru of the Upper Xingú. In *Adaptive responses of native Amazonians,* edited by R. B. Hames and W. T. Vickers, 65–111. New York: Academic Press.
Chernela, J. M., and V. E. Thatcher
1989   Comparison of parasite burdens in two native Amazonian populations. *Medical Anthropology* 10:279–85.
da Rocha, F. J., and F. M. Salzano
1972   Anthropometric studies in Brazilian Cayapo Indians. *American Journal of Physical Anthropology* 36:95–102.
Davies, D. P.
1988   The importance of genetic influences on growth in early childhood with particular reference to children of Asiatic origin. In *Linear growth retardation in less developed countries,* edited by John C. Waterlow, 75–82. Nestle Nutrition Workshop Series, vol. 14. New York: Raven Press.
Delange, F., P. Bourdoux, and A. M. Ermans.
1982   Summary and general conclusions. In *Nutritional factors involved in the goitrogenic action of cassava,* edited by F. Delange, F. B. Iteke, and A. M. Ermans, 84–86. Ottawa: International Development Research Centre Monograph IDRC-184e.
Dricot-D'ans, C., and J. M. Dricot
1978   Influence de l'acculturation sur la situation nutritionnelle en Amazonie Peruvienne. *Ann. Soc. Belge. Med. Trop* 58:39–48.

Dufour, D. L.
n.d.   Anthropometric Characteristics of Tukanoan Indians in the Colombian
            Vaupés Region. MS.
1983   Nutrition in the northwest Amazon: Household dietary intake and
            time-energy expenditure. In *Adaptive responses of native Amazonians*,
            edited by R. B. Hames and W. T. Vickers, 329–55. New York: Academic
            Press.
1984a   The time and energy expenditure of indigenous women horticulturalists
            in the northwest Amazon. *American Journal of Physical Anthropology*
            65:37–46.
1984b   Diet of Tukanoan Indians in the northwest Amazon. Paper presented at
            the 83rd Annual Meeting of the American Anthropological Associa-
            tion, Denver.
1988   Cyanide content of cassava (*Manihot esculenta, euphorbiaceae*) cultivars
            used by Tukanoan Indians in northwest Amazonia. *Economic Botany* 42
            (2): 255–66.
1989   Effectiveness of cassava detoxification techniques used by indigenous
            peoples in northwest Amazonia. *Interciencia* 14 (2): 88–91.
Eveleth, P. B., F. M. Samzano, and P. E. De Lima
1974   Child growth and adult physique in Brazilian Xingu Indians. *American
            Journal of Physical Anthropology* 41:95–102.
Eveleth, P. B., and Tanner, J. M.
1976   *Worldwide variation in human growth*. Cambridge: Cambridge University.
Fagundes-Neto, U., et al.
1981   Observations of the Alto Xingu Indians (central Brazil) with special
            reference to nutritional evaluation in children. *American Journal of
            Clinical Nutrition* 34:2229–35.
FAO/WHO
1973   *Energy and protein requirements*. Technical Report Series No. 522.
            Geneva: World Health Organization.
FAO/WHO/UNU
1985   *Energy and protein requirements*. Technical Report Series No. 724.
            Geneva: World Health Organization.
Flowers, N.
1983   Seasonal factors in subsistence, nutrition, and child growth in a central
            Brazilian Indian community. In *Adaptive responses of native Amazonians*,
            edited by R. B. Hames and W. T. Vickers, 357–90. New York: Academic
            Press.
Frisancho, A. R.
1981   New norms of upper limb fat and muscle areas for assessment of nutri-
            tional status. *American Journal of Clinical Nutrition* 34:2540–45.

Gillin, J.
1948   Tribes of the Guianas. In *The tropical forest tribes*. Vol. 3, *Handbook of South American Indians*, edited by J. H. Steward, 799–860. Washington, D.C.: Smithsonian Institution Press.

Glanville, E. V., and R. A. Geerdink
1970   Skinfold thickness, body measurements and age changes in Trio and Wajana Indians of Surinam. *American Journal of Physical Anthropology* 32:455–62.

Gross, D. R., et al.
1979   Ecology and acculturation among native peoples of central Brazil. *Science* 206:1043–50.

Gupta, M. C., et al.
1977   Effects of periodic deworming on nutritional status of *Ascaris*-infected preschool children receiving supplementary food. *Lancet* 2:108–10.

Habicht, J.-P., et al.
1974   Height and weight standards for children: How relevant are ethnic differences in growth potential. *Lancet* 1:611–15.

Herrera, R., C. F. Jordan, H. Klinge, and E. Medina
1978   Amazon ecosystems: Their structure and functioning with special emphasis on nutrients. *Interciencia* 3 (4): 223–30.

Hill, J., and E. F. Moran.
1983   Adaptive strategies of Wakuenai peoples in the oligotrophic rain forest of the Rio Negro Basin. In *Adaptive responses of native Amazonians*, edited by R. B. Hames and W. T. Vickers, 113–35. New York: Academic Press.

Holmes, R.
1981   Estado nutricional en cuatro aldeas de la selva Amazonica—Venezuela: Un estudio de adaptación y aculturación. M.S. thesis, Instituto Venezolano de Investigaciones Científicas, Caracas.

1984   Non-dietary modifiers of nutritional status in tropical forest populations in Venezuela. *Interciencia* 9 (6): 386–90.

1985   Nutritional status and cultural change in Venezuela's Amazon territory. In *Change in the Amazon Basin*, edited by J. Hemming, 237–55. Manchester: University of Manchester.

Hugh-Jones, P., et al.
1972   Medical studies among Indians of the upper Xingu. *British Journal of Hospital Medicine* (March): 317–34.

James, W.P.T., A. Ferro-Luzzi, and J. C. Waterlow
1988   Definition of chronic energy deficiency in adults. *European Journal of Clinical Nutrition* 42:969–81.

Jelliffe, D. B.
1966   *The assessment of nutritional status of the community*. Geneva: WHO.

Larrick, J. W., et al.
1979   Patterns of health and disease among the Waorani Indians of Ecuador.
            Medical Anthropology 3:147–89.
Lizot, J.
1977   Population, resources and warfare among the Yanomami. Man, new ser.,
            12:497–517.
Martorell, R.
1985   Child growth retardation: A discussion of its causes and its relationship
            to health. In Nutritional adaptation in man, edited by K. Blaxter and
            J. C. Waterlow, 13–30. London: John Libby.
Maybury-Lewis, D.
1974   Akwe-Shavante society. New York: Oxford.
McGregor, I. A.
1982   Malaria: Nutritional implications. Reviews of Infectious Disease 4 (4):
            798–804.
Mclaren, D. S.
1976   Concepts and content of nutrition. In Nutrition in the community, edited
            by D. S. McLaren, 3–12. New York: John Wiley.
Neel, J. V., et al.
1964   Studies on the Xavante Indians of the Brazilian Mato Grosso. Human
            Genetics 16 (1): 52–140.
Neel, J. V., et al.
1968   Further studies on the Xavante Indians. 8. Some observations on blood,
            urine and stool specimens. American Journal of Tropical Medicine and
            Hygiene 17 (3): 474–85.
Niswander, J. D., F. Keiter, and J. V. Neel
1967   Further studies on the Xavante Indians. 2. Some anthropometric, der-
            matoglyphic and nonquantitative morphological traits of the Xavantes
            of Simões Lopes. American Journal of Human Genetics 19 (4): 490–501.
Ortiz Moreno, M. E.
1981   Encuesta nutricional y alimentaria de la comisaria del Vaupés. Instituto
            Colombiano de Bienestar Familiar, Servicio Seccional de Salud del
            Vaupés, Bogotá, Colombia.
Picchi, D. S.
1982   Energetics modeling in development evaluation: The case of the Bakairi
            Indians of central Brazil. Ph.D. diss., University of Florida, Gainesville.
Prance, G. T.
1978   The origin and evolution of the Amazon flora. Interciencia 3 (4):
            207–22.
Reviere, R., D. Comar, M. Colonomos, J. Desenne, and M. Roche
1968   Iodine deficiency without goiter in isolated Yanomama Indians: Prelimi-
            nary note. In Biomedical challenges presented by the American Indian, 120–

23. Washington, D.C.: Pan American Health Organization Scientific Publication No. 165.

Ross, E. B.
1976   The Achuara Jivaro: Cultural adaptation in the upper Amazon. Ph.D. diss., Columbia University, New York.

Salati, E., J. Marques, and L.C.B. Molion
1978   Origen e distribuicao das chuvas na Amazonia. *Interciencia* 3 (4): 200–205.

Stephenson, L. S., M. C. Latham, and A. Jansen
1983   *A comparison of growth standards: Similarities between NCHS, Harvard, Denver and privileged African children and differences with Kenyan rural children.* Cornell International Nutrition Monograph Series Number 12. Ithaca, N.Y.: Cornell University.

Vickers, W. T.
1989   Los Sionas y Secoyas: Su adaptación al ambiente Amazónico. Quito: Ediciones ABYA-YALA.

Waterlow, C., et al.
1977   The presentation and use of height and weight data for comparing the nutritional status of groups of children under the age of 10 years. *Bulletin of the World Health Organization* 55 (4): 489–98.

Weinstein, E. D., J. V. Neel, and F. M. Salzano
1967   Further studies on the Xavante Indians. 6. The physical status of the Xavantes of Simões Lopes. *American Journal of Human Genetics* 19 (4): 532–42.

Werner, D.
1983   Why do the Mekranoti trek? In *Adaptive responses of native Amazonians,* edited by R. B. Hames and W. T. Vickers, 225–38. New York: Academic Press.

Wheeler, E. F.
1980   Nutritional status of savanna peoples. In *Human ecology in savanna environments,* edited by D. R. Harris, 439–55. New York: Academic Press.

WHO Working Group
1986   Use and interpretation of anthropometric indicators of nutritional status. *Bulletin of the World Health Organization* 64 (6): 929–41.

Wray, J. D.
1975   Child care in the Peoples' Republic of China, 1973, Part II. *Pediatrics* 55:723.

Yost, J. A., and P. M. Kelley
1983   Shotguns, blowguns, and spears: The analysis of technological efficiency. In *Adaptive responses of native Amazonians,* edited by R. B. Hames and W. T. Vickers, 189–224. New York: Academic Press.

8

Hunting and Fishing in Amazonia

Hold the Answers, What Are the Questions?

STEPHEN BECKERMAN

Amazonia is one of the world's foremost "ethnographic laboratories." The interpretation of the evidence provided by Amazonian societies has implications beyond regional and subdisciplinary boundaries. Hence, it is of interest to anthropology at large to examine the ethnographic lessons of Amazonia. The lesson to which this chapter is addressed has to do in its most specific sense with our understanding of the archaeology and ethnohistory of Amazonia; in this respect it addresses two questions: *What* do the ethnographic data on fishing and hunting tell us about precontact Amazonia? and *How* are these data informative about the past? In a larger sense the Amazonian lesson addressed here is the question of the use of ethnographic analogy: At what level should the anthropologist draw the analogy—at the level of the specific fact or at the level of the general rule inferred from the pattern of facts?

The main issues in the interpretation of Amazonian archaeology and ethnohistory addressed here by foraging data have to do with the distribution and abundance of the human population of the region. The questions of how many people there were in precontact Amazonia, where they were located and why, and how they had come to be in that distribution in those numbers have a considerable history in anthropology, some of it summarized by Denevan (1976).

Briefly, there is a school that holds that Amazonian populations were always of a size and density indicated at least to an order of magnitude by their contemporary descendants, and that they were held there by the poverty of the natural environment. Proponents of this view may admit local and temporary exceptions to the categorical statement made in the last sentence, but they are united in emphasizing the meager availability of food in the rain forest, given the technical repertoire of native Amazonians (Divale and Harris 1976; Gross 1975; Meggers 1957, 1971; Ross 1978; Steward 1949) This "environmental limitation" perspective on Amazonian populations began with a focus on the fragile and ungenerous nature of Amazonian soils, and then switched to an emphasis on the poverty of its protein resources after Carneiro's (1961) demonstration that ethnographic population sizes were considerably below those allowed by agricultural productivity. In its focus on protein—particularly fish and game—the modern version of this position is called the "protein limitation hypothesis" (Gross 1975).

The other side of this debate holds that the Amazonian environment is more generous than has generally been acknowledged, and that the current ethnographic sparsity of Amazonian populations is due more to postcontact disease, slavery, and warfare than to the niggardliness of the natural environment. In addition to Carneiro (1960, 1961), advocates of this position include Balée (1987), Beckerman (1979), Lathrap (1968), Roosevelt (1987), and Smith (1980).

In recent times, the debate has turned on archaeological evidence that there were (or were not) large, dense populations in the pre-Columbian Amazon; and on ethnographic evidence that there was (or was not) sufficient protein to support large, dense populations there. It is in this context that a modern synthesis of the ethnographic data on the productivity of native fishing and hunting is of interest. The data are arranged here to serve a number of purposes. In the first place, it is of interest to assemble the facts— how many grams per hour does a fisherman fish? In the second place, it is also of interest to note the obvious patterning in the facts—how do returns vary with season, location, and so forth? In the third place, it is perhaps most interesting to ask if there is a less-than-obvious pattern behind the obvious ones—do the decisions of fishermen and hunters follow an inferable rule, are they (perhaps) rate maximizers or time minimizers in the sense of optimal foraging theory?

The fishing and hunting data may tell us, then, first, what contemporary returns for protein acquisition activities are—for it is certainly true, as protein limitation advocates such as Gross have argued, that most contemporary native Amazonians get most of their protein from fish and game. Knowing what return rates are is fundamental to knowing how hard people are working for their protein (a piece—but only one piece—in the puzzle of whether its scarcity limits their populations); and it is a necessary step in combining foraging return rates with the human and faunal demographic data soon to come from Amazonia. When we are able to compare longitudinal changes in the sizes of the human and animal populations of a given area with changes in fishing- and hunting-return rates there, then we will have a much better idea of what size human population could have been supported in its protein needs by fishing and hunting in a given, largely unmodified Amazonian environment.

Second, the fishing and hunting data may tell us about population constraints that are not obvious from average return rates. How much better are some locations than others, and what may this information suggest about population distributions? How much better are some seasons than others, and what may this information tell us about seasonal migrations and seasonal resource ceilings under which populations have to pass?

Third, the data on hunting and fishing may be informative as to when and why people may choose not to hunt and fish for their protein. There is evidence to suggest that some precontact Amazonian populations consumed substantial amounts of maize, thus presumably getting a good deal of their protein in cultivated form (van der Merwe et al. 1981). Is there a pattern in the fishing and hunting data consistent with the considerable switch in subsistence strategy implied by this turn from corn to fish in the last few centuries?

One possible pattern is suggested by optimal foraging theory (Stephens and Krebs 1986), a part of ecological theory that suggests that many foraging organisms are *rate maximizers*, that is, they try to maximize the amount of foraged food they obtain per unit of time during the time they are foraging. If the ethnographic data are largely consistent with such a strategy in contemporary times, then it is not an excessive jump to the suggestion that rate maximization might also have operated in the past to turn people's efforts from fishing to maize and legume gardening, say, under circumstances in which greater protein returns per hour could have been obtained from corn and beans than from fish.

Below, quantitative ethnographic data, most of them quite recent, are assembled and examined within a framework established by the following simplifying assumptions:

1. The greater Amazonian peoples now use fish and game to supply the necessary protein in their diets.

2. In fulfilling this function, fish and game are effectively fungible; their differences in quality and quantity of protein provided per unit weight of flesh have no detectable consequences.
3. There is currently nothing that is substituted for fish and game, to diminish the amounts needed per person.

These assumptions are dubious, to say the least (see Beckerman 1979 on item 1 and Hill 1988 on item 3, and any table of the nutrient contents of foods on item 2). Their value is that they permit the ordering of the data in a predictive model.

The predictions of the model are simplicity itself. An optimally foraging, rate-maximizing, *Homo economicus* ought always to choose the activity that will produce the greatest weight of flesh for the number of manhours invested in foraging. He ought to choose the class of activity, fishing or hunting; the technique he uses for that activity; the place he pursues the activity; and the time he undertakes it so as to bring home the largest load in the shortest time—given the possibilities of his equipment, territory, and season. (These predictions are, to be sure, coarse and simplistic—and that is their virtue. They allow the culling of behavior that is immediately explicable by appeal to "vulgar materialism" from behavior that is not, and thereby indicate where to look for the "pattern behind the pattern.")

Variability

Of the three limiting conditions noted above—equipment, territory, and season—the first two are somewhat less ethnographically prominent than the third, which is almost always acknowledged to produce important changes in the rate-of-return of fishing, and sometimes of hunting as well. Because fishing is more productive than hunting for most (but by no means all) of the peoples considered here (which is to say that its mean hourly return rate for the entire year is higher than the corresponding rate for hunting) and because fishing generally has a lower trip-to-trip variability within a single season, the simplified model predicts that for most of the Amazonian peoples, hunting is driven by fishing; that is, people hunt only when seasonal or other temporal variability has diminished expectable fishing returns to the point where hunting can be reasonably expected to be the more profitable activity. Expectable fishing return rate is driven by water height and clarity, and by fish migration patterns, the latter being very strongly influenced by the former. Water condition, in turn, responds to rainfall, either local or far upriver, depending on the location within the watershed. Thus, for peoples among whom fishing is more productive than hunting, the entire fishing-hunting complex can be predicted to respond to rainfall, although the location of that rainfall may be half a continent away.

One may measure the rate and variability of rate-of-return from hunting and fishing in many ways. One can take the overall rate-of-return for hunting and for fishing as the quotient of total yearly take for each activity divided by total manhours devoted to each activity in a year, as mentioned above; or one can subdivide such a broad picture with varying degrees of refinement, along several dimensions. Dimensions prominently recorded in the literature as important include the following:

> *Time:* This most tractably patterned of the variable dimensions can be examined on a scale ranging from decades (the hunting out and repopulating of a hunting ground), through years (seasonal variation in fish concentration), down to days (the clarity of a river in response to a shower), and even hours (night-roosting birds are mainly crepuscular game).

> *Place:* Fish and game abundances, and the returns that depend on them, are known to be variable at scales ranging from half the continent (black-water vs. white-water river basins) to a few meters (salt licks and rapids concentrate mammals and fish respectively). Technique: Both weapons (e.g., bow and arrow vs. blowgun) and strategy (e.g., waiting in ambush vs. active stalking) are involved in this dimension; and both are known to have effects on mean rate-of-return and probably on variance as well. Characteristics of individual forager: Evidence is beginning to accumulate that there are systematic differences in the rate and variability of returns that respond to such forager characteristics as age; number and kind of dependents; physical fitness, education, and experience as a hunter and fisherman; and talent.

> *Taxon:* Rates of return and variances respond to the level of taxonomic fineness at which they are calculated, from the mean hourly take for all mammals, for instance, to the return rate for juvenile female howler monkeys; many techniques are largely determined by the taxon of the intended prey, so that technique and taxon are often best considered as a single dimension.

To the extent possible, the data are presented below in such a way that when the predictions of the simplified model fail at one level of scale, it is possible to ask whether the predictions are upheld at the next lower level.

Fishing

Because the simplified model predicts that fishing should drive hunting, we begin by examining the fishing data. Average (for all locations, all seasons, all techniques) fishing return figures are recorded in table 8.1.

Table 8.1. Mean Fishing Returns

Society	Grams/Manhour	Source
Pumé	405	Gragson 1989
San Carlos	620	Clark and Uhl 1987
Barí	350	Beckerman 1980, 1983a, 1983b
Shipibo	1,140	Bergman 1980
Cocamilla	2,120	Stocks 1983
Bororo	680	Werner et al. 1979
Xavante	400	Werner et al. 1979
Mekranoti	200	Werner et al. 1979
Kanela	50	Werner et al. 1979
Yanomamo	80–170[a]	Lizot 1977
Siona-Secoya	675–1,000[a]	Vickers 1976
Makuna	300–555[a]	Århem 1976

[a]according to community

What is perhaps most interesting about this compilation of figures is the fact that, even though these rates vary by almost two orders of magnitude, there is a definite clump of (geographically widely dispersed) societies that get their fish at an average rate close to 500 grams/manhour.

Variation Over Time

The variability of fishing returns over the course of the year is well documented for a number of places and cultures. Gragson (1989) found that for the Pumé (Yaruro) of the Llanos de Apure, Venezuela, fishing returns in grams/manhour were well predicted by the depth of water in the *esteros* (marshes) and streams of this area, which is drained by a third-order tributary of the Orinoco and receives moisture both as rainfall and as subsurface infiltration. The relationship is expressed as a simple linear regression, in which Y = grams of raw fish per manhour of fishing and X = water depth in the esteros in centimeters. The equation is $Y = 881 - 6.41X$; $r^2 = .722$; $p = .004$.

The Pumé live in a tropical savanna; comparable data for a rain forest area were collected by Clark and Uhl (1987) in the town of San Carlos del Rio Negro, on the upper Rio Negro in Venezuela, in a typical black water river area. The fishermen here are largely Arawakan speakers who, despite some modern technology such as outboard motors, continue to fish by largely traditional means. The corresponding equation here is $Y = 1203 - 0.58$; $r^2 = .261$; $p = .011$. (These are my calculations from figure 6, Clark and Uhl 1987; as above, $Y =$ grams of raw fish per manhour of fishing and $X =$ water depth).

The Pumé and the Arawakans of San Carlos live in regions where water depth responds to distant rainfall. The Barí of the southwestern Maracaibo Basin in Colombia inhabit a headwater region where only local rainfall has an effect on river depth. There, Beckerman (1983a) found that fishing returns could be predicted directly by using monthly rainfall figures. The equation is $Y = 545 - 0.911X$, where Y, as above, represents grams of fish per manhour of effort, but X now indicates not centimeters of water depth but millimeters of monthly rainfall; $r^2 = .727$; $p = .003$.

It is possible to make similar calculations using Behrens's (1981) aggregation of the data provided in Bergman's (1980) meticulous monograph on the subsistence of the Shipibo of the central Ucayali River of Peru. Here, X, the independent variable, is the height of the river above its lowest level, expressed in centimeters; and Y remains the number of grams of raw fish taken per manhour. The equation is $Y = 1970 - 1.455X$; $r^2 = .687$; $p = .001$.

The data available in Stocks (1983) make it possible to regress fishing returns on both monthly average rainfall and monthly average water height for the Cocamilla, who fish a *várzea* lake on the lower Huallaga River, in eastern Peru. For rainfall, the equation is $Y = 4458 - 12.705X$; $r^2 = .211$; and $p = .133$; that is, rainfall is not a significant predictor of fishing return rate in this area. However, for water height, the equation $Y = 5809 - 7.108$ is both significant ($p = .002$) and expressive of an independent variable that accounts for a good deal of the variance ($r^2 = .628$). (For both these equations $Y =$ grams of fish per manhour; for the first, $X =$ mean monthly rainfall in millimeters; and for the second, $X =$ mean monthly lake height, in centimeters, above an arbitrary point—the X axis of figure 8.2 in Stocks 1983).

The figures so far given pertain to indigenous fishing with wholly (Pumé and Barí) or largely (San Carlos, Shipibo, and Cocamilla) traditional techniques. Catches are small by commercial standards, as shown in table 8.2 below.

For mestizo commercial fishing, the inverse relationship between river height and catch per unit effort is also found in a strikingly dramatic way for the small fishing town of Mapire, on the Orinoco River in Venezuela (Maraven 1983). A somewhat weaker relationship is recorded by Novoa (1982) for commercial fish catches from the Orinoco brought to the city of Ciudad Bolivar, downriver from Mapire. Smith (1981) found only the most tenuous connection between water height and fish catch per unit effort at Itacoatiara,

Table 8.2. Fishing Return Variability

Society	Man Yearly Catch (grams/manhour)	Monthly Maximum	Monthly Minimum
Pumé	405	1,060	100
San Carlos	620	1,100	150
Barí	350	578	122
Shipibo	1,140	2,475	524
Cocamilla	2,120	5,590	620

on the main stream of the Amazon. The difference is probably related to the degree to which modern technology is employed.

In addition to the sources that provide month-by-month documentation of the variation in fishing returns, a plethora of authors has noted, sometimes quantitatively, sometimes qualitatively, the difference in fishing returns between wet season and dry season.

Setz (1983) found for a forest village of Nambiquara that dry season fishing trips had a success rate of 87 percent, whereas wet season trips had a success rate of 66 percent. (Success was defined as the acquisition of any fish at all; the difference was significant at the .01 level.) It is interesting that no significant difference in success rate for fishing trips was found for a nearby Nambiquara village in the *cerrado*, although the problem there may be one of sample size for this Brazilian group.

For the Bara Makú, Silverwood-Cope (1972) recorded the activities of thirteen hunter-fishermen for nine months, divided about equally between wet and dry seasons. In this rain forest region of the Colombian Vaupés, 187 kilograms of fish and eels were taken in the wet season and 220 in the dry.

Also in the Colombian Vaupés, Århem (1976), Goldman (1963), and Jackson (1983) mention the association of low water and abundant fish. Irvine (1987) found some seasonality of catch abundance among a group of Runa (lowland Quichua) on the headwaters of the Payamino River, Napo Province, eastern Ecuador, although she also found no time of real scarcity. Murphy (1960) reports the difficulties of wet-season fishing for the Mundurucú near the Tapajós River in Pará State, Brazil. Siskind (1973) remarks that in the dry season "fishing becomes a more frequent and more important activity" among the Sharanahua of the Purus River in eastern Peru. Meggers (1971) mentions similar patterns among a number of peoples in the greater

Amazon. Examples could be multiplied. It is important to note that despite the obvious connection among the spatial concentration of fish, the greater clarity of water during the low-water part of the year, and the elevated fishing returns, a number of cited authors mention a complicating factor—the migration patterns of some species of fish make them more abundant and accessible during times of high water, particularly during the rising waters that announce the beginning of the wet season. We should also note that for some peoples the seasonality of fishing returns may be unimportant. These caveats notwithstanding, it remains the case for most Amazonian peoples that the seasonal patterning of fishing-return rates is the most regular and important variation in animal food supply.

At the other end of the time scale from the yearly wet-dry alteration of seasons is the short-term fluctuation of water characteristics that affect fishing returns. In speaking of the várzea lakes of the Huallaga River, fishing grounds of the Cocamilla, Stocks (1983) mentions that "a 24-hour period may see the river and its associated lakes rise or fall as much as 2 m." Beckerman (unpublished field data) found that among the Barí of the Maracaibo Basin, even during the *veranillo* (little dry season), when rivers were low and appeared reasonably clear to him, there was sufficient day-to-day variation in clarity apparent to the Barí fishermen that most days were not considered propitious fishing days even in a low rainfall month. Seasonal and monthly return rates are, after all, averages of the fortunes of individual trips, almost all of which, in most Amazonian societies, last only a day or less. It is the fisherman's appreciation of his chances on a particular day that forms the context in which decisions to fish or do something else are made.

Variation Over Space

The temporal heterogeneity of fishing-return rates is compounded by their spatial heterogeneity. The most extensive data on this subject come from Bergman (1980). He found for the Shipibo at the confluence of the Panaillo with the Ucayali that return rates varied with the general class of water fished (the *igapó* [flooded backswamp] yielded 760 grams/manhour; the lakes 1,060 grams/manhour; and rivers 1,830 grams/manhour) and also with the specific spot in each of those general classifications. Within the general classes of water there was a great deal of variability. River spots ran between 900 and 4,000 grams/manhour; igapó spots between 700 and 1,400 grams/manhour; and lake fishing spots between 300 and 1,300 grams/manhour. It must be remembered that there is a temporal weighting to these spatially distinct figures. Fishing spots are differentially utilized around the course of the year.

Additional documentation touching this subject is provided by Chernela

(1983). Her data, provided as catch totals, not rates, show that among the Uanano of the Brazilian Uaupés, about two-thirds of all fish are caught in igapó, and another sizable fraction in cataracts and rapids in the rivers—only two of the six types of fishing sites used. Stocks (1983) shows monthly catch rates for three different lake zones exploited by the Cocamilla near the Peruvian Huallaga. There are strikingly different patterns of temporal variation. In particular, the fishing zone nearest the community, fertilized by refuse, exhibits considerably less variation in catch rate than the other two zones. Here again, there is a temporal weighting to the different spatially distinguished rates of productivity. The different zones are used for different amounts of time as the year turns.

Chernela, Stocks, and Bergman were based in single communities. Their data pertain to spatial variation within the territory of one local group. Spatial heterogeneity is also documented for different communities inhabiting the territory of a single ethnic unit. Usually, these communities are only a day or two distant, one from the other, by foot or canoe.

Vickers (1976) records the differences in fishing-return rates for two Siona-Secoya (western Tucanoan) communities in eastern Ecuador. One of these communities, on a white water river, achieved a return of about 1,000 grams/manhour for the dry season. Little if any fishing took place during the wet season. The other community, on what seems to be an unusually productive black water river, achieved a return of 675 grams/manhour, year round. The combined effects of temporal and spatial variation are nicely illustrated in this example. Although the white water river has at first sight a higher yield, that rate is temporally restricted, whereas the black water river produces year round.

Another example, this time dealing exclusively with black water rivers, is provided by Århem (1976). He studied two Makuna communities in the Colombian Vaupés region, upstream from the Brazilian area where Chernela did her work. The Makuna, like the Uanano and the Siona-Secoya, are Tucanoans. Århem's two communities were on the mainstream and in the headwaters region of the Komeña River.

The settlement on the main stream of the Komeña caught fish at an average rate of about 555 grams/manhour, in a sampling period of thirty-six days spread between May and November. The headwaters settlement seems to have achieved a rate of only about 300 grams/manhour for adjacent periods during the same months, supplying a few assumptions necessary to compute this ratio from Århem's published data.

In March, 1972, among the Barí of the Maracaibo Basin in Colombia, Beckerman (1980) found a fishing return of 536 grams/manhour for a lowland house close to streams that communicated with major rivers within a short distance. In March of 1971, at a highland house in the headwaters region of the same river system, he had found a catch rate of only 138 grams/manhour. (It should be noted that, among the Barí, women are active participants in the great majority of fishing trips, building one of the pair of weirs used to trap the fish; they are therefore counted as full producers in computing the "per manhour" figures. Among most other peoples, women apparently do not participate as actively in fishing as they do among the Barí, and only male labor is used in calculating productivity.)

Variability Over Technique

In addition to temporal and spatial variation, fishing returns are also affected by the techniques used. Clark (1982) provides data that can be manipulated to suggest that in the Rio Negro at San Carlos, the productivity of fishing techniques varies by about a factor of two, from a little over 400 grams/manhour to a little over 800 grams/manhour. The techniques include both traditional and modern methods and are all specific as to season—that is, river height. It is interesting that the variability of technique here is less than the seasonal variability shown for these people in table 8.2, a finding that suggests that people are indeed attempting to maximize the rate at which they procure fish.

Smith (1981) also provides comparative-yield figures for several techniques, both aboriginal and modern, of fishing the Amazon itself. Of the aboriginal techniques, the harpoon gives a yield of 2,000 grams/manhour, and the bow and arrow, 500 grams/manhour. Both techniques are beggared by the modern nylon lampara seine, which produces at the rate of 16,580 grams/manhour.

Hunting

With this summary of fishing-yield regularity and variability, a parallel look at hunting is in order. Because this subject has been reviewed three times in the last ten years (Beckerman and Sussenbach 1983; Redford and Robinson 1987; Vickers 1984), a somewhat briefer examination of the data themselves is required. Table 8.3 shows mean returns in hunting, for the whole year, over all locations included by the author of each citation.

Variation Over Time

In terms of temporal variation, we can distinguish three patterns responding to the march of the seasons: there are societies for which no appreciable

Table 8.3. Mean Hunting Returns

Society	Grams/Manhour	Source
Pumé	810	Gragson 1989
Barí	135	this chapter
Shipibo	1,600	Bergman 1980
Bororo	200	Werner et al. 1979
Xavante	400	Werner et al. 1979
Mekranoti	690	Werner et al. 1979
Kanela	110	Werner et al. 1979
Waorani	2,430	Yost and Kelly 1983
Aché	660	Hill and Hawkes 1983
Bakairi	240	Picchi 1982
Makú	1,520	Milton 1984
Ye'kuana	1,600	Hames 1979
Yanomamo	450	Hames 1979
Siona-Secoya	3,200[a]	Vickers 1988

[a]Nine-year average

difference seems to be made by the change of season from wet to dry, insofar as hunting success is concerned; there are societies for which the wet season brings increased hunting returns; and there are societies for which the hunting gets better in the dry season. The last are by far the most numerous.

Only three peoples have been found for whom moisture differences in the environment seem to cause no significant difference in hourly game returns. The Barí (Beckerman 1980), the Aché (Hill et al. 1984), and the two groups of Nambiquara studied by Setz (1983) apparently practiced a hunting indifferent to rainfall and river level, although in the Nambiquara case the conclusion of a lack of significant difference comes from a comparison of percentages of successful hunting trips (those in which some game was obtained) rather than from an evaluation of hourly return rates.

Setz's results contrast with those of Aspelin (1975), who found among the Nambiquara he studied a clear improvement in hunting-return rate during the wet season, from 340 grams/manhour in the dry season to 700 grams/manhour in the wet season, perhaps a result of substantial animal migration into the savanna-forest ecotone inhabited by these Mamainde Nambiquara, in order to feed on the seasonal fruits of trees of the area.

Data are tabulated here for only one other society in which increased moisture is definitely associated with increased rates of hunting returns. These people are the Shipibo, among whom "land animals begin to concentrate as the amount of dry land on the levees is reduced" (Bergman 1980, 136) during the wet part of the year. Wet-season hunting operated with a return of about 1,250 grams/manhour; whereas dry season hunting, excluding one unprecedented windfall, obtained a rate of about 350 grams/manhour.

Societies for which hunting is said to improve with lower moisture are legion. Silverwood-Cope (1972), Reid (1979), and Milton (1984), working with three different groups of Makú in the Vaupés Basin in Colombia and Brazil, agree that the dry season is the better time for hunting. Campos (1977) records similar sentiments from the Shipibo of the Rio Pisqui (a smaller river than the Ucayali, home of the Shipibo studied by Bergman) although her data and her evaluation of them suggest that seasonal variation is not particularly marked in this case. Nonquantitative statements to the effect that hunting is better in dryer times are made with reference to the Ye'kuana of southern Venezuela by Hames (1980); by Lizot (1978) and Sponsel (1981), for the Yanomamo of the same region; and by Morey (1970) and Metzger (1968), for the Guajibo of the llanos of eastern Colombia–western Venezuela. Århem (1976) records similar sentiments expressed by the Makuna of the black water forests of the Colombian Vaupés.

Quantitatively, Werner (1983) gives yields-per-manhour for the Mekranoti of the forests of central Brazil that combine fishing and hunting returns. Because fishing is practiced for only about a quarter of the time spent in hunting, and because its yield is only a bit over a quarter of that of hunting, most of the contribution to these comparative rates comes from hunting returns. Werner finds that in the rainy season the combined hunting-fishing yield is 450 grams per manhour; that this figure rises to 1,620 grams per manhour in the "intermediate" season; and drops to 490 grams per manhour in the height of the rainy season. The Mekranoti themselves also assert that hunting is easier during the dry season, when animals aggregate around water sources, and are easier to pursue over dry ground than through flooded areas.

Gragson (1989) gives figures for the Pumé of the Venezuelan llanos showing that median hunting returns decline from 1,026 grams/manhour in the dry season to 684 grams/manhour in the wet.

Yost and Kelly (1983) provide the most comprehensive data set on this issue, for the Waorani (Auca) of the rain forests of eastern Ecuador, an interfluvial people. As they remark (Yost and Kelly 1983, 217), "hunting efficiency drops considerably during the rainy months and reaches its peak during the drier months." However, the complications of the relationship between rainfall and hunting yield are such that there is no simple inverse relationship (such as was found above for fishing) at an acceptable level of significance. A linear regression of returns on rainfall for the Yost and Kelly data produces an equation ($Y = 3093 - 5.411X$) that explains little of the variance ($r^2 = .204$) and is no more than suggestive ($p = .14$). A closer look at the data reveals that there is a good inverse relationship between rainfall and hunting-return rates from December through the following June, but that in the months of July, September, and October, rainfall and hunting returns rise and fall together directly, rather than inversely; whereas, in the remaining months of August and November the relationship is inverse again, but at a different scale from that of the December-June run. These authors provide an interesting phenological explanation of these findings. Waorani hunting returns vary from about 1,200 grams/manhour in July to over 2,750 grams/manhour in October. These overall returns are the summation of seasonal patternings in the acquisition of individual game species, the latter also provided by Yost and Kelly.

In a longer time frame, Vickers (1988) found that the hunting yield of a Siona-Secoya village in Ecuador fell from an initial value of about 5,000 grams/manhour (just after the village was founded) to a low of around 2,000 grams/manhour six years later, only to climb again to about 4,500 grams/manhour, nine years after the establishment of the village. (A large part of the absolute difference between the Waorani and Siona-Secoya figures is due to use of traditional weapons—bows and blowguns—by the Waorani, and shotguns by the Siona-Socoya.)

Variation Over Space

Hunting variation over space has also been the object of some attention. Hames (1980) found that Ye'kuana hunters attained a rate of between 120 and 5,430 grams/manhour, depending on what zone they hunted, for those zones in which they got any return at all, in southern Venezuela. The rate of Yanomamo hunters of a settlement associated with these Ye'kuana varied between 300 and 1,430 grams/manhour over the same set of zones. (Here again, differences in absolute values probably reflect a greater use of shotguns by the Ye'kuana.)

Bergman (1980) records returns stretching between 40 and 4,200 grams/manhour for the Shipibo with whom he worked, depending on location, and these figures exclude several zones that had rates of zero return, despite appreciable hunting time spent there.

Romanoff (1976) noted, for the Matses of eastern Peru, a significant difference in the success rate (49 percent vs. 66 percent), the average number of animals taken per hunt (59 vs. 78), and the average size of the animals taken (4 percent large, 41 percent intermediate, 55 percent small vs. 10 percent large, 75 percent intermediate, 13 percent small) for the different zones he labeled "center" and "periphery."

These figures are from people hunting from the same settlement. For spatial variation having to do with different settlements of people from the same culture, there are also a few data. Beckerman (1980) found, in the months of March, 1971, and March, 1972, among the Barí, that at an upland longhouse hunting returns were about 250 grams/manhour, while at a lowland house they were only about 160 grams/manhour. These figures are for bow and arrow only. Århem (1976) found a mainstream group of Makuna hunting at a rate of about 170 grams/manhour, while a headwater group hunted at around 350–400 grams/manhour (if the assumptions supplied to Århem's data to calculate these rates are valid.)

Variation Over Technique

Hunting returns also vary with technique—weapon and strategy—as documented by Yost and Kelly (1983), Hill and Hawkes (1983), and Hames (1979). Yost and Kelly, for example, show that for the Waorani, the spear produces at 3,950 grams/manhour; the shotgun, at 2,540 grams/manhour; and the blowgun, at 1,620 grams/manhour. Because these weapons are skewed toward different animals in terms of the relative frequency of use, and because these animals are sought and encountered with different frequencies at different months of the year, and in differing locations, we have here a particularly nice example of the confounding of all the variables asserted above to have a major effect on hunting-return rates. To emphasize technique-specific variation, it is worthwhile to note that Hill and Hawkes found that among the Ach, the shotgun produced at a rate of 1,600 grams/manhour, and the bow, at 540 grams/manhour. Hames found that the Ye'kuana achieved rates of 1,490 grams/manhour with shotguns, whereas the Yanomamo got 450 grams/manhour with their bows.

Discussion

Compounding Sources of Variation

The intention of the compilation of figures provided here has been, not to vex the reader's memory for numbers, but to demonstrate the wide variation of the critical (according to optimal foraging theory) rates of animal food acquisition. In the interests of space and good will, I have supplied no figures for the final important source of variability—that of individual enthusiasm and talent for fishing and hunting. Such figures are supplied by Gragson (1989) and Silverwood-Cope (1972), for instance. The variability shown in individual differences in foraging rates is at least as great as that produced by time, space, and technique—this much is already demonstrated. *It is also likely that these individual differences are in turn highly sensitive to the changes of time, space, and technique,* although I am unaware of more than anecdotal documentation for this assertion.

The last assertion is crucial enough to the thesis I am developing here that it needs to be spelled out in some detail. The thesis is that in addition to known average variation in foraging-return rates due to seasonally changing water condition and animal migration patterns, to location, and to weapon and strategy; in addition to known average differences in foraging rates due to forager age, to number of dependents, and so on, there is also an idiosyncratic interaction between these sources of variation for each individual. Some foragers will, for example, find that their fishing-return rates go up to higher figures than their hunting-return rates at the beginning of the dry season—while for other foragers fishing, at this season, will remain less productive than hunting.

It is inevitable that every individual man will have some foraging activities in which he is more skillful, or luckier, than in others. The forager is certainly aware of his own skills. Thus, when a forager decides on the activity, location, technique, and potential prey of his foraging activity—indeed, when he decides whether to forage at all on a given day—he brings to the decision not only centuries of cultural knowledge having to do with animals, weapons, and terrain, but also a lifetime of experience with his own abilities vis-à-vis the opportunities the moment offers.

Combining the attention that the individual hunter gives to day-to-day variation in the long-run average return rate for all possible foraging activities with his knowledge of the idiosyncrasies of his own repertoire of skills produces an individualized and highly contingent context in which foraging decisions are made. The picture is further complicated, from the point of view of an anthropologist trying to predict behavior, by incomplete and erroneous information. Nevertheless, a good deal of behavior *can* be predicted, at least in the gross. Most of the authors cited above for quantitative data on seasonal variation in fishing and hunting returns have also shown regularities in the proportions of time dedicated to these activities, regularities that correspond to a goal of foraging rate maximization (cf. Århem 1976; Behrens 1981; Bergman 1980; Gragson 1989; Hill 1988; Stocks 1983; Werner 1983) — although in some cases (e.g., Stocks 1983) there are salient problems.

The suggestion offered here is that these problems cannot be used at this point in our knowledge to reject even the simplifying assumptions with which this article began. When Stocks (1983) finds that, in three months of the year the zones that the Cocamilla fish are "wrong" in that other zones are higher *average* producers at that time, and that, in almost the entire year the proportion of hunting to fishing does not straightforwardly reflect the relative *monthly* return rates of the two foraging options, then the first place to search for an explanation of these anomalies is in a finer-grained examination of day-to-day options. What were the expected return rates in the "best" zones on the days when fishermen chose the "wrong" zones? Were the "best" zones best across-the-board or for only some fishermen? What were the hunting- and fishing-return rates of the particular foragers who chose to hunt instead of fish on a particular day? Did these men have or lack any information about water levels or game sightings that distinguished them from other men? What weapons were available to them?

Even so simple-minded a prediction as the invariable attempt to maximize rate-of-return for foraging hours cannot be rejected until tested by the appropriate data. The thrust of this paper so far has been to suggest that such a data set would allow the assignment of expected rates-of-return for every independently deciding forager with respect to every set of moisture conditions, geographical location, weapons, and intended prey-type that the forager himself is able to distinguish. This complex set of conditions is what the forager has in mind, whether consciously or not, when he decides to spearfish in a particular várzea lake instead of taking his shotgun to a particular terra firme hunting ground on a particular 22 March afternoon following three rainless days but with a shower threatening.

Implications of Compounding

This chapter, then, ends with the same questions with which it began, but now posed in a somewhat more rigorous way. Insofar as what the data tell us about the precontact populations of Amazonia and the resource constraints that may have limited them, that general question can be divided, as above, into three smaller questions.

The first of these individual queries, How many grams per hour does a fisherman fish? (or a hunter hunt?) is a partial question that can give an answer to serve only as a hypothesis for further research. The data suggest that most contemporary Amazonians, with their low population densities, are not working very hard for the fish and game in their diets (cf. tables 8.1 and 8.3). This empirical finding does *not* mean that dramatically larger human populations necessarily could have been sustained on wild Amazonian fauna alone (although some support to such a position is given by the fact that a number of the faunal populations in question also suffer commercial predation by *criollos* [members of national, nonindigenous populations—native-born, Spanish- or Portuguese-speaking participants in the national culture of, e.g., Venezuela or Brazil]). What the overall rate-of-return data provide is a baseline against which future rate-of-return data can be evaluated, when the individual cases are controlled for human population density (and ultimately, it is to be hoped, for faunal density as well).

It might turn out that even though contemporary Amazonians do rather well, they are harvesting close to the maximum sustainable yield of their wild animal resources, and a significant increase in their harvest would send the fauna into a declining spiral and force them to work much harder for their daily protein. By contrast, it may be revealed that, even as native populations grow (as some of them are now doing) and as their territories shrink (as virtually all of them, unhappily, are also doing) their fishing and hunting hourly return rates do not change much, thus suggesting that considerably denser human populations than now evident can be supported on wild Amazonian fauna.

Thus the question, How many grams per hour does a fisherman fish? (or a hunter hunt?) reemerges as, What is the relationship between the mean hourly return rates of fishing and hunting, and the human and faunal regional population densities?

The second individual query, How do returns vary with season, location, and so forth? must, in the first place, be folded into the question immediately above. The relationship between return rates and population densities must be made specific as to habitat, season, and so on. Beyond this obvious elaboration, the patterning of the variability of return rates does suggest, unsurprisingly, that some regions, notably upstream white water regions, are more favored than others, particularly in fishing returns. There is also the suggestion, in the seasonal variability data, that the ordinary indicator of degree of seasonality in the tropics, variation in mean monthly local rainfall, is only a good predictor of variation in monthly fishing-return rate in rather special circumstances. Fishing returns respond to water height (and, often, transparency), and only where these proximate determinants of fishing success directly reflect local rainfall can return rates be adequately derived from rainfall data. There emerges from this finding a cautionary note for cross-cultural, ethnohistorical, and archaeological reconstructions: Local rainfall figures are not in themselves adequate indices of effective seasonality in faunal protein supply for Amazonian peoples; it is variation in water level that really counts.

The third individual question, Is there a hidden pattern behind the obvious ones? can receive only a tentative answer, embodying an elaborate set of questions: We will know if protein acquisition behavior is well described as being a rate-maximization strategy when we also know a number of other things. We cannot reject even an intent always to maximize the rate at which protein is acquired as the single-minded goal of Amazonian foragers on the basis of the data we now have. What we need to evaluate this proposition is (as mentioned above) *both* the data on expected returns for each set of distinguishable conditions in which each forager in a society operates *and* the individual forager's evaluation of his expected returns under all those conditions. It is in the comparison of these two data sets, one from quantitative human ecology and the other from cognitive anthropology, that the test of adherence to a rate-maximization strategy can be made.

If, as I suspect, rate-maximization proves to be widespread and robust, the "default" strategy of foragers, then the pattern behind the pattern will also have clear explanatory use in handling the emerging empirical record, with its evidence that Amazonians have switched from animal to vegetable and back to animal protein in the last couple of millennia.

REFERENCES

Århem, K.

1976   Fishing and hunting among the Makuna: Economy, ideology and ecological adaptation in the northwest Amazon. *Göteborgs Etnografiske Museum Årstryek* 27–44. (Reprinted *El Dorado* [1977] 2[2]:37–54.)

Aspelin, P. L.

1975   *External articulation and domestic production: The artifact trade of the Mamaide of northwestern Matto Grosso, Brazil.* Ithaca, N.Y.: Cornell University Latin America Studies Program Dissertation Series No. 58.

1976   Nambicuara economics dualism: Lévi-Strauss in the garden, once again. *Bijdragen tot de Taal-Land-en-Volkenkunde* 132 :1–32.

Balée, W.

1987   Ka'apor ritual hunting. *Human Ecology* 13:485–510.

Beckerman, S.

1979   The abundance of protein in Amazonia: A reply to Gross. *American Anthropologist* 81:533–60.

1980   Fishing and hunting among the Barí of Colombia. *Working Papers in South American Indians* 2:67–109.

1983a   Carpe diem: An optimal foraging approach to Barí fishing and hunting.
             In *Adaptive strategies of native Amazonians,* edited by R. B. Hames and
             W. T. Vickers, 269–99. New York: Academic Press.
1983b   Optimal foraging group size for a human population: The case of Barí
             fishing. *American Zoologist* 23:283–90.
Beckerman, S., and T. Sussenbach
1983   A quantitative assessment of the dietary contribution of game species to
             the subsistence of South American tropical forest peoples. In *Animals
             and archaeology I: Hunters and their prey,* edited by J. Clutton Brock and
             C. Grigson, 337–50. Oxford: BAR.
Behrens, C. A.
1981   Time allocation and meat procurement among the Shipibo Indians of
             eastern Peru. *Human Ecology* 9:189–220.
Bergman, R. W.
1980   *Amazon economics: The simplicity of Shipibo Indian wealth.* Dellplain Latin
             American Studies 6. Syracuse, N.Y.: Syracuse University Department
             of Geography.
Campos, R.
1977   Producción de pesca y caza de una aldea, Shipibo en el río Pisqui.
             Amazonia Peruana 1:53–74.
Carneiro, R.
1960   Slash-and-burn agriculture: A closer look at its implications for settle-
             ment patterns. In *Men and cultures,* edited by Anthony Wallace, 229–
             34. Philadelphia: University of Pennsylvania Press.
1961   Slash-and-burn cultivation among the Kuikuru and its implications for
             cultural development in the Amazon Basin. In *The evolution of horticul-
             tural systems in native South America: Causes and consequences,* edited
             by J. Wilbert, 47–67. Caracas: Sociedad de Ciencias Naturales La
             Salle.
Chernela, J. M.
1983   Hierarchy and economy of the Uanano (Kotira) speaking peoples of the
             middle Vaupés Basin. Ph.D. diss. Anthropology Department, Columbia
             University, New York.
Clark, K. E.
1982   Subsistence fishing at San Carlos de Rio Negro, Venezuela. MS.
Clark, K., and C. Uhl
1987   Farming, fishing, and fire in the history of the upper Rio Negro region
             of Venezuela. *Human Ecology* 15:1–26.
Denevan, W. M.
1976   The aboriginal population of Amazonia. In *The native population of the
             Americas in 1492,* edited by William M. Denevan, 205–34. Madison:
             University of Wisconsin Press.

Divale, W., and M. Harris
1976   Population, warfare, and the male supremacist complex. *American Anthropologist* 78:521–38.
Goldman, I.
1963   *The Cubeo*. Champaign: University of Illinois Press.
Gragson, T.
1989   Time allocation of subsistence and settlement in a Chu Kho Nome Pume Village of the Llamos of Apure. Ph.D. diss. Anthropology Department, Pennsylvania State University, University Park, Pa.
Gross, D. R.
1975   Protein capture and cultural development in the Amazon Basin. *American Anthropologist* 77:526–49.
Hames, R. B.
1979   A comparison of the efficiencies of the shotgun and the bow in neotropical forest hunting. *Human Ecology* 7:219–52.
1980   Game depletion and hunting zone rotation among the Ye'kwans and Yanomamo of Amazona, Venezuela. *Working Papers on South American Indians* 2:31–66.
Hill, K.
1988   Macronutrient modifications of optimal foraging theory: An approach using indifference curves applied to some modern foragers. *Human Ecology* 16:157–98.
Hill, K., and K. Hawkes
1983   Neotropical hunting among the Aché of eastern Paraguay. In *Adaptive responses of native Amazonians*, edited by R. R. Hames and William T. Vickers, 139–88. New York: Academic Press.
Hill, K., K. Hawkes, M. Hartado, and H. Kaplan
1984   Seasonal variance in the diet of Aché hunter-gatherers in eastern Paraguay. *Human Ecology* 12:101–36.
Irvine, D.
1987   Resource management by the Runa Indians of the Ecuadorian Amazon. Ph.D. diss., Anthropology Department, Stanford University, Palo Alto, Calif.
Jackson, J. E.
1983   *The fish people*. Cambridge: Cambridge University Press.
Lathrap, D.
1968   The "hunting" economies of the tropical forest zone of South America: An attempt at historical perspective. In *Man the hunter*, edited by R. Lee and I. DeVore, 23–29. Chicago: Aldine.
Lizot, J.
1977   Population resources and warfare among the Yanomami. *Man* 12:497–517.

1978   Economie primitive et subsistence. *Libre* 4:69–113.
Maraven
1983   La pesca del Río Orinoco: Mapire, Estado Anazoategui, Venezuela.
              Caracas: Maravan. Photocopied report.
Meggers, B. J.
1957   *Environment and culture in the Amazon Basin: An appraisal of the theory of*
              environmental determinism. Studies in Human Ecology: Social Science
              Monograph No. 3. Washington, D.C.: Panamerican Union.
1971   *Amazonia: Man and culture in a counterfeit paradise.* Chicago: Aldine-
              Atherton.
Metzger, D.
1968   Social organization of the Guajibo Indians. Ph.D. diss., University of
              Pittsburgh, Pittsburgh, Pa.
Milton, K.
1984   Protein and Carbohydrate Resources of the Makú Indians of northwest-
              ern Amazonia. *American Anthropologist* 86:7–27.
Morey, R.
1970   Ecology and culture change among the Colombian Guajibo. Ph.D.
              diss., University of Pittsburgh, Pittsburgh, Pa.
Murphy, R. F.
1960   *Headhunter's heritage.* Berkeley and Los Angeles: University of California
              Press.
Novoa, R. D.
1982   *Los recursos pesqueros del Río Orinoco y su explotación.* Caracas: Corpora-
              ción Venezolana de Guayana.
Picchi, D. S.
1982   Energetics modeling in development evaluation: The case of the Bakairi
              Indians of central Brazil. Ph.D. diss., University of Florida, Gainesville,
              Fla.
Redford, K. H., and J. G. Robinson
1987   The game of choice: Patterns of Indian and colonist hunting in the neo-
              tropics. *American Anthropologist* 89:667.
Reid, H.
1979   Some aspects of movement, growth, and change among the Hupda
              Makú Indians of Brazil. Ph.D. diss., Faculty of Archaeology and Anthro-
              pology. Cambridge University, Cambridge, Eng.
Robinson, J. G., and K. H. Redford
1986   Body size, diet, and population density of neotropical forest mammals.
              American Naturalist 128:665–80.
Romanoff, S.
1976   Informe sobre el uso de la tierra por los Matses en la Selva baja peruana.
              Amazonia Peruana 1:97–130.

Roosevelt, A. C.

1987 Chiefdoms in the Amazon and Orinoco. In *Chiefdoms in the Americas,* edited by Robert Drennan and Carlos Uribe, 153–84. Lanham, Md.: University Press of America.

Ross, E. B.

1978 Food taboos, diet, and hunting strategy: The adaptation to animals in Amazon cultural ecology. *Current Anthropology* 19:1–36.

Setz, E.Z.F.

1983 Ecologia alimentar em um grupo indígena: Compara e ao entre aldeias nambiguara de floreata e de cerrado. Master's thesis. Instituto de Biologia. Universidade Estadual de Campinas, Campinas, Brazil.

Silverwood-Cope, P.

1972 A contribution to the ethnography of the Colombian Makú. Ph.D. diss., Cambridge University, Cambridge, Eng.

Siskind, J.

1973 *To hunt in the morning.* London: Oxford University Press.

Smith, N.

1980 Anthrosols and human carrying capacity in Amazonia. *Annals of the Association of American Geographers* 70:533–66.

Smith, N.J.H.

1981 *Man, fishes, and the Amazon.* New York: Columbia University Press.

Sponsel, L. E.

1981 The hunter and the hunted: An integrated biological and cultural approach to the behavioral ecology of human predation. Ph.D. diss., Cornell University, Ithaca, New York.

Stephens, D. W., and J. R. Krebs

1986 *Foraging theory.* Princeton, N.J.: Princeton University Press.

Steward, J.

1949 South American cultures: An interpretive summary. In *The comparative ethnology of South American Indians.* Vol. 5, *Handbook of South American Indians,* edited by Julian Steward, 669–772. Washington, D.C.: Smithsonian Institution.

Stocks, A.

1983 Cocamilla fishing: Patch modification and environmental buffering in the Amazon *Várzea.* In *Adaptive responses of native Amazonians,* edited by R. B. Hames and W. T. Vickers, 239–68. New York: Academic Press.

van de Merwe, N., A. C. Roosevelt, and J. C. Vogel

1981 Isotopic evidence for prehistoric subsistence change at Parmana, Venezuela. *Nature* 292:536–38.

Vickers, W. T.

1976 Cultural adaptation to Amazonian habitats: The Siona-Secoya of eastern Ecuador. Ph.D. diss., University of Florida, Gainesville, Fla.

1980   An analysis of Amazonian hunting yields as a function of settlement age. *Working Papers on South American Indians* 2:7–29.

1984   The faunal components of lowland South American hunting kills. *Interciencia* 9:366–76.

1988   The game depletion hypothesis of Amazonian adaptation: Data from a native community. *Science* 239:1521–22.

Werner, D.
1983   Why do the Mekranoti trek? In *Adaptive responses of native Amazonians*, edited by R. B. Hames and W. T. Vickers, 225–39. New York: Academic Press.

Werner, D., N. M. Flowers, M. L. Ritter, and D. R. Gross
1979   Subsistence productivity and hunting effort in native South America. *Human Ecology* 7:303–16.

Yost, J. A., and P. M. Kelley
1983   Shotguns, blowguns, and spears: The analysis of technological efficiency. In *Adaptive responses of native Amazonians*, edited by R. B. Hames and W. T. Vickers, 189–224. New York: Academic Press.

PART III   SOCIETY, ECOLOGY, AND
             COSMOLOGY IN CONTEXT

9

Homeostasis as a Cultural System

The Jivaro Case

PHILIPPE DESCOLA

Recent research on time allocation among Amazonian societies has revealed the existence of two conflicting patterns in hunting strategies: time minimization versus energy (protein) maximization. In some societies the acquisition of shotguns and the increased efficiency this entailed led to a decrease in time allocated to hunting, whereas in others the same cause resulted in increased hunting at the probable cost of game depletion. In their discussion of the problem, Hames and Vickers (1983, 16–18) suggest that its resolution is critical for the understanding of Amazonian cultural adaptation; indeed, if native hunters and fishermen are protein maximizers, then game and fish are a crucial limiting factor, whereas if they are time minimizers, protein availability becomes of secondary importance.

In spite of their markedly different consequences, however, both these strategies share a common ground; they are defined by reference to the well-known microeconomic principle that the rational behavior of an economic agent tends to maximize the achievement of some end or to minimize the expenditure of some means. Although this central idea of formalist economic anthropology has been challenged by a wide variety of critics during the past thirty years, it seems nevertheless to have retained its full legitimacy for most anthropologists who advocate an ecological approach. Like the primitive

hunter and fisherman of Ricardo,[1] the native people of Amazonia are perceived by contemporary cultural ecology as individualistic entrepreneurs
economizing their means of labor to further their goals in a closed ecosystem
that has all the features of the capitalist market. As a result, a simple fact has
been overlooked; in economies oriented towards the production of use value,
work schedules as well as labor expenditures are usually determined less by
personal choice than by cultural specifications. In other words, the adjust-
ment of time allocation to changing conditions of production is not necessarily as automatic as orthodox economics will predict.

My aim in this essay is to demonstrate that, contrarily to the maximization/
minimization alternative, work allocation can remain remarkably stable in
all sectors of subsistence, whatever the range of empirical variations in the
conditions of production. Drawing on ethnographic material collected among
the Jivaroan Achuar of Ecuador,[2] I will show that labor expenditure varies
within narrow limits for any given adult, male or female, and that this stability is not affected by otherwise wide local fluctuations in the availability of
natural resources, in the quality and size of gardens, in the work force of the
domestic unit, and in the number of consumers. Finally, I will discuss the
general hypothesis that can be inferred from this result, namely, that the
relative inelasticity in time expenditure might have been an essential factor
of the homeostasis of productive forces among native Amazonian societies.

Ethnographic Setting

Scattered in the upper area drained by the Rio Morona and the Rio Pastaza,
on either sides of the line of the Protocol of Rio de Janeiro (1942) that
delimits the Amazonian territories of Ecuador from those of Peru, the Achuar
(or *Achuales* as they are known in Peru) are one of the four main "tribes," or
sub-groups, of the Jivaroan linguistic family, the others being the Shuar, in
Ecuador, and the Aguaruna and Huambisa in Peru. In Ecuador, the Achuar
number a little more than two thousand persons, distributed on a territory of
approximatively 12,000 km^2 ranging on both sides of the Rio Pastaza; with a
distribution of 0.17 persons/km^2, their overall density is thus one of the
lowest in Amazonia.

Although they live very close to the Andes, the Ecuadorian Achuar occupy
a truly Amazonian habitat, typical of the *hylea amazonica*, with altitudes varying between 400 m (mesas and hills) and 250 m (alluvial valleys), annual
average isotherms superior to 23°c., and rainfall ranging from 2,000 mm to
3,000 mm yearly. A common feature of this ecosystem are the *aguajales*,
swamps covered by colonies of *Mauritia flexuosa* palm trees (*aguajes*); this

element of the landscape is indeed so typical that it serves as an ethnic marker, the ethnonym Achuar meaning "people of the Mauritia (*achu*)."

The Achuar clearly distinguish in their natural environment between a riverine habitat and an interfluvial habitat, respectively called "downriver" (*tsumu*) and "upriver" (*yaki*), or "flat country" (*paka*) and "hilly country" (*mura*). The former biotope is characteristic of the alluvial basins where the aggrading rivers flow, with their low terraces of volcanic black soils, whereas the latter is typical of the hills and mesas, with their network of degrading rivers. Particular traits of the riverine biotope are the high fertility of its alluvial soils, the existence of a specific riparian and aquatic fauna (water-turtle, dolphin, arapaima, black caman, and so on), and the presence of malaria. The interfluvial area, by contrast, can be defined by its high, nonfloodable terraces of sandy or red soils with low fertility, small clear rivers with a low density of fish, a predominantly tree-dwelling land fauna, and the absence of malaria. Although they are quite aware of the superior productive potentialities of the riverine habitat, the Achuar of Ecuador are more or less evenly distributed in both ecosystems. Since roughly 70 percent of their territory is interfluvial, however, the population densities are widely contrasted: 0.44 persons/km^2 in the riverine habitat and only 0.08 persons/km^2 in the interfluvial habitat, that is, roughly equivalent to that of Aboriginal tribes in the desert of central Australia.

The traditional settlement pattern is markedly dispersed; each household consists of a single, and generally polygynous, nuclear family and functions as a politically independent unit of production and consumption. Households occur either in total isolation or in clusters of two or three; the distance that separates them may vary from an hour to a day's trip by foot or by canoe. This extreme residential atomism is nevertheless tempered by the existence of a discrete supralocal unit that I call an "endogamous nexus" (Descola 1981, 1982; Taylor 1983). A nexus is a collection of from twelve to twenty scattered domestic units that intermarry regularly according to a marriage system promoting endogamy through a replication, at each generation, of the parents' alliance. Although a nexus does not receive any particular name that would serve to maintain its specificity through time as a corporate group, its members are generally identified by the name of an important river that designates their territorial baseline.

The domestic units scattered within a nexus can coalesce in times of war to form a temporarily nucleated faction settled in a fortified house under the strategic command of a "great-man" (*juunt*). The nexus does not coalesce as such, that is, as a clearly bounded entity, but rather as the kindred group of a great-man. Based on a reputation of skill and bravery in warfare, the status of an Achuar great-man is very contextual and does not entail any formal political or economic privileges, beyond the high prestige awarded in this society to great warriors. The great-man nevertheless plays a key role in the structuring of social space, because it is through him, rather than through claim to a territorial baseline, that a nexus is temporarily defined and acquires cohesion and relevance.

Jivaroan societies are a good test case for the study of homeostasis since, in contradistinction to many other Amazonian societies whose structures were deeply altered in response to the European conquest, they appear to have remained remarkably stable in their socioeconomic and political structures over at least the past five centuries. After a brief attempt to colonize their territory in the sixteenth century failed, the Jivaro succeeded in preserving their political independence and their territorial autonomy until the first decades of the twentieth century; indeed, the Achuar of Ecuador accepted peaceful contacts with the missionaries only in the 1970s (Descola 1981, 1982; Taylor 1981). The chronicles left by the first Spanish explorers who ventured into Jivaroan country less than fifty years after the discovery of America describe a society whose social organization, settlement pattern, and subsistence system are remarkably similar to those of the contemporary Achuar.

It is of course extremely difficult to ascertain if this plurisecular stability goes back much farther into time, since the prehistory of this area of the upper Amazon appears very confusing. We do know from pollen studies that six thousand years ago there existed in the highest sector of the region presently occupied by Jivaroan societies a population who practiced the extensive cultivation of maize (Bush and al. 1989), but the later archaeological records show that by 2,000 B.C. a population of potters whose staple diet was probably derived from the cultivation of sweet manioc had occupied the whole area; after a period of regional integration at the beginning of the Christian era that has left monumental earthworks in the montaña (Porras 1987), a relative involution seems to have taken place in spite of a renewal of maize cultivation at the beginning of the second millennium A.D. We know also that a pottery of Jivaroan type began to appear only at the end of the first millennium A.D. (last period of the Pastaza phase) and that it coexisted for a long time with very different traditions. Perhaps more significant, however, is the fact that the vast majority of present-day Achuar sites of habitat in the riverine area are littered with potsherds typical of the late Pastaza phase and that, conversely, most archaeological sites known by the Achuar are either settled by them, very close to a settlement, or regarded as desirable places to settle. This remarkable continuity shows that the variations in demographic density, in settlement patterns, and in the use of land have probably been minimal during the present millennium.[3]

Outline of the Economic System

Work processes

Like many other Amazonian societies, the Achuar have a strictly defined sexual division of labor, according to which men are essentially predators (clearing gardens, hunting, fishing, and fighting), whereas women are mainly "transformers" of nature (gardening; cooking; raising children, dogs, poultry, and pets). Basket weaving, canoe and raft making, basketry and woodworking are male tasks, whereas spinning, weaving, and pottery are female tasks.

Slash-and-burn horticulture is of the pioneer type, new plots always being cleared in primary forest, every two or three years in the interfluvial habitat—because of the sharp decrease in fertility—and every time a house is relocated (every ten to twelve years) in the riverine habitat, since horticultural yields otherwise remain constant in the fertile terraces of this ecosystem. I have shown elsewhere (Descola 1981), that there are no limiting factors to horticultural land use among the Achuar (either in quantity or in quality), as can be expected with such low population densities. The main cultigen is sweet manioc, but over a hundred species of domesticated plants are cultivated with a wide range of local cultivars adapted to each habitat.

The gardening work process is highly individualized; in a polygynous household each co-wife—with the help of her daughters—plants, cultivates, and weeds a distinct and clearly delimited portion of the main garden or a separate plot. Each woman, along with her children, consumes the product of her harvest and makes her own manioc beer. The magical preconditions of the work process are also clearly individualized; gardening is viewed as the establishment of a symbolic relationship of motherhood between a woman and her cultivated plants, a replication of the paradigm set up by the garden spirit Nunkui with whom every woman tries to identify (Descola 1986, 237–72).

Achuar men hunt often so as never to let their household pass a day without meat, a relatively easy task since game is quite plentiful. Furthermore, most households have exclusive control over hunting territories that exceed 40 km^2. All men know how to use blowguns with great skill; however, very few know how to make potent curare dart poison, which is preferably purchased from the Peruvian Achuar. Muzzle-loading and breech-loading sixteen-gauge shotguns are also used, but to a more limited extent; indeed, when the supply of ammunition and powder runs short, the Achuar prefer to save it for defense or warfare. Men hunt alone or in the company of one of their wives, who will carry the catch and manage the pack of dogs, since these belong to the women and are raised by them. Symbolically, hunting is conceived of as the establishment of a relation of affinity with the game, either directly or through the animals' representatives: *amana* (the prototype of each species) or the spirits known generically as the "mothers of game" (Descola 1986, 317–30).

Complete autonomy in every domain seems to be the goal of every Achuar household. First, the domestic unit is self-sufficient in terms of the work-force it needs for its material reproduction; mutual cooperative work parties undertaken between households render such tasks as clearing a garden or building a house easier and shorter but are not a necessary condition of their realization. Technically, the only task that cannot be done without supralocal cooperation is the hauling of a large canoe to a watercourse from the spot in the forest where it was manufactured.

The means of labor are produced locally, except for manufactured tools (machete, ax, shotgun, and so on) and hunting poison, which are acquired through trading networks in exchange for blowguns, feather headdresses, and other local artifacts produced partly for exchange. This small production of exchange values as a medium for obtaining tools is in no way a recent phenomenon; formerly, stone axes and metal spear heads were acquired in the same fashion.

The self-sufficiency in the use of most of the means of labor echoes the self-sufficiency in the production of subsistence; except for the occasional piece of game offered by a man to his mother-in-law, there is almost no exchange of food even between very closely related households. The great value placed on the economic and political autonomy of each household is a reflection of the individualistic attitudes of Achuar men and women. Although cooperation within the household is important, the work processes and their preconditions are ultimately defined through a set of individual relationships with nature and supernature.

Productivity

A remarkable trait of the Achuar economic system is its extremely high productivity in relation to both the maximization of the means employed and the satisfaction of its socially determined objectives. One of the first signs of the productive efficiency of the system is the considerable underexploitation of the gardens' productive capacity. Since in all Achuar households, manioc counts for at least 50 percent of the vegetable foods, its cultivation is therefore of vital importance in the balance of the productive system.

Table 9.1 shows the relation between the potential manioc output and the real consumption in six households, drawn from both habitats. In all cases

Table 9.1. Percent of Manioc Productive Potential Effectively Harvested

Households	Riverine Habitat				Interfluvial Habitat	
	1	2	3	4	5	6
Garden size (m^2)	2,437	9,655	15,409	22,642	9,729	31,820
Garden productivity (kg.)	4,570	18,102	28,892	42,452	14,594	47,730
Annual consumption (kg.)	3,650	8,760	10,585	8,935	6,497	8,212
Productive potential effectively harvested (%)	79.9	48.4	36.6	21.0	44.5	17.2

the underuse of the gardens' productive capacities is considerable and systematic, regardless of the habitat. The household (riverine) that adapts its productive capacities most closely to its own consumption exploits only 79.9 percent of its potential output, whereas the household (interfluvial) that obtained the greatest difference between its productive potential and its consumption effectively uses only 17.2 percent of its productive capacities. In all the households there exists a potential surplus of manioc that varies between 20 percent and 80 percent of the productive capacities of the gardens.

Another testimony to the productive efficiency of the economic system is quite simply its adequacy in supplying calories and proteins sufficiently to satisfy nutritional needs. Table 9.2 presents the daily per capita contribution in kilocalories and grams of proteins supplied by the different sectors of production in both habitats.

As an estimate of the daily maximum energetic and proteic needs I choose to use the highest values that J. Lizot calculated for the Yanomami after a detailed anthropometric survey by sex and age; 2,600 kcal and 27.4 gr of proteins (Lizot 1978, 94–95). Table 9.2 shows that in all the households of the sample the average consumption is way above these two maximal values.[4] With a global daily average for all the sample of 3,408 kcal and 104.5 gr of proteins, nutritional needs are covered respectively at 131 percent and 381 percent. However remarkable these results may seem, they are nevertheless very close to data collected in other relatively unacculturated Amazonian societies, Jivaroan (Berlin and Markell 1977, 12; Ross 1976, 149), or non-Jivaroan (for example, Chagnon and Hames 1979; Lizot 1978, 96; Vickers 1976, 135).

Table 9.2. Daily Caloric and Protein Input Per Capita

	Sector of Subsistence										
	Hunting		Fishing		Horticulture		Total	
Habitat	Calories	Protein	Calories	Protein	Calories	Protein	Calories	Protein
Riverine	1,047.0	102.0	106.0	19.0	3,404.0	30.0	4,557.0	151.0
	666.0	65.0	98.0	17.5	2,958.0	26.9	3,722.0	108.5
	0.0	0.0	196.9	35.9	2,111.0	19.0	2,307.0	54.0
	988.9	96.0	227.0	40.0	3,016.0	26.9	4,231.0	162.0
Interfluvial	498.0	49.0	71.0	12.0	2,024.0	18.0	2,593.0	79.0
	429.0	42.0	43.0	8.0	2,567.0	23.0	3,039.0	73.0
Average							3,408.0	104.5

Furthermore, the differences in habitats do not entail important disparities in hunting, fishing, and gardening productivity, despite more favorable conditions in the riverine habitat in terms of soil fertility and availability of natural resources. It is true that caloric and proteic outputs are consistently lower in the interfluvial habitat, but they are still way above the maximum needs. In sum, it seems clear that the Achuar underexploit to a considerable degree the productive capacities of their environment, irrespective of the microlocal constraints of the ecosystem.

Structure of Work Expenditure

Hypothesis

One of the reasons that led me to keep count of work expenditure as well as to study the productivity of the economic system was to ascertain if the differences in the potential productivity of the two habitats exploited for centuries by the Achuar were reflected in a difference in work expenditure. However ethnographic and local, the answer might be of crucial importance for a better understanding of cultural adaptation in the Amazon Basin, since anthropologists as well as archaeologists have claimed that the duality of habitats in this region has generated highly different responses in native populations (for example, Carneiro 1970; Denevan 1970; Gross 1975; Lathrap 1968, 1970; Meggers 1971; Roosevelt 1980; Ross 1976 and 1978). To study the effect of a recognized difference in potential productivity on the structure of work expenditure was then an obvious first step, inasmuch as most ecological explanations of cultural variability rest on the assumption that a complex technical and social division of labor emerges as the means to enhance the carrying capacity of a potentially highly productive habitat.

Starting with this working hypothesis, I therefore undertook to measure the labor output within each of the major subsistence sectors using a sample that included both riverine and interfluvial domestic units. I also had to check how possible differences of labor output in the two habitats might be reflected at the level of the domestic unit, in the distribution of work expenditure between men and women. Finally, given that the demographic composition of peacetime domestic units is highly variable (from five to thirty persons), I wanted to know if these demographic variations had any effect on the average daily work output of adults of both sexes. Apart from the number of consumers in the domestic unit, the parameters that had to be taken into account in this last case were the number and the status of producers and, more particularly, the number of co-wives; indeed, one might think that the more co-wives, the less gardening work for each one of them but the more foraging work for their husband, sole supplier of game and fish.

Another problem also had to be solved, to wit, the relation between the size of gardens and the quantity of female work necessary for their cultivation. This problem stems from the wide variations that can be observed in the size of gardens, which, in turn, require a little explanation. Careful topographic measurements of the garden plots of eleven households have indeed revealed important differences in size, with the largest garden thirteen times the size of the smallest (from 2,437 m^2 for the smallest one to 31,820 m^2 for the biggest). These variations could not be accounted for by differences in the number of consumers, since the average cultivated surface per consumer also showed enormous variations, with the largest seven times the size of the smallest (from 487 m^2 per consumer to 3,535 m^2 per consumer). Nor could the nature of the habitat (differential fertility of the soils) be invoked to explain these disparities, since important variations were found between households exploiting the same ecosystem.

The data presented in table 9.1 partly explain this apparent mystery; in all garden plots the average cultivated surface per consumer is always largely superior to consumer needs. In the case of the smaller gardens, there is a positive balance between production and needs, whereas in the case of the larger gardens, approximately 70 percent of the plot is cultivated uselessly, that is, does not serve for consumption. I have shown elsewhere that this systematic disproportion between needs and the size of gardens is not an adaptive response to technical constraints or crop hazards (Descola 1986, 384–85) but is rather a function of social status; the size of a house and the size of the clearing around it are essential components of a household's prestige.[5] Anyhow, and whatever the causes of these important differences in the size of gardens, the question had to be raised of their effects on female work expenditure; what is the cost, in terms of labor output, of maintaining a very large and partly unused garden?

Time Allocations

Table 9.3 presents a breakdown of the average time devoted daily to the different sectors of material subsistence;[6] due to the hypothesis to be tested, the parameters taken into account are sex and the difference of habitats. Two features of the organization of labor appear immediately: the Achuar are not overburdened by their material reproduction, and the women are not the harassed slaves of their leisurely husbands. Overall, the men work a little less than five hours daily (4 h 44 min), against almost six hours for the women

Table 9.3. Daily Time Allocation by Habitat, Sex, and Activity

	Habitat											
	Interfluvial						Riverine					
	Men			Women			Men			Women		
Activity	H	Min	%	H	Min	%	H	Min	%	H	Min	%
Horticulture	—	28	2.0	2	22	9.9	—	41	2.8	2	—	8.3
Hunting	3	35	15.0	—	38	2.6	1	32	6.4	—	10	0.7
Fishing	—	11	0.7	—	1	0.1	1	20	5.5	—	16	1.1
Collecting	—	8	0.5	—	13	0.9	—	6	0.4	—	5	0.3
Manufacture	1	6	4.5	—	12	0.8	—	21	1.5	—	17	1.2
Cooking and housework	—	—	—	2	50	11.8	—	—	—	2	50	11.8
Sleep and leisure	18	32	77.3	17	44	73.8	20	—	83.4	18	22	76.5

(5 h 57 min), the difference being due mainly to female involvement in domestic work.

The differential allocation of work according to sectors of production and to types of habitat shows the incidence of some ecological factors on the repartition of tasks. Thus, the amount of time spent in hunting and fishing are in an inverse ratio in the two habitats: in the interfluvial area, men spend less time fishing than those in the riverine area (0.7 percent as against 5.5 percent), whereas men spend more time hunting than those in the riverine area (15 percent as against 6.4 percent). In both habitats, however, the productivity per hunting expedition is approximately equivalent; in other words, hunters of the interfluvial habitat usually spend more time (on the average two to three hours more) than hunters of the riverine area (Descola 1986, 304–6) to obtain the same quantity of game. The time thus gained by riverine hunters does not entail any advantage in terms of a possible reallocation of the means of labor economized: following a hunting trip, a man generally does not undertake any important activity before the following day, even if he is back home in early afternoon.

By contrast, the differences between the two habitats in the amount of time devoted to horticulture by either men or women are insignificant: the ecological adaptive advantage of the riverine habitat has no consequence on horticultural labor output.

Quite logically, the differences in the amounts of time allocated by women to foraging activities according to habitats directly correlate with those of men: women in the riverine habitat spend less time on hunting trips than women in the interfluvial area but devote more time to fishing than the latter do. In any case, we can note that the participation of women in hunting activities does not imply for them a great amount of work, given the generalization of polygyny, which distributes the hunting trips alternatively between several co-wives. Even in the case of monogamous domestic units, the increase in labor linked to the obligation of regularly accompanying a husband on hunting trips is relatively low. This appears clearly in table 9.4, which details the labor expenditure of women in relation to the number of co-wives included in the same domestic unit.

It is indeed in the monogamous households of the interfluvial habitat that the percentage of female labor devoted to nonhorticultural sectors of production is the highest, a result perfectly congruent with the fact that the hunting trips and the preparation of manioc beer cannot be shared between several co-wives. This increase in labor, however, is relatively insignificant if one compares it with the average time spent on identical tasks in polygynous households of the same habitat. As for the corresponding labor expenditures

Table 9.4. Average Female Daily Time Expenditure in the Main Sectors of Production According to the Number of Co-wives

Sector	Monogamous				2 Co-wives				3 Co-wives				More than 3 Co-wives			
	I		R		I		R		I		R		I		R	
	H	Min	H	Min	H	Min	H	Min	H	Min	H	Min	H	Min	H	Min
Horticulture	1	25	2	6	2	33	2	24	2	16	1	30	2	52	2	34
Hunting, fishing, collecting, and manufacture	1	20	–	32	1	15	–	48	1	51	1	7	1	10	–	27

Percentage

	I	R	I	R	I	R	I	R
Horticulture	6.0	8.8	10.7	10.0	9.4	6.3	11.9	10.7
Other sectors	5.5	2.2	5.2	3.3	3.5	4.6	4.9	1.9

KEY:
I = Interfluvial habitat
R = Riverine habitat

Table 9.5. Relation Between Size of Plots and Daily
Female Time Expenditure in Gardening

Garden Size	Daily Mean Gardening Time	
(m^2)	H	Min
1,000–2,000	2	39
2,000–3,000	2	10
3,000–4,000	2	14
4,000–6,000	1	45
6,000–8,000	2	11
8,000–13,000	2	30

in the riverine habitat, they tend rather to increase in correlation with the increase in the number of co-wives, at any rate up to the category of households with more than three co-wives, beyond which they decrease below the level of monogamous households.

As for the average amount of labor devoted to gardening, it tends rather to increase with the number of co-wives, whatever the type of habitat. This is easily explainable, since each adult woman forms by herself a small autonomous unit of production: the amount of work she devotes to her garden plot is therefore totally independent of the work of the other co-wives in neighboring plots. These results thus imply that *the increase of the female labor force of a domestic unit will not result in a decrease of labor time for each of its women.*

Another surprising conclusion appears if one attempts to correlate the average amount of feminine labor devoted to gardening with the size of the cultivated plots. It has already been shown that the relative size of the plots individually cared for by a woman depended neither on ecological factors nor on the number of consumers of the domestic unit. Great-men generally have numerous wives, and each one of these tries to keep up the household's reputation by cultivating large plots. Now, one may think that this quest for prestige is expensive, in terms of labor, and that the cultivation of a large garden requires far more time than the cultivation of a small one. Yet, table 9.5 shows that this is not the case.

This table correlates the mean daily time spent on gardening by sixteen women in sixteen plots of different sizes grouped for the sake of convenience along a scale of six categories. Each category includes several plots of approximately the same size and is correlated with a mean labor time calculated on the basis of the average time spent daily by each of the women that cultivate plots in this category.

The table shows that the average time spent in gardening remains almost constant in all the categories, independently of the size of the plots. In other words, *whereas one garden may be as much as thirteen times the size of another garden, the labor expenditure remains the same.*

This startling result calls for an explanation. First, there is a difference between the planted surface of the garden and the much smaller surface used for the daily production of tubers. Only a small part of the planted species in the very large gardens is actually cropped; the rest simply constitutes an enormous surplus that may never be used. Important differences in the size of garden plots thus hide the fact that all women actually use a more or less equivalent surface for their domestic needs. One might object of course that, even if it is used only partially, a very large garden nevertheless requires more work than a small garden since it must in any event be planted, cared for, and weeded. Indeed, large gardens are always carefully weeded, even in those parts that are not intensively used. If the planting and the weeding of large gardens do not entail an increase in labor time, it is simply because the women who exploit these gardens work much faster than the women who cultivate smaller gardens. The former are generally mature women, highly experienced gardeners and hard workers who, in the same amount of time, manage to get a lot more done than easygoing young wives cultivating small plots.[7]

The culturally prescribed differential intensity of labor is therefore an important element to be taken into account in the analysis of factors of production, the more so as it is the intensity of work and not its duration that is socially sanctioned. For exactly the same amount of time daily spent in gardening, one woman will be called "lazy" (*naki*) and "incompetent" (*nekachau*) because she cultivates only a small plot, whereas another will be held up as an example because she cares for a very large garden.

A last question remains to be discussed: the effect on a man's labor expenditure of the number of his wives. Insofar as they are the purveyors of game and fish, men bear the whole weight of production in this highly valued sector of the daily food supply. It would therefore seem logical that an increase of the number of people to be fed in a household entails an increase in the time spent on hunting and fishing.

Table 9.6 correlates the average time spent each day by a man in foraging activities both with the type of habitat and with the number of wives in the household. Here again the variations within the habitats appear insignificant. In the interfluvial area, there is a slight increase in male work time in

Table 9.6. Average Male Daily Time Expenditure in the Main Sectors of Production According to Number of Co-wives

	Type of Domestic Unit															
	Monogamous				2 Co-wives				3 Co-wives				More than 3 Co-wives			
	I		R		I		R		I		R		I		R	
Sector	H	Min	H	Min	H	Min	H	Min	H	Min	H	Min	H	Min	H	Min
Hunting	3	20	–	53	3	53	3	36	4	15	1	7	4	2	2	37
Fishing	–	15	2	46	–	–	–	24	–	40	2	10	–	–	1	7
								Percentage								
	I		R		I		R		I		R		I		R	
Foraging activities	15		15.2		16.2		16.6		20.4		13.6		16.8		15.5	

KEY:
I = Interfluvial habitat
R = Riverine habitat

correlation with the increase in the number of wives; but there is practically no such difference in the riverine area. The stability of labor time allocated to foraging activities is due largely to the unequal aptitudes of hunters: in each habitat hyperpolygamous men (more than four wives) generally supply more game per hunting trip than inexperienced, young, monogamous husbands; indeed, their marital status is partly a function of their efficiency as hunters. Once again, this situation refers to the necessary distinction between the duration of work, which is approximately the same for all, and the variability of productive efficiency. In this case, the criterion of hierarchization is not the relative intensity of work, as in gardening, but the inequality of technical competence.

Conclusions

The time expenditures presented so far reveal a startling result: every Achuar man and woman apparently devotes the same amount of time to the production of material subsistence, without notable deficits or surpluses in any of the households sampled. There are indeed slight differences between habitats in the amount of time allocated to hunting, due to a greater accessibility of game, especially peccary, in the riverine area. The average woman's workday is also longer than man's; however, the difference is probably less important than appears in the first instance, since certain time-consuming activities, like the preparation of manioc beer, are in fact closer to a leisurely social gathering than to a dreary domestic toil.

The obvious conclusion is then that, whatever the variations in personal abilities and individual circumstances, *there exists for everyone an identical superior limit to the amount of time devoted in the long run to material reproduction.* In other words, as was established by the correlation of time expenditure with the number of wives and the size of gardens (tables 9.4, 9.5, and 9.6), the evaluation of labor allocation by a man or a woman is largely independent from the empirically visible productivity of this labor. The evaluation thus does not respond to a mechanistic process of minimization of the means, but is grounded instead in a native norm of the distribution of time between work and leisure.

Since the representation of an overall limit to work time seems to be shared by everyone, there are no major differences in time expenditure between the habitats, between the domestic units and even between the sexes. The individual adjustments are made in terms of relative intensity of effort, or are the result of unequal aptitudes, but they do not affect the global structure of the allocation of time. Intensification of labor does not take the form of an increase in its duration, but rather of an optimization of its conditions of execution. Furthermore, an equilibrium is always maintained between the portions of time assigned to the different sectors of production in accordance with the seasonal and ecological variations of resources, since the total amount of work tends to remain identical irrespective of the specific operations that compose it. This is why the percentage of time devoted by men to foraging activities is so strikingly similar, whatever the specific resources of their habitats and the number of their wives.

The idea that the duration of labor expenditure is socially restricted leads to the hypothesis that the setting of a limit to the increase in labor time may be an essential factor in understanding the so-called homeostasis of productive forces in archaic societies. If the intensification of production has historically implied a progressive increase in the average duration of the workday, any socially instituted barrier to this increase will entail as a consequence, either a "freeze" of the productive forces at a given level, or the orientation of their development towards a progress of the technological system. When, for various reasons, local conditions do not permit such a progress, the existing productive system will then tend to perpetuate itself without any change over long periods of time, provided it continues to fulfill its culturally prescribed objectives. Of course such a phenomenon is neither eternal nor automatic.

In the case of the Jivaro, homeostasis was actualized by the conjunction of a particular set of historical and ecological factors: a vast territory closed to European settlers but linked to the external world through indigenous trade networks; a rich environment in the riverine sector; a regime of limited demographic growth (Taylor 1989); a slow territorial expansion made possible from the eighteenth century onward by the extinction of neighboring tribes and the withdrawal of the missionary frontier.[8] Few Amazonian societies have benefited from a comparable set of conditions for such a long period of time; however, so long as they did, they underwent no *internal* pressure toward a basic reorganization of their socioeconomic structure. Their cultural system thus exerted a homeostatic effect that could be altered only as a result of exterior constraints such as military conquest or the expansion of a market economy.

NOTES

1. "Even Ricardo has his Robinson Crusoe stories. Ricardo makes his primitive fisherman and hunter into owners of commodities who immediately exchange their

fish and game in proportion to the labor time that is materialized in these exchange values. On this occasion he slips into the anachronism of allowing the primitive fisher and hunter to calculate the value of their implements according to the annuity tables used on the London Stock Exchange in 1817" (Marx 1976, 169).

2. Fieldwork on which this essay is based was conducted among the northern Ecuadorian Achuar with Anne-Christine Taylor. Between November 1976 and August 1978, the research was supported by a grant from the Centre National de la Recherche Scientifique and by a scholarship from the Fondation Delheim of the Collège de France. Further fieldwork in 1979 was supported by a grant from the Mission de la Recherche, and in 1984 by a grant from the Fondation Fyssen. In Ecuador the investigation was sponsored by the Instituto Nacional de Antropologia e Historia and by the Department of Anthropology of the Catholic University of Quito (PUCE). The ethnographic present corresponds to the year 1977.

3. For a detailed account of the prehistory and early history of Jivaroan societies see Renard-Casevitz, Saignes, and Taylor-Descola 1986, 212–352.

4. Table 9.2 is based on a sample of six households (four in the interfluvial habitat and two in the riverine habitat) wherein all incoming foodstuff intended for human consumption has been daily weighed during a total period of investigation of sixty-six days.

5. Apart from being a status symbol, an overlarge garden may also be useful to a great-man in periods of war, when the potential manioc surplus is put to use to feed those members of his kindred that have taken residence in his fortified house.

6. Table 9.3 is based on a sample of eight households (four in each habitat) wherein the time expenditure of all adults over the age of sixteen was logged by A.-C. Taylor and myself for a total duration of 87 days. The sample of interfluvial households is based on 216 individual workdays (those of five men and thirteen women), while the sample of riverine households lists 124 individual workdays (those of six men and thirteen women). Because of their utter fragmentation, female domestic chores were not systematically timed with the rest of daily activities. On several occasions, we have kept time of all housekeeping tasks carried out by women during a day (mainly cooking, preparing manioc-beer, sweeping, dish and cloth washing, bringing water, and feeding the chickens), the resulting expenditure varying between a minimum of 2 h 10 min and a maximum of 2 h 50 min. I have thus kept the highest figure (2 h 50 min) as an appropriate estimation for all households, although the actual average time expenditure must be somewhat less.

7. In the logic of Achuar polygyny, women's value for men tends to shift as a function of age: appreciated in the beginning of her marriage for her sexual services, a wife will later be highly esteemed for her gardening abilities and the quality of her manioc-beer.

8. Because of their highly effective techniques of guerrilla warfare, the Jivaro were famous for successfully banning white intruders from their territory almost until the 1940s. In the seventeenth century alone, attempts to penetrate the area from the

Andes met with such high casualties that all subsequent missionary and military expeditions were officially prohibited by the Audiencia de Quito at the beginning of the eighteenth century. During the same period, however, a small group of mostly Jivaroan and Zaparoan Indians began to cluster around the Dominican mission of Canelos, on the upper Bobonaza, where they learned Quichua and became nominally Christianized. They thus formed a sort of buffer group between the Jivaro and the outside world, now known as the Canelos Quichua (see Whitten 1976), which served as an effective trade relay for the procurement of European goods for the Jivaro. Finally, the rubber boom of the late nineteenth century did not greatly affect the Jivaro because white intruders were afraid of them; the full thrust of rubber extraction fell north and northeast of the Jivaroan territory where it provoked the almost complete extinction of local tribes, particularly the Zaparo. With the ebbing of the rubber wave, huge tracts of jungle were thus left devoid of inhabitants, offering the Jivaro an opportunity for territorial expansion.

REFERENCES

Berlin, E. A., and E. Markell
1977   *Parasitos y nutrición: dinámica de la salud entre los Aguaruna Jibaro de Ama-
            zonas, Peru. Studies in Aguaruna Jivaro ethnobiology.* Report no. 4. Berke-
            ley: Language Behavior Research Laboratory, University of California.
Bush, M. B., D. R. Piperno, and P. A. Colinvaux
1989   A 6,000-year history of Amazonian maize cultivation. *Nature* 340:
            303–5
Chagnon, N., and R. Hames
1979   Protein deficiency and tribal warfare in Amazonia: New data. *Science*
            207: 592–93.
Denevan, W.
1970   The Aboriginal population of western Amazonia in relation to habitat
            and subsistence. *Revista geográfica* 72: 61–86.
Descola, P.
1981   From scattered to nucleated settlements: A process of socio-economic
            change among the Achuar. In *Cultural transformation and ethnicity in
            modern Ecuador,* edited by N. Whitten, 614–46. Urbana: University of
            Illinois Press.
1982   Territorial adjustments among the Achuar of Ecuador. *Social Science
            Information* 21, no. 2:299–318.
1986   *La nature domestique: Symbolisme et praxis dans l'écologie des Achuar.* Paris:
            Fondation Singer-Polignac/Editions de la Maison des Sciences de
            l'Homme. Published in English translation under the title *In the society
            of nature: A native ecology in Amazonia* (Cambridge: Cambridge Univer-
            sity Press, 1994).

Gross, D.

1975 Protein capture and cultural development in the Amazon Basin, *American Anthropologist* 77:526–49.

Hames, R., and W. Vickers

1983 Introduction. In *Adaptive responses of native Amazonians*, edited by R. Hames and W. Vickers, 1–26. New York: Academic Press.

Lathrap, D.

1968 The hunting economies of the tropical forest zone of South America: An attempt at historical perspective. In *Man the hunter*, edited by R. Lee and I. De Vore, 29–39. Chicago: Aldine.

1970 *The upper Amazon*. London: Thames and Hudson.

Lizot, J.

1978 Economie primitive et subsistance: Essai sur le travail et l'alimentation chez les Yanomami. *Libre*, no. 4: 69–113.

Marx, K.

1976 *Capital*. Translated by B. Fawkes. Vol. 1. London: Penguin Books.

Meggers, B.

1971 *Amazonia: Man, and culture in a counterfeit paradise*. Chicago: Aldine.

Porras, P.

1987 *Investigaciones arqueológicas a las faldas del Sangay*. Quito: Centro de Investigaciones Arqueológicas de la Universidad Católica.

Roosevelt, A. C.

1980 *Parmana: Prehistoric maize and manioc subsistence along the Amazon and Orinoco*. New York: Academic Press.

Renard-Casevitz, F. M., Th. Saignes, and A. C. Taylor-Descola

1986 *L'Inca, l'Espagnol et les sauvages. Rapports entre les sociétés amazoniennes et andines du XV au XVII siècle*. Paris: Editions Recherches sur les Civilisations.

Ross, E.

1976 *The Achuara Jivaro: Cultural adaptation in the upper Amazon*. Ann Arbor, Mich.: University Microfilms.

1978 Food taboos, diet, and hunting strategy: The adaptation to animals in Amazon cultural ecology. *Current Anthropology* 19 (1): 1–36.

Taylor, A.-C.

1981 God-wealth: The Achuar and the missions. In *Cultural transformation and ethnicity in modern Ecuador*, edited by N. Whitten, 647–77. Urbana: University of Illinois Press.

1983 The marriage alliance and its structural variations in Jivaroan Societies. *Social Science Information* 22 (3): 331–53.

1989 L'évolution démographique des populations indigènes de la haute Amazonie du XVI au XX siècle. In *Equateur 1986*, edited by D. Delauney and M. Portais, 227–38. Paris: Editions de l'ORSTOM.

Vickers, W.
1976   *Cultural adaptation to Amazonian habitats: The Siona-Secoya of eastern
              Ecuador.* Ann Arbor, Mich.: University Microfilms.
Whitten, N.
1976   *Sacha Runa. Ethnicity and adaptation of jungle Ecuadorian Quichua.*
              Urbana: University of Illinois Press.

10

Farming, Feuding, and Female Status
The Achuar Case

PITA KELEKNA

Anthropological inquiry conducted in diverse habitats across several continents attests to the relative gender egalitarianism of nomadic hunter-gatherer
groups (Dahlberg 1981; Downs 1966; Ehrenberg 1989; Friedl 1975; Goodale
1971; Kayberry 1970; Leacock 1978; Lee 1984; Marshall 1959; Martin and
Voorhies 1975; Radcliffe Brown 1948; Turnbull 1961; Woodburn 1968).
Band organization is mobile and flexible and, because of female economic
salience, leverage in marriage, and prominent role in decision making, female status is high. By contrast, in many agricultural societies women occupy
low status. Research of recent years tends to link this apparent evolutionary
decline in female status not to the beginnings of extensive agriculture but to
the later development of intensive agriculture, in which, with the adoption
of the plow, men came to play a central subsistence role with resultant economic peripheralization of women (Boserup 1970, 50; Ember 1983, 285–86;
Whyte 1978, 139, 172).

   This chapter challenges this interpretation. Although it is true that female
status remains high in some extensive horticultural, nonpastoral societies of
temperate regions (Aberle 1961; Brown 1975; Grumet 1980), this does not
hold for the tropics. In many tropical zones throughout the world, particularly
in New Guinea and Amazonia, where internal warfare is prevalent, small-
scale societies practicing extensive swidden horticulture are characterized by

marked gender asymmetry (Chagnon 1977; Goldman 1963; Langness 1967; Lindenbaum 1976; Maybury-Lewis 1967; Meggitt 1964; Strathern 1972; Turner 1979a). In the upper Amazon, the Jivaroan Achuar are one such internally feuding horticulturist society. Data will be presented to show that in this acephalous society of shifting horticulturists, women play a central role in agriculture yet occupy markedly low social status. In this analysis, I will examine gender asymmetry in three main areas, the economic, the political, and the psychological. I will consider the sociopolitical factors contributing to the development of marked gender role differentiation, the political ramifications of the male-female economic divide, and its impact on family organization and childhood development. I will argue that in Achuar social organization, female segregation and subservience are integral components of the Jivaroan warring complex.

Setting

First documented by anthropologists a half-century ago (Karsten 1935; Stirling 1938), the Jivaroans comprise several dialect groups that occupy the eastern jungles of the Ecuador-Peruvian frontier region (Harner 1973). The most numerous are the Shuar of the Ecuadorian *montaña*. To the south, the Aguaruna and the Huambisa inhabit the Peruvian montana. Far to the east in the interior, the Achuar straddle the border area. The Mayna, now significantly reduced in numbers, inhabit the lowland Peruvian interior.

Because of the relative isolation of the Achuar area, warfare entailing blood-revenge feuds has persisted until the present. Explanations for this pattern of warring, once widespread in lowland South America, vary. In ecological analysis, the recurrent warfare characteristic of rain forest groups is considered by some (Denevan 1966; Gross 1975; Harris 1974; Lathrap 1970; Ross 1978) to be a social mechanism effecting optimal demographic distribution in areas of low-density protein availability. Feuding causes communities to disperse over wide areas, thus minimizing the impact of human predation and regulating population numbers according to availability of strategic resources. The inadequacy of dietary protein in Amazonia is, however, disputed by other anthropologists (Chagnon and Hames 1979; Lizot 1978), Beckerman (1979) in particular noting the diversity of reptilian, invertebrate, and plant sources. Dufour (1983) finds generally adequate protein levels but remarks irregular fluctuations in animal protein availability. In these latter analyses, warfare is varyingly explained as functioning to preserve the sovereignty of independent villages (Chagnon 1968) or to serve as a retaliatory mechanism whereby personal insults are punished and deaths avenged (Lizot

1978). Sparse, dispersed settlement is furthermore viewed by Beckerman (1979) as a direct result of white advance into Amazonia.

In the Jivaroan case, at least, there is every indication that warfare and dispersed settlement are precontact in origin. It is well documented that in the fifteenth century the Jivaroans roundly defeated two Inca invasions of their territory (Karsten 1935, 3–4; Stirling 1938, 38–42). In the mid-sixteenth century, the first Spanish detachments entering the zone reported scattered settlements, intratribal war, and fierce resistance to colonial intrusion (Salinas 1897). Before the end of the sixteenth century, Jivaroan resistance culminated in the complete rout of the Spaniards and their definitive expulsion for three centuries. This feat, unparalleled in the annals of white-Amerindian military confrontation, bespeaks a native martial tradition of no mean consequence. The practice of shrunken head trophies, the antiquity of which is well documented archaeologically for the montaña and the Coast, is further indicative of the long-standing history of armed conflict among the Jivaroans. With regard to protein, evidence of game scarcity is reported for areas of heavy settlement in Jivaroan territories (Brown 1986, 70; Harner 1973, 56; Kelekna 1981, 10), although in more sparsely settled zones adequate animal protein resources are encountered (Descola 1985, 390–92).

Settlement

The martial character of Jivaroan Achuar culture is reflected in the atomistic settlement pattern. In the absence of centralized political integration, settlements are dispersed and for purposes of defense almost always situated away from the major rivers. The traditional long house, or small cluster of houses, is typically located on high ground overlooking a tributary stream, the elevation affording defensive advantage in times of attack. In periods of intensive war, additional fortifications, ten-foot-high palisades, surround the settlement.

Subsistence

The forest adjoining the settlement is cleared by slash-and-burn techniques for which men are largely responsible, along with the planting of heavy trees. But once these measures are completed, the routine subsistence tasks of planting, weeding, harvesting, transportation, and processing garden produce are performed exclusively by women. Horticultural output in which manioc and plantains are the principal cultigens accounts for more than one-half of total food production. Men's major economic commitment is to the hunt, in which the primary game are peccary, agouti, armadillo, monkeys, and birds.

Men use blowguns for arboreal fauna and spears and guns for terrestrial. On long treks a woman accompanies her husband, but she does not utilize fire-arms; her job is to handle the dogs and to transport the meat home. Fishing, an important source of protein, is undertaken by both sexes, but specific tasks are conducted separately by men and women. Overall, in food production a marked gender-role segregation prevails, with men specializing as hunters and women as horticulturalists.

Compatibility of Women's Work and Child-Rearing Responsibilities

As horticulturalist, a woman's role differs significantly from that of the woman gatherer. In the foraging context, women enjoy considerable mobil-ity, efficient subsistence effort that allows ample leisure, and a wide range of social contacts (Lee 1984; Turnbull 1962; Goodale 1971). In the shift to swidden horticulture much of this changes. With the labor intensification inherent in horticulture, increased work effort is required from the woman cultivator. Important to note is that this intensified commitment to subsis-tence by women is complicated by several factors.

For the nomadic woman gatherer, accustomed to range long distances in the course of subsistence, child transport is onerous, and raising more than one infant at a time is problematic (Lee 1972). Birth spacing is therefore a crucial factor. Inhibiting ovulation by prolonged lactation significantly low-ers fertility (Kolata 1974; Konner and Worthman 1980; Lee 1980) and, prac-ticed in combination with infanticide, effectively limits the number of chil-dren a woman forager mothers in her lifetime. Sedentarization, however, radically transforms this situation (Sussman 1972).

In shifting horticulture, certain wild products continue to be gathered, but the bulk of carbohydrates is derived from gardening. Since full mobility no longer is required from women, birth spacing ceases to be critical. With bland cultigens from her garden, a woman is able early to introduce supple-mentary foods into an infant's diet, to reduce nursing, and to terminate breast feeding after the first year (Howell 1979). Achuar women, for example, once a child has begun to walk, often smear a hot peppery substance on their breast to discourage nursing. Without the check of protracted lactation, fertility increases as births occur at more frequent intervals. More infants survive, since with the increased work effort required in horticulture, children are viewed as valuable additions to the work force (Cavalli-Sforza 1983) and infanticide consequently becomes less likely. As a result of sedentism there-fore, women bear and rear more children and must come to reconcile their intensified subsistence activities, on the one hand, with increased maternal responsibilities on the other (Draper 1975).

Political Dimensions of Male-Female Role Differentiation

In a shifting adaptation to the tropical rain forest, male mobility in hunting continues whereas female mobility is reduced, and many of women's economic activities are concentrated in the area immediately adjacent to the household. In this way, a mother is able to interrupt her work periodically to attend to her more numerous dependent children or, as older siblings assume caretaking duties, to be minimally at hand should some crisis develop (Brown 1970). As Ember (1983) has emphasized, in raising more children, the female subsistence and maintenance effort intensifies. With more numerous offspring, a mother necessarily produces more food—food that must be planted, tended, harvested, transported, processed, and served. Larger families entail larger houses, more housework, more firewood and fuel to be fetched. Also, as evidenced in the archaeological record, looms and pots invariably first appear in association with sedentism. The additional tasks of weaving and pottery manufacture are commonly the lot of women, and, in fact, Achuar women devote much of their time to these activities.

In a comparative survey of Amazonian groups, Carneiro (1983) notes a positive correlation between male involvement in warfare and hunting and low participation in horticulture. In the Jivaroan context, Shuara military expansion and population movement eastward from the montaña has placed unrelenting pressure on the Achuar of the lower altitudes. In such a situation of armed confrontation, the disproportionate assumption of routine horticultural activities by women confers an important advantage; it effectively frees men to specialize as warriors. With men away on war expeditions, women's undertaking almost the entire bulk of horticultural work assures the settlement economic self-sufficiency in terms of a steady supply of carbohydrates and certain protein-rich crops such as maize, beans, and peanuts. In the event of distant or prolonged warring, women are further able to supplement their garden produce with protein obtained by fishing or by engaging in minimal hunting. Since women do not have access to weapons (Godelier 1986, 12), this latter activity is accomplished simply by running down with dogs the agouti and paca that infest a woman's gardens.

Thus men's economic commitment revolves around clearing land for gardens, felling trees for canoe manufacture or house building, and hunting, all of which, with the exception of hunting, occur sporadically and, if necessary, can be postponed at will. Hunting is performed regularly, yet the skills developed by the hunter—tracking, stalking, running, shooting—are precisely those employed in warfare. The gender asymmetric dichotomy of horticulture/hunting is therefore one that has the immediate effect of ensuring male combat proficiency and maximal readiness in warfare.

The Subsidiary Nature of Women's Work

This bifurcation of male and female activities in which routine, repetitive tasks commonly fall to women clearly enhances male competence and solidary effort in war. But it also results in greater prestige being attached to male undertakings and less recognition being accorded women's work. In foraging societies, men and women depart the camp each on independent subsistence assignment. At the end of the day each returns conspicuously and independently bearing the fruits of his or her labor (Draper 1975). In the sedentary environment, the man departs regularly on the hunt; on occasions his wife accompanies and assists him. But for the most part, in their subsistence effort, women remain restricted to the immediate vicinity of the settlement and as a result enjoy less economic salience than men. This asymmetric situation among horticulturalists thus differs markedly from that of foragers, among whom tasks assigned to the sexes are not ranked, but rather the efficiency with which the task is performed by the individual, regardless of whether it is a man or a woman (Martin and Voorhies 1975).

Apart from disparities in mobility and economic salience, men's and women's activities are also differentially structured in terms of type and style of work undertaken. Men's productive activities typically involve long-range projects that require planning and discussion, in contrast to women's activities, which tend to be short-term, repetitive tasks. Furthermore, tasks performed by men—raiding, clearing the forest, canoe manufacture, house building—often entail cooperation, and, as Shapiro (1972) has noted for the Yanomamo, even when coordinated effort is not intrinsically required in the work situation, the tendency for men to operate in groups persists.

Among the Achuar, when a group assembles for a communal project, men's work is often staggered so that only a few individuals are working at one time while the others are seated, drinking beer and conversing. A generally festive air pervades the gathering. The greatest ceremony, of course, surrounds the raiding party, which entails elaborate planning, cunning, and ingenuity and is marked by dramatic and sacred ritual. Compared to the structured world of male bonds, the female social universe is relatively diffuse. Whereas sororal co-wives are more likely to coordinate their work efforts, in general there is little cooperation among other women in tackling subsistence tasks, and female activities go largely unmarked by public ritual.

Segregation of Male/Female Activities—Spatial and Behavioral

Contrasts in male and female behavior are clearly evident in the Achuar household. In the sixty-foot long house, capable of accommodating some forty individuals, male and female activities are spatially demarcated. Two distinct zones, the *tankamash* and the *ekent* are separately designated for men and women (Descola 1985; Kelekna 1981).

The front of the Achuar house is the male section. Conspicuously displayed in the tankamash are many accoutrements of male enterprise: spears and guns are left leaning against the wall; blowguns are tied to a central post; canoe paddles are stashed in the roof thatch; quivers containing bamboo darts and small gourd containers of curare hang from the posts; and a log signal drum is slung in the entrance way. Here, seated on a sculpted stool, the male head of the household ordinarily presides over the conversation of men assembled as they engage in such tasks as basketry, the manufacture of hammocks, the filing of arrows, bead work, and feather work. The exterior space adjoining the tankamash is used for the drying of skins, woodworking, and the manufacture of blowguns. The tankamash is the focus of men's activities while in the settlement; it is also the public sphere in which political debate and decision occur.

While the tankamash is the political hub of the settlement, the ekent, the women's section, located in the rear of the house, is the private-domestic sphere. As noted above, the pattern of female labor is individual and particularized. In the ekent, each wife maintains a personal hearth where she prepares food. Ordinarily, a mother eats separately here with her children. Surrounding the hearth are the utensils of her everyday work—gourd water containers, beer fermentation jar, back strap loom, and equipment for pottery manufacture. Female activities extend outside to the cleared land behind the house, where corn is husked, beans shelled, peanuts dried, and calabashes scraped and incised. In the garden beyond the cleared area, each wife has her separate garden plot that she works independently.

Within the Achuar household, individuals have varying access to the tankamash and ekent. If at home during the day, the male head of the household is encountered in the tankamash interacting with his mature sons, sons-in-law, and male visitors. Solely men of the Achuar extended family are allowed access to the female section of the house, where they may frequent only those areas surrounding the hearths of their wives, mothers, or sisters. Entrance to the ekent is totally prohibited to all other men under pain of severe penalty. Correspondingly, female access to and movements within the tankamash are also constrained. When men are assembled, a woman enters the tankamash only at the express bidding of her husband. At home, men never help themselves to food, so the woman most commonly is summoned to serve manioc beer or a meal.

When visitors arrive from afar, many formalities are observed. Barking dogs normally alert the settlement to the visitors' presence; it is also customary for travelers to fire a shotgun to announce their arrival. As the party enters, carrying shotguns, formal salutations are pronounced. Men file into the tankamash and are seated on stools facing their host. A wife of the house appears to sweep the floor ceremonially, with head bowed and with wide elaborate gestures of deference. After an initial silence, the host engages the principal guest in the *aujmatin,* a ceremonial discourse. The Achuar consider oratory an esthetic accomplishment and eloquence in public speaking an essential social skill. The aujmatin is a ritual confrontation between two men. In this dialogue host and visitor exchange news of recent events, generally with reference to warfare, and, in a series of stylized assertions and rejoinders, postures and gestures, each man challenges the other as to his allegiance and intent (Bourdieu 1977).

Proceedings of the tankamash are characteristically boisterous. Whether men are engaged in heated debate or friendly banter, animation prevails, as exclamations, wisecracks, and loud laughter occur and reoccur. But women play no active part in these flamboyant displays. Unlike the woman forager, who participates energetically in group discussions and decision making (Lee 1982, 44), the Achuar woman must remain silent. With subdued stance and eyes averted, the women meticulously avoid close contact with men. On occasions an older woman, whose grown sons are present, may comment shrilly from the rear of the house, but this is essentially a contribution from the sidelines which receives scant acknowledgment by men.

Manioc beer, the Achuar staple beverage, is emblematic of female horticultural production and wifely accomplishment. The finely decorated, polychrome pottery drinking bowls presented to the visitors in the tankamash reflect the wealth and industry of the house. Yet in serving manioc beer, the woman deliberately refrains from all manner of direct confrontation with her guests. A man signals his wish for more beer by extending his bowl at the same time leaning away from the woman; she reciprocates by turning away as she pours the beer. Here the woman's position differs significantly from that of the woman gatherer, whose salience in society is marked by her absence from the home base during food procurement, conspicuous return with the gathered product, and the control the woman exerts in the distribution of food (Sanday 1973). In the Achuar case women deliver the food they labor to produce, but their mode of presentation is anonymous, since it is men who direct distribution. Thus, a wife dutifully complies with her husband's direction, providing generous or niggardly portions to individuals according to her husband's political disposition. And in the event that her husband is absent from the house, under no circumstance does she ever serve a male visitor. Male control of distribution and female anonymity are displayed even in guest behavior. A woman accompanying her husband on a visit is not permitted to enter the tankamash. Instead, she must remain outside, squatting on the ground with her burdens. There she is not formally served by her hosts but must depend on her husband to hand her refreshment periodically.

Gender Hierarchy

It becomes evident that, in Achuar society, role dichotomization along gender lines provides a framework for male priority. The spatial and functional separation of economic activities establishes male and female as contrasting elements. In the everyday situation of routine interaction, the dichotomous patterning of male/female roles is elaborated by the preeminence of men in the public sphere and the relative confinement of women to the domestic-private sector. As men arrive and depart, they exchange formal greetings with distinctive cadence and vocabulary. No comparable form of stylized greetings or oratory is observed between men and women or between women. Men's decorative apparel and ornamentation, bold demeanor, the weapons they monopolize and brandish are the insignia of male ascendancy, and the dramatic ceremony accompanying their conferences and work groups bespeak the political power men wield in society (Godelier 1986, 10).

Women's work effort and subsistence contribution are economically important yet deemed socially insignificant. Men are dominant, and women occupy subsidiary status. In relation to male tasks, horticulture and domestic duties are subsidiary undertakings that can be interrupted at a man's whim. A husband addresses a wife with stern commands that are social displays of male privilege and the ability to control. Obedience is expected from a wife at all times. Delay or failure on her part to comply or to behave in a properly compliant manner is met with severe verbal recrimination. Women's work is largely menial: the unremitting toil of horticulture, the transportation of heavy burdens, the fetching of water, the disposal of garbage. And a wife's servility is exhibited in public by the ceremonial sweeping of the floor during the reception of important guests. Thus, at many levels, social behavior is governed by rules of female deference to men that are ritualized expression of male authority structure and female inferior status.

Male Monopoly of Specialized Occupations

Achuar men's and women's lives are further differentiated in that only men have access to the specialized occupations of trader, shaman, and warrior. Centralized political authority is notably absent in Achuar society. Nevertheless, these occupations—from which women are excluded—allow a man with initiative to maneuver adroitly to gain prestige and standing in the wider society. These roles are not hereditary; therefore, any male is free to engage in these pursuits. Yet despite the generalized nature of these activities, it is recognized throughout Achuar society that certain persons excel in these roles. Such men are highly disciplined, enterprising individuals, whose resourcefulness enables them to wield influence both within and outside their home communities and to command the respect and deference of others.

Trader

By distributing commodities throughout the forest zone, trading chains in the Jivaroan area fulfill a far-reaching economic function. However, as Harner has noted (1973, 126), the Jivaroans engage in trade not solely for material profit but also from political motive. A trader dispenses goods to increase status and to incur obligation in the form of reciprocated goods, services, or support. Trade generally promotes sociability among groups by serving as a formal channel of communication in a society of scattered settlements of frequently inimical disposition. When men are unable to secure wives in their home vicinity, the trader can play an intermediary role in the arrangement of extralocal marriage. As a traveler, familiar with different sectors of society, the trader also serves as arbitrator in disputes. Trading relations are further integrative in that they facilitate safe passage through a hostile zone. The personal protection extended by a trading partner and the sanctuary afforded by his home are of crucial importance in allowing individuals to undertake long-distance travel (Harner 1973, 131). The trading partner's home also provides a refuge to the man beleaguered by fighting at home and a haven to his family in distress. And in times of war, it is the trader who furnishes the link whereby the terms of truce between enemy groups are negotiated and conciliation effected (Kelekna 1985).

Among foragers, trade has been described as a mechanism for lubricating social relations, maintaining ecological balance, and reducing risk (Lee 1984; Wiessner 1982). Many of these elements obviously persist in horticultural society, although among the Jivaroans, trade is clearly intertwined with war. What is remarkable, though, is that, whereas among foragers women are very active in trading and consequently very mobile throughout society (Shostak 1981; Wiessner 1982), among the Achuar, only men are traders. Due to the prevailing climate of hostilities, a trader often travels alone; at times, however, he is accompanied by his wife, her presence on the trip signifying the amicable intent and deep trust the man feels toward his trade partner. A woman takes advantage of the trip to exchange small domestic commodities with the women of the households they visit. But since on subsequent trips the husband may travel alone or accompanied by a different co-wife, female exchanges by comparison are of an intimate character and lack the long-term consistency, formality, and political intrigue characteristic of male exchanges. Achuar women, furthermore, never undertake trading trips independently.

Shaman

Another prestigious occupation from which Achuar women are excluded is that of the shaman. The Achuar attribute sickness and death resulting from sickness to malign witchcraft. The shaman is believed to possess the powers both to inflict and to cure sickness. To obtain shamanic power, a man must undergo apprenticeship with established shamans in different locations for which, depending on the fame of the shaman, he pays a high price. Returning home as a practitioner, the shaman is greatly valued by members of his community and generously paid for his services. Due to the payments the shaman receives from his patients and the initiates under his tutelage, he is able to amass more material wealth than other members of society. A shaman is appreciated for his curing skills, but he is also feared for the supernatural powers he might wield against others. Men are therefore more careful to defer to him and not to expect that same reciprocity of exchange they demand of their fellows. The shaman also acts as a diviner. When a patient cannot be cured or actually dies, the shaman, in hallucinogenic trance, identifies the malign sorcerer and thus directs the vengeance of the raiding party against the enemy.

Warrior

The greatest distinction in society is achieved as a warrior. Accusations of witchcraft and disputes over women are the major causes for the outbreak of hostilities among the Achuar. Warring can take place as a series of swift successive attacks or may extend over a period of many years, raids being undertaken by as few as two or three men or as many as several canoeloads of warriors.

In planning an assassination, the principal warrior draws upon his own sons, his sons-in-law, brothers, brothers-in-law, and men whose raids he has accompanied in the past. As emissaries, his sons and sons-in-law are sent to different households, where each messenger states the warrior's intent in the ritual *anemartin,* a chant in which grievances are declared and men invited to join the war. This invitation is not extended lightly and is declined rarely, for given the strategic value of secrecy, rejection is tantamount to a declaration of hostility.

In this acephalous society, a man who leads assassination raids with repeated success gains renown. As a respected warrior, he is known as *kakaram* (strong man) and is invited to organize war expeditions in other sometimes distant locations, for which he is richly recompensed. Upon completion of a raid, a war party commonly disperses. With strong affinal alliance, however, political alignment may persist for a significant time period. Since with each successful assassination a warrior is believed to increase his spiritual vigor (Harner 1973, 141), the kakaram customarily commands a strong following at home, where, due to his reputed invincibility, few dare to oppose his decree.

Marriage and Family Organization

Nowhere is the principle of male superordination more apparent than in marital arrangements. Achuar society lacks lineal descent groups and operates along the flexible lines of the cognatic kindred. The marriage pattern is the Dravidian type in which the prescribed spouse is a classificatory same-generational affine, true bilateral cross-cousin being the ideal. Polygyny is frequent, sororal polygyny occurring most commonly in that uxorilocal residence is required at marriage. Due to the high rate of polygyny, women are a scarce resource through control of which a man may dominate other men.

Since horticulturalists have more cohesive groupings than bands, greater concern and emphasis are attached to reproductive and marital matters (Meillassoux 1981, 38). An Achuar father is regarded as the owner of his daughter, and it is he who determines her disposition in matrimony, although he is often influenced by his mature sons, who, in exchange for their sisters, hope to gain wives themselves. A woman is not easily ceded in marriage. First, the father must be approached by an intermediary. In negotiation, the suitor's diligence, ability as a hunter, and readiness in warfare are evaluated. If the suitor's reputation and demeanor are satisfactory, the prospective groom visits the household to assist in routine activities and is expected to deliver a large game animal to the girl's mother. The mother leads the bride to the man's bed in the evening. The marriage, however, is not immediately consummated. For three or four nights, the bride's brother sleeps between the bride and groom, his presence in the matrimonial bed symbolizing the strong bonds of cooperation that are forged between male affines. The exchange of women is merely the first step in a long series of obligations, presentations, and services that signify alliance between affines and constitute a pattern of mutual assistance.

Immediate tasks incumbent upon the new husband are clearing the forest for his wife's garden and carrying large logs for his wife and her mother's fires. His major obligations, though, are toward his father-in-law. This relationship invariably involves certain tensions. The older man has already established his position in society. By ceding his daughter in marriage he feels he has bestowed upon the younger man a valuable gift. In return, as Turner has noted for the Gê and the Bororo (1979b, 159), he demands that his son-in-law owes him maximal support in warfare, industry in economic activities, and deference in daily interaction. The son-in-law is relegated the most strenuous and least desirable tasks, which he is expected to do without complaint. A father-in-law's attitude in this regard may be extremely exigent, and if not satisfied with the young husband's behavior, he will in fact reclaim his daughter.

Despite the tensions existing between them, father and son-in-law seek to avoid open confrontations of hostility and strive to maintain solidarity, for each man stands to benefit from the relationship. In the case of the father-in-law, his own sons must leave the household at marriage and he must recruit fresh manpower to his family unit. In the case of the younger man, he is maneuvering to make his way in the world, and polygyny is a central component of his strategy. By submitting to his father-in-law's testiness and criticism, he has the expectation that his allegiance and diligence will be rewarded by the concession of additional daughters as wives. In return for his economic and political commitment, the son-in-law anticipates receiving all the daughters of his wife's mother. However, this does not always come about. The father may find it expedient to assign his daughters to others in order to cement military alliance. As a consequence, in-marrying husbands are often at odds among themselves, also vis-à-vis consanguineally related men within the settlement. Coresidents, these men are in direct competition over the same women and are jealous of one another's privileges.

Widespread polygyny results in a relative scarcity of marriageable women, so that often young men are obliged to postpone marriage, whereas the reverse obtains in the case of females, who are snapped up as soon as they are nubile; sometimes, they are taken even earlier—as young as seven or eight, when they are clearly extremely docile and malleable. In relation to her father, brothers, and husband, a woman is the link that facilitates male alliance. She is the important strategic resource exchanged by men, her importance lying in her procreative and economic capabilities. As the connecting link in alliance between affines, she is expected to subordinate her personal inclinations to the political interests of men. Women vary in their response to arranged marriage. Some adjust well and take pride in their premature wifely role. Others energetically resist the marriages forced upon them. When a woman opposes a father or brother in this manner, she is severely penalized. She is harassed mercilessly and reproached for her obduracy. And should she persist in her defiance, she is subject to violent intimidation. Rather than confront men's wrath directly, women contrive to escape to seek refuge with distant kin or asylum with an enemy group. But such escape is difficult, for often, the flight is anticipated and intercepted, and the female fugitive is brought back at gunpoint by her male kin.

Male domination continues during marriage. Since men customarily marry at a later age than women, the husband's authority is enhanced by his seniority. Wives owe their husband obedience and deference at all times. Within the polygynous extended family, however, the respective positions of co-wives vis-à-vis one another and their husband are not explicitly defined, nor are the norms that regulate and equilibrate a man's responsibilities to his different wives. While many men recognize the general advisability of spending time with each of their wives and of distributing equal amounts of meat and trade goods among them for the maintenance of a harmonious household, some feel free to favor one wife and to neglect the rest. A man may elect to associate with the most recent addition to his polygynous family and to provide her with more presents at the expense of his other wives. The effects of this partiality for the younger, more sexually attractive wife at times inflict real hardship on the older women.

Understandably, tensions among co-wives arise that reach peak expression in the nonsororal polygynous situation. As rivalry erupts, co-wives of inimical disposition rigorously exclude one another's children. This divisiveness is further exacerbated when interpersonal friction prevails among in-marrying husbands who are in competition for additional wives or between an in-marrying husband and the father-in-law. Growing up, children become early attuned to the varying currents of amity and antagonism pervading the family environment and accordingly adjust their behavior to the tensions and rifts that later in life lead to the feuds and fissions of the wider society.

Men, of course, are free to contract as many wives as they can procure; by contrast polyandry is unknown. Women, furthermore, are not permitted to seek divorce, and as Harner (1973) has noted the penalties for extramarital liaisons are severe. For suspected though unproven adultery, the punishment entails slashing of the wife's scalp; for adultery, shooting of the unfaithful wife and her lover. In general severe restrictions surround female sexuality.

Whereas boys boisterously romp naked until the age of eight or nine, even minimal genital display on the part of small girls is rigorously interdicted and immodesty is promptly punished. Correspondingly, sexual play is strongly disapproved of in mixed children's play groups, and any behavior of this sort is swiftly forestalled. Premarital sex in youth, although a less serious offense than adultery, is still firmly censured. All incidents of illicit sexual activity involving young people during the time of fieldwork resulted in extreme public indignation and outrage on the part of the girl's male kin, in one case escalating almost to the level of armed confrontation. This situation differs very markedly from the sexual permissiveness tolerated in hunter-gatherer children play groups and the flexible serial marital patterns of foraging societies (Radcliffe Brown 1948; Shostak 1981; Turnbull 1961; Goodale 1971).

Among the Achuar, male coercion persists even after marriage. When a man dies, his brothers stand to inherit his widows in the levirate. In the case of immediate kin, procedures are relatively straightforward. But in their absence, a woman may find herself precariously situated as her classificatory kin dispute her appropriation—especially if she attempts to assert initiative of her own. Overall, in Achuar kinship and marital arrangements, female subordination is dramatically evident. Men seek continually to expand their sphere of social ties through affinal linkage, and women are the medium through which these new relationships are established. Yet as Rubin (1975) remarks in her discussion of Lévi-Strauss's theory of alliance, women are the conduit of the marriage relationship rather than partner to it, and their rights are residual compared to those of men, who are the major beneficiaries of marital exchange.

Cross-Sex Identification

Perhaps, even more potent a factor, in promoting the development of aggression during maturation, than the cracks of interpersonal rivalries within the extended family, is the gulf that separates the spheres of men's and women's activities. A cross-cultural survey of husband-wife patterns of interaction (Whiting and Whiting 1975) has remarked the coincidence of male-female role segregation and societal belligerence. In this comparative study, it is shown that in the majority of cultures husbands and wives participate in an "intimate" pattern of interaction—that is, they share many activities, and fathers have frequent contact with infants and young children. In 29 percent of the cultures, however, strict division of labor along sex lines and general segregation of men and women's activities are encountered. This less common, dual economic-domestic arrangement occurs predominantly in societies at a middle-level range of development where male organization is needed for defense of property or territory, yet no state-directed militia exists to provide this protection. Whiting and Whiting submit that, in these middle-level, primarily horticulturalist/pastorialist societies, husband-wife "aloofness" is conducive to the development of cross-sex identification in boys, compensatory hypermasculine behavior, and high levels of violence in society.

The construct of cross-sex identification, which has evolved over the course of more than thirty years of research by Whiting and his associates, maintains that father disengagement from the domestic sphere and nonparticipation in early child rearing cause a boy to identify strongly with his mother. During the first few years, interacting preponderantly with the mother and minimally with the father, the boy perceives his mother as being in control of desired resources, such as food, warmth, love, information, success (Burton and Whiting 1961). He envies her control, covertly practices her role, and consequently develops a feminine optative identity (Whiting 1965). As the boy matures and is required to operate in contrastive male spheres of activity, he finds his perception of the relative power of men and women to be distorted. He then develops the need to dis-identify with his mother, to reject his underlying feminine identity (Greenson 1968; Stoller 1974; Tyson 1982); this need becomes manifested in compensatory hypermasculine displays of aggressive behavior.

Additionally, Whiting (1969) shows that polygynous societies, in which dual economic-domestic patterns most commonly occur, are more likely to place high value on virtues such as valor, recklessness, and fighting skills than other societies.

Male Initiation

As earlier discussion has shown, marked disjunction between male and female characterizes many facets of Achuar culture. Consequently, a young boy is reared in a female-dominated environment. Yet, at puberty he must begin to make the transition to the male adult world. To facilitate this transition, male initiation rites are enacted that emphasize seclusion from women, isolation, and tests of manliness; their functions are to break primary identification with the mother and to ensure acceptance of the male adult role (Whiting, Kluckhohn, and Anthony 1958).

Achuar puberty rites initiate the youth into the sacred *arutam* cult. Among hunters, initiation rites stress virility and hunting prowess, but Achuar rites in addition underscore the importance of warring. Arutam refers to "forefather" or "ancestor." Often, an older, experienced warrior accompanies a small band of youths as they undertake a trek of several days far into the forest. As on a war expedition, the boys are required to endure hunger, thirst, sleeplessness, and exposure to the elements. The group constructs lean-tos alongside a forest trail the arutam ancestor is expected to pass. The eminent warrior presides. Tobacco is smoked or masticated; juice squeezed from the bark of *maikua* (*Datura arborea*) is imbibed. In a visionary ordeal, the initiate must withstand the violent effects of the hallucinogen and confront in dreams menacing specters that appear in the form of spinning stars, boas, jaguars, anteaters, eagles, or condors. In this encounter, the neophyte must bravely strike the apparition with his staff. If he is not manly enough to perform this aggressive act, he will eventually be destroyed by the power he fails to overcome. If he succeeds, the youth receives from the august ancestor the arutam power that will ensure his success in war and in life.

The shift from boyhood to manhood in Achuar culture is thus celebrated by formal disassociation from the female domestic sphere, by remote seclusion in the forest, and by participation in rites that emphasize valor and aggression as essential virtues of male adult life. Periodically, boys and men return to the forest to increase their arutam power that will enable them to achieve longevity, fecundity, and military success. Spiritual vigor is also sought during the *natemamu*, a world renewal festival that is observed at ten-year intervals by the Achuar. At this great celebration, male and female again are segregated. Under the mother's tutelage, girls' fertility rites are conducted in the garden. By contrast, boys hike far away from the settlement to obtain from the forest the *natem* vine. On their return, when imbibing the hallucinogen, they are subjected to ordeals of hazing, kicking, and pummeling by their fathers and older men. Perhaps the major ordeal facing the Achuar youth, however, is the, assumption of uxorilocal residence at marriage. Embarking on adulthood, the young man must leave the domesticity and familiar security of his natal settlement and, as in-marrying husband subject to the scrutiny and exigency of his father-in-law, address the internal competition and hostilities of his affinal household and the threat and challenge of war in the wider society.

Conclusion

Initially, it was noted that with the transition to sedentism, increased family size among horticulturalists required from women intensified subsistence and maintenance effort in conjunction with greater commitment to child rearing.

Consequent concentration of women's activities within the immediate settle-ment area and preponderant responsibility for horticulture, in the situation of armed conflict, allow men to achieve maximal preparedness and proficiency in war. As Gelber suggests (1986, 55–56), the "separateness" of women may also afford men a sense of fellowship and cohesiveness in circumstances where in fact they are subject to internal differences and stress. Social and economic segregation of men and women, restriction of boys during early childhood to the female sphere, and emphasis placed on hypervirility and male aggressive-ness during puberty initiation—traits undoubtedly selected for in the context of resource competition—further assure men's ranks a regular supply of junior warriors.

But women's "separateness" or confinement to the domestic environment prevents them from developing important extralocal networks of communica-tion and political endeavor and thus profoundly undermines female status in society. In male competition, female labor and childbearing are viewed as valuable economic assets. Through polygynous marriage a man greatly in-creases his power and prestige, and through the allocation of women in mar-riage a man is also able to control other men. A father cedes a daughter in marriage to recruit fresh manpower to his household. Women are alterna-tively exchanged for wives by their brothers, inherited in the levirate, ab-ducted in raiding, given as reward for war exploits, or as payment for shaman's services. Alliance groupings among men are formally expressed and upheld through the exchange of women (Taylor 1983). Access to this connubium is jealously guarded and fiercely defended. Disregard for marital prescriptions, violation of the levirate, or female resistance to coercive marriage is not toler-ated; in this context, adultery constitutes the ultimate challenging offense against male ownership of women. Recurrent disputes over women signifi-cantly elevate levels of violence in Achuar society and contribute directly to the persistent pattern of fission and feuding.

The tradition of warfare among Jivaroans is admittedly pronounced. But many of the practices described above are commonly observed among Amazo-nian groups and have parallels in tropical forest swidden horticultural societies elsewhere in the world. Data presented here indicate that Achuar women do *not* have parity with men. In this shifting hunting-horticulturalist society, their predicament differs markedly from the more equitable role played by women among foragers. It is contended that the decline in female status had its beginnings in human society long before the adoption of inten-sive agriculture. Sedentism and concomitant increase in human fertility set the stage for profound changes in male-female relations. In the acephalous political context of internal fissioning and feuding, among tropical swidden horticulturalists, marked gender asymmetry is functionally significant and is inextricably linked with the emergence and promotion of militarism.

ACKNOWLEDGMENTS

The author is indebted to the Comision Fulbright del Ecuador, the Organization of American States, Sigma Xi Research Society of North America, and the Frieda Butler Foundation of the University of New Mexico, whose financial support made possible the research on which this article is based.

I am also deeply grateful for the interest and critical feedback given this work by Dr. Patricia Draper and Dr. Nina Swidler. Earlier drafts of this chapter were presented at the South American Indian Caucus at Bennington College, Vermont, and at the seminar of Ecological Systems and Cultural Evolution at Columbia University.

REFERENCES

Aberle, D.
1961   Matrilineal descent cross-cultural perspective. In *Matrilineal Kinship*, edited by David M. Schneider and Kathleen Gough, 655–727. Berkeley and Los Angeles: University of California Press.
Beckerman, S.
1979   The abundance of protein in Amazonia: A reply to Gross. *American Anthropologist* 81:533–60.
Boserup, E.
1970   *Women's role in economic development*. New York: St. Martins.
Bourdieu, P.
1977   *Outline of a theory of practice*. Translated by R. Nice. Cambridge: Cambridge University Press.
Brown, J. K.
1970   A note on the division of labor by sex. *American Anthropologist* 2:1073–78.
1975   Iroquois women: An ethnographic note. In *Toward an Anthropology of Women*, edited by R. Reiter, 235–51. New York: Monthly Review Press.
Brown, M.
1986   *Tsewa's gift: Magic and meaning in an Amazonian society*. Washington and London: Smithsonian Institution Press.
Burton, R., and J. Whiting
1961   The absent father and cross-sex identity. *Merrill-Palmer Quarterly of Behavior and Development* 7:85–95.

Carneiro, R.
1983   The cultivation of manioc among the Kuikuru of the upper Xingu.
            In *Adaptive responses of native Amazonians,* edited by R. Hames and
            W. Vickers, 65–111. New York: Academic Press.
Cavalli-Sforza, L. L.
1983   The transition to agriculture and some of its consequences. In *How
            humans adapt,* edited by D. Ortner. Washington: Smithsonian Institu-
            tion Press.
Chagnon, N.
1968   Yanomamo social organization and war. In *War: The anthropology of armed
            conflict and aggression,* edited by M. Fried, M. Harris, and R. Murphy,
            105–59. New York: Natural History Press.
1977   *The Yanomamo: The fierce people.* New York: Holt, Reinhart, and Winston.
Chagnon, N., and R. Hames
1979   Protein deficiency and tribal warfare in Amazonia: New data. *Science*
            203:910–13.
Dahlberg, F., ed.
1981   *Woman the gatherer.* New Haven and London: Yale University Press.
Denevan, W. M.
1966   A cultural-ecological view of the former aboriginal settlement in the
            Amazon Basin. *Professional Geographer* 18 (6): 346–51.
Descola, P.
1985   *La nature domestique: Symbolisme et praxis dans l'écologie des Achuar.* Paris:
            Editions de la Maison des Sciences de l'Homme.
Downs, J.
1966   *The two worlds of the Washo: An Indian tribe of California and Nevada.* New
            York: Holt, Rinehart and Winston.
Draper, P.
1975   !Kung women: Contrasts in sexual egalitarianism in foraging and seden-
            tary contexts. In *Toward an anthropology of women,* edited by R. Reiter,
            77–109. New York: Monthly Review Press.
Dufour, D.
1983   Nutrition in the northwest Amazon: Dietary take and time-energy
            expenditure. In *Adaptive responses of native Amazonians,* edited by
            R. Hames and W. Vickers, 329–90. New York: Academic Press.
Ehrenberg, M.
1989   *Women and prehistory.* London: British Museum Publications.
Ember, C.
1983   The relative decline in women's contribution to agriculture with inten-
            sification. *American Anthropologist* 85:285–304.
Friedl, E.
1975   *Women and men: An anthropologist's view.* New York: Holt, Rinehart and
            Winston.

Gale, F., ed.

1974   *Women's role in aboriginal society.* Canberra: Australian Institute of
            Aboriginal Studies.

Gelber, M. G.

1986   *Gender and society in the New Guinea highlands: An anthropological per-
            spective on antagonism toward women.* Boulder and London: Westview
            Press.

Godelier, M.

1986   *The making of great men: Male domination and power among the New
            Guinea Baruya.* Cambridge: Cambridge University Press.

Goldman, I.

1963   *The Cubeo: Indians of the north west Amazon.* Illinois Studies in Anthro-
            pology 2. Urbana: University of Illinois Press.

Goodale, J.

1971   *Tiwi wives: A study of the women of Melville Island, North Australia.*
            Seattle: University of Washington Press.

Greenson, R.

1968   Dis-identifying from mother: Its importance for the boy. *International
            Journal of Psychoanalysis* 49:370–74.

Gross, D. R.

1975   Protein capture and cultural development in the Amazon Basin. *Ameri-
            can Anthropologist* 77:526–49.

Grumet, R. S.

1980   Sunksquaws, shamans, and tradeswomen: Middle Atlantic coastal
            Algonkian women during the 17th and 18th centuries. In *Women and
            colonization: Anthropological perspectives,* edited by E. Leacock and
            M. Etienne, 43–62. New York: Praeger.

Harner, M. J.

1973   *The Jivaro: People of the sacred waterfalls.* Garden City, N.Y.: Doubleday/
            Anchor Press.

Harris, M.

1974   *Cows, pigs, wars, and witches: The riddle of culture.* New York: Random
            House.

Howell, N.

1979   *Demography of the Dobe !Kung.* New York: Academic Press.

Karsten, R.

1935   *The headhunters of western Amazonas: The life and culture of the Jibaro
            Indians of eastern Ecuador and Peru.* Helsinki: Societas Scientarum Fenica
            Commentationes Humanarum Litterarum Vol. 19 (5).

Kayberry, P.

1970   *Aboriginal woman: Sacred and profane.* London: Routledge and Kegan
            Paul.

Kelekna, P.
1981   *Sex asymmetry in Jivaroan Achuara society: A cultural mechanism promoting belligerence.* Ph.D. diss., Department of Anthropology, University of New Mexico.
1985   Achuara trade: counterpoise and complement to war. In *Political anthropology in Ecuador: Perspective from indigenous cultures,* edited by Jeffrey Ehrenreich, 217–56. Society for Latin American Anthropology and The Center for the Caribbean and Latin America, State University of New York Albany Press.

Kolata, G. B.
1974   !Kung hunter-gatherers: Feminism, diet, and birth control. *Science,* 13 September, 932–34.

Langness, L.
1967   Sexual antagonism in the New Guinea highlands: A Bena Bena example. *Oceania* 37 (3): 161–77.

Lathrap, D. W.
1970   *The upper Amazon.* New York: Praeger.

Leacock, E.
1978   Women's status in egalitarian society: Implications for social evolution. *Current Anthropology* 19:247–75.

Lee, R.
1972   Population growth and the beginnings of sedentary life among the !Kung Bushmen. In *Population growth: Anthropological implications,* edited by B. Spooner, 329–50. Cambridge, Massachusetts: MIT Press.
1980   Lactation, ovulation, infanticide, and women's work: A study of hunter-gatherer population regulation. In *Biosocial mechanisms of population regulation,* edited by M. N. Cohen, R. S. Malpass, and R. G. Klein. New Haven, Conn.: Yale University Press.
1982   Politics, sexual and non-sexual, in an egalitarian society. In *Politics and history in band societies,* edited by E. Leacock and R. Lee, 37–59. Cambridge: Cambridge University Press.
1984   *The Dobe !Kung.* New York: Holt, Rinehart and Winston.

Lindenbaum, S.
1976   A wife is the hand of man. In *Man and woman New Guinea Highlands,* edited by P. Brown and G. Buchbinder, 54–62. Washington, D.C.: American Anthropological Association.

Lizot, J.
1978   Population, resources, and warfare among the Yanomamo. *Man* 12:497–517.

Marshall, T. E.
1959   *The harmless people.* New York: Random House

Martin, K. M., and B. Voorhies
1975   *Female of the species.* New York and London: Columbia University Press.

Maybury-Lewis, D.
1967   *Akwe Shavante society.* Oxford: Clarendon Press.
1979   *Dialectical societies: The Ge and Bororo of central Brazil.* Cambridge,
            Mass.: Harvard University Press.
Meggitt, M.
1964   Male-female relationships in the highlands of Australian New Guinea.
            In *New Guinea: The central highlands,* edited by J. B. Watson. *American
            Anthropologist* 66 (4, pt. 2): 204–24.
Meillassoux, C.
1981   *Maidens, meals, and money: Capitalism and the domestic community.* Cam-
            bridge: Cambridge University Press.
Radcliffe Brown, A. R.
1948   *The Andaman Islanders.* Glencoe, Ill.: Free Press.
Ross, E. B.
1978   Food taboos, diet, and hunting strategy: The adaptation to animals in
            Amazon cultural ecology. *Current Anthropology* 19:1–16.
Rubin, G.
1975   Traffic in women: Notes on the political economy of sex. In *Toward an
            anthropology of women,* edited by R. R. Reiter, 157–210. New York:
            Monthly Review Press.
Salinas, L.
1897   Descubrimientos, conquistas, poblaciones de Juan de Salas Loyola. In
            Relaciones geográficas de Indias, 4:45–101. Madrid: Publicaciones del Mis-
            terio deFomento.
Sanday, P. R.
1973   Toward a theory of the status of women. *American Anthropologist* 75:
            1682–1700.
Shapiro, J.
1972   *Sex roles and social structure among the Yanomama Indians of northern Brazil.*
            Ph.D. diss., Department of Anthropology, Columbia University.
Shostak, M.
1976   *Nisa: The life and words of a !Kung woman.* Cambridge, Mass.: Harvard
            Univerity Press.
Stanner, W.
1965   The dreaming. In *Reader in comparative religion,* edited by W. Lessa and
            E. Vogt, 269–77. New York: Harper and Row.
Stirling, M.
1938   *Historical and ethnographical material on the Jivaro Indians.* Bureau of
            American Ethnology Bulletin 117. Washington, D.C.: Smithsonian
            Institution.
Stoller, R.
1974   Symbiosis anxiety and the development of masculity: A cross-cultural
            contribution. *Journal of American Psychoanalytic Association* 30:29–59.

Strathern, M.
1972   *Women in between*. London: Seminar Press.
Taylor, A.
1983   The marriage alliance and its structural variation in Jivaroan societies.
              Social Science Information, 331–53. London: Sage.
Turnbull, C.
1961   *The forest people: A study of the Pygmies of the Congo*. New York: Simon
              and Schuster.
Turner, T.
1979a   The Gé and Bororo societies as dialectical systems: A general model. In
              Dialectical Societies: The Ge and Bororo of central Brazil, edited by D.
              Maybury-Lewis, 179–214. Cambridge, Mass.: Harvard University Press.
1979b   Kinship, household, and community structure among the Kayapó.
              Dialectical societies: The Ge and Bororo of central Brazil, edited by D.
              Maybury-Lewis, 147–78. Cambridge, Mass.: Harvard University Press.
Tyson, P.
1982   A development line of gender identity, gender role, and choice of love
              object. *Journal of the American Psychoanalytic Association* 30:61–86.
Whiting, B.
1965   Sex identity conflict and physical violence: A comparative study. *American Anthropologist* 67 (6, part 2): 123–40.
Whiting, J.
1969   The place of aggression in social interaction. In *Collective violence*,
              edited by J. Short and M. Wolfgang. Chicago: Aldine.
Whiting, J., R. Kluckhohn, and A. Anthony
1958   The function of male initiation ceremonies at puberty. In *Readings in
              social psychology*, edited by E. Maccoby, T. Newcomb, and E. Hartley,
              359–70. New York: Holt.
Whiting, J., and B. Whiting
1975   Aloofness and intimacy of husbands and wives: A cross-cultural study.
              Ethos 3 (2): 183–201.
Whyte, M. K.
1978   *The status of women in preindustrial societies*. Princeton, N.J.: Princeton
              University Press.
Wiessner, P.
1982   Risk, reciprocity, and social influences on !Kung San economics. In *Politics and history in band societies*, edited by E. Leacock and R. Lee, 61–84.
              Cambridge: Cambridge University Press.
Woodburn, J.
1968   Stability and flexibility in Hazda residential groupings. In *Man the hunter*,
              edited by Richard B. Lee and I. DeVore, 103–10. Chicago: Aldine.

II

Subsistence Strategy, Social Organization, and Warfare in Central Brazil in the Context of European Penetration

NANCY M. FLOWERS

Cultural evolution in the Amazon Basin has most often been discussed in terms of the agricultural potential of two habitats: the floodplains of the Amazon and some of its major tributaries, and the tropical forest interfluvial areas (Carneiro 1970, 1973; Gross 1975; Lathrap 1970, 1977; Meggers 1954, 1971; Roosevelt 1980, 1987). A third major natural division of Amazonia, the *cerrado* region of central Brazil, has seldom been considered in these discussions. The cerrado contrasts sharply in climate and vegetation with the tropical forest. There is a winter dry season of three to five months with practically no rainfall. Cerrado flora is botanically distinctive (Eiten 1972), adapted to survive the rainless months and the brush fires that sweep across the land at the end of the dry season. However, in the gallery forests, usually only narrow strips along watercourses, a number of species grow that are also found in the tropical forest.

The peculiar features of the cerrado habitat have, until recently, seldom been considered important in explaining the contrast between the social elaboration of many central Brazilian societies with aggregation in large villages, and subsistence technologies in which seasonal nomadism and wild food collection played a major role. At most, the cerrado was held to be a marginal habitat, stultifying the technological development of its inhabitants and therefore likely to lead to the devolution of groups forced to migrate there from more favored regions.

Steward and others (Lowie 1948, 5; Martin 1969; Steward and Faron 1959, 378) argued that the central Brazilians had acquired most of their advanced cultural features (including farming) from their tropical forest neighbors in relatively recent times. Lévi-Strauss (1967, 48) held that the Nambiquara, the Bororo, and the Gê-speakers formed in central Brazil a "kernel of primitiveness" surrounded by tribes of higher cultures. He suggested that the central Brazilians should be seen as "pseudo-archaic," having devolved under unfavorable circumstances from a "higher type of social and material organization." He believed that the egalitarian social forms found in many groups masked constructs that were more complex and hierarchical and presumably, were survivals from the past.

A number of anthropologists, including D. Maybury-Lewis and his students (Maybury-Lewis 1974, 1979, 1989), have undertaken field studies among these groups that have led to new data and interpretations of their social structures. Views that suggest that the complex social structures of central Brazilian societies are anomalous imply a theory of social evolution in which "stages" correlate with degree of agricultural commitment. More recent ideas stress adaptation to specific environments through exploitation of resources at a given technological level (Layton et al. 1991). Gross (1979) has suggested a view of central Brazilian adaptation in which their complex but egalitarian social organizations are seen as integral factors in their adjustments to a habitat characterized by varied ecological zones, climatic unpredictability, and competition for resources, especially in the context of European expansion.

In 1976 Gross organized a comparative field study of four central Brazilian societies: the Bororo, the Kanela, the Xavante, and the Mekranoti Kayapó. A number of publications (Flowers 1983a, 1983b; Flowers et al. 1982; Gross 1983; Gross et al. 1979; Rubin et al. 1986; Werner 1978, 1980, 1981a, 1981b, 1982a, 1982b, 1983a, 1983b, 1984; Werner et al. 1979) resulted from this study.

Another important line of research that is doing much to elucidate prehistorical and historical adaptation to the cerrado habitat is the archaeological and ethnoarchaeological work of Wüst and her colleagues (Wüst 1984, 1987, 1990, n.d., and this volume).

In this essay I describe some features that, in my opinion, distinguish human adaptation to the cerrado, using illustrations from the literature and from my field observations. I then summarize some ethnohistorical evidence relating to the response of the Xavante and other Gê groups to contact. This evidence suggests that their flexible subsistence strategies and widespread social networks favored the survival of these groups as they faced successive fronts of European penetration.

After the initial contact between Indians and whites, the frequency of unpredictable disturbances increased. Resources might disappear, as game was driven away, or access to gallery forests along rivers was blocked by cattle raisers and mining settlements. The entire population of a village might be killed or enslaved, or a local population might be practically wiped out by an epidemic. The partially nomadic groups appear to have had a certain survival advantage over those that were more sedentary due to greater agricultural commitment, since the flexibility of their economies and social structures allowed them to resist by abandoning some resources from which they were cut off by colonial settlement and adopting others, including predation on the colonists' crops and cattle. As Irons (1974) showed for pastoral nomads, when mobility allows people to defend themselves effectively against external threats, it is valued as a means of maintaining their political independence.

The Cerrado Habitat

D. Harris (1980b, 3) places the Brazilian cerrado in the Intermediate Tropical or Savanna Zone, which he defines according to the length of the dry season, for while savanna plant communities vary, "all tropical savanna ecosystems are adapted to a winter dry season that checks plant growth."

Not only are savanna habitats temporally variable, since the amount of rainfall tends to vary from year to year, they also are geographically patchy. These general features of savanna environments are factors that shaped human adaptation to savanna living, favoring "seasonally scheduled exploitation of a mosaic of resources" (D. Harris 1980a, 31).

The cerrado is even more diversified in vegetational forms than most other savanna regions (Parsons 1980, 268), ranging from closed-canopy forest to grass with or without scattered trees and shrubs. Relatively dense low scrub is the most common form. "As a rough estimate, in 70 percent of the cerrado area today (discounting the up-to-now small fraction deliberately cleared by cutting) the woody plants are too dense to permit a jeep to be driven through" (Eiten 1972, 202).

According to Eiten, cerrado vegetation grows back vigorously after burning, and the taller shrubs and trees, protected by their thick, corky bark, sprout again from their burned trunks and branches. D. Harris points out that fire has a number of different ecological effects and that humans have used it purposefully since earliest times: "There can be little doubt that fire was early used to drive game and to attract animals to the salty ash and fresh herbaceous growth of burned ground. Fire set during the dry season after tuberous plants have accumulated starch in their underground organs, also makes foraging for roots, tubers, and other plants easier" (D. Harris 1980a, 32).

Medina (1980, 310) notes that, as well as increasing aboveground organic matter by about 30 percent, fire apparently increases the activity of plant root systems and thus stimulates higher nutrient uptake from the soil.

It would appear that the cerrado presents varied opportunities for human subsistence. The patchy nature of resource distribution suggests that these resources would best be exploited by extensive strategies involving a large territory for each group.

Agriculture

Central Brazilian groups have been considered "incipient agriculturalists" in that they depended to a large extent on gathering wild foods. Yet there is little reason to believe that they were hunter-gatherers only recently converted to cultivation. Archaeological investigation in Mato Grosso, in a region occupied historically by Bororo groups, has demonstrated that agriculture was practiced by groups, probably of the Uru tradition, by the beginning of the Christian era (Wüst 1987, and this volume). It appears, however, that in historical times the procurement of wild species, including game, plant foods, and materials for manufacture, was often at least as important a determinant in central Brazilian scheduling of activities as were the requirements of agriculture. Although cerrado groups varied in their degree of reliance on agriculture, none of them, until recently, was reported to be dependent year-round on crops for its food supply.

Even the Apinayé who, according to Nimuendaju (1967, 87–90), raised an extensive repertoire of crops, did not intensify agriculture to the point where it would interfere with seasonal trekking. After planting their clearings, most of the villagers went on trek until harvest time, leaving only two ritual guardians to watch over and perform ceremonies to promote the growth of the crops.

The Crop Complex

It appears that manioc was less important for most cerrado groups than for those in the tropical forest. Maize was the staple of the Bororo and the Xavante, although according to Nimuendaju (1946, 58) both the Northwestern and Central Gê emphasized sweet potatoes and yams.

The familiarity of the Northwestern Gê with manioc seems to be well documented; Nimuendaju (1946, 58) points out that they probably did not borrow its use either from the Tupi or the Karajá, "whose methods of employment and preparation are totally distinct." He further cites the term *kwur* for manioc as distributed over the entire Northwestern Gê branch. It is curious that the present-day Xavante use the word *upá* for manioc, and Martius (1867, 141), in his Xerente vocabulary collected early in the nineteenth century, cited *kupá* as the Xerente term for that crop. Nimuendaju (1946, 59) tells us that kupá is a distinctive cultigen, a creeper (*Cissus* sp.) with starchy tendrils that are baked in earth ovens: "It does not occur wild; is restricted, so far as my information goes, to the Eastern and Western Timbira and the Xerente, all of them Gê tribes; and is pronouncedly xerophil. Accordingly, it is probably a very old cultivated species peculiar to these tribes, which could not have borrowed it from either Neobrazilians or any of their present Indian neighbors."

Posey (1983, 235) identifies kupá as *Cissus gonglyloses*, and found four domesticated varieties of kupá cultivated by the Kayapó. The Kayapó also collect wild kupá and plant it in forest fields along trekking routes. It seems possible that the Xavante/Xerente, when introduced to manioc, used for it the term for the cultigen with which they were more familiar.

In the 1950s the Xavante were probably among the most nomadic of central Brazilian groups. The only crops they grew were maize, beans, and pumpkins. When Maybury-Lewis (1974, 49) asked the Xavante why they did not grow manioc, since they were so fond of eating the manioc flour that the Indian Protection Service distributed to them after pacification, some replied that the cultivation of manioc required too much attention, and it would prevent them from going out on trek.

The Xavante preference for short-term crops does not imply a recent acquaintance with agriculture. One indication that they have been cultivating for a long time is that the Xavante, like several other central Brazilian groups, grow an archaic variety of maize known to botanists as "interlocked soft corn." This race of maize is found only around the western and southern margins of the Amazon Basin (Brieger et al. 1958, 199–214). Brieger collected samples of this corn variety from the Bororo, the Tapirapé, and the Xavante. He suggests that the interlocking of adjacent alveoli in this unique variety is not the result of recent breeding but is "a primitive character, dating from the very early days of breeding and domestication" (Brieger et al. 1958, 211), which had the favorable effect of increasing the number of kernels per ear. The limited geographic distribution of interlocked varieties might be explained by climatic adaptation. "If the genes for interlocking and for climatic adaptation were correlated after a first period of adaptation in the Amazon Basin, this would explain that genes neither spread outside the region nor became lost within the region" (Brieger et al. 1958, 211).

Although the Xavante have now adopted upland rice as their staple, largely for commercial reasons, maize continues to have great ceremonial importance for them. When Maybury-Lewis (1974, 47) was with them in the late 1950s the Xavante cultivated seven named strains of maize, distinguished by color. In 1977, when I lived with the same group, they continued to keep the seed of the varieties separate in gourds carefully stoppered with beeswax, and since all the maize was used for food in the same ways, their reason for doing so appeared to be aesthetic. Maize loaves, baked in the ashes of household fires, are an important ceremonial food. As Maybury-Lewis (1974, 42) wrote, "the Shavante, in common with other Gê tribes, value meat and maize as the basis of all ceremonial prestations. They cannot in theory be substituted by any other food of which they may happen to have a surplus."

An interesting aspect of Xavante use of maize is that this, perhaps the most completely domesticated of all crops, was the primary food during periods of aggregation when its symbolic role was to reinforce the solidarity of the community through ceremonial redistribution. By contrast, tubers, which are found in wild, domesticated, and semidomesticated forms, were their staple during periods of nomadism.

The exchange of maize varieties may also have played a role in intergroup trade. The Xavante are especially fond of a variety of maize with bright red kernels. An older man told me that the Xavante acquired seed of the red maize from the "Tepe Tede'wa"—that is, the "Fish People" (Karajá or Canoeiro?)—with whom they traded on the banks of the Araguaia. The Fish People would appear suddenly in the river holding ears of maize out of the water. If they were startled or didn't want to trade, the Fish People would submerge and swim away under water. But sometimes they came out on the bank and traded. The Xavante exchanged game for their fish, and the Tepe Tede'wa gave the Xavante seeds of their red maize.

Hunting

Whether game resources are more likely to be abundant in savanna regions than in the tropical forest is a question that has been debated (Kiltie 1980, 543), and there seems to be little agreement. Hershkovitz (1972, 397) states that the fauna of central Brazil is more varied than that of any other part of the South American continent. He refers to the Brazilian uplands as a "faunal center" where the terrestrial animals that now occupy all of Amazonia evolved. In any case, because of greater visibility and the use of fire to surround game in the dry season, group hunting is probably more effectively practiced in the cerrado than in the tropical forest.

My data (Flowers 1983b, 362) indicate that collective hunting is considerably more productive for the Xavante than individual hunting. One of the reasons for this may be that the principal species captured, in numbers, is white-lipped peccary. White-lipped peccary run in herds, and are highly mobile, so that their appearance in any one place tends to be rare and unpredictable (Kiltie 1980, 542). This would place a premium on cooperation and exchange of information among hunters (Dyson-Hudson and Smith 1978, 24–25).

Productive group hunting might tend to exhaust game species in a given area, but since central Brazilian groups spent much of their time on trek, moving over a wide area, predation was spread over a range of hunting zones. This extensive exploitation would be less likely to affect game resources than the typical tropical forest pattern of exploitation in which hunting parties depart year-round from a fixed settlement (Hames 1980; Vickers 1980).

Gathering

Another aspect of central Brazilian subsistence was the extent to which wild plant resources, especially tubers, were exploited. "[Tubers] are gathered in large quantities in certain parts of the savanna and provide a nourishing, if starchy, diet. Usually the roots are brought in during the late afternoon or at dusk, the fires are lit (or revived) and half the tubers are put over them to boil in a pot while the other half are roasted in the embers" (Maybury-Lewis 1974, 44).

Giaccaria and Heide (1972, 65), in their ethnography of the Xavante, give native names for fourteen different kinds of roots that the Xavante distinguish as edible. They also make the intriguing comment: "Two or three varieties of these roots are gathered and also cultivated; the small tubers are kept in baskets hung on the posts of the hut, or placed outside on poles until planting." Posey (1983) describes a similar custom among the Gorotire Kayapó of planting wild tubers in "forest fields." It seems that both the Xavante and the Kayapó practiced a form of "nomadic agriculture," to supply themselves while on trek.

It appears that edible tubers are most abundant in tropical savannas, like the cerrado, that have pronounced wet and dry seasons, since they survive drought by accumulating starch in their roots or stems during the season of rain and growth (D. Harris 1977, 209). For example, although the heart of manioc cultivation is most often believed to be the lowlands of northern Colombia (Lathrap 1977; Sauer 1952), more wild manihot species are found in an area that stretches from northeastern Brazil to Mato Grosso and into parts of Paraguay than in any other South American region (Rogers 1963, 52). In reviewing evidence concerning the area of origin of manioc as a crop plant, Renvoise (1972, 356–57) shows that this region has relatively few cultivars of sweet or bitter manioc. It seems possible that cerrado groups, having at their disposal a wide variety of tubers that could be gathered for immediate consumption and replanted for later use, found less need to develop highly productive cultivars.

This stress on gathered plant foods as subsistence staples contrasts with tropical forest groups, who collect a great variety of plants for various purposes (Boom 1987; Carneiro 1970), but not as dietary staples. Tropical forest communities, since they depended almost entirely on their gardens for vegetable food, were forced to plant new gardens whenever they moved, whereas cerrado groups could remain nomadic for an indefinite period because they could provide themselves with plant foods wherever they camped.

Werner (1978, 1983a) found that the Mekranoti, who belong to a Kayapó branch that moved into the tropical forest from the cerrado sometime around the beginning of the nineteenth century, still go on trek, but carry garden produce—sweet potatoes, bananas, manioc roots, and processed manioc flour—with them. However, according to Lukesch (1976, 247), his Kayapó informants maintained that when their people lived on the cerrado, they subsisted entirely on wild food when on trek, and Posey (1983, 242) found that men on hunting treks from the Gorotire Kayapó village relied on foods, principally semidomesticated tubers, planted in "forest fields" along established hunting trails.

Xavante treks, as observed by Maybury-Lewis in the late 1950s, were far from being haphazard; they were carefully planned by the elders to exploit specific resources and might last from six weeks to three or four months (Maybury-Lewis 1974, 53). Maybury-Lewis's map (1974, 54) of Xavante trek routes in 1958 indicates that they traveled as far as eighty miles from their base village. On one trek the specific resources to be collected were scleria seeds, to manufacture ceremonial regalia, and arrow canes. A band that traveled in a different direction was attracted by the abundance of game to be found there. It seems, however, that wherever they went, they could count on gathered plant foods for subsistence.

Even at the present day, when confinement to a reservation limits the area available for wild food collection and dependence on agriculture is greatly increased, the Xavante at Pimentel Barbosa spend much of their dry season subsistence labor time in gathering wild foods. According to my time allocation data, collected in 1976–77 (Flowers 1983a), throughout the dry season, hunting, fishing, and gathering parties left the village for periods from a day to a week or more, often bringing back substantial quantities of food, much of which was shared. During this period, collecting wild food occupied 38 percent of men's subsistence time and 49 percent of women's subsistence time.

Resources, Settlement Pattern, and Warfare

The earliest historical description that we have of a Gê or related group (Barleus 1940; Marcgrave 1942) dates from the seventeenth century. This Dutch account of a "Tapuya" group in northeastern Brazil indicates that they had a mixed economy, alternating seasonal agriculture with periods of nomadism, each accompanied by its corresponding aspect of ceremonial life. The central Brazilian type of social organization, as indicated by the presence of log races and other ceremonial competitions, was apparently fully developed at this time. This suggests that central Brazilian patterns of subsistence and social organization were already established when these groups began their struggle to maintain their resource base and political independence against the advance of the colonial frontier. It seems plausible, as Balée (1984, 253) points out, that some aspects of the cerrado complex, such as large settlements, may have pre-Columbian origins in the competition between Tupians and cerrado groups to control productive riverine and coastal areas.

There are numerous reports of large central Brazilian villages in historical times. Nimuendaju (1967, 6) writes that in the early nineteenth century the population of Apinayé villages ranged from four hundred to fourteen hundred. A plan of a Bororo village drawn at the beginning of the twentieth century shows 140 houses in three concentric circles (Wüst n.d.). A pictorial map reproduced in Chaim (1974), probably drawn around the middle of the eighteenth century by Jesuit missionaries, shows two villages in eastern Goiás. The villages are composed of beehive-shaped houses arranged in horseshoe formation, which indicates that they belonged to Central Gê groups. Captions give the number of houses in the first village as 276, and 396 in the second village, implying a population of well over a thousand for each of them.

There is also archaeological evidence for large villages. The diameter of the agricultural village sites investigated by Wüst (1987) suggests that the largest may have had a population of up to a thousand.

An interesting point is that the Bororo, the Kayapó, and the Xavante all have traditions of a very large village that has great significance in their collec-

tive memory as an "ideal type." In all cases this village broke up, probably as
a result of indirect contact, which as Posey (this volume) points out, may
cause depopulation and social disruption long before so-called "pacification."
The large village of the Eastern Xavante was at a place called "Tsereprê," to
the north of the present Pimentel Barbosa reservation where I did fieldwork.
Apowẽ, the elderly chief, said that he grew up and was initiated there, probably around 1920. He maintained that the village split up, not because people
were quarreling, but because the village had grown very large, and if every-
body stayed, they would eventually start fighting. Apowẽ and his brothers
moved apart and founded new villages but remained on friendly terms.

Do these large villages indicate high overall population density, or rather
a strategy to maintain relatively large territories giving access to varied resources? Such a strategy might imply alliances for defense as well as hostilities with neighboring groups. The presence of large villages that could mobilize two to three hundred warriors might force smaller groups to coalesce
for resistance.

Success in warfare would favor the development of large, well organized
local groups, even though regional population density might not increase if
the groups remained mobile and continued to exploit the resources of their
territory by extensive methods.

Subsistence and Social Ties

Aggregation of nomadic hunter-gatherers into multiband groupings at certain
seasons and dispersal at others are commonly referred to in the literature
(e.g., Lee 1972; Stuart 1977; Wilmsen 1973). In almost all cases the larger
groups are formed when some resource is seasonally concentrated. These
periods of concentration are characterized by more intense social interaction
and economic cooperation (Lee 1972, 181; Steward 1976, 135).

The formation and maintenance of social ties for exchange of information
about the location of resources becomes particularly important in a habitat, like the cerrado, characterized by patchy spatial distribution of resources
and temporal unpredictability. As Kurland and Beckerman (1985, 82) point
out: "The more widely dispersed but more profitable a given food type, the
greater will be the optimal size of the group of foragers who should look for
and share it."

This seasonal pattern of aggregation and dispersal may continue even
when agriculture is considerably developed, as long as the seasonal cycle
includes a period of dependence on wild foods. Cultivation might provide
food to support a large group at a season when another resource could be most

profitably exploited through cooperation. A concentrated supply of vegetable foods would allow hunters with their families to stay together during the period of cooperative hunting. Collective hunts with the use of fire to drive game are described for the Xavante (Flowers 1983b, 362; Maybury-Lewis 1974, 42). Similar game drives are reported by Nimuendaju (1967, 90–93) for the Apinayé, and by Nimuendaju (1946, 65) and Paula Ribeiro (1841, 188) for the Eastern Timbira. These game drives were held after the harvest, at the end of the dry season and, as Maybury-Lewis (1974, 43) notes, were usually held in conjunction with ceremonies, with formal distribution of meat to the entire village.

Practically all central Brazilian groups have elaborate, though basically egalitarian, social structures. Organizational units may include lineages, clans, nondescent moieties, age sets, age grades, and men's societies. Individuals may have special ascribed roles and have "formal friendship" links with other individuals. Both social complexity and ceremonialism appear to vary with group size, since ceremonial life disappears when villages become depopulated, and there is little ceremonial activity during periods of dispersal into foraging bands (Gross 1979; Werner 1984). Organizational complexity finds expression in ceremonials during the season of aggregation.

Johnson (1982) suggests that as an egalitarian group grows larger it has an increasing tendency to disintegrate because of communication breakdown. This problem may be dealt with, at least up to a point, by increasing the size of operational units. Johnson refers to this type of organizational principle as "sequential hierarchy," since, "If consensus were achieved first within nuclear families, then within extended families, a group decision would only require consensus among extended families" (Johnson 1982, 403).

Consensus arrived at through sequential hierarchy is likely to be unstable, however, since a break at any point in the chain can block the achievement of group consensus and lead to splitting away from the larger group of one or more of the organizational units. In fact, one of the characteristics of central Brazilian societies was frequent fission. A disaffected group—sometimes a group of extended families, sometimes a clan, or a men's society (Werner 1980)—might leave to found a new village, or join another.

Central Brazilian social organization, with kin and nonkin sodalities and dyadic ties that extended throughout the tribe, tended to maintain relations among distant villages, even though these relations were often hostile. They formed the basis for political alliances between communities that were economically autonomous and wove a social network around each individual that linked him to distant villages (see Deetz 1968, 284). Maybury-Lewis noted that the Xavante were keenly interested in news from other villages:

"They felt that what happened in other Shavante communities, however remote, politically affected them, especially since they might want to transfer to them at any time" (Maybury-Lewis 1974, 205). If the balance of power shifted in any community, the weaker faction might have to flee or be killed. Right of asylum was universally granted as a matter of reciprocity, for those who granted it might need it themselves at some future time. Those already there accepted into the community on equal terms newcomers, who aligned themselves politically as they saw fit.

As long as the Xavante maintained their exogamous clan system, feuding might have the effect, not of isolating communities, but of linking them more closely; for when a village split left a village demographically dominated by one lineage, young men would have to leave their home village to find wives, in accordance with the matrilocal residence rule (Flowers 1983a, 179). For example, in the early 1950s a group of classificatory brothers came from Marawatsede, a village some two hundred miles to the north, and married five daughters of Apowẽ, the chief of the village at São Domingos.

Other central Brazilian societies put greater stress on nonkin relationships. According to Werner (1980) the Mekranoti could define factions in several different ways: with relatives, through membership in men's societies, or, in one documented case, by age-grade affiliation. On one occasion, a Mekranoti community accepted a previously hostile group into the village because the newcomers shouted "ceremonial friend" to one of the Mekranoti men (Werner, personal communication).

Conflict and Survival

A recurring theme of the Wenner-Gren conference "Amazonian Synthesis: An Integration of Disciplines, Paradigms, and Methodologies" was the profound changes in the social and subsistence systems of native populations brought about by European conquest. However, as Whitehead (1988 and this volume) shows, the impact of contact was unevenly felt, and some groups maintained their autonomy much longer than others. The effects of contact depend, not on the contact situation alone, but on previous patterns of subsistence, settlement, and social organization of the groups involved (see Bates and Plog 1990, 435–40).

There is evidence from historical sources that, as the sedentary Tupians near the coast were wiped out by disease and Portuguese slaving, more mobile peoples from the cerrado expanded eastward, where they raided the European farms and cattle ranches of Bahia. By the early seventeenth century Portuguese settlers were moving up the rivers into the interior of the country, and as they controlled the riverbanks they deprived the Indians of soils most suitable for agriculture. At the same time the Portuguese provided resources that could be captured by mobile groups—fields of crops to raid and cattle that could be hunted as game or driven off to Indian villages and held as a supply of food. Not being dependent for their food supply on growing crops, seminomadic cerrado Indians could join together to attack settlements and then disperse. After arduous marching, during which they were harassed by Indians who killed from ambush, the soldiers who pursued them found only empty villages to burn. As Ferguson and Whitehead (1991, 19) point out, mobility is often a major advantage of indigenous groups resisting state expansion.

At the end of the eighteenth century, when part of the Portuguese population of Goiás emigrated as a result of the exhaustion of the gold mines, Indians abandoned the missions, and a number of groups expanded their territory and intensified their raiding activities.

It is quite possible, as Gross (1979) has suggested, that central Brazilian villages became larger and social organization more elaborate as a result of colonial warfare. At times the Indians were apparently able to organize a large number of warriors to attack settlements in force. In 1762 the Governor of Goiás reported that a large band of Xavante warriors had besieged a mining settlement for several days (RIHGB 1918, 83). The Indians outnumbered the three hundred miners available for defense, who therefore feared to counterattack. Gardner (1970, 319) wrote that in 1788 a mission village was attacked by two hundred Xerente, who killed forty people.

At other times groups were scattered and might wander for several years in the cerrado without planting crops. When they did this, it was usually because they had recently been attacked, had made a raid, or had suffered some other disturbance, such as an epidemic. For example, Xavante informants told me that in 1946, after men from Apowẽ's group killed several members of the first Indian Service team sent to pacify them, they abandoned their village and spent two years on trek without planting crops for fear of reprisals from the whites. Giaccaria and Heide (1972) collected from Xavante informants several accounts that indicate more or less extended periods of nomadism following epidemics and intervillage attacks.

These wandering periods were undoubtedly times of stress and considerable hardship, but the tactic must often have allowed groups to survive catastrophic events, which became more frequent after the invasion of their territory by white colonists. Since the very fact of contact with whites was disruptive, it is not surprising that Western observers who met such groups often believed them to be completely nomadic foragers.

After the gold strikes in south Goiás, the Southern Kayapó became the scourge of the mule trains that traversed the road between Goiás and Cuiabá. As time went on they were increasingly described as treacherous and elusive. In 1760 Governor Mello (RIHGB 1918, 61) wrote: "[The Kayapó] have no fixed dwellings, but wander continuously around the cerrado, living on game and wild fruits." They may indeed have become more nomadic, or merely have appeared so because they had moved their villages westward, as the Xavante did a century later, and were raiding far from them. Social ties with their unpacified kin probably helped some Indians to survive the periodic attempts at settlement in *aldeias* during the eighteenth century. As long as these ties were maintained, settled Indians could rebel and leave when ill-treated, often taking with them the firearms they had learned to use, and resume hostilities. As Governor Mello (RIHGB 1918, 59) commented sourly in a letter to Lisbon: "These [Akroá] are astute and inconstant heathen. They came to the aldeias to see what advantage they could gain; they stayed there only as long as Your Majesty supported them at the cost of the Royal Treasury; none of them cared to learn a trade or to cultivate the soil."

In spite of numerous attempts to make cerrado Indians economically useful, economic ties failed to develop between central Brazilian native groups and the settlers. In the mines black slaves were employed, for the Indians were not only unwilling workers, they quickly died from diseases; nor did cerrado Indians make good boatmen, for, with the exception of the Karajá, they did not build or use canoes. Unlike the tropical forest, the cerrado had few commercialized wild products, such as valuable hardwoods, spices and cacao, and later rubber, that Indians could gather for their masters (see Boxer 1964, 278). As we showed (Gross et al. 1979), it is only recently, with increased circumscription and degradation of their habitat, that some central Brazilian groups have entered the regional market economy.

Conclusions

I have shown that native groups of the cerrado region of central Brazil shared subsistence practices and social systems related to both their physical and sociopolitical environments. Some of these common characteristics are:

1. The exploitation of seasonally and geographically varied resources, including cultivated crops.
2. A settlement pattern that was alternately nucleated and dispersed, and the exploitation of a large territory by each group.

3. A regional rather than localized view, demonstrated by social interaction among geographically scattered groups.

4. Persistence of some regional populations over time, in spite of unpredictable disturbances that led to the extinction of local groups.

Adaptation of central Brazilian native peoples to their environment and to surrounding groups has not come to an end; rather, it has entered a new phase. As central Brazilians interact increasingly with the regional and national economies and political structures, their communities are beginning to support one another in their struggle to retain control over the land that they see as their economic base.

I believe that the emerging definition of broad goals by Xavante, Kayapó, and other native leaders can be explained not only in terms of their present situation, but also by the history of their relationship with their physical and human environment, which, as I have shown, was characterized by opportunistic exploitation of a varied range of resources and by social interaction among geographically dispersed groups.

ACKNOWLEDGMENTS

I should like to thank all the participants in the Wenner-Gren conference, "Amazonian Synthesis: An Integration of Disciplines, Paradigms, and Methodologies," for many hours of productive discussion and exchange of ideas, and especially Anna Roosevelt and Sydel Silverman, who brought us all together.

Much of the research on which this article is based was done as a participant in the project, "Human Ecology in Central Brazil," organized by Daniel Gross and supported by grants from the National Science Foundation and the City University of New York. My work has profited greatly over the years from Dan Gross's continued support, cooperation, and criticism.

REFERENCES

Balée, W.

1984   The ecology of ancient Tupi warfare. In *Warfare, culture, and environment,* edited by R. B. Ferguson, 241–65. New York: Academic Press.

Barleus, C.

1940   *História dos feitos recentement praticados durante oito anos no Brazil e noutras partes.* Translated by Cláudio Brandão. (Original *Rerum per octennium in Brasilia et albi nuper gestarum.* Amsterdam 1647.) Rio de Janeiro: Serviço Gráfico do Ministério da Educação.

Bates, D. G., and F. Plog
1990   Cultural anthropology. 3d ed. New York: McGraw-Hill.

Boom, B. M
1987   Ethnobotany of the Chacobo Indians, Beni, Bolivia. Advances in Economic
        Botany, No. 5. New York: New York Botanical Garden.

Boxer, C. R.
1964   The golden age of Brazil: 1695–1750. Berkeley and Los Angeles: Univer-
        sity of California Press.

Brieger, F. G., J.T.A. Gurgel, E. Paterniani, A. Blumenschein, and M. R. Alleoni
1958   Races of maize in Brazil and other eastern South American countries.
        National Research Council Publication No. 593. Washington, D.C.:
        National Science Foundation.

Carneiro, R. L.
1970   The transition from hunting to horticulture in the Amazon Basin. In
        Eighth congress of anthropological and ethnological sciences, 244–48. Tokyo:
        Science Council of Japan.
1973   Slash-and-burn cultivation among the Kuikuru and its implications for
        cultural development in the Amazon Basin. In Peoples and cultures of
        native South America, edited by D. R. Gross, 98–123. Garden City,
        N.Y.: Natural History Press.

Chaim, M. Matos
1974   Os aldeamentos indígenas da Capitania de Goiás: Sua importância na política
        de povoamento (1749–1811). Goiânia: Oriente.

Deetz, J.
1968   Hunters in archaeological perspective. In Man the hunter, edited by
        R. B. Lee and I. DeVore, 281–85. Chicago: Aldine.

Dyson-Hudson, R., and E. A. Smith
1978   Human territoriality: An ecological reassessment. American Anthropolo-
        gist 80 (1): 21–41.

Eiten, G.
1972   The cerrado vegetation of Brazil. The Botanical Review 38:201–341.

Ferguson, R. B., and N. L. Whitehead
1992   The violent edge of empire. In War in the tribal zone, edited by R. B.
        Ferguson and N. L. Whitehead, 1–30. Santa Fe, N.Mex.: School of
        American Research Press.

Flowers, N. M.
1983a   Forager-farmers: The Xavante Indians of central Brazil. Ph.D. diss., City
        University of New York.
1983b   Seasonal factors in subsistence, nutrition and child growth in a central
        Brazilian Indians community. In Adaptive responses of native Amazonians.
        edited by R. B. Hames and W. T. Vickers, 357–90. New York: Academic
        Press.

Flowers, N. M., D. R. Gross, M. L. Ritter, and D. W. Werner

1982   Variation in swidden practices in four central Brazilian Indian societies. *Human Ecology* 10 (2): 203–17.

Gardner, G.

1970   *Travels in the interior of Brazil, principally through the northern provinces, and the gold and diamond districts, during the years 1836–1841.* New York: AMS Press.

Giaccaria, B., and A. Heide

1972   *Xavante: Auwẽ Uptabi (Povo Autêntico).* São Paulo: Editorial Dom Bosco.

Gross, D. R.

1975   Protein capture and cultural development in the Amazon Basin. *American Anthropologist* 77:526–49.

1979   A new approach to central Brazilian social organization. In *Brazil: Anthropological perspectives: Essays in honor of Charles Wagley,* edited by M. L . Margolis and W. E. Carter, 321–42. New York: Columbia University Press.

1983   Village movement in relation to resources in Amazonia. In *Adaptive responses of native Amazonians,* edited by R. B. Hames and W. T. Vickers, 429–49. New York: Academic Press.

Gross, D. R., G. Eiten, N. M. Flowers, F. M. Leoi, M. L. Ritter, and D. W. Werner

1979   Ecology and acculturation among native peoples of central Brazil. *Science* 206:1043–50.

Hames, R. B.

1980   Game depletion and hunting zone rotation among the Ye'kwana and Yanomamö of Amazonas, Venezuela. In *Studies in hunting and fishing in the neotropics,* edited by R. B. Hames, 31–66. Working Papers on South American Indians No. 2. Bennington, Vt.: Bennington College.

Harris, D. R.

1977   Alternative pathways toward agriculture. In *Origins of agriculture,* edited by C. A. Reed, 179–243. The Hague: Mouton.

1980a   Commentary: Human occupation and exploitation of savanna environments. In *Human ecology in savanna environments,* edited by D. R. Harris, 31–39. New York: Academic Press.

1980b   Tropical savanna environments: Definition, distribution, diversity, and development. In *Human ecology in savanna environments,* edited by D. R. Harris, 3–27. New York: Academic Press.

Hershkovitz, P.

1972   The recent mammals of the neotropical region. In *Evolution, mammals, and southern continents,* edited by A. Keast, F. C. Erk, and B. Glass, 311–431. Albany: SUNY Press.

Irons, W.

1974   Nomadism as a political adaptation: The case of the Yomut Turkmen. *American Ethnologist* 1 (4): 635–58.

Johnson, G. A.
1982   Organizational structure and scalar stress. In *Theory and explanation in archaeology: The Southampton Conference*, edited by C. Renfrew, M. J. Rowland, and B. A. Seagrave, 389–421. New York: Academic Press.

Kiltie, R. A.
1980   Note on Amazonian cultural ecology. *Current Anthropology* 21:541–44.

Kurland, J. A., and S. J. Beckerman.
1985   Optimal foraging and hominid evolution: Labor and reciprocity. *American Anthropologist* 87 (1): 73–93.

Lathrap, D. W.
1970   *The upper Amazon*. New York: Praeger.
1977   Our father the cayman, our mother the gourd; Spinden revisited: Or a unitary model for the emergence of agriculture in the New World. In *Origins of agriculture*, edited by C. A. Reed, 713–51. The Hague: Mouton.

Layton, R., R. Foley, and E. Williams
1991   The transition between hunting and gathering and the specialized husbandry of resources. *Current Anthropology* 32 (3): 255–63.

Lee, R. B
1972   Work effort, group structure, and land use in contemporary hunter-gatherers. In *Man, settlement, and urbanism*, edited by P. J. Ucko, R. Tringham, and G. W. Pimbleby, 176–85. London: Duckworth.

Lévi-Strauss, C.
1967   The social and psychological aspects of chieftainship in a primitive tribe: The Nambikuara of Mato Grosso. In *Comparative political systems*, edited by R. Cohen and J. Middleton, 45–62. New York: Natural History Press.

Lowie, R. H.
1948   The tropical forests: An introduction. In *Handbook of South American Indians*. Vol. 3, edited by J. H. Steward. Washington, D.C.: Smithsonian Institution.

Lukesch, A.
1976   *Mito e vida dos Indios Caiapós*. São Paulo: Livraria Pioneira Editora.

Marcgrave, J.
1942   *História natural do Brasil*. Translated by José Procópio de Magalhães. São Paulo: Imprensa Oficial do Estado. (Original *Historia Naturalis Brasiliae*. Amsterdam/Leyden 1648.)

Martin, M. Kay
1969   South American foragers: A case study in cultural devolution. *American Anthropologist* 71:243–60.

Martius, C.F.P. von
1867   *Beitrage zur ethnographie und sprachenkunde Amerika's zumal Brasiliens*. 2 vols. Leipzig: Friedrich Fleischer.

Maybury-Lewis, D.
1974   *Akwẽ-Shavante society.* New York: Oxford University Press.
1989   Social theory and social practice: Binary systems in central Brazil. In *The attraction of opposites: Thought and society in the dualistic mode,* edited by D. Maybury-Lewis and U. Almogor, 97–116. Ann Arbor: University of Michigan Press.
Maybury-Lewis, D., editor
1979   *Dialectical societies: The Gê and Bororo of central Brazil.* Cambridge, Mass.: Harvard University Press.
Medina, E.
1980   Ecology of tropical American savannas: An ecophysiological approach. In *Human ecology in savanna environments,* edited by D. R. Harris, 297–319. New York: Academic Press.
Meggers, B. J.
1954   Environmental limitations on the development of culture. *American Anthropologist* 56:801–24.
1971   *Amazonia: Man and culture in a counterfeit paradise.* Chicago: Aldine.
Nimuendaju, C.
1946   *The eastern Timbira.* University Publications in American Archaeology and Ethnology No. 41. Berkeley and Los Angeles: University of California Press.
1967   *The Apinayé.* Oosterhout, The Netherlands: Anthropological Publications.
Parsons, James J.
1980   Europeanization of the savanna lands of northern South America. In *Human ecology in savanna environments,* edited by D. R. Harris, 267–89. New York: Academic Press.
Posey, D.
1983   Indigenous ecological knowledge and development of the Amazon. In *The dilemma of Amazonian development,* edited by E. Moran, 225–57. Boulder, Colo.: Westview Press.
Renvoise, B. S.
1972   The area of origin of *Manihot esculenta* as a crop plant—a review of the evidence. *Economic Botany* 26:352–60.
Revista do Instituto Histórico e Geográphico Brasileiro (RIHGB)
1918   Subsídios para a história da Capitania de Goyaz (1756–1806). 84:41–294.
Ribeiro, F. da Paula
1841   Memória sobre as nações gentias que habitam o continente de Maranhão—escripta em 1819. *Revista do Instituto Histórico e Geográphico Brasileiro,* Vol. 3.

Rogers, D. J.
1963   Studies of Manihot esculanta crantz and related species. Bulletin of the
            Torrey Botanical Club 90:43–54.
Roosevelt, A. C.
1980   Parmana: Prehistoric maize and manioc subsistence along the Amazon and
            Orinoco. New York: Academic Press.
1987   Chiefdoms in the Amazon and Orinoco. In Chiefdoms in the Americas,
            edited by R. D. Drennan and C. A. Uribe, 153–84. Lanham, Md.: Uni-
            versity Press of America.
Rubin, J., N. M. Flowers, and D. R. Gross
1986   The adaptive dimensions of leisure. American Ethnologist 13 (3):
            524–36.
Sauer, C. O.
1952   Agricultural origins and dispersals. New York: American Geographical
            Society.
Steward, J.
1976   Theory of culture change. Urbana: University of Illinois Press.
Steward, J. H., and L. C. Faron.
1959   Native peoples of South America. New York: McGraw Hill.
Stuart, D. E.
1977   Seasonal phases in ona subsistence, territorial distribution, and organiza-
            tion: Implications for the archaeological record. In Theory building in
            archaeology, edited by L. R. Binford, 251–83. New York: Academic
            Press.
Vickers, W. T.
1980   An analysis of Amazonian hunting yields as a function of settlement age.
            In Studies in hunting and fishing in the neotropics, edited by R. B. Hames,
            7–29. Working Papers in South American Indians No. 2. Bennington,
            Vt.: Bennington College.
Werner, D. W.
1978   Trekking in the Amazon. Natural History 87 (9): 42–55.
1980   The making of a Mekranoti chief: The psychological and social deter-
            minants of leadership in a native South American society. Ph.D. diss.,
            City University of New York.
1981a   Are some people more equal than others? Status inequality among the
            Mekranoti Indians of central Brazil. Journal of Anthroplogical Research 37
            (4): 360–73.
1981b   Gerontocracy among the Mekranoti of central Brazil. Anthropological
            Quarterly 54 (1): 15–27.
1982a   Chiefs and presidents: A comparison of leadership traits in the United
            States and among the Mekranoti-Kayapó of central Brazil. Ethos 10 (2):
            136–48.

1982b   Leadership inheritance and acculturation among the Mekranoti of central Brazil. *Human Organization* 41 (4): 342–45.

1983a   Why do the Mekranoti trek? In *Adaptive responses of native Amazonians*, edited by R. B. Hames and W. T. Vickers, 225–38. New York: Academic Press.

1983b   Fertility and pacification among the Mekranoti of central Brazil. *Human Ecology* 11 (2): 227–45.

1984   *Amazon Journey.* New York: Simon and Schuster.

Werner, D. W., N. M. Flowers, M. L. Ritter, and D. R. Gross

1979   Subsistence productivity and hunting effort in native South America. *Human Ecology* 7:303–15.

Whitehead, N. L.

1988   *Lords of the tiger spirit: A history of the Caribs in colonial Venezuela and Guyana 1498–1820.* Dordrecht, Holland: Foris.

Wilmsen, E. N.

1973   Interaction, spacing behavior, and the organization of hunting bands. *Journal of Anthropological Research* 29:1–31.

Wüst, I.

1983   A pesquisa etnoarqueólogica entre os Bororos do Mato Grosso. *Estudos Goiânos* 10 (2): 155–63.

1984   A pesquisa etnoarqueológica entre os Bororos do Mato Grosso. *Arquivo do Museu de História Natural.* Universidade Federal de Minas Gerais 8/9:285–96.

1987   A ocupação pre-colonial em uma area nuclear Bororo entre os Rios Vermelho e Garças, Mato Grosso. Paper presented at the Meeting of the Sociedade Arqueológica Brasileira, Santos, September, 1987.

1990   Continuidade e Mudança: Para uma interpretação dos grupos ceramistas pre-coloniais na bacia do Rio Vermelho, MT. Ph. D. diss., Universidade de São Paulo.

n.d.   A pesquisa arqueológica e etnoarqueológica no território Bororo, Mato Grosso: Primeiros Resultados. MS.

12

Environmental and Social Implications of Pre- and Postcontact Situations on Brazilian Indians

The Kayapó and a New Amazonian Synthesis

DARRELL ADDISON POSEY

Modern indigenous societies probably bear little resemblance to their precontact antecedents. Drastic depopulation due to European diseases and dominance left only remnants of aboriginal societies. The Northern Kayapó, for example, once lived in large villages with a complex age-grade and lineage organization. As a result of epidemics prior to first recorded face-to-face "contact" with the whites, large groups split into small, dispersed villages. This dispersion had significant effects on regional flora and fauna, as well as provoking major social changes. Since many of these modifications are recent, old village sites can still be located and excavated, thereby giving unique opportunities to combine ethnohistory, archaeology, ethnography, and ethnoecology to trace and document dramatic changes in indigenous populations during the transition from pre- to postcontact times. The Kayapó case provides an excellent opportunity to test many of the theories that are proposed for a new Amazonian synthesis.

Studies suggest that aboriginal populations in the New World tropics were considerably larger than previously assumed (Denevan 1976; Dobyns 1966; Hemming 1978; Lathrap 1968; Myers 1973, 1974; Sweet 1974). Indigenous agricultural and ecological management systems have likewise been shown to be more sophisticated and productive than expected (Alcorn 1981; Balée 1989a, 1989b; Balée and Gély 1989), and consequently, offer a higher aboriginal population potential (Barbira-Scazzochio 1981; Moran 1981).

Other prevailing misconceptions have also been undermined. For example, it is no longer accepted that indigenous agricultural systems of interfluvial, lowland tropical groups were simple and poorly developed or "marginal" (Balée 1989b; Goodland and Irwin 1975; Posey 1985; cf. Meggers 1971); nor that all tropical ecological zones are insufficiently fertile to sustain substantial human populations (Moran 1979, 1981; Roosevelt 1989a, 1989b; Smith 1980).

Scientists have also underestimated the importance of gathered products and obscure sources of proteinlike insects and nuts (DeFoliart 1990; Ramos-Elorduy 1990). Generally overlooked are the extensive categories of semi-domesticated plants and animals from secondary reforestation vegetation (usually misleadingly named "abandoned fields"), "nomadic agriculture," and "forest fields" (Posey 1983, 1985). Thus, it is evident that the long-standing debates concerning "carrying capacity" and "protein capture" are based on inadequate data at best. In short, a new synthesis is necessary to establish more accurate models of subsistence and diet, especially in relation to political and social organization of aboriginal Amazonians.

Disease, Contact, and History

Kayapó History

"Initial contact" is frequently assumed to be the first recorded episode of face-to-face interaction. A mistaken corollary is that what was observed during initial contact was a pristine Indian population free from European influence. Descriptions of social and political organization, rituals and artifacts, as well as population estimates are frequently based upon these assumptions. According to Ribeiro (1970), for example, the Gorotire Kayapó were first contacted in 1936. Verswijver (1985, 41), however, shows that some Kayapó groups had contact with Europeans nearly a century earlier. Horace Banner, the missionary who established "first contact" in 1936, wrote in his unpublished diary[1] that the Kayapó were "pacificado" because they were too weak from European diseases and resulting intergroup warfare to further resist whites. Frei Gil Vilanova, a Dominican priest, established the Mission of Santa Anna Nova in 1860 to serve the Kayapó who lived along the Araguaia River. He helplessly watched the Indians die off due to successive epidemics (Krause 1911). Nonetheless, when Coudreau arrived at the Mission in 1896, he still found five thousand Pau d'Arco Kayapó living in four villages, the largest of which had approximately fifteen hundred inhabitants (Coudreau 1897).[2] Only fifty years after Coudreau's visit, however, the Pau d'Arco were extinct as a group (Dobyns 1966, 413–14; Vellard 1956, 78–79).[3]

Disease and Effects

Typhus, yellow fever, and malaria are frequently written into historical epidemiological records (Crosby 1972, 73–121; Dobyns 1966; McNeill 1976, 176–207). The effects of European "childhood" diseases like mumps, measles, whooping cough, and flu were disastrous (cf. Crosby 1972; Davis 1977; McNeill 1976). It is not uncommon to find 85 to 90 percent of any given Indian group destroyed by a rapid series of epidemics (Dobyns 1966; Hemming 1978, 139, 492; Myers 1974; Sweet 1974, 78–80, 589–82).

In one epidemic of measles in a Northern Kayapó village (Kokrajmoro), 34 percent of an inoculated population died within two weeks. The dead included everyone over the age of forty, except for two old women (Earl Trapp, personal communication). This particular epidemic took place in a village that had been officially contacted for nearly twenty years. One can only imagine what effect such epidemics had upon uninoculated populations. The village was left with no one to tend the crops or even gather ripened produce. The village was weakened to the point that, had it not been for emergency medical aid from a missionary team, the entire group would have disappeared. Kokrajmoro did survive, but with its cultural and social systems severely disrupted, since grandparents play central roles in cultural transmission (Murphy 1991). There were no elders to teach the essential rituals to insure healthy crops, or anyone to perform the ceremonies of naming that perpetuate the unique inheritance system.

The Kayapó have ceremonial activities that are highly differentiated, with specialized roles being performed by representatives of specific lineage groups (Lea 1986). Rapid depopulation, therefore, can provoke the elimination of entire ceremonies, and rituals disappear as elders and their knowledge disappear. Kokrajmoro, like villages of many other indigenous groups before and after it, fell instantly into the throes of chaotic deculturation. Subsequently, in an attempt to reestablish cultural transmission, village leaders brought an elder male (Manduka), known for his traditional knowledge, from Kikretum village (some 380 kilometers distant) to live and teach in Kokrajmoro. No matter how knowledgeable the elder, he could pass on only a small part of the richness of Kayapó male tradition.

A Disease-Contact Typology

Diseases can be analyzed based upon the ways they are transmitted. Diseases do not always have to have direct human carriers, since epidemics can easily precede initial face-to-face contact (Crosby 1972, 51). As described in detail elsewhere (Posey 1987), "contact" situations can be separated into three

categories based on the epidemiological nature of interaction between Indians and Europeans:

1. Indirect contact, which includes disease transmission without any human
   intermediaries, such as through insect and animal reservoirs and vectors.
2. Intermediate contact, which depends upon temporary or chance contact
   with groups or individuals such as traders, soldiers, rubber tappers, run-
   away slaves, and other Indians who have already been in contact with
   Europeans and their diseases.
3. Direct contact, which comes from sustained contact with missionaries,
   white communities, hostages and marriage partners from other groups
   already in contact.

A Schism and Dispersal Model

Present-day Northern Kayapó groups lived in one ancestral village, Pyka-
tô-ti, at the beginning of this century. The "Great" or "Beautiful Village"
(Kri-mêx) had two Men's Houses, one oriented toward the east (sunrise) and
the other toward the west (sunset). Each was headed by a Benadjwyàrà-rax
(strong chief) and subdivided into numerous subgroups with their own chiefs.
Complementary female chiefs and organizations mirrored those of the men
(Posey 1979, 1985).

Although Pyka-tô-ti was permanently inhabited, trekking groups would
leave for trips that ranged from a few weeks to several months. The travelers
would return to the village with captives, valuable feathers, ritual items,
booty, and abundant meat for the festivals and ceremonies that inevitably
followed (and often prompted) such treks. Pyka-tô-ti would swell with inhabitants during these ceremonial periods, often utilizing structures in all
three of its concentric circles. Due to udjy (sorcery) and kane (disease), the
great village began to break up from fear of the karon (spirits) of the many
who began to die from unknown diseases. The Kayapó traditionally abandon
a house if multiple deaths occur; and an entire village site can be abandoned
if many households are afflicted with death as during an epidemic.

Some Indians would periodically return to the great village in order to
maintain their old fields, or to unite temporarily with scattered subgroups
and relatives to enact important annual and name-giving ceremonies. Eventually (probably by 1919), Pyka-tô-ti was totally abandoned as hostility between subgroups increased. By the time that missionaries and the National
Indian Foundation (FUNAI) "contacted" the Gorotire Kayapó in 1936, Pyka-
tô-ti was history. Only fragmented, disintegrated remnants of the once highly
organized Kayapó could be observed.

Disease and mortality in Kayapó villages still lead to accusations of udjy. Turner (1965, 210), Verswijver (1978, 1985) and Bamberger (1966, 35–39) documented specific cases where individual Kayapó were accused of causing disease outbreaks. Under such situations, the accused must either flee the village with family and loyal relatives or face being killed. If one insists on innocence, then the accused and perhaps his extended kin group may choose to fight (*aben tak*) the accuser and the accuser's extended kin. The loser in this dramatic, stylized, and deadly serious battle must leave the village. Thus, major chunks of a village population were split due to accusations of udjy; other groups fled in fear of the karon or for other reasons.

Impact of Dispersion and Deculturation

Sociocultural Reduction

The dispersal of Kayapó groups led to the immediate collapse of the traditional *ngà-be* (east-west Men's House) system. Two Benadjwyàrà-rax were inadequate to coordinate the several scattered subgroups, leaving former subchiefs to assume responsibility. Since the breakup of Pyka-tô-ti, the Kayapó have not been able to establish a single village with both Men's Houses, or agree upon, who, in modern times, should be the Benadjwyàrà-rax.

Individual villages were associated with either the eastern or western ngà-be, except for Gorotire, which became an "attraction post" (*posto de atraição*), or FUNAI post to entice Kayapó groups to make peaceful contact with whites. Gorotire became filled with representatives of all the Kayapó subgroups, and consequently, became a microcosm of Kayapó beliefs and practices. A single Men's House was established in Gorotire, but, in fact, its members come from both eastern and western traditions. This can be illustrated by the burial practices of peoples from the different Men's Houses. The Eastern House buries with the head facing east; the Western House buries facing west. In Gorotire, however, burials occur in both orientations (personal communication, Kwyrà-kà Kayapó).

As a result of its diverse mixture, Gorotire shows great variations in the myths, songs, stories, and rituals that are presented in the village. Debates over which version is the *djyjarejn kumrenx* ("true" tradition) are frequent. These variations reflect the special knowledge held by individuals and family groups that, at the time of breakup, were differentially distributed by chance and historical occurrences.

Kayapó ceremonies and festivals are characterized by the complex integration of many specialized ritual parts "owned" by *nekrêx* (inheritance groups) (Lea 1986). If the nekrêx is without a representative in any given village, the festival that requires that specialized missing part cannot be performed. In some cases, entire festivals have died out due to lack of surviving ritual specialists to perform essential parts, The We-We (Butterfly) Festival is such an example. Kayapó elders can name many festivals that are no longer practiced for this reason.

Thus, dispersal of Kayapó groups led to a reduction of festivals due to the lack of a critical mass and necessary ritual specialists to carry out the ceremonies. The same process must have occurred in other areas of knowledge and practice, resulting in cultural fragmentation and reduction.

One can speculate on the preponderance of "Bep" names as one possible example of this reduction process. Bep names are given during the Bemp festival and were once thought to be the highest status names of the Kayapó. But as other naming ceremonies became more difficult or impossible to perform, Bemp remained relatively easy to perform due to the survival of Bemp "knowers." As a result, the name "Bep" is now very common, and although it is still considered an *idjy mêx* (beautiful name), it no longer connotes such a high status.

The clearest evidence of knowledge reduction is with Kayapó shamans and traditional medicine knowers. They have special powers and deal with physical and spiritual illnesses (Elisabetsky and Posey, 1989; Posey 1982). Most of the *wayanga kunrenx* (true shamans) died or were killed due to epidemics and inter- or intragroup fighting. In their place came the apprentices, "weak" shamans, and those with little experience. By default, the title of "wayanga" fell onto those who in past generations would have been considered unprepared, or undesirable for such an important role.

The deculturation/disintegration process stimulated the appearance of many *mẽkute-pidjà-mari* (plant knowers), who do not claim to deal with spirits but only with the curative properties of certain plants. These "knowers" specialize in certain families of plants (Elisabetsky and Posey 1989; Poser 1982) and the diseases they cure. In the village of Gorotire, over 25 percent of the population claims to be a mẽkute-pidjà-mari. One can hypothesize that the abundance of such specialists was stimulated by the loss of "true shamans" and, as a result, loss of medical advice during a time of increased illness.

Contact with FUNAI and missionaries provoked other changes that resulted in creation of alternative social structures and loss of traditional Kayapó ways. In Gorotire, for example, the mission church has its own organization centered around the Indian pastor and church leaders. The church structure sometimes competes with the chiefs for power, attention, and resources, creating conflicts between the Crentes (Christians) and the rest of the community. On two occasions over the past fifty years, the missionaries have been expelled from Gorotire, always to be invited back because of their access to merchandise, transport, and medicines. The Brazilian FUNAI has favored male leaders as *the* spokespersons for the villages. Consequently, female chiefs have disappeared, and those males who speak Portuguese have climbed to positions of greatest importance. Most modern male chiefs do not even know the ceremonial language, or Ben, for which their office was named (*mẽbenadjwyrà*, or "giver of the Ben").

Both the missionaries and FUNAI encouraged the Kayapó to wear clothes. But Kayapó themselves decided to abandon some of their most characteristic traditions, such as the *amuh mẽtôrô* (Wasp Dance), during which warriors are repeatedly stung by wasps during a ceremonial "fight." The Tep Djwa (fish tooth), a gourd paddle embedded with very sharp fish teeth and used for scarification of young boys who misbehaved, was also discarded. Use of large ear spools and lip plugs also died out. All of these losses were due to the same reason; the Kayapó felt *pia'am* (ashamed) of such practices because of the way they were viewed by whites.

Nomadic Agriculture

With the dispersal of Kayapó subgroups, useful biological species and natural-resource management strategies also spread. Agricultural plots could be maintained for permanent and semipermanent villages like Pyka-tô-ti, but nomadic groups depend more heavily upon other types of management, such as trail-side plantings and "forest fields." Trail systems were extensive in the Kayapó area, and their margins served as areas for planting, transplanting, and spreading numerous semidomesticated plant species used for food, medicine, building materials, dyes, scents, insect repellents, and so on. Forest fields were made either by felling large trees in the forest or by utilizing *bà-krê-ti* (natural forest openings) into which seeds, cuttings, seedlings, and tubers of useful species were introduced. These concentrations of useful resources required little or no human care after planting.

Special "war gardens" (usually known as *krai-kam-puru*) were planted in forested hills near trails, villages, or campsites (Gottsberger and Posey, in preparation, Posey, 1983, 1985). These secret gardens not only served as emergency sources for food, but also as germplasm banks where stocks of useful species could always be found if necessary.

The strategy of producing hidden "resource islands" extended to the production of *apête*, or islands, of resources in the campo-cerrado (Anderson and Posey 1985, 1989; Posey and Gottsberger forthcoming). Apête were produced by introducing colonizing plants into small mounds of enriched planting material in the savanna. These plantings grew and were further molded to provide forest "islands" filled with requisite species for human and animal survival.

Trailside plantings, forest fields, war garden, and apête form part of an ancient Kayapó "nomadic agriculture" system (Posey 1983, 1985). The system allowed warriors to have food sources during long treks and war raids. Other Kayapó used them on extended family treks and during journeys to distant villages. This system gave the Kayapó needed flexibility during periods when agricultural plots were abandoned or inaccessible due to enemy activity. As soon as feasible, Kayapó groups would reestablish their regular agricultural plots. As long as intra- and intergroup raids existed, however, dependence on agriculture remained difficult. The prevalence of *puru* (fields) probably shrank and grew as a function of warfare and peace. Today, with no open hostilities remaining, "nomadic agriculture" has been all but abandoned; only a few older people can describe the system in detail. In contrast, agriculture is flourishing in all Kayapó villages.

Ecological and Biological Consequences

Dispersal of Kayapó groups meant the dispersal of domesticated and semidomesticated species traditionally exploited by the Kayapó (for a partial list see Posey 1984; Anderson and Posey 1985; Posey and Gottsberger forthcoming). Possibly, with the greater range of Kayapó groups, the number of varieties or species drastically increased as new plants were encountered. Certainly, many varieties traditionally used by different family groups were carried wherever its members went.

Informant Kwyrà-kà told of his treks between the Araguaia and Tapajós rivers as a young warrior. He described a special basket used by the old men to carry roots, seeds, and cuttings for planting along the trails or at home villages. Transportation of germ plasm was one of the major functions of any trek; tribal elders alone were entrusted with this important task.

Near Gorotire village, Anderson and Posey (1985, 1989) found that useful species from an area the size of Western Europe had been concentrated into a ten-hectare apête study area. In recent years, Chief Pombo (Tut) was seen many times wandering off into the old fields and apête of Gorotire to snatch up cuttings for his new village downstream. Plants remain one of the most common gifts exchanged between Kayapó visitors from different villages. Establishment of new villages always means the establishment of a stock of necessary plants from the parent villages.

Cognitive maps by Kayapó informants show that Brazil nut, babaçu, açai and bacaba groves are associated with ancestral villages and campsites. Planting these trees is part of an ancient tradition and often marks sites of human occupation. Such trees are but a few of the most easily recognizable markers of habitation sites. Shaman Beptopup took an English film crew and me to film old village sites near Conceição do Araguaya in 1988.[4] He had little difficulty locating the sites by interpreting the vegetation, though the sites had been abandoned for approximately fifty years.

Archaeobotany has been little utilized by scientists to locate, characterize, and interpret prehistoric and historic Indian sites. Yet, in most cases, characteristic plants can be identified easily by informants and surveyed with traditional botanical collection methods. Aerial, or even satellite, images can also be used once the botanical diagnostic profile has been completed for old village, camp, and field sites.

As periodically used campsites turned into permanent villages, forest areas used for agriculture also began to be transformed into *ibê* (old fields). Old fields are important links in the overall Kayapó management process, since they are filled with semidomesticated species as well as with animals that are attracted to their low, bushy vegetation. Ibê are difficult to detect except by the trained eye and are frequently confused with "natural forest." Probably, much of what has been considered "natural" in the Amazon is, in fact, modified by prehistorical and historical Amerind populations (Balée, 1989a, 1989b; Posey 1985). Although some efforts have been made to map and locate secondary growth and old fields with satellite imagery, little published data is available.

Likewise, soil-management methods led to improvements in agricultural soils and the formation of "terra preta dos Índios." The extensive accumulation of these rich anthropogenic (anthrosols) soils is most important along the banks of the Amazon River (Smith 1980). Similar processes also occurred in interfluvial areas, such as with the Kayapó (Hecht and Posey 1989, 1990). As scattered villages grew and peace allowed for the flourishing of agricultural activities, more land came under cultivation, and consequently, more soils were affected.

The Past Meets the Future: Steps to the New Synthesis

A New Scientific Synthesis

Given the richness of oral tradition and memory of elders who actually lived in old villages such as Pyka-tô-ti, the Kayapó offer a unique opportunity to compare oral tradition with archaeological and ethnobiological information. Since 1982, the Kayapó Project has accumulated extensive data on ethnobiological aspects of Kayapó culture, including extensive soil, botanical, and zoological collections; ethnoecological, ethnopedological, ethnomedical,

ethnopharmacological, and agricultural studies, as well as classic sociopolitical research, make the Kayapó one of the best documented Amazonian indigenous groups. It is therefore possible to correlate archaeological theory and
subsistence models with living and historic populations.

For example, comparative soil analyses can show how modern soil modifications led to the formation of "terra preta dos Índios." Likewise, old camp
and village sites, as well as trail systems, can be mapped and located using
living informants and checked with botanical indicator species also provided
by the Kayapó.

In some cases, myth and legend can be correlated with historical events to
provide ethnohistorical markers. For example, the Kayapó myth of the origin
of agriculture offers a unique opportunity to correlate celestial markers with
actual astronomical dates. According to the myth, agriculture was given to
the ancestors by the daughter of the rain, Nhàk-pôk-ti, represented by the
planet Venus. This event occurred when Venus appeared in the midday sky
during a total eclipse of the sun. The exact position is recorded as being in
the southeast quadrant of an area defined by the east-west path of the sun and
moon, cut at approximately a ninety degree (90°) angle by the Milky Way.
Using astronomical data, one can calculate dates in the past when this event
could have occurred (Campos and Posey 1990). This date, in turn, can be
correlated with archaeological evidence from the actual site.

A new scientific synthesis for Amazonia depends upon interdisciplinary
research and, in turn, the correlation of that research with oral tradition and
actual ethnographic practice.

A New Indigenous Synthesis

The Kayapó themselves are trying to reconstruct and restructure their own
society. They still speak frequently about the building of a Kri-mêx or Great
Village, with two Men's Houses. There is a great desire to build up the Kayapó
population to compensate for losses during the decades of epidemics and
warfare.

Two recent events show how the old structures of Kayapó society have been
adapted for modern use: The first was in 1988 during the demonstration of
Kayapó warriors against the prosecution of two of their chiefs, who had gone
to the World Bank to oppose construction of dams on their Xingu River lands
(cf. Posey 1989a, 1989b). Traditional war oratory and dances were used by the
demonstrators as they closed some of the main arteries in Belém, the regional
capital. Representatives of most Kayapó subgroups were present and were
organized with remarkable precision and control under village leaders and
special war chiefs. The event showed how the Kayapó were not only capable of

effectively reintegrating their society, but also of adapting their organization and culture to manipulate the mass media that covered the demonstration.

Shortly thereafter (February 1989), an even larger media event was held in Altimira, Pará, the proposed site of the dams. The "Altimira Encounter" was one of the most significant events in the history of the environmental and indigenous movements. The Kayapó were able to mobilize representatives of many indigenous peoples from all over the Americas to discuss with human rights and environmental leaders a unified strategy to protect natural ecosystems and native peoples (Posey, 1989a, 1989b).

For the Kayapó themselves, it was the first time that so many from dispersed groups were able to meet peacefully together. It was, in a sense, a modern re-creation of Pyka-tô-ti. After so many decades of separation and differences, it was amazing to see how easily and efficiently the subgroups could reintegrate to form a unified and highly organized social event. The complex model of Pyka-tô-ti organization had been long abandoned but not in the least forgotten.

Conclusion

Aboriginal population densities have been considerably underestimated because of failures to assess properly the effect of Europeans' diseases on Amerindian peoples. Likewise, assumptions that observations made at "initial contact" reflect Indian societies unaffected by European influence ignore the various effects that foreign trade items and diseases can have prior to face-to-face contact. For the Northern Kayapó, European artifacts and epidemics arrived decades (if not centuries) before missionaries made their first observations. Trade networks, warfare, raids, missionaries, and explorers all introduced elements of change into the hinterlands. Indirect, intermediate, and direct contact in the Amazon Basin form a typology of contact perhaps generally applicable to other parts of the Americas.

Oral tradition, historical documents, and archaeological remains combine to provide a model for cultural disintegration and reintegration. Rapid depopulation due to epidemics thrust the Kayapó society into chaos. Political structures disintegrated, social rules collapsed, and ceremonial life disappeared as death took away knowledgeable elders with specialized ceremonial roles. The ancient village of Pyka-tô-ti fragmented through various stages into mutually hostile groups. Accusations of witchcraft flourished because of unexplainable death from unknown diseases and created enemies from neighbors; beliefs in spirits led to abandonment of houses or whole villages due to spiritual contamination by the dead. The Kayapó thus appeared to outsiders, unaccustomed to Kayapó history and culture, to be unduly warlike and no-madic. This skewed impression has colored perceptions of the Kayapó and other indigenous people ever since. Cultural degradation led to the disap-pearance of "true" shamans and the rise of many "weak" shaman and "plant knowers" who appeared to fill a needed gap in medical care. Similar reduc-tions occurred in other areas of ceremonial and cultural knowledge.

Agriculture was less evident in the direct-contact period due to increased nomadic warfare activity. A much greater dependence on "semidomesticated" products of "nomadic agriculture" was necessary. These products escaped European eyes because they fell between the paradigms of hunter-gatherers and agriculturalists, leaving the scientific data inadequate for the evaluation of indigenous diet. "War gardens," "forest fields," trail-sides, and "apête" went unnoticed, since they fell outside the Western concept of natural-resource management. Consequently, many areas of Amazonia considered to be "nat-ural" are probably products of aboriginal and historic human presence. Agri-cultural plots began to thrive again only when relatively peaceful times were restored. This led to a decreased dependence on semidomesticated foods and the decline of the war-adapted "nomadic agricultural" system.

It is clear that, although demographic and cultural degradation was rapid and severe, the Kayapó society resisted in remarkably strong ways. Specialized knowledge, elaborate rituals, and a complex system of inter- and intragroup organization allowed the Kayapó not only to survive in the white world, but to take a leadership role in it, as the Altimira Encounter proved. A conscious new synthesis of Kayapó society by the Kayapó themselves already includes the abstract notion that they are conservers of nature and that their tradi-tional knowledge is important for the future of Amazonia. Perhaps this means that the Kayapó will be one of the first indigenous groups to work together with scientific specialists to provide the true Amazonian synthesis: One in which Indian knowledge and Western scientific data can be used together to interpret the past, analyze the present, and prepare for the future.

NOTES

1. Horace Banner's widow, Eva Banner, graciously allowed me to study and photo-copy his diaries during a five-month period in 1981.

2. These population estimates have been routinely dismissed as exaggerated, al-though recently rediscovered photographs of Araguaia villages prove that such esti-mates were possible (Verswijver, personal communication).

3. Some survivors were moved to Gorotire village, where the last Pau d'Arco Kayapó died in 1965 (Turner 1965).

4. The film *Jungle Pharmacy* was produced by Herbert Guiradet for TV Trust for the Environment.

REFERENCES

Alcorn, J. B.

1981   Huastec noncrop resource management: Implications for prehistoric rain forest management. *Human Ecology* 9:395–417.

1989   Process as resource: The traditional agricultural ideology of Bora and Huastec resource management and its implications for research. In Posey and Balée 1989, 63–77.

Anderson, A. B., and D. A. Posey

1985   Manejo de Cerrado Pelos Índios Kayapó. *Boletim do Museu Paraense Emílio Goeldi, Botânica* 2 (1): 77–98.

1989   Management of a tropical scrub savanna by the Gorotire Kayapó of Brazil. In Posey and Balée 1989, 159–73.

Balée, W. L.

1989a   The culture of Amazonian forest. In Posey and Balée 1989, 1–21.

1989b   Cultura ne vegetação da Amazônia. *Boletim do Museu Paraense Emílio Goeldi,* Coleção Eduardo Galvão: 95–109.

Balée, W. L., and A. Gély

1989   Managed forest succession in Amazonia: The Ka'apor case. In Posey and Balée 1989, 129–48.

Bamberger, J.

1967   Environmental and cultural classification: A study of the Northern Cayapó. Ph.D. diss., Harvard University, Cambridge, Mass.

Barbira-Scazzocchio, F.

1981   *Land, people, and planning in contemporary Amazonia.* Cambridge: Cambridge University Press.

Campos, M. d'O., and D. A. Posey

1990   Ethnoastronomy and ecological calendars of the Kayapó. Paper read at the Second International Congress of Ethnobiology, October 1990, Kunming, China.

Coudreau, H.

1897   *Voyage au Tocantins-Araguaya.* Paris: Lamure.

Crosby, A. W., Jr.

1972   *The Colombian exchange.* Westport: Greenwood Press.

Davis, S. H.

1977   *Victims of the miracle.* New York: University Press.

DeFoliart, G.

1990   Insects as food in indigenous populations. In *Ethnobiology: Implications*
            and applications, proceedings of the first International Congress of Ethnobiol-
            ogy, edited by D. A. and W. L. Overal, 345–54. Belém: Museu Paraense
            Emílio Goeldi/cnpq.

Denevan, W.

1976   *The native population of the Americas in 1492*. Madison: University of
            Wisconsin Press.

Dobyns, H. F.

1966   Estimating aboriginal American population. *Current Anthropology*
            7:395–416.

Elizabetsky, E., and D. A. Posey

1989   Use of contraceptive and related plants by the Kayapó Indians (Brazil).
            Journal of Ethnopharmacology 26:299–316.

Goodland, R. J., and H. S. Irwin

1975   *Amazon jungle: Green hell or desert?* Amsterdam: Elsevier Scientific
            Publishing.

Gottsberger, G., and D. A. Posey

n.d.   *A brief description of a tuber "war-garden" of Gorotire (Kayapó) village,*
            Pará, Brazil. Forthcoming.

Hecht, S. B., and D. A. Posey

1989   Preliminary results on soil management techniques of the Kayapó
            Indians. In Posey and Balée 1989, 174–88.

1990   Indigenous soil management in the Latin American tropics: Some impli-
            cations for the Amazon Basin. In *Ethnobiology: Implications and applica-*
            tions, proceedings of the first International Congress of Ethnobiology, edited
            by D. A. Posey and W. L. Overal, 344–53. Belém: Museu Paraense
            Emílio Goeldi/cnpq.

Hemming, J.

1978   *Red gold: The conquest of the Brazilian Indians*. Cambridge, Mass.:
            Harvard University Press.

Irvine, D.

1989   Succession management and resource distribution in an Amazonian rain
            forest. In Posey and Balée 1989, 223–37.

Krause, F.

1911   *In den Wildnissen Brasilians: Bericht und Ergebnisse der Leipsiger Araguaya-*
            Expedition. Leipzig, 1908.

Lathrap, D.

1968   Aboriginal occupation and changes in river channel on the central
            Ucayali, Peru. *American Antiquity* 33:62–79.

Lea, V.
1988   *Nomes e nekrets Kayapó: uma concepçao de riqueza.* Ph.D. diss., Museu
            Nacional, Postgraduate Program in Social Anthropology, Federal
            University of Rio de Janeiro, Brazil.
McNeill, W. H.
1976   *Plagues and peoples.* Garden City, N.Y.: Anchor Books.
Meggers, B.
1971   *Amazonia: Men and culture in a counterfeit paradise.* Chicago: Aldine
            Press.
Moran, E. F.
1979   *Human adaptability: An introduction to ecological anthropology.* North
            Scilerate, N.J.: Duxbury Press.
1981   *Developing the Amazon.* Bloomington: Indiana University Press.
Murphy, I. I.
1990   *Indigenous knowledge transmission in an oral society: A study of indigenous
            education among the Kayapó Amerindians of central Brazil.* Ph.D. diss.,
            School of Education, University of Pittsburgh, Pittsburgh, Pa.
Myers, T. P.
1973   Toward reconstruction of prehistoric community patterns in the Amazon
            Basin. In *Variation in anthropology,* edited by D. Lathrap and J. Douglas,
            123–28. Urbana: Illinois Archaeological Survey.
1974   Spanish contacts and social change on the Ucayali River, Peru. *Ethnohis-
            tory* 21 (2): 135–57
Posey, D. A.
1982   The journey of a Kayapó shaman. *Journal of Latin American Indian Litera-
            ture* 6 (3): 13–19.
1983   Indigenous knowledge and development: An ideological bridge to the
            future? *Ciência e Cultura* 35 (7): 877–94.
1984   Os Kayapó e a natureza. *Ciência Hojê* (SPPC, São Paulo) 12:36–41.
1985   Indigenous management of tropical forest ecosystems: The case of the
            Kayapó Indians of the Brazilian Amazon. *Agroforestry Systems* 3 (2):
            139–58.
1987   Contact before contact: Typology of post-Columbian interaction with
            Northern Kayapó of the Amazon Basin. *Boletim de Museu Paraense Emílio
            Goeldi, Serie Antropológica* 3 (2): 135–54.
1989a   The Kayapó on trial for speaking out. *Index on Censorship* 18 (6/7):
            16–20.
1989b   From warclubs to words. *NACLA* 23 (1): 13–19.
Posey, D., and W. Balée, eds.
1989   *Resource management in Amazonia: Indigenous and folk strategies.*
            Advances in Economic Botany, no. 7. Bronx, N.Y.: New York Botanical
            Garden.

Posey, D. A., and G. Gottsberger
n.d.   *Initial observations on creation and management of forest islands (Apêtê) in Campo-Cerrado by the Gorotire Kayapó, Pará State.* Forthcoming.

Ramos-Elorduy, J.
1990   Edible insects: Barbarism or solution to the hunger problem. In *Ethnobiology: Implications and applications, proceedings of the first International Congress of Ethnobiology,* edited by D. A. Posey and W. L. Overal, 87–398. Belém: Museu Parense Emílio Goeldi/CNPq.

Ribeiro, D.
1970   *Os Índios e a civilização.* Ed. Civilização Brasileira.

Roosevelt, A. C.
1989a   Resource management in Amazonia before the conquest: Beyond ethnographic projection. In Posey and Balée 1989, 30–62.

1989b   *Panama: Prehistoric maize and manioc subsistence along the Amazon and Orinoco.* New York: Academic Press.

Salick, J.
1989   Ecological basis of Amuesha agriculture, Peruvian upper Amazon. In Posey and Balée 1989, 189–212.

Smith, N. J.
1980   Anthrosols and human carrying capacity in Amazonia. *Science* 70 (4): 553–58.

Smole, W.
1989   Yanoama horticulture in the Parima highlands of Venezuela and Brazil. In Posey and W. Balée 1989, 189–212.

Sweet, D. G.
1974   *A rich realm of nature destroyed: The middle Amazon Valley, 1640–1750.* Ph.D. diss., University of Wisconsin, Madison.

Turner, T.
1966   Social structure and political organization among the Northern Cayapó. Ph.D. diss., Harvard University, Cambridge, Mass.

Vellard, J.
1956   *Causas biological de la desaparición de los Indios Americanos. Boletín del Instituto Rive-Aguero,* No. 2. Pontifica Universidad Católica del Perú.

Verswijver, G.
1978   *Enquête enhnographique chez les Kayapó-Mekrangnoti: Contribution a l'étude de la dynamique des groupes locaux (scissons e regroupements).* Thesis, École des Hautes Études en Sciences Sociales, Paris.

1992   *The club-fighters of the Amazon: Warfare among the Kaiapo Indians of central Brazil.* Rijksuniversiteit, Ghent.

13

Beyond Resistance

Comparative Study of Utopian Renewal in Amazonia

MICHAEL F. BROWN

> Thus the Tukuna told me that forty or fifty years ago the prophecies of a
> girl in Peruvian territory resulted in a gathering of Indians from both Peru
> and Brazil. One day Neobrazilians [non-Indian settlers] surrounded the
> assembly and attacked it with firearms, killed some Indians, thrashed the
> rest, and carried off the girl prophetess to an unknown fate.
>
> Curt Nimuendajú, *The Tukuna* (1952)

The experiments in social change that anthropologists classify as crisis cults,
revitalization movements, or millenarian episodes have played a conspicuous
role in the history of aboriginal South America.[1] Observers have long been
struck by the singularity of millenarian movements, evident in their radical
divergence from everyday practice and their fusion of such apparently opposed qualities as spirituality and materialism, egalitarianism and apotheosis.
As a result, descriptions of millenarian episodes draw on a vocabulary of
detonation ("explosion," "outburst," "eruption") that marks them as dramatic breaks with a history otherwise assumed to be stable (Schwartz 1976, 7).

Contemporary inquiry into millenarian movements has shifted toward the
recognition that each is shaped by deep cultural currents that transcend the
particulars of a specific historical moment. In their analysis of a series of
millenarian movements in the northwestern Amazon, for instance, Wright
and Hill (1986) note both the movements' innovative features and their
continuity with indigenous ritual practice. More specifically, Wright and Hill
argue that millenarianism uses myth as an idiom for the expression of resistance to Western political domination. Their analysis exemplifies the importance that the concept of resistance has assumed in interpretations of utopian
renewal put forward in the past decade.[2]

As an analytical concept, however, resistance has some significant flaws. The term is freighted with moral overtones that can distract us from the subtleties and contradictions of strategies for cultural survival. After all, don't we feel greater admiration for those who resist overwhelming power than for those who bend to its pressures, despite the survival advantages that are sometimes conferred by selective accommodation? In studies of Amazonian millenarian movements, resistance is usually invoked to label the struggle of Indians to reframe their vision of a world increasingly dominated by Western states. But millenarian struggle often turns inward as well, for indigenous societies have their own internal fields of conflict and points of contention. Because millenarian movements advocate a "radical change in the distribution of power, status, and wealth" (Scott 1985, 333), they may threaten the internal status quo as much as they challenge the power of outsiders. To the extent that the notion of resistance blinds us to these complex social processes, it recalls anthropology's love affair with "acculturation" in the 1960s. Now, of course, we regard the concept of acculturation as far too blunt an instrument to dissect the nuances of intercultural exchange.

In the spirit of intellectual synthesis that inspires the present volume, this chapter explores issues of resistance and change through a comparative survey of millenarian movements in Amazonia.[3] To frame my analysis, I first review recent developments in the study of Amazonian prehistory that cast doubt on the assertion that millenarian movements can be attributed solely to the crisis sparked by the arrival of Europeans. Drawing on the work of Hélène and Pierre Clastres, I review the case for a long-standing tension between hierarchical and egalitarian tendencies in Amazonian societies. These opposed tendencies may play themselves out in *longue durée* cycles of political consolidation punctuated by self-limiting episodes of millenarian and messianic enthusiasm. This is followed by summaries of five cases of utopian renewal chosen for the richness of their documentation and the degree to which they represent the diversity of indigenous responses at various historical moments. I search them for common themes and explore the possibility that our view of them may have been distorted by the colonial lens, lending them an eventness that disguises underlying social processes and exaggerates elements that appear to constitute resistance to Western society.[4]

Amazonian Millenarian Movements Prior to Western Contact

Since the 1970s it has been common to identify millenarian movements as forms of social protest and reactions to the deterioration of native life almost universally experienced under European colonialism (see, for example, Adas

1979; Fields 1985; Stern 1987). Indeed, many scholars have identified the appearance of millenarian movements with the introduction of Christianity, a religion held to be uniquely prone to messianic, millenarian, and revolutionary dreams (Burridge 1979, 209; see also Burridge 1985; Worsley 1968). Yet, although few New World peoples seem to have shared the European idea that history is moving ineluctably toward a moment of ultimate transcendence, we now know that other historical visions can comfortably accommodate millenarian anticipation. In his reflections on the historical consciousness of native South Americans, Jonathan Hill (1988, 7) observes a pattern in which "history is understood in relation to a few 'peaks,' or critical periods of rapid change, rather than a smoothly flowing progression." In some cases, these critical periods include social movements of a messianic or millenarian variety.[5]

Unfortunately, the scarcity of written sources dating to precontact times limits our knowledge of possible instances of millenarianism prior to the arrival of Europeans. The few anecdotal cases that exist—for instance, the claim of Fry (1985) that there is evidence of revitalization movements among the Postclassic Maya—are projections of contemporary categories onto suggestive but ambiguous archaeological data.

Advances in Amazonian archaeology and ethnohistory have challenged the idea that the conquest represented an isolated shock to the region's Indians, whom scholars had long thought to exist in a state of untrammeled sameness prior to contact with the West (see Roosevelt 1987; Whitehead 1989). The archaeological record discloses the rise and fall of Amazonian social systems, the replacement of egalitarian societies by highly stratified ones marked by an uneven distribution of wealth and power—in short, the kinds of brusque changes that might have precipitated cultural crises long before the sixteenth century. These intra-Amazonian encounters were less calamitous than were later contacts with the Spanish and Portuguese, which often led to staggering mortality due to the introduction of new diseases, but they were surely traumatic enough to have produced internal crises in the affected societies. Amazonian populations must have been confronted from time to time with new and powerful religious ideologies emanating from Andean polities to the west or from emerging Amazonian chiefdoms closer to home. They would have had to respond to the challenge of these alternative symbol systems by modifying their own worldview to accommodate (and appropriate powerful elements of) new ritual patterns and political forms.

The best-documented studies of movements with precontact roots concern the Tupí Guaraní societies of eastern South America, peoples renowned for their millenarian inclinations.[6] Métraux (1927, 21) notes that as early as

1549 three hundred Tupis from the Atlantic coast of Brazil arrived in Chacha-
poyas, in the Peruvian Andes, a decade after they had begun walking west in
search of a "land of immortality and eternal rest"—more commonly referred
to in Portuguese sources as the Terra Sem Mal, "Land Without Evil." Brazilian
chronicles are littered with instances of other Tupí Guaraní groups undertaking similar migrations as recently as the early twentieth century. Fairly soon
after the arrival of Europeans, however, Tupian movements incorporated elements of Christian symbolism. Pereira de Queiroz (1969) describes several
Tupí Guaraní messianic movements in the late sixteenth century that identified native messiahs with Christian saints, and there is little doubt that
later Tupian millenarianism represented, at least in part, a strong reaction to
colonial oppression (Shapiro 1987, 131). Balée (1984, 256) declares that
seventeenth-century Tupian migrations westward were in essence a "massive
exodus from the centers of human extinction" associated with Portuguese
settlement.

The preconquest origins of Tupí Guaraní millenarianism have provoked
reflection on the indigenous social forces that sporadically prompted thousands of Indians to abandon their villages and follow charismatic leaders into
the unknown. The most influential analyses of this phenomenon are found
in two separate but interrelated monographs by Pierre Clastres (1987) and
Hélène Clastres (1978). Although the work of Pierre Clastres is probably
more familiar to English-speaking readers, that of Hélène Clastres represents
a more historically and ethnographically detailed analysis that proves useful
for the purposes of the present chapter.[7]

The argument of Hélène Clastres, reduced to its principal schematic elements, is that Tupí Guaraní migrations were inspired not by ordinary shamans
but by prophets called caraís or caraíbas, whom other Indians regarded as
god-men. These prophets were wandering figures who lived on the perimeter
of Tupi communities, both physically and in terms of prevailing social and
political norms, which immediately before European conquest were characterized by marked social ranking and a complex village organization. As marginal men, caraís could visit the villages of enemies without fear of harm.
When a prophet's vision, presented in metaphorically charged language,
moved people to renounce settled life for a journey to the Land Without Evil,
the prophet exercised political control that, at least for a time, surpassed that
of local headmen.[8] (This state of affairs led some European observers to label
caraís as "provincial chiefs.") Clastres (1978, 60) argues that the goal of these
migrations was "not to halt social disorganization but, on the contrary, to promote it" (my translation). Prophetic movements thus rejected social ranking
and implicitly advocated the "abolition of all forms of power" (Clastres 1978,

113). By leaving sedentary life behind, the Tupi abandoned the prevailing social structure in search of a place beyond secular space and time. Eventually, the movements lost their momentum, the wisdom of specific prophets was thrown in doubt, and the social norms of sedentary life reasserted themselves.

There are several parts of this analysis to which I shall return in the following review of other instances of Amazonian millenarianism. Of particular interest are the outsider status of the prophet or messianic leader and the paradoxical way that the prophet uses a rhetoric of radical egalitarianism to establish greater hierarchy than had existed before. The Tupian case also raises the possibility that episodes of utopian renewal are less "events" than instantiations of a cyclical process of political struggle internal to Amazonian societies.

Case Studies

Case 1: Asháninka, Central Peru, 1742–1965

The Asháninka (more widely known in the anthropological literature as "Campa"), an Arawakan people of Peru's upper Amazon, represent an example of what Wilson (1973, 327) calls a "spasmodic cult," in which episodes of millenarian fervor are separated by long periods of quiescence.[9] The best-known instance of millenarian enthusiasm among Asháninkas began in 1742, when a highland Indian named Juan Santos Atahualpa convinced them, as well as neighboring Arawakan and Panoan peoples, to throw off the yoke of Spanish colonial rule and expel the Franciscan missionaries who were its most important local representatives.

Prior to the arrival of Juan Santos Atahualpa in 1742, there had been several Asháninka uprisings sparked by conflicts between missionaries and the local headmen upon whom they depended. But the rebellion of Juan Santos was far more widespread and dangerous to Spanish interests. A Quechua Indian educated by priests, possibly in a Jesuit seminary, Juan Santos seems to have traveled to Europe and Africa. His utopian program called for the expulsion of the Spanish from Peru, restoration of the Inca empire with him as its head, and replacement of Spanish priests by Indian clerics, who would take charge of Christian practice in the new empire. With the help of Asháninkas and other rebels, including renegade blacks, highland Indian settlers, and neighboring Amazonian peoples, Juan Santos decisively defeated Spanish military forces in several encounters. Although there were no large-scale military engagements between Spaniards and rebels after 1752, native belligerence closed the central jungle area of Peru to settlers for nearly a century.

Because no Spanish records of life among Asháninkas during this period have surfaced, we know little about the impact of the movement on their politics and religion, nor do we know what they thought about the neo-Inca ideology of the messiah, which must have been as alien to them as the Christianity advanced by Franciscan missionaries. Scholars have been quick to see the roots of the movement in a pan-Andean belief in Inkarrí (the Inca king, who will return to overthrow European colonists and establish a native utopia) and even in the apocalyptic millenarianism of the Franciscans. It seems more likely, however, that Asháninkas drew on millenarian roots in their own tradition, though these were no doubt modified by social contacts with the Andean Indians, Franciscans, and black slaves who resided in mission settlements.[10]

The millenarian currents exploited by Juan Santos in the eighteenth century stirred again in the nineteenth and twentieth. Explorers' accounts from the 1890s suggest that Carlos Fitzcarrald, a legendary rubber baron, may have been regarded as the Son of the Sun (Itomi Pavá) by some Asháninkas. In the 1920s, a Seventh-Day Adventist missionary named F. A. Stahl inspired a large-scale crisis cult that anticipated the end of the world (Bodley 1972). Finally, oral histories collected in Satipo Province establish that in 1965 some Asháninkas regarded Guillermo Lobatón, regional commander of a leftist guerrilla organization called the Movement of the Revolutionary Left (MIR), as the Son of the Sun, a helpful spirit sent to lead the Indians in militant appropriation of whites' material wealth. The Peruvian government's counterinsurgency campaign against Lobatón and his followers, which included the use of napalm against peasant and Indian villages, led to the death of scores of Asháninkas and virtually all of the guerrillas. The 1965 movement provoked opposition from within the Asháninka population itself, and some Asháninkas—in most cases people who were long-standing enemies of Lobatón's native allies—assisted the counterinsurgency forces in tracking down the guerrillas (Brown and Fernández 1991).

Asháninka support for the MIR guerrillas alarmed the government and focused national attention on the plight of Indians in zones of intensive colonization. This concern undoubtedly contributed to the promulgation of a progressive Native Communities Law in the early 1970s. Today, however, Asháninkas are locked in an even more violent struggle with elements of two leftist guerrilla groups, the Shining Path and the Túpac Amaru Revolutionary Movement (Benavides 1990; Gorriti 1990). It is not yet known whether this new conflict has millenarian undercurrents.

A common theme emerges from the episodes of Asháninka millenarianism about which information exists: each was sparked by the arrival of a charismatic outsider. Juan Santos was an educated highland Indian; Fitzcarrald was of mixed Andean and Irish ancestry; F. A. Stahl was an American; Guillermo Lobatón, the MIR's local commander, was a black intellectual from the Peruvian coast. Somehow these outsiders succeeded in creating temporary alliances that transcended local kinship groups; in some cases, however, Asháninkas eventually turned on the messiah and contributed to his downfall. As Asháninkas themselves say about their prophet-leaders, "There is always someone who doubts."

Case 2: Tukanoan and Arawakan Indians, Upper Río Negro region, Venezuela-Colombia-Brazil, ca. 1857–84

The mid to late nineteenth century was a turbulent period for the Tukanoan and Arawakan Indians of the Río Negro. Native communities and their traditional institutions had been shattered by aggressive missionary campaigns, labor conscription, debt servitude, and epidemics. Into this unhappy circumstance stepped a visionary named Venancio Aniseto Kamiko. Hemming (1987, 321) identifies Venancio as a mestizo woodcutter; Wright and Hill (1986, 35) state that he was born of the Arawak-speaking Baniwa. Venancio's guardian was a black preacher named Don Arnao or Arnaoud, a Christian evangelist to whom the Baniwa attributed shamanistic powers. After miraculously surviving a serious illness (apparently an attack of catalepsy compounded by excessive alcohol consumption) in 1857, Venancio reported having a vision in which he was directed to inform Indian people that they must refuse to work for whites and that their debts would be forgiven if they made gifts of food to him (Wright and Hill 1986, 35, 37). Later, he took on a priestly role, organizing feasts and wedding ceremonies and eventually predicting the destruction of people, notably whites, who refused to follow his teachings. Despite relentless suppression of the movement by Brazilian authorities, interest in Venancio's message spread to the Vaupés and Xíe rivers, where Indians danced in expectation of a coming day of judgment.

Wright and Hill (1986; see also Hill and Wright 1988) note that Venancio's influence drew on traditional Arawakan beliefs about fasting, the signs of a shamanistic calling, and on myths of world destruction and renewal. Stephen Hugh-Jones (1981, 34) detects traces of the Tukanoan Yuruparí (or Juruparí) cult in the movement, including an emphasis on shamanistic revelation and large-scale manioc beer feast. Venancio's teachings also incorporated elements of rural Christianity; indeed, according to Hemming (1987, 322), Venancio "assumed the title Christo and he appointed elderly men and women as his ministers, giving them the names of Christian saints." Wright and Hill (1986, 44) see this use of Christian symbols as a "transformation of indigenous ritual activities into a form of ritual protest against colonial institutions."

Yet it is hard to see why this notion of "protest" would have been meaningful to the Indians, who had no reason to think that white authorities would be moved by an expression of native displeasure. Wright and Hill (1986, 37) seem closer to the mark when they note that the Christian content of the movement allowed the Indians "to conduct their own marriages and baptisms . . . hence, they no longer had any use for Christian missionaries."

Although Venancio managed to elude the government expeditions sent to capture him, his power waned by late 1858. His movement seems to have passed into obscurity, but Venancio himself lives on in native history as a figure who "redefin[ed] . . . the indigenous ancestor cult into a cult of historical opposition to external domination" (Wright and Hill 1986, 51).

New messianic movements that echoed the teachings of Venancio Christo arose in the same region. Three other "Christos," named Alexandre, Anizetto, and Vicente, appeared between 1858 and 1885 on the Içana and Vaupés rivers. Vicente began teaching in 1880. He announced that he was the "Supreme Shaman" in charge of all Christian missionaries. According to Hugh-Jones (1981, 34; my translation), Vicente "predicted the elimination by force of all white people who mistreated Indians and proclaimed an inversion of the social order to one in which the Indians could be bosses and the whites their slaves." Local authorities tried vigorously to suppress each of these movements, and there is little evidence that the experience had any long-term impact on the way the native participants dealt with whites in economic and political terms.

Case 3: Canela, Maranhão, Brazil, 1963

The Canela (also known as "Ramkokamekra"), a Gê-speaking people who inhabit a region of closed savannas in northeastern Brazil, underwent a messianic movement in 1963 that has been extensively documented by William H. Crocker (1967, 1989). The movement began when a pregnant woman named Kee-khwëi received prophetic messages from the child in her womb, whom she predicted would be born a girl. The child identified herself as the sister of Auké, a mythical hero, and announced that with her birth the roles of Indians and whites would be reversed. Indians would enjoy extraordinary material wealth, while whites would descend into poverty. As news of the prophecies spread among the Canela, some Indians began to rustle cattle from nearby ranches, a move that Kee-khwëi eventually supported, arguing that cattle belonged to everyone. The Canela commenced a period of frantic dancing, alternating between indigenous dance styles and the dances of the Brazilian peasantry, on the assumption that "he who danced the most would be the richest when the great day came" (Crocker 1967, 73).

In a matter of weeks, the prophetess became the focus of a cult that sup-
planted the society's traditional leadership, leading Crocker (1989, 19) to
remark that "she had become a leader of great power . . . stronger than the
traditional chiefs had been" while establishing "one united tribal community." The Indians sold their shotguns, machetes, and metal cooking pots in
order to buy trade clothing, make-up, jewelry, and cane alcohol for themselves and for Kee-khwëi. The prophetess attracted a group of fifty retainers
drawn from among "high-status" young people (Crocker 1967, 72). She was
carried between villages by her followers, seated in state in village plazas, and
honored by visitors who would kiss her abdomen, the site of the spiritual
being whom she promised to bring forth. Under her direction, the community also experimented with changes in traditional patterns of sexual behavior, including the abolition of taboos on intercourse with some prohibited
categories of kin.

The cult faced a crisis when Kee-khwëi delivered a stillborn male baby
rather than the promised spirit-girl. The prophetess and her followers found
a way to account for this unexpected event, and they continued to consoli-
date their influence. Crocker's description of the cult characterizes this post-
birth period as a shift toward folk Catholicism accompanied by intensifying
assertions of Indian superiority over, and aggressiveness toward, Brazilian
settlers. Eventually, ranchers whose cattle were being stolen attacked Canela
settlements, leaving six Indians wounded and five dead.[11] The Indian Protection Service moved the Canela to another location for their own safety; Kee-
khwëi was discredited and the movement died.

Crocker's original interpretation of the movement focuses on its unusual
features: first, that the cult began when the Canela were enjoying economic
prosperity; second, that they had long been among the most conservative of
Brazilian tribal groups, maintaining a positive self-image and a "traditional"
worldview. More recently, Crocker (1989) has modified his assessment, presenting a mixed picture of the status of the Indians at the time of the movement. He notes, for instance, that the Indians were bewildered by the declining generosity of the Indian Protection Service in the months preceding
Kee-khwëi's vision. In broad terms, however, Crocker sees the movement as a
response to a crisis of acculturation, during which the cult attempted to smash
many traditional practices and effect a transformation to Brazilian custom.

In a reinterpretation of Crocker's work, Manuela Carneiro da Cunha
(1973) asserts that the movement represented an act of mythic praxis paral-
leling the Canela myth of Auké, who was said to have originally given Brazilian settlers the wealth that the Canela coveted. (Melatti [1972] notes that
the same myth had a central role in a different messianic movement among

the closely related Krahó in the early 1950s.) Rather than mimicking the
culture of Brazilian settlers, Carneiro da Cunha argues, the cult applied traditional Canela symbolic structures to the confrontation between Indian and
settler attitudes toward reciprocity, sexual relations, and social hierarchy with
the goal of restoring a life-giving balance in the relations between the two
societies (see also Turner 1988, 265).

Case 4: Orden Cruzada, Peru and Brazil, 1971 to the Present

In the early 1970s, a visionary named José Francisco da Cruz (born José
Nogueira in the Brazilian state of Minas Gerais) began to proselytize in communities along the Amazon and its tributaries in Peru. His movement, which
is called the "Orden Cruzada" or the "Hermandad de la Cruz" in Spanish and
the "Irmandade da Santa Cruz" in Portuguese, has attracted a significant
following among the Tikuna (Tukuna) and Cocama peoples, and to a lesser
extent among the Yagua.[12] Sources within the movement insist that the
Orden Cruzada has ten thousand followers in Peru and Brazil (Agüero 1985,
134). The reliability of this figure is uncertain, but even unsympathetic observers admit that the church's native membership has experienced sustained
growth.

The visions of da Cruz came at a time of cultural disorganization for the
Tikuna and Cocama. Regan (1988, 134–35) notes that the Amazonian oil
boom of the late 1960s had caused dislocations in the local economy and a
precipitous decline in traditional agriculture; deforestation of Amazonian
watersheds to the west produced a series of highly destructive floods in the
native communities downriver.

The teachings of da Cruz emphasized the power of the Christian cross and
asserted that world destruction was imminent. Until his death in 1982, da
Cruz insisted that on the instructions of Jesus Christ he was instituting the
"Third Universal Reform of Christianity" to help people prepare for the coming apocalypse, which will be survived only by members of the Orden Cruzada. The post-apocalypse world will be one of abundance and peace.

The theological and cosmological underpinnings of the Orden Cruzada
bear little outward resemblance to their native Amazonian counterparts.
Ritual life centers on veneration of the cross, the singing of Christian hymns,
and Bible study. The "brothers and sisters" of the Orden Cruzada dress in
white garments and, through a rejection of such practices as alcohol consumption and dancing, attempt to live a life free of the "prostitution" that prevails
in the profane world. The life of Orden Cruzada communities, called *villas*,
centers on a daily and monthly round of religious observances and prayer.
Each villa fits into a larger political and religious hierarchy culminating in a

Peruvian "patriarch," whose seat is in the city of Iquitos. The "Mother Central Church" of the order is on the Río Juí in Brazil. The existing ethnographic sources do not make it entirely clear how the Peruvian communities relate to their leaders in Brazil, though apparently some funds tithed in Peru make their way to the Mother Central Church (Regan 1983, 2:140).

Despite the explicitly Christian character of the movement, Regan (1988) sees in the cosmology of Orden Cruzada believers a direct link to the Tupian search for the Land Without Evil. (The Cocama, many of whom have joined the movement, speak a Tupian language.) Apparently various groups of Orden Cruzada pilgrims have set off in search of what they call the "Tierra Santa"—Holy Land—a terrestrial paradise (Regan 1988, 132).

In his analysis of the Orden Cruzada movement among the Cocama, Oscar Agüero (1985) argues that, far from being acculturative in its effects, the cult is counter-acculturative. Villas are founded on the principle of isolation from the contaminating influence of the national society. The internal politics of each villa is relatively democratic, and many community economic activities follow traditional Cocama labor-exchange practices. Orden Cruzada groups actively avoid engagement with merchants and wage-labor recruiters—indeed, with all "gentiles." The messianic and millenarian traditions of the Cocama and the Tikuna certainly find contemporary echoes in the movement.[13] Cocama believers see themselves as occupying a sacred space and time that contrast with the profane space and time of the rest of Peru. All observers agree that the Orden Cruzada has had a major impact on the economy, social organization, settlement pattern, and cosmology of the native peoples who have embraced it. These changes appear to be of long duration, though Agüero argues that the movement is ultimately doomed to extinction because it has no political program in the conventional sense.

Case 5: Kapon and Pemón, Guyana-Venezuela-Brazil, Mid-Nineteenth Century to the Present

In superbly documented studies, Colson (1971, 1985) and Thomas (1976) analyze the origins and spread of closely related religious movements called "Hallelujah," "Chochimu," and "San Miguel" among Carib-speaking peoples living in the area known as Circum-Roraima, a region straddling the shared borders of Guyana, Venezuela, and Brazil (see also Colson's earlier work, Butt 1960). The Hallelujah movement was apparently inspired by the teachings of a Makusi prophet named "Bichiwung" (or Pichiwön), who visited England under the sponsorship of a British missionary. Upon his return to what was then British Guiana, Bichiwung began to preach of his personal visions, which included the revelation that white men were hiding God's word from

Indians. "So Bichiwung got Hallelujah from God then, and God also gave him a bottle of white medicine and words and songs and also a piece of paper which was the Indian Bible," as the Indians say (Butt 1960, 69). Bichiwung's teachings, which had a strongly Christian character, were adopted and modified by other native prophets, some of whom were drawn from the pool of traditional shamans. In many instances, the new prophets repudiated what were perceived as the negative aspects of shamanism (e.g., its association with sorcery) but maintained some of its key features, notably, direct contact between prophets and God.[14] The rituals of Hallelujah include modified forms of pre-Christian dancing and feasting and the performance of special chants. According to Colson (1985, 137), this new form of Christian belief "was passed on in the same way as indigenous knowledge, and so converted into a new set of concepts and associated practices." Hallelujah prophet-leaders follow a Big Man model of personal prestige: they and their close kin "have to own extensive gardens and be energetic food providers in order to give extraordinary hospitality during frequent and long church festivals" (Colson 1985, 141).[15]

A detailed discussion of the evolution of this complex syncretistic movement is beyond the scope of the present chapter. Suffice it to say that Hallelujah and its successors are strongly nativistic in character (emphasizing Indian hostility to the subordination of native peoples by non-Indians), highly selective in their use of Christian symbolism and concepts, and occasionally marked by a cargo-cult-like fascination with the material wealth of Europeans. According to Colson, the relative isolation of the Indians during the movement's gestation prevented its suppression by colonial authorities and missionaries, allowing it to achieve a cosmological and political stability rare in other indigenous New World millenarian movements. Hallelujah, she writes, "is at once a Christian religion in its basic details and an indigenous conceptual system . . . that began as an enthusiastic movement and . . . has now become an indigenous church" (1985, 142). The movement redefined and intensified exchange relations, according to Colson (1985, 104), thus effecting a "common accord between regional groups." In other words, Hallelujah and its local variants helped to integrate formerly hostile ethnic units and strengthen their positions vis-à-vis the dominant society.

Thematic Similarities and Differences

There are, of course, many points of comparison among these cases, ranging from their specific historical contexts to the subtleties of the cosmological vision enunciated by each. For the purposes of my analysis, however, I will focus on the general theme of resistance as it is played out in native responses to the ideological challenge of Christianity, the movements' programs for the hierarchical reorganization of society, and the ways indigenous people conceptualized the future place of non-Indians in the postmillennial world.

Christianity

All the case studies include the integration of Christian symbols and concepts into a millenarian vision, a practice sometimes interpreted as a form of acculturation. Pierre Clastres (1987, 160–61), for instance, laments the creation of an "impoverishing syncretism where, under the mask of an always superficial Christianity, indigenous thought seeks only to postpone its own demise." Yet he presents no evidence of how or why this "impoverishment" occurs. On the contrary, in Amazonian millenarian movements we see robust efforts to wrestle control of Christianity from whites while reshaping it to meet the spiritual needs of Indian peoples. Juan Santos Atahualpa advocated an indigenous clergy; the Orden Cruzada claims that its religious practice represents the third great reformation of the Catholic church; Venancio Christo took on a priestly role so that his followers would be free of meddling friars. Vigorous appropriation of Christianity is consistent with a view that ritual knowledge is something to be exchanged and shared—an attitude perhaps best illustrated by the wide circulation of indigenized Christianity among Carib-speakers in Guyana. This openness to exotic spiritual knowledge is so widely distributed in the New World that it probably existed long before contact with Europeans.

The indigenization of Christian concepts and symbols surely represents resistance to the missionary's demand for theological exclusivity. Yet it is also the sincerest form of flattery. By appropriating Christianity, Amazonian peoples acknowledge the power of its authors. One might go so far as to say that the integration of Christian symbolism represents an implicit, if muted, critique of indigenous modes of explanation and ritual action; at the very least, it is an admission that native systems are not closed symbolic worlds. Consider the two case studies of movements that have demonstrated long-term durability. Members of the Orden Cruzada of Peru and Brazil reject both the corruption of the dominant society and elements of native society that they find objectionable, including drunkenness and sorcery (Regan 1988, 136). The result is a religion that is far more Christian than Amazonian. The Hallelujah movement of Carib-speaking peoples represents a less drastic break with indigenous society than the Orden Cruzada, but it expresses similar uneasiness about the dark side of shamanism, namely, sorcery (cf. Brown 1988). In sum, participants in Amazonian millenarian movements demonstrate less "resistance" to Western society than the thousands of Indians who, without benefit of millenarian enthusiasm, proved remarkably unyielding to Christian missionary efforts (Pollock 1993).

The millenarian assimilation of Christianity has sometimes followed paths laid down by indigenous religion or mythology, and it is not unusual for the leaders of such movements to be shamans, presumably the members of the affected population most thoroughly versed in traditional religious practice. In other instances, though (e.g., the movement sparked by Venancio Christo in the upper Río Negro and the rebellion of Juan Santos Atahualpa among the Asháninka), prophets or messiahs were marginal to native society through birth or upbringing. They gained their following by virtue of their ability to convey Christian ideas within a native idiom. Outsider status seems to have enabled these prophets to bypass the political constraints of existing social units and achieve a higher level of social integration.

Social Ranking

Four of the five movements summarized above include attempts to institute forms of social ranking that had little precedent in the societies where they arose. Both Venancio Christo and the Canela prophetess Kee-khwëi demanded food as tribute, and it is by no means clear that the redistribution of this food was equitable. If we accept that tributary use of food is a key element of chiefly societies (see, for example, Kirch 1984, 39), we are drawn inescapably to the conclusion that both movements represented a flirtation with chiefly politics. By joining forces with Juan Santos Atahualpa, the Asháninka of Peru pledged themselves to an imperial political model, though there is reason to doubt that they were truly committed to this aspect of Juan Santos's social program; later Asháninka messiahs seem to have had a broader field of influence than ordinary political leaders, although there is no evidence for the collection of tribute. The situation of the Orden Cruzada is contradictory: the egalitarianism that reportedly characterizes individual communities contrasts sharply with the hierarchical structure of the church organization that knits communities together into one movement.

Emphasis on social ranking calls to mind the paradox noted by Hélène Clastres in her analysis of Tupí Guaraní prophetic movements: that the destruction of a prevailing social order correlates with the adoption (however transitory) of greater social distance between leader and follower. A sharp tilt in the direction of a ranked society can, I believe, be seen as an intensification of more subtle oscillations in organizing principles observed in contemporary Amazonian societies. Jonathan Hill (1984) found among the Wakuénai of northwestern Amazonia two "modes of structuring behavior," an egalitarian mode associated with ordinary subsistence activities and a hierarchical mode activated during ritual enterprises. Hill's observation is paralleled by Jean Jackson's (1983, 212) work in the same region. Waud Kracke's (1978, 70–71) study of leadership among the Kagwahiv, a Tupi-speaking people of the Rio Madeira in Brazil, notes "fundamental contradictions in Kagwahiv values and social structure" between two models of leadership, one egalitarian and conciliatory, the other self-aggrandizing and oriented to resource control.

Ritual often provides the context for a shift from egalitarianism to hierarchy, since it demands attention to degrees of ceremonial purity and hence of ranked distinctions (Jackson 1983, 103). Because participants in millenarian movements see themselves as entering into sacred space and time, they may quickly reshape their social world to follow a hierarchical model. In most cases, however, this hierarchy collapses with the intrusion of the profane world into the life of the participants. A notable exception is the case of the Orden Cruzada, which has sustained intercommunity hierarchy by balancing it with local egalitarianism.

Research on millenarianism in other world regions (e.g., Worsley 1968) associates crisis cults with nascent nationalism or pan-tribalism. When prophets draw followers from across ethnic boundaries, they set the stage for the creation of new and larger political units that are better able to confront the state (Pereira de Queiroz 1969, 242–43). Most postcontact millenarian movements in Amazonia, however, were suppressed before they could achieve higher levels of political integration. Even when the state did not completely interrupt the trajectory of utopian renewal, the precarious circumstances in which Indians found themselves seem to have inhibited whatever regional cohesion the movements promoted. Alliances established between the Asháninka and other tribes during the rebellion of Juan Santos, for instance, did not survive the stresses of jungle colonization in the nineteenth century. Of the case studies explored here, only the Hallelujah movement of Circum-Roraima has been able to forge stable links between formerly atomistic social units (Colson 1985).

The Direction of Indian-White Relations

The case studies demonstrate great variability in native views on the future of Indian-white relations, no doubt because of wide differences in colonial and postcolonial experience with outsiders. The Asháninka allies of Juan Santos Atahualpa sought the expulsion of whites from Peru. The Canela apparently expected to *become* whites. Members of the Orden Cruzada isolate themselves from the corrupting influence of white society in anticipation of a final day of reckoning.

All of the movements have anticipated a major shift in the status relations of Indians and whites, as when a messiah from the Río Vaupés announced that he was the leader of all white missionaries and that "Indians could be bosses and the whites their slaves" (Hugh-Jones 1981, 34). Amazonian peoples show less concern with trade goods and material things in general than their counterparts in Melanesia and other colonized parts of the world. Nevertheless, cargo-cult tendencies are evident in some of the case studies (for instance, in the Canela movement and the earliest phases of the Hallelujah religion) as well as elsewhere in the Amazonian ethnographic record (e.g., Vinhas de Queiroz 1963). In general, Amazonian Indians have been less interested in appropriating the ultimate source of all wealth than with ending the exploitative relations that forced them to work so hard to get modest amounts of the goods that whites possessed in abundance. This is most clearly expressed in the separateness sought by the Orden Cruzada, which isolates its followers from the impurity and exploitative tendencies of non-Indian "gentiles," and by Venancio Christo's denial of the validity of white debt claims against Indians. The nativistic renunciation of Western goods that Curt Nimuendajú saw among Guaraní pilgrims in 1912 has been remarkably rare. They attributed their failure to fly to the Land Without Evil to their contamination by European clothing and food, which made them too heavy to take wing (Métraux 1941, 54).

The explicitly stated aim of reversing the dominance hierarchy of the colonial system in favor of the Indians is arguably the most powerful expression of resistance to outsiders in Amazonian millenarian movements. In their analysis of the Venancio Christo movement, Wright and Hill (1986, 51) argue that a major consequence of the movement was "a reorientation of social and economic relations in which the refusal to cooperate with the external, dominating order of the white man became elevated to the status of a sacred cosmological postulate." It is doubtful that this sacred postulate did much to change native reality, however. Hemming (1987) reports that the exploitation of the Indians of the Río Negro continued unabated from 1858, regardless of the teachings of Venancio and the native "Christos" who followed him; nor is there any evidence that former adherents to the movement were somehow better equipped to resist the advances of Western civilization than Indians who had never subscribed to Venancio's message.

The circumstances of state control in the Amazon ensured that the situation of missionaries, labor recruiters, settlers, and government officials was often precarious. Colonists held exaggerated fears of the Indians' inherent savagery (Taussig 1987), and agitation within native communities caused by millenarian movements was therefore likely to arouse a prompt and brutal response far out of proportion to the actual danger posed by the natives' utopian dreams. Of the five case studies, only the Asháninka (led by Juan Santos Atahualpa in 1742 and by the Castroite guerrilla leader Guillermo Lobatón in 1965) undertook outright rebellion. Others elaborated ideologies of avoidance, nativist self-vindication, or repudiation of debt that were more threatening to whites' economic interests than to their physical safety. When violence broke out, it was nearly always initiated by state authorities attempting to apprehend a prophet-leader, suppress antisettler rhetoric, and "restore order." As Scott (1985, 332) puts it, "Millennial and utopian thought typically make their appearance in the archives only when they take the form of sects or movements that pose a threat to the state." There have doubtless been many episodes of utopian renewal that escaped the historical record because colonists found them unthreatening and therefore unworthy of note.

What impact did forcible suppression have on native narratives about these movements that survive today? Surely it intensified the image of the movements as explicit episodes of active resistance to Western society, at the same time obscuring those aspects of the movements that challenged traditional authority or advocated the abandonment of specific rituals. We will never learn of countless instances of cultural redefinition that may have expressed little overt resistance to outsiders but considerable criticism of indigenous society itself.

Conclusion

Drawing on case studies of indigenous Amazonian millenarianism, I have identified links between precontact and postcontact episodes of utopian renewal. Such points of continuity include tension between hierarchical and egalitarian models of leadership, periodic questioning of traditional rituals and political systems, and openness to the ritual knowledge of other ethnic groups. These processes exemplify resistance to *internal* realities as well as to those imposed by Euro-American society. For even as indigenous millenarian movements ratify the hopes of native peoples, they represent a break with, and an implicit critique of, specific indigenous practices, if not always with their underlying structure.

In each of the case studies presented here, Indians reached out to powerful outsiders in search of new insights and conceptual categories. This openness to exotic knowledge is part of the highly nuanced, dialectical process by which Amazonian peoples incorporate and, at the same time, define themselves against the differences of others. In the colonial period, selective borrowing (what used to be called "acculturation") became an even more necessary strategy for cultural survival. The militant appropriation of Christianity is a critique of the failure of indigenous models in the face of a vastly changed world, an assertion of subjecthood (as against the passivity promoted by missionaries), and a vital moment in a long-term, underlying cycle within which native peoples actively explore alternatives to their own structures of power.

The growth and consolidation of the Hallelujah religion of Circum-Roraima, which was never suppressed by the local authorities, exemplify the capacity of Amazonian millenarian movements to steer native societies through the rough waters of their own internal contradictions: tendencies toward hierarchy versus a fierce commitment to equality; the continuity of myth versus the need for change in response to new circumstances; ethnic boundary maintenance versus regional integration; resistance to new symbol systems versus their active assimilation. This capacity was fully realized in only a handful of cases in the recorded history of Amazonia. More often, the search for utopia drew a violent response from terrified colonists, and an indigenous social process was forcibly abridged.

NOTES

The research on which this chapter is based was supported by the School of American Research, Santa Fe, New Mexico, and by grants from the National Endowment for the Humanities and the Harry Frank Guggenheim Foundation. For their help in refining these ideas, I would like to thank the participants in the "Amazonian Synthesis" conference, especially the symposium organizer, Anna C. Roosevelt, as well as my fellow resident scholars at the School of American Research. Additional suggestions were kindly provided by Ellen Basso, William H. Crocker, Gertrude Dole, Eduardo Fernández, Shepard Krech III, Priscilla Rachun Linn, David J. Thomas, Neil L. Whitehead, and Norman E. Whitten, Jr. This chapter originally appeared in a slightly different form in *Ethnohistory* 38 (4), 1991; it is reprinted here with permission.

1. I use "millenarian movement" as a general cover term that includes such specific subtypes as messianic and nativistic movements (see Wallace 1956; La Barre 1971). Since most Amazonian revitalization movements contain elements of each of these ideal types, little purpose is served by taxonomic hairsplitting.

2. For essays exploring this issue in a South American context see Hill 1988 and Stern 1987.

3. For economy of expression, in this chapter I use "Amazonia" to include both the Amazon Basin proper and adjacent lowland areas of South America. Although I am aware of no other comparative studies of Amazonian millenarianism in the recent

literature, notable works dating to the 1960s and earlier include Métraux 1941; Pereira de Queiroz 1969; Ribeiro 1962; and Schaden 1965.

4. Let me here acknowledge my debts to the work of Fogelson (1989) and Turner (1988), who in different ways address the problematic distinction between "event" and "process."

5. Hill's assertions are echoed in Nancy McDowell's provocative analysis of Melanesian cargo cults. McDowell (1988, 124) asserts that the rapid social transformations associated with such movements may derive from local assumptions about change. For many Melanesian people, she says, "there is no gradual, cumulative, evolutionary change; change is always dramatic, total, and complete."

6. This analysis of the Tupí Guaraní case draws on the following works: H. Clastres 1978; P. Clastres 1987; Diaz Martinez 1985; Métraux 1927, 1941; Pereira de Queiroz 1969; Shapiro 1987; Susnik 1975; Viveiros de Castro 1986; Wilson 1973. To save space, I cite individual works in the text only when making reference to specific arguments or passages.

7. For a brief analysis and comparison of these works and their implications for Tupian research, see Viveiros de Castro 1986, 103–5.

8. Pierre Clastres (1987, 218) echoes this observation when he observes that "the insurrectional act of the prophets against the chiefs conferred on the former, through a strange reversal of things, infinitely more power than was held by the latter."

9. For this summary of Asháninka messianic movements, I draw primarily on Bodley 1972; Castro Arenas 1973; Fernández 1986; Flores Galindo 1988; Lehnertz 1974; Loayza 1942; Stern 1987; Varese 1973; and Zarzar 1989. Brown and Fernández (1991) review this history in much greater detail and present new information on the millenarian roots of the alliance between Asháninkas and MIR guerrillas in 1965.

10. Some important sources on the Andean belief in Inkarrí include Flores Galindo 1988; Ossio 1973; Stern 1987; Zarzar 1989. References to the Amazonian variations on this and similar themes include Fernández 1984, 1987; Roe 1988; Weiss 1986. Messianic currents in Franciscan thought are discussed in Phelan 1970 and Zarzar 1989.

11. These casualty figures, which differ slightly from those reported in Crocker 1967, were provided by Priscilla Rachun Linn (personal communication, 1990). She also reports that "numerous deaths took place after the relocation because the Canela found life in a woodland ecosystem intolerable."

12. The principal sources for this case study are Agüero 1985 and Regan 1983, 1988; to a lesser extent, I also draw upon Chaumeil 1981 and Seiler-Baldinger 1984. These sources focus on the situation of the Orden Cruzada in Peru. Unfortunately, a recent study of the Brazilian followers of Francisco da Cruz (Oro 1989) came to my attention too late to be included in this analysis.

13. Instances of Tikuna messianism dating to the 1940s are discussed in Nimuendajú 1952.

14. Thomas (1976) discusses indigenous ambivalence about traditional shamanism and the role it has played in the evolution of San Miguel, a modification of the Hallelujah religion that Thomas studied among the Pemón.

15. Thomas (1976, 5), however, notes that among the Pemón, "leaders of religious movements [presumably including Hallelujah] have had influence over a much larger geographic area than have the *capitanes* (political leaders or 'chiefs')."

REFERENCES

Adas, M.
1979   *Prophets of rebellion: Millenarian protest movements against the European colonial order.* Chapel Hill: University of North Carolina Press.
Agüero, O.
1985   El milenio en la Amazonía Peruana: Los hermanos cruzados de Francisco da Cruz. *Amazonía Peruana* 12:133–45.
Balée, W.
1984   The ecology of ancient Tupi warfare. In *Warfare, culture, and environment,* edited by R. Brian Ferguson, 241–65. New York: Academic Press.
Benavides, M.
1990   Levantamiento de los Asháninka del río Pichis: Organización nativa contra guerrilla del MRTA? *Pagina Libre* (Lima), 11 July, 11–33.
Bodley, J. H.
1972   A transformative movement among the Campa of eastern Peru. *Anthropos* 67:220–28.
Brown, M. F.
1988   Shamanism and its discontents. *Medical Anthropology Quarterly* 2:102–20.
1993   Facing the state, facing the world: Amazonia's native leaders and the new politics of identity. *L'Homme* 33 (2–4): 311–30.
Brown, M. F., and E. Fernández
1991   *War of shadows: The struggle for utopia in the Peruvian Amazon.* Berkeley and Los Angeles: University of California Press.
Burridge, K.
1979   *Someone, no one: An essay on individuality.* Princeton, N.J.: Princeton University Press.
1985   Millennialism and the recreation of history. In *Religion, Rebellion, and Revolution,* edited by Bruce Lincoln, 219–35. New York: St. Martin's Press.
Butt, A. J.
1960   Birth of a religion. *Journal of the Royal Anthropological Institute* 90:66–106.
Carneiro da Cunha, M.
1973   Logique du mythe et de l'action: Le mouvement messianique Canela de 1963. *L'Homme* 13 (4): 5–37.

Castro Arenas, M.

1973   *La rebelión de Juan Santos*. Lima: Carlos Milla Batres.

Chaumeil, J.-P.

1981   *Historia y migraciones de los Yagua de finales del siglo diez y siete hasta nuestros días*. Lima: Centro Amazónico de Antropología y Aplicación Práctica.

Clastres, H.

1978   *Terra sem mal: O profetismo Tupi-Guaraní*. São Paulo: Brasiliense.

Clastres, P.

1987   *Society against the state: Essays in political anthropology*. New York: Zone Books.

Colson, A.J.B.

1971   Hallelujah among the Patamona Indians. *Antropológica* (Caracas) 28:25–58.

1985   Routes of knowledge: An aspect of regional integration in the Circum-Roraima area of the Guiana Highlands. *Anthropológica* (Caracas) 63–64:103–49.

Crocker, Wm. H.

1967   The Canela messianic movement: An introduction. *Atas do Simpósio sôbre a Biota Amazônica* 2:69–83.

1989   Was Maria lying? MS.

Diaz Martinez, N.

1985   La migration Mbya (Guaraní). *Dédalo* (São Paulo) 24:148–65.

Fernández, E.

1984   La muerte del Inca: Mitologia Asháninca. *Anthropologica* (Lima) 2: 201–8.

1986   *Para que nuestra historia no se pierda: Testimonios de los Asháninca y Nomatsiguenga sobre la colonización*. Lima: Centro de Investigación y Promoción Amazónica.

1987   Los Asháninca y los Incas: Historia y mitos. *Anthropologica* (Lima) 5:333–56.

Fields, K.

1985   *Revival and rebellion in colonial central Africa*. Princeton, N.J.: Princeton University Press.

Flores Galindo, A.

1988   *Buscando un Inca*. 3d ed. Lima: Editorial Horizonte.

Fogelson, Raymond D.

1989   The ethnohistory of events and nonevents. *Ethnohistory* 36:133–47.

Fry, R. E.

1985   Revitalization movements among the postclassic lowland Maya. In *The lowland Maya postclassic*, edited by A. F. Chase and P. M. Rice, 126–41. Austin: University of Texas Press.

Gorriti, G.
1990   Terror in the Andes: The flight of the Asháninkas. *New York Times
            Magazine*, 2 December, 40–48, 65–72.
Hemming, J.
1987   *Amazon frontier*. London: Macmillan.
Hill, J. D.
1984   Social equality and ritual hierarchy: The Arawakan Wakuénai of Vene-
            zuela. *American Ethnologist* 11:528–44.
Hill, J. D., ed.
1988   *Rethinking history and myth: Indigenous South American perspectives on the
            past*. Urbana: University of Illinois Press.
Hill, J. D., and R. M. Wright
1988   Time, narrative, and ritual: Historical interpretations from an Amazo-
            nian society. In *Rethinking history and myth: Indigenous South American
            perspectives on the past*, edited by J. D. Hill, 78–105. Urbana: University
            of Illinois Press.
Hugh-Jones, S.
1981   Historia del Vaupés. *Maguaré* (Bogotá) 1:29–51.
Jackson, J. E.
1983   *The fish people: Linguistic exogamy and Tukanoan identity in northwest
            Amazonia*. Cambridge: Cambridge University Press.
Kirch, P. V.
1984   *The evolution of the Polynesian chiefdoms*. Cambridge: Cambridge Univer-
            sity Press.
Kracke, W.
1978   *Force and persuasion: Leadership in an Amazonian society*. Chicago: Univer-
            sity of Chicago Press.
La Barre, W.
1971   Materials for a history of studies of crisis cults: A bibliographic essay.
            Current Anthropology 12:3–44.
Lehnertz, J. F.
1974   Lands of the infidels: The Franciscans in the central montaña of Peru,
            1709–1824. Ph.D. diss., University of Wisconsin, Madison.
Loayza, C. A.
1942   *Juan Santos, el invencible*. Lima: Pequeños Grandes Libros de Historia
            Americana.
McDowell, N.
1988   A note on cargo cults and cultural constructions of change. *Pacific
            Studies* 11:121–34.
Melatti, J.
1972   *O messianismo Krahó*. São Paulo: Editora Herder.

Métraux, A.

1927   Migrations historiques des Tupi-Guaraní. *Journal de la Société des Améri-canistes de Paris,* new ser., 19:1–45.

1941   The messiahs of South America. *Interamerican Quarterly* 3 (2): 53–60.

Nimuendajú, C.

1952   *The Tukuna.* University of California Publications in American Archaeology and Ethnology, No. 45. Berkeley and Los Angeles: University of California Press.

Oro, A. P.

1989   *Na amazônia um messias de indios e brancos: Traços para uma antropologia do messianismo.* Petrópolis, Brazil: Editora Voces y Editora da Pontificia Universidad Católica do Rio Grande do Sul.

Ossio, J., ed.

1973   *Ideología mesiánica del mundo andino.* Lima: Ignacio Prado Pastor.

Pereira de Queiroz, M. I.

1969   *Historia y etnología de los movimientos mesiánicos.* Mexico, D.F.: Siglo Veintiuno Editores.

Phelan, J. L.

1970   *The millennial kingdom of the Franciscans in the New World.* 2d ed. Berkeley and Los Angeles: University of California Press.

Pollock, D. K.

1993   Conversion and "community" in Amazonia. In *Conversion to Christianity: Historical and anthropological perspectives on a great transformation,* edited by Robert W. Hefner, 165–98. Berkeley and Los Angeles: University of California Press.

Regan, J.

1983   *Hacia la tierra sin mal: Estudio de la religión del pueblo en la Amazonía.* 2 vols. Iquitos, Peru: Centro de Estudios Teológicos de la Amazonía.

1988   Mesianismo cocama: Un movimiento de resistencia en la Amazonía Peruana. *América Indígena* 48:127–38.

Ribeiro, R.

1962   Brazilian messianic movements. In *Millennial dreams in action,* edited by S. Thrupp, 55–69. The Hague: Mouton.

Roe, P. G.

1988   The *josho nahuanbo* are all wet and undercooked: Shipibo views of the Whiteman and the Incas in myth, legend, and history. In *Rethinking history and myth: Indigenous South American perspectives on the past,* edited by J. D. Hill, 106–35. Urbana: University of Illinois Press.

Roosevelt, A. C.

1987   Chiefdoms in the Amazon and Orinoco. In *Chiefdoms in the Americas,* edited by R. D. Drennan and C. A. Uribe, 153–85. Lanham, Md.: University Press of America.

Schaden, E.
1965   Aculturaçao indígena: Ensaio sôbre fatôres e tendências da mundança
            cultural de tribos índias em contacto com o mundo dos Brancos. *Revista
            de Antropologia* (São Paulo) 13 (1–2): 1–315.
Schwartz, H.
1976   The end of the beginning: Millenarian studies, 1969–75. *Religious
            Studies Review* 2 (3): 1–14.
Scott, J. C.
1985   *Weapons of the weak: Everyday forms of peasant resistance.* New Haven:
            Yale University Press.
Seiler-Baldinger, A.
1984   Indianische Migrationen am Beispiel der Yagua Nordwest-Amazoniens.
            Ethnologica Helvetica (Berne) 8:217–67.
Shapiro, J.
1987   From tupã to the land without evil: The Christianization of Tupi-
            Guarani cosmology. *American Ethnologist* 14:126–39.
Stern, S. J.
1987   The age of Andean insurrection, 1742–1782: A reappraisal. In *Resis-
            tance, rebellion, and consciousness in the Andean peasant world, eighteenth
            to twentieth centuries*, edited by S. J. Stern, 34–93. Madison: University
            of Wisconsin Press.
Susnik, B.
1975   *Dispersión Tupí-Guaraní prehistórica: Ensayo analítico.* Asunción,
            Paraguay: Museo Etnográfico "Andrés Barbero."
Taussig, M.
1987   *Shamanism, colonialism, and the wild man: A study in terror and healing.*
            Chicago: University of Chicago Press.
Thomas, D. J.
1976   El movimiento religioso de San Miguel entre los Pemón. *Antropológica*
            (Caracas) 43:3–52.
Turner, T.
1988   Ethno-ethnohistory: Myth and history in native South American repre-
            sentations of contact with Western society. In *Rethinking history and
            myth: Indigenous South American perspectives on the past*, edited by J. D.
            Hill, 235–81. Urbana: University of Illinois Press.
Varese, S.
1973   *La sal de los cerros.* 2d ed. Lima: Retablo de Papel Ediciones.
Vinhas de Queiroz, M.
1963   "Cargo cult" na Amazônia: Observação sobre o milenarismo Tukuna.
            América Latina (Rio de Janeiro) 6 (4): 43–61.
Viveiros de Castro, E.
1986   *Areweté: Os deuses canibais.* Rio de Janeiro: Jorge Zahar Editor.

Wallace, A. F.C.

1956   Revitalization movements: Some theoretical considerations for their comparative study. *American Anthropologist* 58:264–81.

Weiss, G.

1986   Elements of Inkarrí east of the Andes. In *Myth and the imaginary in the New World*, edited by E. Magaña and P. Mason, 305–20. Amsterdam: Centre for Latin American Research and Documentation.

Whitehead, N. L.

1989   The ancient Amerindian polities of the lower Orinoco, Amazon, and Guayana coast. Paper prepared for the Wenner-Gren International Symposium No. 109, June 1989, at Novo Friburgo, Brazil. Currently the Whitehead essay in this volume.

Wilson, B.

1973   *Magic and the millennium: A sociological study of religious movements of protest among tribal and Third World peoples.* New York: Harper and Row.

Worsley, P.

1968   *The trumpet shall sound: A study of "cargo" cults in Melanesia.* 2d ed. New York: Schocken.

Wright, R., and J. D. Hill

1986   History, ritual, and myth: Nineteenth-century millenarian movements in the northwest Amazon. *Ethnohistory* 33:31–54.

Zarzar, A.

1989   *Apo Capac Huayna, Jesús Sacramentado: Mito, utopía, y milenarismo en el pensamiento de Juan Santos Atahualpa.* Lima: Centro Amazónico de Antropología y Aplicación Práctica.

PART IV STRATEGIES FOR INTEGRATIVE RESEARCH

14

The Eastern Bororo
from an Archaeological Perspective

IRMHILD WÜST

Compared to the present Indian societies, archaeological and ethnohistorical information suggests the existence of more complex sociopolitical systems in the Amazon Basin and the Chaco area in the late prehistoric and early historic periods (Roosevelt 1987; Susnik 1972, 1978). Until recently, explanations for the factors involved in this cultural evolution and the decline of some of these systems prehistorically have been limited to essentially environmental factors. In Amazonia the ecological conditions of the floodplains (várzea) have been considered more favorable for the development of complex societies than the interfluvial "terra firme," where soils are poorer in nutrients and protein availability is generally lower (Gross 1975; Meggers 1975). It is clear that any explanatory model of cultural development in precontact Amazonia must go beyond the possible ecological factors and take into account historical and demographic variables, including what happened outside of the restricted area along the main rivers. However, the degree to which nonecological factors, for instance "social circumscription" (Carneiro 1970), provide compelling explanations for cultural development in Amazonia and elsewhere remains to be demonstrated. From an archaeological point of view, we do not yet know much about those societies and are especially ignorant about the prior forms of sociopolitical and economic organization from which the more complex forms emerged in the Amazon and adjacent areas.

The purpose of this paper is to present some of the results of archaeological and ethnoarchaeological investigations in the Bororo area of Central Brazil that may contribute not only to a better understanding of cultural development along the border of the Amazon Basin but also to a reconsideration of some variables and research strategies not yet sufficiently explored in lowland archaeology. In Central Brazil, large circular villages with considerable populations are known to have existed since at least A.D. 800. There is also evidence for the existence of extensive social networks among the various preconquest groups in the region (Prous 1986; Schmitz et al. 1982; Wüst 1983, 1989), as well as evidence suggesting village site hierarchies and the division of labor between domestic units within villages (Wüst 1990). The ethnographically known Bororo, however, underwent significant cultural change in settlement patterns, subsistence strategies, and demography following the first direct contact with national—that is, Western—society. As a result, however, an image of the Bororo as "primitive" hunter-gatherers confined to savanna areas still permeates ethnographic literature. This erroneous classification of the central Brazilian tribes as "marginals" (Steward 1946) has drawn attention away from this area, and the archaeology of the Amazon region has not taken into consideration the evidence from it.

Data from the Bororo area demonstrate that the portrayal of these societies as "marginal" hunters and gatherers is false and that the Bororo and many other native central Brazilian groups were, in fact, settled agriculturalists living in large, more or less permanent villages. Furthermore, extensive interaction between groups from various regions and complex patterns of population movements and migrations—sometimes accompanied by warfare and/or the fusion of different cultural and ethnic groups—attests to the complex and dynamic nature of the sociopolitics of the region. These findings help us to place in perspective the emergence of the complex social structures of the Bororo and other central Brazilian Gê-speaking groups, long considered anomalous.

Research Strategies

The research area is situated in the southeastern part of the state of Mato Grosso (53° 30' to 55° 30' W and 15° 30' to 17° 30' S) in the Lourenço River Basin, which comprises a large part of the traditional Bororo territory.

Archaeological interpretations depend to some degree on the use of analogous models derived from other fields, like geography, physics, and anthropology. However, the validity of reasoning by analogy is still a sharply debated matter in the epistemology of the social sciences (Murray and Walker 1988).

To avoid the common pitfalls of such reasoning, ethnoarchaeological data are used here to formulate alternative working hypotheses. Cultural continuity between the present Bororo Indians and their ancestors of at least three centuries, based on archaeological evidence, permits us to take a direct historical approach. Nevertheless, other models of more general scope are also employed here, particularly in discussing precolonial societies of the more remote past. Most of the ethnoarchaeological data used here was obtained during fieldwork conducted in January 1977 in the village of Córrego Grande and from January 1983 to August 1984 in the village of Tadarimana.[1] The Bororos' sustained contact with the national society has contributed to a general cultural decline and a near abandonment of the use of ceramic and lithic artifacts over the past 30 years. The focus of ethnoarchaeological investigation has been on aspects of territorial behavior, demographic parameters, and an emic view of sociocultural processes because these are the traits most susceptible to study.

The life histories of the elders of this society and their emic geographical maps furnished important insights into the location of old villages, the density of occupation, social networks, mobility, and the hierarchical aspects of settlement structure and system. The emic maps were based on the toponomy of rivers, lakes, mountains, regions, and local geographical features like river bends and bedrock outcroppings. Most of the informants were able to draw mental maps of the region on the ground that were extremely useful in plotting old village sites and specific resource areas. When Bororo Indians accompanied archaeological researchers, the names of geographical features could sometimes be checked, but such information is still sparse for a large part of their territory. We have some information about specific resources, like wild tobacco, native tubers, and various plant species used in handicraft manufacture. In the future, specific ecological studies of animal and plant resources will be of importance for evaluating resource potentials and for determining the extent to which place names are correlated with areas of major occurrence of specific resources. Additionally, data about population fluctuations, relationships between villages, patterns of domestic space in relation to demographic aspects, and the dynamics of spatial organization at the village level have been obtained during the project's population census and through the measurement and mapping of structures in the Tadarimana village.

Oral traditions—specifically mythology—may be found to contain historical elements when adequately decoded. The collection and interpretation of myth cycles (instead of isolated myths, as presented by Albisetti and Venturelli 1969 and Colbacchini and Albisetti 1942) and of songs and informal oral traditions provide us with an insight into the Bororos' emic vision about their history, as well as their cultural processes and the nature of relationships among various social and ethnic groups through time (see Viertler 1986).

Data about the disposal of those materials that might survive in the archaeological record have been obtained primarily by direct observation and interviewing. At present, however, it is difficult to evaluate the real behavior associated with many of these artifacts during their use-life, including their involvement in social networks within and between settlements, due to fundamental changes in material culture as a result of contact (e.g., the abandonment of ceramic manufacture). For example, intriguing correlations related to the differential use of ceramic vessel forms based on social structure, specifically in terms of clan units, has been obtained almost exclusively through interviews.

The ethnohistorical documents contain relatively poor ethnographic information, are generally limited to the description of conflicts, and reflect the foreigner's ideology in regard to the indigenous people. Even if the demographic data furnished by missionaries and government entities have to be handled with care, however, initial comparisons of the relationship between floor area and population show significant changes in this ratio, at least when contact with the national society became more intensive about 1940. This means that any population parameters obtained in a recent ethnographic context have to be used with caution for precontact situations, for they will likely be underestimates.

Additional ethnohistorical information about the relationship between the Bororo and the national society, and the cultural impact of contact with the first colonizers of the Rio Vermelho and Garças region, has been obtained from today's population, and in some cases it has been possible to compare the information with testimony of the individuals involved. However, in the past few years research conditions in most of the Bororo villages have become extremely difficult, which is why I pay more attention here to the archaeological investigation itself.

Our archaeological approach to this area, whose prehistory is still relatively unknown, began with a research design for an intensive surface examination of sampling areas of about 20 × 15 km located in the various ecological zones. To date, 14 sampling areas have been surveyed, especially in the basin of the Vermelho River, one of the major affluents of the São Lourenço River, resulting in the discovery of 145 archaeological sites. These include open-air camps of hunter-gatherers, rock shelters with pictographs and paintings, and villages of ceramic-using agriculturalists. Based on their material culture, 33 of the sites are identified as old Bororo villages and camps, nearly all relating to the historic period.

A preliminary chronological sequence of precolonial occupation, based on 23 absolute dates,[2] permits the formulation of several hypotheses concerning changes in the territorial behavior of groups with different subsistence systems and technological traditions. It has also been possible to establish some links between distinct classes of sites and, most important, to document the first presence of the ethnographically known Bororo in the Rio Vermelho Basin.

The main purpose of archaeological investigations has been to gain an understanding of cultural systems and processes over time from the first precolonial occupation up to the time of the historically documented Bororo Indians. Theoretical and methodological inquiry focuses on spatial analysis at regional, local, and site-specific levels, which we consider here as a powerful instrument for formulating questions about sociocultural changes in past societies. Large-scale excavations at some of the sites will be crucial for the testing of specific hypotheses, especially those concerning differences in the use of space, the composition of domestic units, the nature of contacts between groups of different subsistence and technological bases, and social stratification at the level of the site.

Ethnohistorical and Ethnoarchaeological Data

Some Historical Considerations

The first ethnohistorical references to the Bororo date back to 1649 when the *bandeirante*[3] leader Antônio Rapôso Tavares mentions the Coxipônes (Siqueira 1898–99, 8–10), who may be considered a group of Bororo Indians. With the beginning of the gold rush to the region of Cuiabá in 1718, mutual hostilities characterized relations with Brazilian society until the end of the nineteenth century (Coelho 1872, 139–40; Mello Rego 1895, 92). Some villages soon surrendered, however, enabling Antônio Pires de Campos to create an army of 600 Bororo in 1728, which raided other native societies such as the Payaguá and Southern Kayapó (Carvalho 1946, 92). The division of the Bororo into eastern and western groups during the eighteenth century, with the two groups separated by the Paraguay River, resulted from the pressures of contact with national society (Albisetti and Venturelli 1962, 217–18). The region along the Vermelho River represented the last place of refuge for the "free" Bororo. To attract the groups that were still independent at the end of the nineteenth century, military posts were established on the São Lourenço River but they were soon replaced by Salesian missions (Albisetti and Venturelli 1962, 218–20; Steinen 1894).

Finally, around A.D. 1900 the last uncontacted Bororo of the Vermelho and Garças rivers came into direct contact with Brazilian society when a telegraph line was constructed between Goiás and Mato Grosso (Rondon 1949, 92) and when settlers from the state of Goiás crossed the Araguaia River to establish cattle ranches in southeastern Mato Grosso. During the first half of this century, most of the traditional villages disintegrated due to decimating massacres and epidemics of infectious diseases such as measles and influenza. The remaining Bororo Indians became general laborers on the settlers' farms, where they sometimes established small camps with four or five houses and where they maintained remnants of their traditional culture. In general, their relationship with the settlers can be described as pacific, but the minimal payment they received for their work—primarily cloth, tobacco, and liquor—and drastic changes in their diet contributed to a rapid decline leading to cultural and biological decadence. The Brazilian informants we interviewed about the native labor force describe the Bororo of the 1930s and 1940s as small, scattered groups without any agriculture and as a miserable band of human beings.

When Indian reservations were established by the Serviço de Proteção ao Índio (SPI)[4] in 1940, most of the Bororo came back to some of their traditional village areas. Demoralized by the contact situation, the inefficiency of Indian policy, the loss of most of their traditional territory, their demographic decline due to epidemics, and the resulting radical change in lifestyle, the Bororo resorted to widespread infanticide, still clearly perceptible in demographic curves (Wüst 1990).

Today the Bororo live in five main villages and number about 700 people (Novaes and Grupioni 1986), more than half of whom live in Salesian missions. After suffering from the disastrous economic projects of the Fundação Nacional do Índio (FUNAI)[5] during the 1980s they returned to their former system of slash-and-burn agriculture (see Serpa 1988), although traditional maize cultivation has been largely replaced by rice and manioc cultivation. Fishing and hunting small mammals still furnish most of the Bororo's protein requirements. Their dependence on cooking oil, sugar, coffee, and manufactured goods has stimulated handicraft production and husbandry of small domestic animals, which are sold in local towns.

Traditional Bororo Territory and Neighbors

The largest expanse of Bororo territory mentioned in the nineteenth-century sources extended from the southwestern part of the state of Goiás to the Paraguay River and from the Rio das Mortes to the city of Campo Grande (Colbacchini and Albisetti 1942, 29). Great geomorphological and ecological diversity is characteristic of this large area, which includes savanna, extensive gallery forests along the main streams, and swamps along the middle and lower part of the São Lourenço River. In the higher altitudes, water is found only near stands of *buriti* palms (*Mauritia* sp.). The occurrence of "ecotones" throughout the region, which are frequently the product of soil conditions, make a complicated mosaic of vegetation cover.

Nearly all the traditional Bororo villages are situated along the main rivers, where fish are abundant and soils are more fertile than in the savanna regions. Distances between neighboring villages in the Rio Vermelho Basin varied in the first half of this century between 18 and 28 km. A nearest-neighbor analysis indicates a mean spacing of 21.9 km, which, in terms of their subsistence pattern, can be interpreted as a mature phase of occupation.

In contrast to other central Brazilian groups like the Shavante (Maybury-Lewis 1967), Bororo villages constitute relatively stable sociopolitical and economic units, with little evidence of village splitting and intervillage hostility. Strong ceremonial ties, especially in the event of funerals, link members of often distant populations and facilitate the exchange of the varied resources of diverse ecological zones. Steinen (1894, 481), for instance, mentions the exchange of tobacco, cotton, and gourds for arrows between people living along the Vermelho and São Lourenço rivers. The villages from Córrego Grande up to the headwaters seem to have been part of a unique "ceremonial province," whereas the occupants of the Lower São Lourenço at Pirigara and the communities near Cuiabá formed distinct ceremonial provinces.

Population flux is still very common among the Bororo villages. During the period of observation at Tadarimana, nearly a third of the inhabitants changed their residence over the course of a year and a half. The individuals' motives for moving included personal quarrels, deaths, dissatisfaction with the food supply, and pressure from the national society. The migrants carry most of their household goods, even domestic animals, away with them. Life histories of older Bororo reveal that a similar pattern existed earlier and may not be related solely to present situations of stress. Most of the people interviewed had lived in about nine different villages. This elevated mobility among widely separated villages might eventually produce an extremely high homogeneity of material culture and genetic patterning that might be detectable in the archaeological record.

Settlements in the Bororo territory are hierarchically ordered; however, whereas site hierarchies are normally expressed by demography, settlement size, functional diversification (Flannery 1976), or even geographic location (Chernela 1986), the hierarchical position of Bororo settlement is considered a function primarily of the presence of shamans and the number of funerals held. The shaman is an extremely important person in Bororo society, and the presence of one or more of these ritual specialists seems related to population size. In fact, the absence of a shaman results in severe dietary restrictions, because most of the meat, some fruits, and the first maize harvested have to be blessed by the shaman before consumption. Nonetheless, the extreme population mobility—including that by shamans—changes the hierarchical order of villages frequently and therefore may obscure this pattern archaeologically. Likewise, although funerals stimulate visits between villages, the visitors, when staying for an extended period, live with their relatives, and no new houses are constructed.

Until the 1950s the Bororo still practiced a kind of trekking, though villages were not totally abandoned. Smaller groups without any specific clan or moiety affiliation (Crocker 1967, 30) wandered along preestablished routes, frequently including visits to other villages. These expeditions during the dry season might last up to three months and were executed mainly to obtain a variety of feathers, specific types of wood, and fibers that did not exist in the village catchment area. Camps were constructed within a day's travel of each other. People brought their smaller household implements with them, so it may be possible to detect some of the resting places archaeologically. Shorter expeditions might take place even during the rainy season before crops were ripe in the gardens.

Life histories revealed still another kind of collective excursion through the Bororo territory. Before receiving their penis sheaths, boys would travel up to two years to quite distant places, accompanied by their sponsors. During this time they learned the names of geographic features and the location of rich resources sometimes referred to in mythology.

Traditional neighbors of the Bororo are linguistically and culturally distinct. In early historic times, most were characterized by large settlements and complex village organization, occasionally associated with the incorporation of alien groups. To the north and northwest lived manioc cultivators like the Bakairi (Carib) and the Paresi (Arawak).[6] Both experienced considerable displacement during the past hundred years (Gruenberg 1970, 685; Oberg 1953, 33–39; Schmidt 1914, 168–72) and were reduced in 1978 to 349 and 685 people respectively (Moonen 1983). To the west and southwest are the Guató and Xarae.[7] By the nineteenth century the Xarae had ceased to exist (Susnik 1978, 32–33), and the few surviving Guató families (totaling about 220 people) occupy a marginal position in contemporary society (Moonen 1983). To the south are the Payaguá, Guaikuru, and Mbayá of the Guaiaki linguistic family. To the southeast were the Southern Kayapó, now extinct, and to the east and northeast the Karajá, and since the nineteenth century, the Shavante (of the Macro-Gê family).

Ethnohistorical data from the Chaco region show that the expansion of the Inca Empire and the penetration of Europeans along the Paraguay River in the first half of the sixteenth century caused considerable displacement of native groups (Susnik 1972, 1978), which may have been responsible for the appearance of the Bororo in their present habitat. Hence, the relatively stable picture outlined by the map of Nimuendajú (1982) seems to be of little direct relevance for possible correlations between ethnic groups and archaeological evidence from this period and before.

Demographic Aspects

Demographic patterns are an important indicator of the degree of sociopolitical complexity. For eastern Brazil, Steward and Faron (1959, 51–60) suggest an aboriginal population density not exceeding 0.12 persons per km^2, with community sizes of 150 people or less. These population estimates are based on ethnographic projections from the postcontact situation and are extremely low. Ethnohistorical data for the Bororo, the Southern Kayapó (da Silva and Souza 1874, 452–55), and other tribes mentioned above do not sustain such a picture, at least with respect to village populations before the first half of the eighteenth century. Indeed, there are references to Bororo villages formed by six or more concentric rings of houses (Colbacchini and Albisetti 1942, 35). A plan from the first half of this century (Rondon and Faria 1948) still shows 140 houses forming three concentric circles. Using a mean of 10.7 persons per house (the mean of Córrego Grande in 1910) we arrive at an estimate of about 1,500 individuals for this village. Only archaeological investigation can reveal whether these large settlements were exceptional or constituted the common pattern.

The scarce ethnographic data on intravillage demographic aspects and village plans permitted me to establish only tentative parameters on the number of persons per house. Mean ratios of house floor to population show significant changes over time, with a clear decline in population per house unit, accompanied by a reduction of house floor size. For the period from 1905 to 1919, the mean number of persons per residential unit was 10.7 (lowest, 3.6; highest, 16.7; $N = 17$), and decreased to 6.1 (lowest, 3.3; highest, 11; $N = 24$) from 1936 onward. In Tadarimana this mean oscillated between 49 and 6.5 during 1983 and 1984 (Wüst 1990).

House size in Tadarimana varies from 16 to 52 m^2, with a mean of 31 m^2 ($N = 11$). Larger houses seem to have existed in the past, and Lévi-Strauss (1970, 208) mentioned that one house of 60 m^2 remained in Kejare in 1935. In Tadarimana, the mean size of the house floor per person varies from 7 to

8.2 m², but when the rate of 3.5 m² per person is reached, additional covered areas are constructed.

Accurate population estimates for the entire traditional Bororo territory are not yet available. The predominant linear occupation along the main streams and the relatively little space between the villages before the first half of this century suggest that population density varied considerably between riverine zones and the hinterland. The highest actual population estimate for the Eastern Bororo accounts for about 10,000 individuals (Cook 1908). This would mean a population density of only 0.029 persons per km² for the entire Bororo territory, unrealistically low even for the conservative estimation of Steward and Faron (1959).

In addition, Cirilo Bororo mentioned the presence of other hostile groups like the "Baridiragudo" and the "Raraidoge," who occupied rock shelters and sometimes stole Bororo women and children. This would indicate an overlap of exploitive territories by different groups in the more distant interfluves, only sporadically explored by the Bororo, and a higher regional population.

The Village and the Village Plan

Bororo society is characterized by the presence of two exogamous matrilineal moieties (Ecerae and Tugarege). Each moiety is divided into four clans, and the predominant residential pattern is matrilocal. Among the clans, other subdivisions, such as lineages, determine the hierarchical positions of individuals in society (Crocker 1967; Viertler 1976). Houses are arranged in a circle around a large plaza with the *baimanagejéwu* (the men's clubhouse) in the center. The main axis of this rectangular structure is oriented to the north, perpendicular to the river. On the west side of the men's clubhouse is the *bororo*, a semicircular area where most of the ceremonies are held and where the primary burial service is carried out.

In contrast to other central Brazilian Indians, the Bororo social order is visible in the layout of the village. Houses of Ecerae women are situated in the northern half of the settlement, and those of Tugarege women in the southern half. The residential units of each clan follow a preestablished order by which those of higher prestige are situated at the end of each of the semicircles (Viertler 1976, 174–76). An imaginary line divides the village from east to west, with the west axis extended by a straight path (the *aije rea*), which terminates within about 30 m with the *aije muga*, a ceremonial place used for some of the male initiation rites.

When a new settlement is built, preference is given to a place where there is some savanna and forest and where the terrain slopes gently to the west[8] following the direction of the main river, which should not be far away. The presence of a water hole or creek is important as a water supply when the rivers become dirty during the rainy season. Construction begins with the central house, whose size depends on the number of adult men in the village. Nowadays, all central houses are composed of only one internal row, but Kasimiro Bororo remembered the village called Koitoguru, where there existed four such internal segments. Subsequently the houses of the Baadogeba clan were built, and afterward the residence units of the other members. With population growth, new residential units are constructed in a second circle so that some of the married daughters come to live behind the mother's house. When a house becomes old and rotten, a new one can be raised behind the first. Sometimes a provisional house at some distance from the inner circle can be replaced by a permanent one on the prescribed locale in the circle. The former house still may be used for some handicraft activities or for raising small domestic animals. When someone dies, the house is burned and another is built nearby.

Today, village diameters vary from 110 meters in Tadarimana to 140 in Córrego Grande. The distance between the eleven houses in Tadarimana varies from 7 to 27 meters, the ideal spacing between residential units corresponding to the length of a house. Thus, a village like Tadarimana could theoretically support 25 houses in the inner circle, which means there could be a maximum of 221 persons for a single-row village. However, during the observation period the population never exceeded 54 persons, and at any one time only about 60 to 70 percent of the archaeologically detectable house floors were occupied in this village (see fig. 14.1).

A settlement is abandoned when it becomes too dirty, when houses are falling down, or when there are too many deaths. A new village is then constructed, usually within a distance of a hundred meters. The name of the village does not change, so it can be considered more a designation for a community than for a specific locality. This practice sometimes makes it difficult to obtain an exact archaeological identification of a specific village mentioned in ethnohistorical sources.

The morphological aspects and dynamics of settlement outlined above have important implications for archaeological interpretation. The houses of the inner circle are not always the oldest structures, and the recovered habitation floor do not necessarily express simultaneous occupations, so their number has to be used with caution in preparing population estimates. However, the existence of several kinds of units that reflect population—including number of hearths, house size, the number and length of house rings, and the size of the men's clubhouse—makes population estimates independently verifiable.

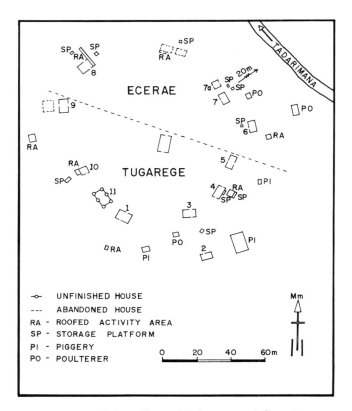

Figure 14.1. The layout of the village of Tadarimana, July 1983.

The Use of Space

Traditionally, the Bororo house (fig. 14.2) represents a multifamily residence without inner partitions, in which each nuclear family occupies a specific section, physically represented by a platform made of wooden rods. Nowadays there is only one fireplace, but in ancient times it is said that each nuclear family had its own fireplace situated along the main axis of the house (Colbacchini and Albisetti 1942, 37). In modern rectangular houses there are two entrances, generally not centered, one facing the central place and the other, somewhat sloping, on the back. In more traditional houses, one entry is placed on the side of the house and another faces the back.

The smaller section of the house is used mainly for subsistence activities, like preparing, processing, and storing food. Near the fireplace, which is centered between the doors, most of the vessels are stored on a special platform situated on the back or a side wall. In this section, predominantly female activities like cooking are carried out, but occasionally activities by men, such as splitting coconuts with stone tools or the polishing of bone tools, take place here.

The larger part of the house is used for sleeping, making fiber and wooden artifacts, and storing personal objects along the walls and under the roof. Sometimes larger receptacles containing beverages for ceremonial purposes are stored here, where they are secure from the traffic of people and animals. In this part of the house there is no clear sexual division in the use of space. Most of the activities are carried out on the platforms. At night during the colder period of the year, a small temporary fire is made beneath the platforms. The walls facing the central area are more valued than the back walls because people can see what is going on in the village. Therefore, a relation between the position of the platforms and social rank can be presumed. The center of the house, marked by a huge post, is for social and ritual functions and visitors.

The front of the house is kept clean, and only occasional work is carried out there by men when there is shade. It is the place where the members of

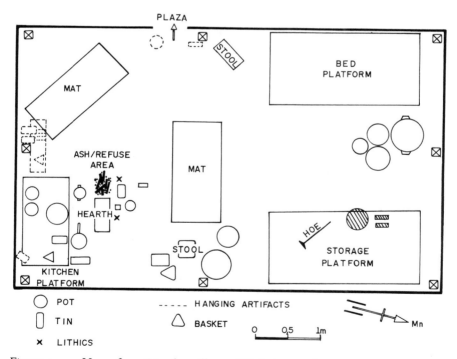

Figure 14.2. Housefloor 6 in the village of Tadarimana, January 1983.

the household assemble during public ceremonies when not directly engaged in them. The area behind the house is intensively used for innumerable dirty tasks: cleaning animals and fish, cooking in larger pots, even by men, and preparing babaçu leaves (Orbygnia sp.) over a fire. The leaves are used for making mats, bags, and fans. The domestic waste is scattered all over this area up to a distance of ten meters from the house. Here fires are not usually made in a fixed location. Instead, new fires are prepared for each task.

Nowadays some little platforms behind or at the side of the house are used to store dishes and food for a short time. In some cases there is already a separate structure beside the house where domestic activities are carried out and where most of the day is spent. Domestic animals are kept near the back of the house, and some plants are grown there as well. At some distance from the house in the direction of the water, there is an area where physical elimination functions are carried out.

From each house, separate paths lead to the nearest water and to the garden plots. In Tadarimana, fields are no farther than half an hour from the village, whereas in Córrego Grande some of them can be reached only by a two-hour walk. When fields are more distant, the whole family may stay there for some time in a garden house.

In the men's clubhouse, men conduct ceremonial activities, make wooden and bone artifacts, and spin cotton, which among the Bororo are exclusively male tasks. Except for some stone polishers, implements used here are stored in the individual houses. Generally there are no platforms, and mats or hammocks are used for sitting and sleeping. There are two opposed fireplaces, which are used for heating some food carried in vessels from the houses. During ceremonies, the main participants are grouped around the heavy wooden post that forms the center of the structure, while the members of the community who are assisting in the ceremonies remain near the longer walls.

The major discard activities of the bororo are related to primary burial, ceremonial meals, and the burning and smashing of personal objects during secondary burial. Only the vessels of the shaman escape this process. They are deposited in a distant place near a large tree in the forest. Today the deposition of the funeral bag—which contains the ornamented bones of the dead, some personal objects, and part of the stone and glass splinters used during the mourning rite—occurs in a nearby lake or in an inundated area of a spring. In former times, burials also took place in rock shelters (Albisetti and Venturelli 1962, 537) or even on the riverbank in shallow holes covered with nettles, as in the village of Arigao Bororo (information from Simiro Bororo).

From the other areas outside the village circle, frequented only by males for some ritual performances, we expect to find archaeologically only some tools, especially those linked to the preparation of wood. At *aije muga* men make bull-roarers and perform initiation rites, and at *todúio bororo*, which is generally situated east of the village, logs for ceremonial purposes are prepared.

Ceramic Artifacts

The Bororo ceased the regular production of ceramic vessels 20 to 30 years ago, but we observed the few that remain during ritual performances. Pottery making is a female task and is carried out especially in the early dry season before clay becomes too difficult to dig. Traditionally, pottery was produced inside the houses and the refuse was thrown into the fireplace.

There are four principal vessel categories: two sizes of simple bowls and two sizes of pots with necks. Clay is tempered with the ash or charcoal of wood from various trees, depending on the ecological zone near the village. Smaller pots are modeled, and the larger ones are produced through coiling. Most vessel walls are between 0.5 and 0.9 cm thick. The bottoms are round, and there are no thickened rims. Treatment with plant juice after burning gives a somewhat dark brown color to the vessels (Muccillo and Wüst 1978).

Beyond the common vessel forms used by all members of the society, there are some special ones associated with specific clans. Most of these distinctive clan-owned vessels belong to the Tugarege moiety. They are characterized by some appliqué decoration and are oblong, globular, or even oval in shape. The only special form, attributed to members of the Ecerae moiety, is a shouldered water pot. These specific vessel forms express social codes, but due to the ritual ties, which frequently involve the loan and use of implements with clan connotation by an individual's counterpart in another clan, we should not expect spatial exclusivity at the house of their real owner.

An Emic View of Tribal History

Mythology plays an important role in justifying social relations in Bororo society and includes some important historical information when adequately decoded. The following interpretation of mythology and informal oral tradition is intended to reveal the Bororos' view of their past (for a more detailed discussion, see Viertler 1986).

The first stage was characterized by the absence of agriculture and the presence of hostility between local communities. These hostile relations were slowly replaced by an exchange system in which women were an important element. According to Cirilo Bororo, the 54 recorded villages, which are located in distinct regions within the Bororo territory, were clan property prior to the final process of confederation. Such a clan attribution may indicate the political predominance of the respective proto-clans in such areas or may reflect a former situation in which ancestors of some *iedaga mage* (matrilinear groups) occupied these specific areas. A simple mental projection of the village plan and social relationships seems unlikely since the myths reveal that hostilities between clan protagonists occurred, especially between those said to have occupied adjacent territories, and the quarrels ceased with confederation.

According to the emic view, the real Bororo came into existence only when all these scattered local groups were united by Akaruio Bokodori (the mythical hero of the Ecerae moiety) at the village called Arua Bororo. The mythical hero of the Tugarege moiety ceded his power to his counterpart in the Ecerae moiety. Secondary burial was established, and the cultural values and norms of Tugarege (considered the real Bororo) were imposed on all. Some other hostile alien groups were incorporated, such as the Koróge, who entered the Paiow clan, and the Karówe and Kayapó, who entered the Iwagudo clan (Viertler 1976, 156). By the establishment of ritual names and a general reciprocity between members of both moieties, internal peace became part of the new "morality." Based on the same myths, Zerries (1953) described the Bororo in a somewhat simplistic manner as the product of the fusion of two different culture groups: the Ecerae (sedentary agriculturalists) and the Tugarege (hunter-gatherers and the conquerors).

Another myth describes a similar process when a second village called Arigao Bororo was established by the same cultural hero, Akaruio Bokodori, near the confluence of the Vermelho and Tadarimana rivers. When this village no longer supported the construction of new residential units, village splitting occurred. Seven new settlements arose along the Tadarimana, Vermelho, and São Lourenço rivers. Their names survived until the first half of this century and designated communities established in proximity to the first villages. The spatial distribution of these villages in relation to Arigao Bororo indicates a dispersion in all directions except southward. The nearest villages formed after the dissolution of Arigao Bororo are situated 23 to 33 km away, and the most distant one 60 km away.

The Archaeological Evidence

The earliest occupation of this area is represented by three campsites of hunter-gatherers which may date back to the beginning of the Holocene. The sites are situated in savanna regions near large rivers rich in fish. A comparison of stone tools indicates that these sites were associated with the Itaparica tradition, which has been dated in southeastern Goiás at 9000 to

6500 B.C. Food remains from sites of this tradition indicate a generalized hunting and gathering subsistence (Schmitz 1987, 66–73).

The characteristic tools at these sites are well-retouched unifacial scrapers, denticulated scrapers, perforators, and unmodified flakes used for cutting. Chert, in the form of river cobbles, is the predominant raw material. Site density seems to be low, and the relative uniformity of the technology over a vast region (from northeastern Brazil to southeastern Mato Grosso) may indicate a common origin. With the rise of the Altithermal, this technological tradition disappears in the research area.

Between these older groups and the producers of another lithic tradition, predominantly established in the savanna areas, there is an enormous gap. Dates between 4000 and 1020 B.C. —for the lower layers of some rock shelters—are associated with a simple flake industry of chert and quartzite characterized by direct and indirect percussion. Most of the rock paintings and some of the geometric engravings may be attributable to this period.

Another lithic tradition is dated at around 600 B.C. Open-air sites and rock shelters of this period are now in ecotones between savanna and forest. The more permanent camps can reach up to 250 meters in length but seem to represent successive reoccupations. This lithic industry is characterized by thick flakes of quartzite with occasional retouching, used mainly to scrape and cut. Based on dates from rock shelters, the preceramic stage seems to have continued until at least 160 B.C. In the upper layers of one open-air site (at a depth of 15 cm) dwelling floors of burned clay were encountered, and above them, in association with the same lithic tradition, ceramic fragments and polished stone tools begin to appear. There is no evidence for a local development of this ceramic, and its presence may have been due to contacts with ceramic-using groups. The processes of contact and the possibility that ceramic artifacts were introduced in combination with an agricultural food-producing system are still unclear, as well as the nature of exchange systems, as proposed by Spielmann (1986), and require further investigation.

The transition from hunter-gathering to agriculture appears to be commonly related to stress situations (see for example, Redding 1988) and some of our empirical data seem to support this supposition. The location of small temporary camps (still of the preceramic period) on the top of elevated hills with a high degree of visibility, articulated with the more permanent camps, may be the expression of defensive strategies in which various groups may have occasionally exploited the same territories, a probable indicator of increased population density and perhaps crowding. Furthermore, frequent reoccupation of the same base camps and the increasing preference for ecotones may be evidence of a need to diversify subsistence strategies and that dispersion could not be used as an escape mechanism in the event of conflicts. Therefore, internal stress, contacts with ceramic-bearing groups of possible food producers, and the adoption of a new settlement strategy may have favored the transition from a hunter-gatherer stage to agriculture in this region.

Rich carbon layers in the riverbank sediments of the Vermelho River with absolute dates of A.D. 230 are attributed to human burning (Emmerich 1988, 106–7). The presence of moister soil conditions and a well-developed gallery forest, which certainly existed in this period, seem to exclude the possibility that these layers represent hunting activities and suggest the beginnings of agriculture. Sediments in the subsequent level indicate (similar to the findings of Hammen [1982] and Saldarriaga and West [1986]) for Amazon region) the beginning of a somewhat drier period here estimated at between A.D. 450 and 750. The extent to which these climatic changes were responsible for a delay in the development of effective agriculture in this region, however, needs further inquiry.

We still have no botanical evidence for cultivated species, but the oldest circular ceramic-age sites here attributed to agricultural groups have been dated to A.D. 800. Pottery from these villages can be identified as a local variation of the Uru tradition established for middle and southern Goiás (Schmitz et al. 1982). The ceramics are generally plain, with occasional red slip and appliqué ornaments. The predominant temper is a siliceous ash called *cariapé*. Vessels generally have curved contours, and rims vary from direct to thickened. Most of the bases are plain, and vessel walls are 1.0 to 1.8 cm thick. Huge bowls and jars are the predominant vessel forms. Griddles appear only in the later sites, dated from the thirteenth century onward.[9] Tubular pipes and spindle whorls indicate the processing of tobacco and cotton.

The villages of these groups are generally situated on the upper or middle part of gentle slopes in interfluve areas characterized by savanna vegetation. They vary from 110 to 410 m in diameter, and consist of from one to three concentric house rings. Some better-preserved sites show one or two ceramic concentrations in the center, probably identifiable with specific activity areas like the men's clubhouse, and in these areas only a limited range of vessel forms are present. The proportion of small and large sites furnishes only slight evidence for village splitting, and difference in site size is thought to be related more to temporal evolution. Shallow refuse (20–30 cm), the short distances between sites (sometimes less than 0.5 km), and even an overlapping of plans from sites of the same ceramic tradition exclude the possibility of concomitant occupation and seem to indicate short site longevity and relatively frequent movement of a village within a restricted area. The relatively poor soil conditions and the sometimes great distance from rivers with plentiful fish suggest a dependence on agricultural products that did not require nutrient-rich soils (e.g., manioc) and on hunting.

A few early sites of the Uru ceramic tradition, nevertheless, are situated along main streams, which represents a deviation from the general settlement pattern. Absolute dates demonstrate the concomitance of these sites with interfluvial ones. Ceramics of the polychrome Tupiguarani pottery tradition (generally ascribed to canoe-bearing people) are present in some of these riverine Uru sites. Therefore, their exceptional location may be related to a defensive strategy against Tupiguarani invasions from riverine areas rather than to the exploitation of distinct ecozones to permit the exchange of differentially available resources to offset ecological stress situations.

The existence of population pressure or conflict in the latter half of the fourteenth century is suggested by the establishment of two small circular villages and a funeral shelter on the top of at least one mesa situated 480 m above the surrounding valley where access is extremely difficult. The ceramic assemblage of these sites can be considered a variant of the Uru ceramic tradition, but some of the vessel forms resemble those of the later Bororo tradition.

The upper layers of some rock shelters situated near open-air sites with dates between A.D. 800 and 1010 indicate an articulation between these two kinds of sites. Morphology, shallow refuse, the predominant lithic waste due to recycling, and the near absence of larger vessels in the rock shelters seem to exclude their serving as habitation sites. Despite significant changes in the rock art—now predominantly figurative (animal and human images)—the stone implements indicate cultural continuity with the former preceramic stage. However, only the genetics of the skeletal remains of both the preceramic and the ceramic groups will allow us to clarify whether the population changed or if local cultural evolution took place.

The last precolonial occupation of the area can be identified with the ancestors of the ethnographically known Bororo Indians. All the traditional Bororo villages archaeologically detected in the Vermelho River Basin are situated along the main streams, where gallery forests may reach a considerable extent. Some older Bororo villages, somewhat westward on the São Lourenço River, are located in a prevailing savanna zone where agricultural land is relatively scarce.

Their first settlement along the Vermelho River—called Arigao Bororo and identified by the contemporary Bororo—is dated to A.D. 1720 ±70 (Wüst 1990). Analysis of the ceramic artifacts at this site shows that Bororo and Uru traditions are stratigraphically associated within a layer 30 cm thick. From surface evidence, this site has a diameter of 450 m, which indicates a considerable total population. From this period onward, villages of the Uru tradition no longer exist, although in some still precontact Bororo sites we find some polychrome Tupiguarani pottery. The mutual loaning of technological and morphological aspects in ceramic production, even within the same sites, seems to indicate that members of both ceramic traditions occupied these villages simultaneously. In most archaeologically identified Bororo settlements, the presence of industrial artifacts shows first contacts with the national society.

Significant changes in settlement pattern, village size, and material culture occurred with the intensification of contact with Brazilian society during the first half of the twentieth century. Settlements of this period were usually established in savanna areas far from main streams and on or near settlers' farms in places where soil conditions do not allow for traditional agriculture. The decline and final abandonment of ceramic production and lithic artifacts were associated with the growing adoption of industrial products.

Despite profound changes in material culture and demography, the present-day Bororo actively reinforce their cultural identity, especially through the revitalization of funeral rites that directly relate to cosmology, traditional interregional integration, and a historical consciousness of their remote past.

Discussion and Perspectives on Future Research

The lack of a direct relationship between ethnic groups and material culture (Hodder 1978, 3) permits one to treat archaeological similarities and differences of stylistic variability only at the level of local communities. Within a normative concept of culture, a heterogeneity of technological traditions has frequently been interpreted as indicating the presence of relationships among different societies, and homogeneity at the regional level has been attributed to strong social ties among communities that share the same stylistic elements (Braun and Plog 1982). Furthermore, changes in material culture under certain circumstances, even when migrations have taken place, demonstrate an additional difficulty in identifying social units from the archaeological record alone, especially when only a small part of the material culture has survived. Ceramic style does not always remain unchanged in migrant groups who come to dominate others, especially when the style did not carry a specific social significance in the homeland (Collet 1987, 106). Therefore, our ability to establish whether local developments or external influences are the cause of stylistic variation is still weak at present.

In our case study of the Bororo region, ethnoarchaeological and ethnohistorical data enable us to attribute at least one of the ceramic complexes and its respective settlements to these ethnographically known Indians. There is no continuity with the older Uru ceramic tradition after the establishment of Arigao Bororo. The archaeological record indicates strong homogeneity among Bororo pottery all over the region. There is no evidence for local evolution in ceramic style, and the cultural disruption in vessel forms and function, along with a change in the settlement pattern, seems to indicate an outside influence. However, in a few precontact Bororo villages the presence of Uru and polychrome Tupiguarani pottery may be interpreted in terms of the initial cultural diversity of their occupants. Lévi-Strauss's observation (1970, 217) that in former times Bororo vessels were painted may be related to our archaeologically identified polychrome sherds. Even if these decorated vessels are identified with the Tupiguarani tradition, their producers may have been considered Bororo at the community level. Therefore, the incorporation of different cultural groups, as referred to in Bororo mythology, seems to be more plausible than the existence of trading networks. Yet the migration of the bearers of the Bororo ceramic tradition still has to be demonstrated by contextual analysis in a larger region. Further, it has to be shown that the system of ideas present in this aspect of material culture is more likely to have come from the outside. The disappearance of the Uru ceramic tradition and polychrome decoration may have been related to the imposition of new aesthetic and cultural patterns, and some of the ceramic attributes linked to specific clans seem to indicate that this item of material culture was important not only as a means of symbolizing social positions but also as a means of reinforcing group identity.

The relatively recent date for the establishment of the first Bororo site in the Vermelho Basin and the dispersion of the "daughter villages" that resulted from its dispersal in all directions except the south may indicate that pressures from colonial society may be partly responsible for the conquest of this new territory. Time depth and ethnohistorical data seem to sustain the idea that the Bororo entered the region when a dualistic clan system was already established but was still in a process of consolidation. The increasing complexity of the Bororo social system, as referred to in mythology, seems to have taken place in a somewhat earlier period, perhaps on the middle and lower course of the São Lourenço River. Only archaeological investigation in this region can clarify some of the aspects involved in this process. Nonetheless, the localization of villages with clan attribution in the Rio Vermelho Basin prior to the establishment of the ethnographically known social system, as conceived by the emic view, suggests that at least some of the Uru tradition villages may represent proto-clans of the future Bororo society.

Historical processes, especially when they involve minority populations, may not necessarily be expressed in the archaeological record (Hodder 1978, 7), and cultural imposition by the conquering group may eliminate nearly all material evidence for ethnic diversity at the community level, as seems to have been the case for the more recent precolonial societies in the region of the Vermelho River. Linguistic and physical anthropological data (Loukotka 1939 and Albisetti and Venturelli 1962, 285–86, respectively) also support cultural and ethnic diversity among the Bororo, but more systematic research in these fields needs to be carried out to strengthen this hypothesis.

Study of the cultural processes involved in the distribution of artifact styles and settlement patterns depends on the size of the research area. Moreover, a large part of traditional Bororo territory and adjacent areas is archaeologically unknown, and on the other hand sufficient data are not yet available concerning variability in the spatial distribution of culture material at the site level. Nonetheless, understanding the cultural processes outlined above requires additional information about settlement patterns, stratigraphy, and site contents. Further, contributions from physical anthropology will be indispensable to our understanding of precolonial cultural dynamics. Going beyond system analysis, archaeology has shown some interest in the study of the mutual interrelationship of neighboring societies and the degree to which interaction plays a role in internal cultural development (Trigger 1986). Therefore, we still have to look for both more certain indicators to establish the contemporaneity of settlements and also better material culture evidence of the social relationships among communities and domestic units. In this sense, correlating the functional types of pottery and lithic artifacts with their stylistic and technological attributes in relation to social structure and ideology seems to be an important key. Ethnoarchaeology is surely one of the most promising instruments in research on this kind of question (Kramer 1979, 1–20), especially in situations in which traditional material culture still constitutes an integral part of current social relations and in which territorial behavior has not been totally constrained by pressure from the national society.

NOTES

1. The results presented in this paper were obtained during the first five years of the Archaeological and Ethnoarchaeological Project of São Lourenço River Basin (1983–1987) and was sponsored by the Fundação de Amparo a Pesquisa do Estado de São Paulo (FAPESP) and the Conselho Nacional de Pesquisa (CNPq). The project was conducted by teachers and postgraduate and graduate students from the Universidade

de São Paulo and the Universidade Federal de Goiás. Renate B. Viertler provided a special ethnological contributions to the project, and this paper has benefited from our discussions about various aspects of the research. The author also thanks Michael Heckenberger, who provided helpful comments on the manuscript.

2. The ^{14}C dates have been furnished by the Radioisotopic Institution (Japan), Beta Analytic (United States), and Hannoverisches Landesamt für Bodenforschung (Germany).

3. The term *bandeirante* means a member of an expedition to hinterland areas in search of Indians or gold.

4. The National Service for the Protection of Indians, founded in 1910.

5. FUNAI was created in 1967 to replace the SPI.

6. The first ethnohistorical data on the Paresi mention high village density during the early part of the eighteenth century. Settlements were formed of 10 to 30 large, circular, dome-shaped houses 10 to 30 m in diameter (Pires de Campos 1862, 443–44). According to Métraux (1942, 163), each house was occupied by 30 to 40 persons, which suggests a maximum population of about 1,200 people. Paresi villages represented autonomous units, though they were linked by close commercial ties facilitated by large pathways. Their social organization was based on a two-class system in which the lower class engaged in the harder work. Some other tribal groups, like the Nambiquara, had been incorporated into Paresi society, and the Aruak language and culture was forced on them (Métraux 1942, 162–64). A similar social system is also described for the Mbay in the south, who submitted the Chan to a kind of vassalage in an effort to obtain agricultural tribute payments (Susnik 1978, 114–15).

7. The Guató were organized into small family bands scattered along the Paraguay and lower São Lourenço rivers and occupied small artificial earth mounds before the beginning of our century (Schmidt 1922–23, 119). They lived mainly on fish and wild rice (*Oryza subulata* sp.) collected by canoe (Métraux 1942).

The Xarae, neighbors of the Guató, formed large population aggregates. In the sixteenth century their settlements were characterized by "suburbs," each with its own chief subordinated to a general overall headman. There could be 140 to 445 houses and up to 420 families in each settlement. One of their villages, representing a confederation of three ethnic groups (Xarae, Aucus, and Paresi), counted 610 houses, with 1,850 families living in 8 sectors, for a total of 7,500 individuals (Susnik 1978, 29–30). The Xarae played an important role among all the neighboring groups because of their commercial relations with the Andean area, intermediated by the Chané, whose traders supplied the groups as far as the upper Paraguay with metal objects (Susnik 1978, 33). These large village confederations had already disintegrated by the end of the sixteenth century. In the eighteenth century the Xarae were established in small villages along the upper Paraguay River (Susnik 1978, 32–33).

8. The spatial orientation of village plan follows not only an east-west direction but also the course of the main stream and the slope of terrain so that the *bororo* is oriented downstream. According to Bororo cosmology, the land of the dead and the home of dangerous water spirits (*aije-doge*) lie to the west and downstream. The

position of the deceased has to be oriented east-west too, especially for the ritual consumption of his flesh by these spirits, who enter the village from the west (see Viertler 1991).

9. The presence of griddles in the later sites of the Uru tradition seems to indicate manioc processing. Since griddles or plates may occur in ethnographical contexts in which subsistence is based either on manioc or maize (De Boer 1975; Roosevelt 1980), it is still not clear whether any significant change in agricultural products had taken place during this period, and only a secure identification of domestic plants from the earlier and later settlements may clarify this question.

REFERENCES

Albisetti, C., and A. J. Venturelli
1962   Enciclopédia Bororo. Vol. 1. Campo Grande: Museu Regional Dom
             Bosco.
1969   Enciclopédia Bororo. Vol. 2. Campo Grande: Museu Regional Dom
             Bosco.
Braun, D. P., and S. Plog
1982   Evolution of tribal social networks: Theory and prehistoric North Amer-
             ican evidence. American Antiquity 47:504–25.
Caldas, J. A.
1887   Memória histórica sobre os indígenas da província de Matto-Grosso. Rio de
             Janeiro: Polytechnica de Moraes e Filhos.
Carneiro, R.
1970   A theory on the origin of state. Science 169:733–38.
Carvalho, S.
1946   O grande bandeirante Antônio Pires de Campos (1716–1756). Revista
             do Instituto Histórico de Mato Grosso [Cuiabá] 53–56:92–96.
Chernela, J. M.
1986   Pesca e hierarquização tribal no alto Uaupés. In Suma Etnológica Brasi-
             leira, vol. 1: Etnobiologia, edited by B. Ribeiro, 235–49. Petrópolis,
             Brazil: Editora Vozes.
Coelho, F.J.N.
1872   Memórias chronológicas da capitania de Mato Grosso principalmente
             da provedoria da fazenda real e intendência do ouro. Revista do Instituto
             Histórico e Geográphico Brasileiro [Rio de Janeiro] 13:137–99.
Colbacchini, A., and C. A. Albisetti
1942   Os Bororos Orientais: Orarimugodoge do planalto oriental de Mato Grosso.
             São Paulo: Companhia Editora Nacional.
Collet, D.
1987   A contribution to the study of migrations in the archaeological record:
             The Ngoni and Kololo migrations as a case study. In Archaeology as Long-

Term History, edited by I. Hodder, 105–31. Cambridge: Cambridge University Press.

Cook, W. A.

1908   *The Bororo Indians of Mato Grosso, Brazil* . Smithsonian Miscellaneous Collections 50, pp. 48–62. Washington, D.C.

Crocker, C. J.

1967   The social organization of the eastern Bororo. Ph.D. diss., Harvard University.

da Silva e Souza, L.

1874   Memória sobre o descobrimento, governo, população e coisas mais notáveis da Capitania de Goyáz. *Revista do Instituto Histórico e Geográfico Brasileiro* [Rio de Janeiro] 13:429–510.

De Boer, W. R.

1975   The archaeological evidence from manioc cultivation: A cautionary note. *American Antiquity* 40:419–33.

Emmerich, K.-H.

1988   *Relief, Böden und Vegetation in Zentral- und Nordwest-Brasilien unter besonderer Berücksichtigung der känozoischen Landschaftsentwicklung.* Frankfurter Geowissenschaftliche Arbeiten, ser. D: Physische Geographie 8. Frankfurt: Johann-Wolfgang Goethe Universität.

Flannery, K. V., ed.

1976   *The early Mesoamerican village.* New York: Academic Press.

Gross, D. R.

1975   Protein capture and cultural development in the Amazon Basin. *American Anthropologist* 77:526–49.

Gruenberg, G.

1970   Beiträge zur Ethnographie der Kayabi Zentralbrasiliens. *Archiv für Völkerkunde* 24:21–186.

Hammen, T. van der

1982   Paleoecology of tropical South America. In *Biological Diversification in the Tropics*, edited by G. T. Prance, 60–66. New York: Columbia University Press.

Hodder, I.

1978   Simple correlations between material culture and society. In *The Spatial Organization of Culture*, edited by I. Hodder, 3–24. London: Duckworth.

Kramer, C., ed.

1979   *Ethnoarchaeology: Implications of ethnography for archaeology.* New York: Columbia University Press.

Lévi-Strauss, C.

1970   *Tristes trópicos.* Buenos Aires: Editora Universitaria.

Loukotka, C.

1939   Línguas indígenas do Brasil. *Revista do Arquivo Municipal* [São Paulo] 54:153.

Maybury-Lewis, D.
1967   The Akwê-Shavante society. Oxford: Clarendon Press.
Meggers, B. J.
1975   Some problems of cultural adaptation in Amazonia, with emphasis on
            the pre-European period. In Tropical forest ecosystems in Africa and South
            America: A comparative review, edited by B. J. Meggers et al., 311–20.
            Washington, D.C.: Smithsonian Institution Press.
Mello Rego, M. do C.
1895   Índios de Matto Grosso: Os Bororos Coroados. Revista Brazileira [Rio de
            Janeiro, São Paulo] 3:5–12; 91–100.
Métraux, A.
1942   The native tribes of eastern Bolivia and western Matto Grosso. Bureau of
            American Ethnology, Bulletin 134. Washington, D.C.: Smithsonian
            Institution.
Moonen, F.
1983   Pindorama conquistada: Repensando a questão indígena. João Pessoa,
            Brazil: Editora Alterantiva.
Muccillo, R., and I. Wüst
1978   Aspectos da tecnologia cerâmica Bororo. Arquivos do Museu de História
            Natural [Belo Horizonte] 6–7:323–28.
Murray, T., and M. J. Walker
1988   Like WHAT? A practical question of analogical inference and archaeo-
            logical meaningfulness. Journal of Anthropological Archaeology 7:248–
            87.
Nimuendajú, C.
1982   Mapa etno-histórico de Curt Nimuendajú. Rio de Janeiro: Fundação
            Instituto Brasileiro de Geografia e Estatística.
Novaes, S. C., and L.D.B. Grupioni
1986   Relatório de censos das aldeias Bororo. Unpublished MS in possession of
            the authors.
Oberg, K.
1953   Indian tribes of north Mato Grosso, Brazil. Smithsonian Institution, Publi-
            cation No. 15. Washington, D.C.
Pires de Campos, A.
1862   Breve notícia que dá o Capitão Antônio Pires de Campos. Revista do
            Instituto Histórico e Geográphico Brasileiro [Rio de Janeiro] 25:437–58.
Prous, A.
1986   L'archéologie au Brésil: 300 siècles d'occupation humaine. L'Anthropolo-
            gie [Paris] 98:257–306.
Redding, R. W.
1988   A general explanation of subsistence change: From hunting and gather-
            ing to food production. Journal of Anthropological Archaeology 7:56–97.

Rondon, C.M.S.

1949   Relatório dos trabalhos realizados de 1900 a 1906 pela comissão de linhas telegráficas do estado do Mato Grosso. Rio de Janeiro: Imprensa Nacional.

Rondon, C.M.S., and J. B. Faria

1948   Esboço gramatical e vocabulário da língua dos Bororo. Conselho Nacional de Proteção aos Índios, Publicação No. 77. Rio de Janeiro.

Roosevelt, A. C.

1980   Parmana: Prehistoric maize and manioc subsistence along the Amazon and Orinoco. New York: Academic Press.

1987   Chiefdoms in the Amazon and Orinoco. In Chiefdoms in the Americas, edited by R. D. Drennan and C. A. Uribe, 153–86. Lanham, Md.: University Press of America.

Saldarriaga, J. G., and D. C. West

1986   Holocene fires in the northern Amazon Basin. Quaternary Research 26:358–66.

Schmidt, M.

1914   Die Paresi-Kabisi: Ethnologische Ergebnisse der Expedition zu den Quellen des Jauru und Juruna im Jahre 1910. Baessler Archiv 4:167–250.

1922–23 Die Anfänge der Bodenkultur in Südamerika. Zeitschrift für Ethnologie 60:85–124.

Schmitz, P. I.

1987   Prehistoric hunters and gatherers of Brazil. Journal of World Archaeology 1:53–126.

Schmitz, P., et al.

1982   Arqueologia do centro-sul de Goiás: Uma fronteira de horticultores indígenas no centro do Brasil. Pesquisas, Série Antropologia 33. São Leopoldo: Instituto Anchietano de Pesquisas.

Serpa, P.

1988   Boe Epa. O cultivo de roça entre os Bororo do Mato Grosso. Master's thesis, Universidade de São Paulo.

Siqueira, J. da C.

1898–99 Chrônicas de Cuyabá. Revista do Instituto Histórico e Geográphico de São Paulo 4.

Spielmann, K. A.

1986   Interdependence among egalitarian societies. Journal of Anthropological Archaeology 5:279–312.

Steinen, K., von den

1894   Unter den Naturvölkern Zentralbrasiliens. Berlin: Dietrich Reimer Verlag.

Steward, J. H.

1946   Handbook of South American Indians. Vol. 1. Washington, D.C.: U.S. Government Printing Office.

Steward, J. H., and L. C. Faron
1959   *Native peoples of South America*. New York: McGraw-Hill.
Susnik, B.
1972   *Dimensiones migratorias y pautas culturales de los pueblos del Gran Chaco y de su Periferia*. Asunción, Paraguay: Universidade Nacional del Nordeste.
1978   *Los aborigenes del Paraguay, I: Chaco Boreal y su Periferia (Siglos XVI y XVII)*. Asunción, Paraguay: Museo Etnográfico Andres Barbero.
Trigger, B. G.
1986   Prospect for a world archaeology. *World Archaeology* 18:1–20.
Viertler, R. B.
1976   *As aldeias Bororo: Alguns aspectos de sua organização social*. Coleção Museu Paulista, Série Etnologia 2. São Paulo.
1982   Aroe-Jaro: Implicações adaptativas das crenças e práticas funerárias dos Bororo do Brasil central. Livre Doc. diss., Universidade de São Paulo.
1986   A formação da sociedade Bororo: Mitologia e considerações etno-históricas. *Revista de Antropologia* [São Paulo] 29:1–39.
1991   *A Refeição das almas: Una interpretação etnológica do funeral dos índios Bororo—Mato Grosso*. São Paulo: Editora da Universidade de São Paulo.
Wüst, I.
1983   Aspectos da ocupação pré-colonial em uma área do Mato Grosso de Goiás: Tentativa de análise espacial. Master's thesis, Universidade de São Paulo.
1989   Aspectos da ocupação pré-colonial em uma área nuclear Bororo entre os Rios Vermelho e Garças, MT. *Dédalo* [São Paulo] Publicações Avulsas 1:161–71.
1990   Continuidade e mudança: Para uma interpretaço dos grupos ceramistas da bacia do Rio Vermelho, Mato Grosso. Ph.D. diss., Universidade de São Paulo.
Zerries, O.
1953   The bullroarer among South American Indians. *Revista do Museu Paulista* [São Paulo], new ser., 7:275–310.

15

Genetic Relatedness and Language Distributions in Amazonia

HARRIET E. MANELIS KLEIN

In the last several years, a significant linguistic controversy focusing on the question of genetic relatedness has embroiled American Indian–language specialists. In 1987, Joseph Greenberg, in his book *Language in the Americas*, brought to the attention of the public the importance of American Indian languages for their potential role in reconstructing the past history of the languages and cultures of the continent. Although the conclusions about relationships that Greenberg draws in his work cannot be accepted by serious scholars of indigenous languages, the work nevertheless serves to highlight the many problems that exist in trying to reconstruct or deduce the linguistic past.[1]

This essay has grown out of an interest in the theoretical and methodological battle over what type of evidence to use in establishing language relationships as well as out of a familiarity with the language distributions in Amazonia. As a heuristic device to familiarize a nonlinguistic audience with the linguistic composition of the geographic region addressed in this volume and to explain the inherent problems in determining genetic relatedness, the structure of this essay is as follows: First, I present an overall view of the languages of Amazonia, followed by a discussion of the methods of approaching the past, and then a discussion of how some of these approaches have yielded results in terms of analyses of contemporary Amazonian languages. I conclude with an indication of the enormous amount of work that must still be done so as to integrate the historical dimension and understanding of the past into language, demographic, and cultural analyses in order to arrive at a better statement of language distributions of the Amazon.

Geographical Definition and Linguistic Composition: The Amazon

There is a considerable amount of diversity of languages and language families to be found in Amazonia. Two opposing features have characterized this region. On the one hand, we find a high degree of intertribal acculturation, largely a result of linguistic exogamy, which results in a high degree of autochthonous multilingualism. This high degree of linguistic adaptation, and concomitant absorption of individual languages, has had a major impact on the contemporary linguistic picture. On the other hand, this pattern is offset by an opposing feature, that of "dialect" endogamy—that is, members of isolated tribes tend to marry among those who speak their own dialect. This endogamous adaptation has come about largely from continuing but occasional contact, sometimes hostile but frequently friendly. This contact has resulted in language spread or language death, and linguistic endogamy is expected to stop these processes. There is a massive presence of languages of the Arawakan, Cariban, Panoan and Tupian families in this region (see fig. 15.1), as well as many languages (e.g., Tukanoan) with a more restricted distribution, but which are generally exclusively Amazonian.

The area where the other great lowland language family is spoken, that is, the Chibchan grouping, is in northern Colombia. This family is found primarily in the northern part of South America and overlaps with Central America. Also found in heavily dispersed northern coastal areas are the remains of some Arawakan languages, whereas in the coastal jungle area of Ecuador, the Colorado and Cayapa languages are found.

Historically, the indigenous languages spoken in lowland South America were even more numerous in the fifteenth century than they are today. But such factors as disease, warfare, slavery, and the assimilation of native groups by other indigenous groups or into the national society have resulted in the extinction of many Indian languages. For example, over a century ago there were more than thirty-five tribes and languages in the Río Branco–Río Orinoco region of Venezuela; today, there are only twenty. There were eighty-five ethnic groups at the beginning of the century in lowland Peru; today, there are sixty-three. And at the time of the Spanish conquest of Ecuador there were thirty Indian languages; today, there are twelve. Even with the

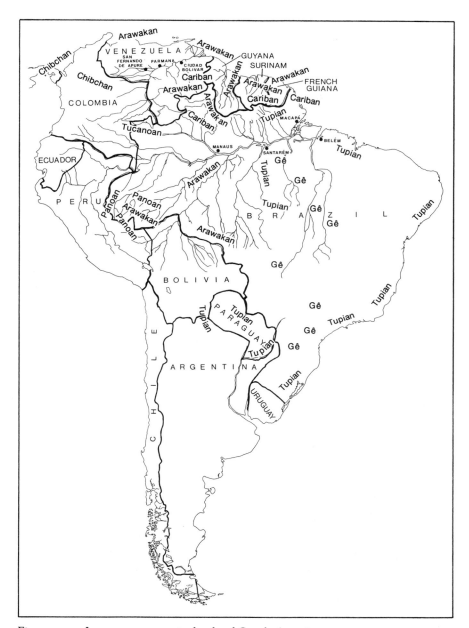

Figure 15.1 Language groups in lowland South America.

loss of so many languages in the lowland area, however, there are still 170 native languages currently spoken in Brazil (Klein 1990).

Linguistic Methods of Approaching the Past

This section must begin with a discussion of how to determine if languages are genetically related. In other words, if we assume that we have a set of languages that are related, how do we test that assumption? There are two parameters that can be used for organizational purposes: temporal and spatial.

Temporal Methods: Comparative Method

The comparative method is utilized to investigate the history of particular words and therefore the relationship between specific languages. It assumes as a positive finding that the end result will be the establishment of genetic relationships. The first step, then, is to look for and set up etymologies. An *etymology* can be defined as a set of *morphemes* taken from languages that we are comparing and that we hypothesize derive from one form or from a set of forms in a protolanguage. Additionally, an etymology is equivalent to a set of *cognates*. Morphemes are cognate by virtue of having been in each of the languages containing them from the time before their ancestors began to diversify. Cognates are by definition not due to borrowing.

How do we find these etymologies and the cognate morphemes? If we have between one and two thousand vocabulary items for a language family and we are dealing with a time depth of under five thousand years, we should be able to find at least five hundred valid etymologies that allow us to reconstruct a portion of the protolanguage (Kaufman 1990). This has indeed been done for some Amazonian languages, such as Panoan (Shell 1975) and Takanan (Girard 1971; Key 1968).

Additionally, when we have language families of up to three thousand years of time depth, we are able to ascertain not only lexical detail, but also considerable grammatical detail, and a large number of linguistic traits that are unique to a particular family. Furthermore, Kaufman has noted:

> As time depth increases, grammatical changes can have the long-term effect of changing the typological profiles of some or all the daughters of a given protolanguage, and more reliance will have to be placed on irregularities and suppletions, especially in minor morphemes. Even after 6000 or even 7000 years however, it is reasonable to expect the possibility of reconstructing large parts of most of the grammatical subsystems of a protolanguage, as long as it has enough descendants. (1990, 20)

Thus, if we can show genetic relatedness, and clearly, we frequently can, the conclusion is that there was a protolanguage, spoken by specific people, in a specific place, at a specific time (Thomason and Kaufman 1988).

We also need to determine the distribution of the languages of a genetic group, and, almost simultaneously, we must ascertain the sources of borrowing from other languages. Then, if we can accomplish a lexical reconstruction that unambiguously corresponds to a certain kind of natural environment, we even have the possibility of determining the probable homeland for a protolanguage.

Both the comparative method and reconstruction allow one to recognize genetic relationships for languages with known relatives. There are, however, other components that languages contain. These include elements borrowed from other languages. Since they involve spatial notions, I discuss borrowing and the diffusion of borrowed elements under spatial methods.

Temporal Methods: Glottochronology

Glottochronology has been called "probabilistic" or "stochastic" (Hockett 1953, 149).[2] It is a method of measuring time. With it we can state that "the parent language of A, B, C, and D was being spoken about A.D. 500 plus or minus 600 years." What this says is that the parent language was most probably being spoken at about A.D. 500; it was less probably but still plausibly spoken a hundred years before or after that date; and it was least probably spoken before 100 B.C. or after A.D. 1100.[3]

What the glottochronological method purports to do, then, is to determine the point when genetically related languages first separated. The method assumes that 86 percent of 100 basic word items will be retained over a thousand-year period. That is, after a thousand years, only 14 percent of the words will no longer be found in the language. Though there has been considerable controversy among linguists as to the validity of this method, among archaeologists, this method has been considered as a useful concomitant proof for a time relationship. For example, Lathrap (1970) in *The Upper Amazon* used lexicostatistical data to corroborate his arguments for the time span involved in the waves of expansion of tropical forest culture. Furthermore, Swadesh, considered the progenitor of the method (1955, 123–4) claimed that:

> There is already sufficient evidence that lexicostatistically estimated time depths are to some degree approximately related to actual time. This is shown by a number of correlations, including several historical dates and a few archaeological ones, including some obtained by the carbon method.

And there is further evidence of general correctness in the inner consistency of lexicostatistic dates found among the languages of a family or stock.

This method of lexicostatistics is based on the assumption by Swadesh that the basic or fundamental vocabulary of any language changes at a constant rate. He defined as basic a vocabulary consisting of two hundred items whose meaning was considered universal to all societies, and which, Swadesh felt, was that segment of language that was most pressured toward change. Cultural vocabulary, which he defined as the opposite of basic, changed slowly. Thus, his underlying principle was that:

> linguistic symbols are of floating character, capable of unlimited gradual change: That under usual conditions in the life of language there are multiple strong factors pushing them one way and another either individually or in sets. Furthermore, the communicational function of language sets some sort of an upper limit on the rate of change affecting the symbols, both individually and as sets. (Swadesh 1962, 145)

The problems inherent in this method are many, and no sooner was the method publicized than a barrage of objections was voiced. "If it is argued that the recently proposed 'glottochronology' techniques have value, it must first be established what that value is" (Hoijer 1956, 52).

The first objection deals primarily with the problem of basic vocabulary. There is no sure way of separating basic from cultural vocabulary for specific languages, and therefore, in the end, there is no way to establish a list that is translatable into any language without inevitable and perhaps overwhelming difficulties. Some of the more recent studies, discussed below, deal with the problem in an interesting way.

The second objection, a corollary to the first, deals with the test list itself.

> It is doubtful that any test list will provide a division of the experience of mankind into one hundred easily identifiable broad concepts, which can be matched with simple terms in most languages, for there is no way which we can utilize to rule out in advance the peculiarities of individual cultures. It is this unavoidable defect of the test list that counts for the error of use of the method. When there is a great choice for an item in several languages and different items are chosen, the losses of vocabulary are indicated where with different choices this might not be the case. Only a few errors of this sort will produce percentages of retention and times of separation that are quite illusory. (Hoijer 1956, 60)

The third objection, a logical extension of the first two, is that even if the vocabulary is actually noncultural and adequate, "the fact remains that all that can be measured by it is extent of vocabulary change. Language structure, language relationship, the ties between language and the rest of culture — all these *are not* and *cannot* be measured by vocabulary counts" (Trager 1953, 115).

Besides these strong objections, which deal primarily with vocabulary, there are some further disclaimers to Swadesh's other assumptions. As has already been stated, Swadesh assumed that the rate of change was uniform. Bergland and Vogt indicate that their findings clearly disprove that assumption (1962, 126–27). There also appears to be some evidence that the hypothesis might not work when the languages occupy an area that is almost unbroken, unusually compact, and heavily populated. Problems of ecology, demography, and history were not taken into account in the formulation of the theory.

Some linguists point out other problems with the method. Thus, with languages that have little or no written history, as is the case with almost all Amazonian languages, there appears to be a real danger of overestimating time depths. This is caused by a failure to recognize actual cognates as such (Taylor and Rouse 1955, 106). Gudschinsky (1955, 149) noted that, although lexicostatistical material led to very useful implications as to the historical sequence in which dialect differences developed, it did not account for reborrowing from other dialects following a change in the lines of communication or a shift of cultural and economic dependence. The evidence thus was so distorted that it no longer accurately reflected the true historical development.

Lyle Campbell, in his review of Greenberg's *Language in the Americas* (1988, 596), notes that glottochronology neither finds nor tests distant genetic relationships; rather, it assumes the relationships exist and then attaches a date. He feels that the method should not be utilized for proposing remoter affiliations.[4]

There are those, however, who have viewed glottochronology more positively. Hockett (1953), for one, pointed out that if Swadesh had not been using the method to date languages as well as evidence for languages that are by no means known to be related, the glottochronological method would have been fine. Kroeber (1955) suggested that our primary concern should be with relatable sets of phenomena; of vocabulary with structure, and of languages with their known historic territories; of a set of datings with a history of linguistic developments. Thus, we might hope that after much more data is gathered, the glottochronological method would perhaps give new insight.

There have been a variety of linguists since the 1950s who in some measure or other have utilized the glottochronological method and who have dealt with the problem of nonhomogeneity in the test list (Embleton 1986, 62ff).

Van der Merwe (1966), for example, deals with that problem by splitting the test list into lexical classes, and establishes for each class its own replacement rate. Dyen (1964) and Dyen, James, and Cole (1967) argue that each meaning is associated with its own meaning replacement rate. They suggest the use for analysis of variance techniques so as to estimate simultaneously the replacement rates and the divergence times from the language family under consideration. Brainerd (1970) further generalized the problem of rate of replacement. He used the terms *recurrent cognation* (the situation where a word "elicited at the end of the time interval is 'cognate' to the word for the same meaning at the beginning of the time interval, but there have been one or more replacements involving noncognation in the interval") and *chance cognation* (where words may coincidentally be phonologically similar).

Another modification to Swadesh's method involves accepting the notion of nonindependence for the evolution of related languages. After two languages separate (that is, from their common source), Embleton postulates that there is an initial period of "inertia" where the degree of parallelism changes between one language and the other (63).

Still another improvement concerns Swadesh's assumptions that we can elicit exactly one word for each test-list meaning and that the replacement process for any given word must be instantaneous.[5]

A position that I find less acceptable is that of Sankoff (1983, 111), who argues that the genetic aspects of linguistic relationships gradually become less important than the diffusion aspects. Comrie (1981, 111) notes that "it is probably impossible ever to *prove* that two languages are genetically unrelated; with the passage of time, genetically related languages grow farther and farther apart, until eventually the level of similarity would be no greater than that due to chance." However, as another linguist notes: "My own experience in applying glottochronology to the Mayan and Mixe-Zoque languages leads me to the belief that whenever external evidence for dating is plausibly associable with linguistic inferences, the calibration provided by glottochronology is impressively robust" (Kaufman 1990, 27).

Wilbert (1962) used the hundred-word list for sixteen Gê languages spoken in eastern Brazil. The glottochronological results of his analysis correspond to cultural resemblances and to the geographical placement in the area (Embleton 1986, 48).

What can be done, then, to improve the method? Longer test lists give results comparable to the short list. Longer lists also minimize the effect of bad cognate judgments and of semantic or cultural problems that may cause the elimination of some items from the test list. Concern continues about the construction of the test-list—questions persist about the elimination or reduction in the number of meanings that are susceptible to borrowing. "Many of the early studies in glottochronology detected skewing of time depths due to borrowing. Lexicostatistical studies based on data from test-lists but using techniques *other* than Swadesh's method . . . have also found 'disappointing results for the time estimates' due to 'intimate borrowing' and 'widespread literary influence' of prestige languages" (Dobson 1978a, 63–64 in Embleton, 67).

It is by no means clear that any meaning exists that is completely immune from borrowing, especially if we were to try to apply lexicostatistical techniques to situations of large-scale language contact.

One concludes, then, that it is probably impossible to construct a satisfactory test list and that lexicostatistics must find a way to incorporate borrowing rates. Yet, by accounting for borrowing, one can diverge from Swadesh's two-hundred-word list and use lists that are basic to specific cultures (Embleton 1986, 151). Finally, as Embleton concludes, lexicostatistics should be used to provide "a first approximation to a tree which can then be validated using the more traditional methods" (157).

Spatial Methods

Internal reconstruction and comparative linguistics were attempts at placing language in a time framework; the glottochronological method tried to locate the time axis more specifically.[6] It has been left, however, to those interested in linguistic paleontology, in problems of diffusion, drift (i.e., tendencies within a language to change due to a lack of balance in its structure), trends, and dialect geography to locate language in space as well.

Linguistic paleontology or "cultural reconstruction by linguistic comparison . . . has been a valuable adjunct of prehistory in Europe" (Swadesh, 1964, 552). The procedure consists of comparing the words used for different artifacts, techniques, and social concepts, along with features of the physical environment, in all the languages of a set based on common origin. Where cognate expressions are used, we can infer that we are dealing with artifacts of concepts known to the peoples in some earlier common period of their history. If a clear pattern of areal distribution can be shown, then we can infer that the item referred to came in when the dialects were already separate and without complete contact among them. This method has also been used by Marija Gimbutas in her studies on the Indo-European homeland (1970). Colin Renfrew has serious misgivings, however, about the theoretical foundations of linguistic paleontology and urges caution in accepting the conclusions that have been based entirely on that method (1987, 18–19).[7]

Another source for concepts about prehistoric migrations comes from the geographical distribution of related languages. Sapir, in "Time Perspective in Aboriginal American Culture," noted that a

> cultural phenomenon whose distribution is studied must have originated but once in the area of distribution and have gained its present spread by a gradual process of borrowing from tribe to tribe. . . . But the spread . . . may, for environmental or resistant cultural reasons, be much more rapid in one direction than in other, so that the culture centre is far removed from the actual geographical centre. . . . Movements of population within the area of distribution, furthermore, may bring about an easily misinterpreted type of culture distribution. (1949, 411–12)

If there has been diffusion of any sort, there is every reason to suppose that some loan words must also exist (Sapir 1949, 411–12). We can then infer borrowing between unrelated languages by certain types of evidence, such as similar form and meaning; by absence of similar forms in related languages on one side of the comparison, presumed to be the received; with phonetics at odds with what is usual in the borrowing language (Swadesh 1964, 538–39).

As an additional way to understand the history of a language or language family, diffusion acts as a complement to genetic studies. Diffusion can not be studied, however, until internal reconstruction and the comparative method are first carried out. This is so because the diffused elements to be studied can not be determined until they are given their status as anomalous to the genetically related forms. With that status, one can then look for places and languages from which the diffused forms came. They thus provide a different but complementary source for linguistic interaction.[8] The most important point to be made here is that one must distinguish between similarity that is due to common origin and similarity that is due to contact (Klein 1982).

A problem connected with this is how to measure linguistic diversity. Thus, it has been stated that in areas of high linguistic diversity, communication is poor, and that the "increase of communication that goes with greater economic productivity and more extensive political organization will lead typically to the spread of a lingua franca, whether indigenous or imported, resulting in widespread bilingualism and the ultimate disappearance of all except a single dominant language" (Greenberg 1956, 110).[9]

Another interpretation of linguistic diffusion was proposed by Hymes (1958, 154). He suggested that languages sometimes shift from one point of resemblance to another through intercommunication. This type of shift is called "tradition trend." It is different from borrowing or drift because it is a change in basic style or patterning, rather than in individual traits. Tradition trend is basically a concept proposed by Willey for use in historical interpretation. It is a "phenomenon resulting from historical contacts whose evidences may, or may not, be readily perceived. It appears to be subject to certain limitations of geographically continuous space in the same manner as the pottery tradition" (Willey 1954, 13). What this seems to mean is that a particular style keeps changing in time and space and that it is part of a pattern of change. It is also evidence that various individual traditions were not historically independent, but comprised a unified tradition. In languages it means, for example, that when two speech communities are either prefixing or suffixing (morphemes are added to stems at either the beginning or the end), then when there is a shift to the reverse, we have an instance of tradition trend (Hymes 1958, 153).

It is appropriate here also to mention two other foci of interest in this area of methodology. The wave model, which Renfrew (1987) expanded upon in his recent controversial work, provides a view opposed to comparative linguistics by focusing on the spatial aspects of language distribution. A more acceptable approach, especially to linguists, is that of linguistic area. This approach also has a spatial component and deals with commonalities in nonrelated languages that arise from fairly sustained contact (see Klein 1987b for details on the Chaco area).

Spatial and Temporal Methods

Embleton (1986, 68ff.) presents a model that deals with the problems of both space and time. She discusses, in formulaic terms, independently evolving languages, that is, languages that at one point in time have become independent of one another. These languages reflect a temporal element. Non-independently evolving languages occur when languages, after they have separated, influence one another. Here one refers to a spatial element, in that each of the languages must have some kind of border in common.

Embleton also concentrates on the borrowing that occurs between languages that are contiguous. In her study, which focuses on quantitative models for historical linguistics, she concludes that the replacement rate should be allowed to vary for each language because it allows one to decide whether the presence, for example, of an affix in one word but not another (when roots are cognate), should affect cognateship decision. Thus, the decision on rates is not predetermined by the method and its need to have a universal value for the rate.[10] She also notes that the borrowing rate should be allowed to vary for each language pair and that the borrowing between languages is not necessarily equal. That is, one must allow for instances of unequal reciprocal borrowing rates between pairs of languages (Embleton, 96). Clearly, the decision on what the borrowing rate should be must be decided upon by linguists knowledgeable about the languages.

Other linguists also discuss both parameters in their discussions of language change. Kaufman (1990), for example, notes that borrowing is related to the amount of contact, and contact tends to be related to space. Furthermore, contact decreases as space between languages increases (Cavalli-Sforza and Wang 1986).

Features of Amazonian Languages

Having explained what possibilities exist at the theoretical and methodological level for analyzing Amazonian languages, I now want to discuss some interesting structural properties of the languages. Among these languages, the following linguistic features are shared to varying degrees. Interestingly, these shared features seem to derive from similarities in patterns of social interaction, general lifestyle, and ecological adaptation, as well as from diffusion and contact, rather than from genetic relationships. These include: (*a*) a common pattern of discourse redundancy; (*b*) a structure in which most, except for a few Arawak languages, are or were ergative languages, and have a transitive verb phrase pattern of the O(bject)V(erb) type, with the subject either preceding the object or following the verb, that is, S(ubject)O(bject)V(erb) or O(bject)V(erb)S(ubject); and (*c*) the absence of a formal distinction between active and passive; rather, apposition and nominalization are utilized, and adjoining rather than embedding produce the equivalent of relative clauses (e.g., in Chibchan).

Other features of lowland languages, especially Arawak, include a high degree of synthesis, that is, many affixes. Carib languages show the least degree of synthesis. There are also some languages that are classified as isolating (e.g., languages of the Je and Maku families).

Other morphological characteristics include the compounding of verbs to produce a very rich verbal morphology. Noun roots may also be compounded, but seem to be a less productive process. Indeed, nominal morphology is less complex than verbal morphology in lowland languages. Additionally, the Amazon region, in particular, is known for having form-shape noun classification systems that reflect diffusionary as well as genetic relationships. These classificatory systems have many different adpositions. In some languages they are suffixed to nouns directly, to numerals, to demonstratives, or are even incorporated into verbs and demonstrate both inflectional and derivational processes. The types of systems that occur are numeral, concordial, and verb-incorporated classifiers, which also serve an anaphoric discourse function. Very few simple adjectives occur, and descriptive processes are accomplished through the use of classifiers or nouns and through affixes on non-modified stems.

For the Amazon region, there is now also a renewed interest in historical and comparative linguistics. In part this is due to the increased quantity of good descriptive work done in the 1980s (Derbyshire and Pullum 1986 and Payne 1990). As a result, a number of new comparisons between families are being made. Thus, Tupi and Je languages can be compared in terms of similarities in the phonology, in which a parallel series of voiceless stops, /p, t, c, k/, and nasals, /m, n, ñ, ŋ/, occurs, and in terms of the lexicon.

Lexical similarities between Tupi and Carib languages, now being restudied, have been pointed out since early in the twentieth century. The comparison of some languages of Tupi stock with some languages of the Carib family have led to the establishment of regular phonological correspondences. Not all similarities between these languages, however, can be ascribed to genetic relationship, that is, the most obvious lexical similarities seem to be the result of borrowing. Yet there are a sizable number of lexical items that can be shown to be cognates linked by regular phonological correspondences. Most of these belong to semantic domains for which loanwords would be less likely to occur.

As a result of recent studies, some identical structural features of the phonologies and grammars of Tupi and Carib can be noted: (a) a six-vowel vocalic system with three high vowels and three nonhigh vowels, (b) postpositions, genitive-noun phrases, and basically verb-final clauses are the norm; (c) prefixal person markers occur in nouns and verbs, other inflections being suffixal; (d) possessor markers and object markers are generally the same; (e) there is a clear distinction between reflexive and nonreflexive third person, as well as between inclusive and exclusive first person; and (f) the verb morphology and syntax are predominantly ergative.

Interesting conclusions about language universals can be drawn from recent work on nasalization in Mura, Tupi, and other Amazon languages, where pause tends to nasalize contiguous vowels. The study of tone in some of the central Amazon languages, such as Pirahã, Gavião and Nambiquara is providing new information for language typology.

Discussion

What directions should linguists and other interested culture historians take to further their investigation of language history in the Amazon region? For purposes of future study, the highest priority should be given to languages in danger of extinction. The subsequent level of priority should be given to languages that do not belong to a known family or that are distantly related to the remaining languages of their family. The next level of priority should be given to those languages that are in the second category, that is, those languages that have changed least, that are most conservative. And lowest priority should be given to those languages that are not very different from well known languages and will therefore not provide as much useful information for reconstruction.

One excellent source for future work comes from the South American Indian Languages Documentation Project. This project is assembling a standard set of lexical data for every South American language (using around eight hundred items of universal and stable basic vocabulary, and about a thousand items of regional and cultural core vocabulary). Data collectors are also using a thirty-three-page list of rubrics and specific questions.

As a result of this source, it will be possible to find data to reconstruct phonology and basic vocabulary. Using some new, specially developed software, one will be able to map the distribution of linguistic traits on a continentwide scale. In this way, zones of diffusion will be identifiable, and, it is to be hoped, correlations so far unthought-of will also became apparent.

The source for lexical items is derived from a questionnaire based on languages of the world. The seven hundred items that occurred with the greatest frequency are considered the universal basic vocabulary. These items are known to be stable and as close to universal as possible (Kaufman 1990, 29).

The end result of this project will be to provide scholars with the information they need to reconstruct the linguistic history of known genetic groups as well as to do the traditional reconstructive linguistic jobs discussed above. It should also allow for the time-depth estimates of glottochronology, which is still of major interest to researchers. Finally, the data set should allow for comparison by computer and for the generation of hypotheses of remote genetic relationships.

NOTES

I am grateful for the helpful suggestions made by fellow participants in the symposium, "Amazonian Synthesis: An Integration of Disciplines, Paradigms, and Methodologies," and especially those of the organizer, Anna Roosevelt. This version also gained much from the comments of Perry Kalick and Carol Kramer, but its present form is solely the author's responsibility.

1. Greenberg compares simultaneously a large number of words from a basic vocabulary list and grammatical morphemes from all the languages of the Americas. The work is flawed because he does not utilize materials that are accurate.

2. The technique for determining the closeness of the relationship between two genetically related languages is called "lexicostatistics," the statistical study of vocabulary. Its greatest utility is in showing the general relationship between these languages; it cannot be used to establish a precise chronology for language change. It can be distinguished from glottochronology (a narrower field) as "anything to do with the reconstruction of the sequence of past events," which obviously includes "the calculation of probable time depths" but also the application of "clustering and splitting algorithms . . . to such lexicostatistical data." (Embleton 1986, 2) In this essay, however, I follow typical precedent, which is to use the two terms interchangeably.

3. The archaeological analogue to glottochronology is the method of radiocarbon dating in that there is a wide standard deviation (a range of plus or minus) for each dated specimen (or language) (Adams 1968, 1192). The standard deviation for carbon 14 is not the same, however, as that allowed for glottochronology.

4. Some scholars have tried to establish other statistical means for deciding issues of distant genetic relationship, such as what proportion of some particular list of vocabulary items may turn out by chance to be similar. Such studies make the assumption that when vocabularies (of the sort specified by the method) of compared languages show a significantly higher number of similarities than those expected by chance (by their calculations), the languages in question are (probably) genetically related. It is also worth mentioning that many scholars take basic vocabulary as a necessity to arrive at successful distant genetic proposals. Campbell (1988, 596) notes that it is generally accepted that basic vocabulary tends to change less dramatically and is preserved longer than more abstract or culturally charged vocabulary. Therefore, distant genetic proposals that lack basic vocabulary among postulated potential cognates are suspicious.

5. Embleton notes that data frequently include multiple synonyms that are arranged by the analyst in order of decreasing frequency. Thus, one should use the principal synonym for comparison but retain the information.

> There is a constant probability per unit time that a new word may be introduced
> (initially at a low frequency) for a meaning. During each small interval of time, the
> . . . frequency for a word has equal probabilities of increasing or decreasing by a small
> increment. Occasionally a word drops to zero frequency, thus becoming permanently
> obsolete. To compare a set of synonyms at one time or in one language with a partially
> different set at another time or in another language, we can use either of two strategies
> . . . (1) Always choose only the most frequently used synonym or (2) Compute a
> metric distance between the frequency distribution of the two sets. Apparently the outcomes of both are equal. (Embleton 1986, 64)

6. Other types of quantitative methods for tree reconstruction have also been explored, but none have the notoriety or even the dubious acceptance that glotto-

chronology has. An interesting but not unqualified success has been attempted in the *Nearest Neighbor, Farthest Neighbor, Group Average Classification* method, which tries to show degree of relationship among languages in a language family (Embleton 1986, 30ff). This method was utilized by Spielman, Migliazza, and Neal (1974, 643) to conclude that linguistic data and genetic data both prove that the Yanomama languages have been diverging from one another for about a thousand years.

7. But note Yoffee's comments in "Before Babel: A Review Article," (1990) which provide evidence to refute Renfrew's model (and incidentally Gimbutas as well). At the same time Yoffee suggests that linguistic and archaeological analyses, representing different kinds of human behavior, need to be handled independently.

8. Renfrew (1987, 120–23, 286) deals with some of these issues in his processual approach to explaining language change.

9. This phenomenon and its opposite are also discussed above in "Geographical Definition and Linguistic Composition: The Amazon."

10. For example, for Waukeshan languages, Embleton (1986, 41) establishes the replacement rate (r) as 22 percent per millennium, the borrowing rate (b) as 8 percent per millennium for pairs of high borrowing, at 4 percent per millennium for low borrowing, and at o where there is no relationship.

REFERENCES

Adams, R. McC.
1968   Archaeological research strategies: Past and present. *Science* 160.3833:
            1177–92.
Bergsland, K., and H. Vogt
1962   On the validity of glottochronology. *Current Anthropology* 3 (2):
            115–29.
Brainerd, B.
1970   A stochastic process related to language change. *Journal of Applied Probability* 7:69–78.
Campbell, L.
1988   Review of Joseph Greenberg's *Language in the Americas. Language* 64 (3):
            591–615.
Cavalli-Sforza, L. L., and Wm. S. Y. Wang
1986   Spatial distance and lexical replacement. *Language* 62:38–55.
Comrie, B.
1981   The genetic affiliation of Kamchadal: Some morphological evidence. In
            Studies in the languages of the USSR, edited by B. Comrie, 109–20.
            Edmonton: Linguistic Research.
Derbyshire, D., and G. Pullum, eds.
1986   Handbook of Amazonian languages. Vol. 1. Berlin: Mouton de
            Gruyter.

Dyen, I.

1964 On the validity of comparative lexico-statistics. In *Proceedings of the Ninth International Congress of Linguists*, edited by H. Lunt, 238–52. The Hague: Mouton.

Dyen, I., A. T. James, and J. W. L. Cole

1967 Language divergence and estimated word retention rate. *Language* 43: 150–71.

Embleton, S. M.

1986 *Statistics in historical linguistics.* Bochum: Studienverlag Brockmeyer.

Gimbutas, M.

1970 Proto-Indo-European Culture: The Kurgan Culture during the fifth to the third millennia B.C. In *Indo-European and Indo-Europeans*, edited by G. Cardona, H. M. Hoenigswald, and A. Senn, 155–98. Philadelphia: University of Pennsylvania Press.

Girard, V.

1971 *Proto-Takanan phonology.* University of California Publications in Linguistics, 70. Berkeley and Los Angeles: University of California Press.

Greenberg, J. H.

1956 Measure of linguistic diversity. *Language* 32 (1): 49–60.

1987 *Language in the Americas.* Stanford, Calif.: Stanford University Press.

Gudschinsky, S. C.

1955 Lexico-statistical skewing from dialect borrowing. *Current Anthropology* 2:138–49.

Hockett, C. F.

1953 Linguistic time perspective and its anthropological uses. *International Journal of American Linguistics* 19:146–52.

Hoijer, H.

1956 Lexicostatistics: A critique. *Language* 32 (1): 49–60.

Hymes, D. H.

1958 Tradition trend in archaeology and linguistics. *Southwestern Journal of Anthropology* 14:152–55.

Kaufman, T.

1990 Language history in South America: What we know and how to know more. In *Amazonian linguistics: Studies in lowland South American languages*, edited by D. L. Payne, 13–73. Austin: University of Texas Press.

Key, M. R.

1968 *Comparative Tacanan phonology: With cavinena phonology and notes on Pano-Tacanan relationship.* The Hague: Mouton.

Klein, H. E. Manelis

1982 Typological classification of the Indian languages of the Gran Chaco. MS.

1987a Evidence for a Toba-Kadiweu relationship. MS.

1987b Chaco Indian languages: Areal features. MS.

1990   South American languages. In *International encyclopedia of linguistics*,
            4:31–35. Oxford: Oxford University Press.
Klein, H. E. Manelis, and L. R. Stark, eds.
1985   *South American Indian languages: Retrospect and prospect*. Austin: Univer-
            sity of Texas Press.
Kroeber, A. L.
1955   Linguistic time depth results so far and their meaning. *International Jour-
            nal of American Linguistics* 21 (2): 91–104.
Lathrap, D. W.
1970   *The upper Amazon*. New York: Praeger.
Payne, D. L., editor
1990   *Amazonian linguistics: Studies in lowland South American languages*.
            Austin: University of Texas Press.
Renfrew, C.
1987   *Archaeology and language: The puzzle of Indo-European origins*. New York:
            Cambridge University Press.
Sankoff, D.
1973   Mathematical developments in lexico-statistic theory. In *Current Trends
            in Linguistics* 11, edited by T. Sebeok, 93–113. The Hague: Mouton.
Sapir, E.
1949   Time perspective in aboriginal American culture: A study in method. In
            Selected Writings of E. Sapir, edited by D. G. Mandelbaum, 389–462.
            Berkeley and Los Angeles: University of California Press.
Shell, O. A.
1975   Estudios Panos 3: Las lenguas pano y su reconstrucción. *Estudios Lingüís-
            ticos Peruanos* No. 12.
Spielman, R. S., E. C. Migliazza, and J. V. Neel
1974   Regional linguistic and genetic differences among Yanomama Indians.
            Science 184:637–44.
Swadesh, M.
1955   Towards greater accuracy in lexico-statistic dating. *Current Anthropology*
            2:121–37.
1962   Response to Bergsland and Vogt. *Current Anthropology* 3 (2): 143–45.
1964   Linguistic overview. In *Prehistoric man in the New World*, edited by J. D.
            Jennings and E. Norbeck, 527–56. Chicago: University of Chicago
            Press.
Taylor, D., and I. Rouse
1955   Linguistic and archeological time depth in the West Indies. *International
            Journal of American Linguistics* 55 (2): 105–15.
Thomason, S. G., and T. Kaufman
1988   *Language contact, creolization, and genetic linguistics*. Berkeley and Los
            Angeles: University of California Press.

Trager, G.
1953 Linguistics and the reconstruction of culture history. In *New interpretations of aboriginal American culture history: Seventy-fifth anniversary volume.* Anthropological Society of Washington, 110–15. Washington, D.C.

van der Merwe, N. J.
1966 New mathematics for glotto-chronology. *Current Anthropology* 7:485–500.

Wilbert, J.
1962a Preliminary glottochronology of Gê. *Anthropological Linguistics* 4:17–25.

Willey, G. R.
1954 Tradition trend in ceramic design. *American Antiquity* 20:9–14.

Yoffee, N.
1990 Before Babel: A review article. *Proceedings of the Prehistoric Society* 56:299–313.

16

Language, Culture, and Environment

Tupí-Guaraní Plant Names Over Time

WILLIAM BALÉE AND DENNY MOORE

We may note, in passing, that the double or compound names are the most doubtful. They may consist of two mistakes; one in the root or principal name, destined almost always to indicate the geographical origin, some visible quality, or some comparison with other species. The shorter a name is, the better it merits consideration in question of origin or antiquity; for it is by the succession of years, of the migrations of peoples, and of the transport of plants, that the addition of often erroneous epithets takes place.

Alphonse de Candolle, *Origin of Cultivated Plants*
[orig. Fr. 1886]

Both because of its many languages and associated indigenous peoples as well as its extraordinary biological and ecological diversity, Amazonia constitutes an ideal setting for investigating relationships among language, culture, subsistence, and habitat. Several recent studies have been made of linguistic and cognitive systems that Amazonian peoples illustrate in naming and classifying the organisms and habitats of their immediate surroundings (e.g., Berlin 1992; Grenand 1980; Posey 1983). This essay contributes a diachronic (temporal) dimension to such studies. We examine many synchronic (current) linguistic and cultural practices in order to help better comprehend diachronic processes, which, through their inferred action over time, have apparently generated many of the interrelationships among language, culture, and environment in Amazonia that one discerns today.

Specifically, this essay assesses patterns of plant naming in the Tupí-Guaraní family of languages. Since by definition these languages are descended from a common mother language, Proto-Tupí-Guaraní, the measure of similarity among them (excluding resemblances due to borrowing, which appears to be relatively insignificant) in terms of plant names should also indicate the degree to which these names have been retained from the mother language through time.

In the semantic domain of plants, one can estimate the proportion of names from Proto-Tupí-Guaraní, a language spoken in Amazonia at about the time Latin was spoken in Rome, that somehow survived the vicissitudes of time and history. In addition, it is most intriguing that the plants whose names have most tended to endure through time seem to possess certain common, culturally defined features.

As for the five languages represented in this study, it is striking that some plant names, such as those for a medium-sized copal tree (*Hymenaea parvifolia* Huber, Caesalpiniaceae family), which is most often found in old fallows (sites where indigenous peoples had swiddens more than forty years ago), are very similar, whereas others, such as those for a large tree, 'moela de mutum' (*Lacunaria jenmani* [Oliv.] Ducke, Quiinaceae family), which is usually seen only in high, primary forests (forests that lack evidence for past swidden horticulture), are highly divergent:

LANGUAGE	COPAL TREE	'MOELA DE MUTUM'
Araweté (Ar)	*yúta'i*	*iwá-pedi*
Asurini (As)	*yeta-'iwa*	*iwa-kaw-'iwa*
Ka'apor (K)	*yeta-'i*	*kupapa-'iran-'i*
Tembé (T)	*zuta-'i-'iw*	*iwa-zu-'iw-ran*
Waypi (W)	*yita-'i*	*mit-'ay*

If a pair-by-pair comparison among the five languages is carried out for these two plant species, it can be shown that there are ten pairs of similar words for the copal tree yet no pair of similar words for 'moela de mutum' among these languages. The present essay seeks to explain why words for certain plant species in these five related languages display stability and genetic similarity, as with these words for the copal tree, whereas words for certain other plant species, such as 'moela de mutum,' in the vocabularies of these same languages, seem to be labile and highly unlike. In other words, we seek to identify certain linguistic and cultural processes involved in the observed patterns of similarity and dissimilarity for a common corpus of plant names in these five different yet related languages.

The data (which are fully presented in Balée and Moore 1991), consist of 625 words for 167 botanical species native to the neotropics in the Araweté (henceforth Ar), Asurini do Xingu (henceforth As), Ka'apor (henceforth K), Tembé (henceforth T), and Wayãpi (henceforth W) languages of eastern Amazonia (see Appendixes 1, 2, and 3). These data are highly appropriate for isolating the factors related to similarity and dissimilarity in plant names among different languages of the same family for many reasons.

First, the five languages are dispersed in four linguistic subgroupings of Tupí-Guaraní (A. R. Rodrigues 1984/85; A. R. Rodrigues, personal communication, letter, 1988), with only W and K being classified within the same subgrouping. Second, these five languages are spoken in three ecologically diverse regions: the Xingu River Basin of north central Brazil for Ar and As, the Gurupi/Turiaçu River Basins of extreme eastern Amazonia for K and T, and the Oiapoque River Basin of northern Amazonia for W. Third, although all five groups practice horticulture, they exhibit significant differences in crop staples and utilization of nondomesticated species. For example, the Ar rely heavily on maize (Viveiros de Castro 1992), in contrast to the other groups who traditionally are more dependent on tubers, especially manioc. Fourth, collections and scientific determinations of voucher plant specimens for the vast majority of the 167 plant species in this sample were obtained for the five languages—identifications for the other plants either took place in the field or are based on dictionary references. In particular, as for W, all plant words were obtained from the monograph by Pierre Grenand (1980). Finally, the corpus of data is large enough to test statistically propositions concerning similarity and dissimilarity among plant words in the five languages.

The present study differs in methodology from that of Berlin et al. (1973) [also see Berlin 1992, 255–56], which, with respect to two Mayan languages, concluded that names for plants of significant cultural importance were more likely to be retained than names for plants of negligible cultural importance. The present essay compares data from five languages instead of two, which yields a comparison of ten pairs of languages instead of one pair. It is organized, moreover, according to botanical referents (that is, plant species themselves), rather than indigenous names. We listed these referents and then counted similarities and dissimilarities among indigenous words for them on a plant-by-plant basis among each of the ten pairs of languages, rather than list folk generic names for botanical species held in common between languages and then count the pairs of similar words. The dissimilar as well as the similar terms are also presented in our data, with morpheme-by-morpheme glosses, in order to facilitate insights into the patterns of naming plants and the relationships that these patterns may have to culture. The results of this study indicate that the retention rate of plant names is not directly determined by cultural importance, but rather by the *type* of name, and that cultural practices that are associated with the degree of domestication of a plant ultimately determine the type of name that the plant receives.

Method of Comparison

Measuring similarity and variation of vocabulary between related languages is different from the procedures of historical linguistics—reconstruction using the comparative method. This exercise first asks the questions, given a botanical species, what are the words for it in various languages of the same family and are these words similar or different? These questions reflect well the common sense notion of what one means by similarity, and their answers can be quantified in a straightforward way. In historical linguistics, by contrast, one searches for cognate terms showing systematic sound correspondences, allowing, if necessary, a considerable degree of semantic "shift" of the referent. There is no concern with determining noncognacy, which is difficult with incomplete collections and without knowledge of the full range of meaning for each word.

In order to determine whether words in two languages are similar or different, it is necessary to specify a comparable range of meaning for them (such as the biological species) to prevent problems of overlapping (see Alcorn 1984, 270). Consider, for example, the K and T names for *jarana* and *caçador*, which are two species in the Brazil nut family:

	K NAME	T NAME
Lecythis cf. *chartacea* Berg	iwɨri-'ɨ	iwɨri-'ɨw ("jarana")
Lecythis idatimon Aubl.	yaši-amɨr	iwɨri'ɨw-pitā ("caçador")

If the range of meaning were not restricted and were one permitted to count as being similar those pairs of words that occurred in vertically different positions, then from the point of view of T, both words would have one similar K counterpart (the K word for *Lecythis* cf. *chartacea*), on the basis of the initial morpheme, iwɨri. And both words would have one dissimilar K counterpart (the K word for *Lecythis idatimon*), insofar as neither T word shares any of its constituent morphemes with yaši-amɨr. That is to say, there would be two pairs of similar words and two pairs of dissimilar words between K and T for these two species. Such a result would be meaningless for the purposes of determining lexical similarity for plant names between the two languages. This is because from the point of view of K, only one of the two words has similar counterparts in T. Such nonrestricted comparison would become yet more confusing upon considering five instead of two languages. Further, a skewing could result insofar as a pair of languages having relatively complete plant collections would offer greater opportunity for finding similar words than would a pair of languages having relatively incomplete plant collections.

Therefore, it is necessary to restrict the range of meaning of the referent, and then examine whether the words for it are similar or dissimilar on a pair-by-pair basis. We decided to restrict referents to the taxonomic rank of botanical species, mainly because one may argue that the botanical species is the most objective level of abstraction for distinguishing between individual plants. The species is more objective than higher order units, such as tribes, genera, and families, given that "rank is not inherent in supraspecific groups" (Cronquist 1968, 31). We subscribe to the view that species are natural units, moreover, not merely products of mind or fantasy (see Gould 1980, 204–13).

Species, for the purposes of this analysis, are also more suitable referents for comparing indigenous plant names than are taxa of infraspecific ranks. For example, the classification of many neotropical cultivars (i.e., varieties) of a single botanical species is still far from possessing taxonomic exactitude. In their taxonomic revision of the genus *Manihot* (which includes cultivated manioc, *Manihot esculenta* Crantz) Rogers and Appan (1973, 34) poignantly noted that, "It is impossible to apply formal subspecific taxon epithets to fleeting variants which are not related to some precise geography or ecological region."

Names for species that were introduced to the neotropics within the last two thousand years are excluded from the list of plant names under study since these names would not, by definition, be of Tupí-Guaraní origin. There is some doubt, nevertheless, about the origins of a few species included in our analysis, all of which are domesticates. These include papaya (*Carica papaya* L.) (Storey 1976, 23; Sousa 1974, 99), bananas and plantains (*Musa* spp.) (Smole 1980; Lery 1960, 157; Lisboa 1967, 122; Sousa 1974, 98; Vasconcellos 1865, 136), and bottle gourds (*Lagenaria siceraria* Mol.) (Sousa 1974, 95; Heiser 1979, 114–16). All domesticates included in the analysis, however, are of sufficient antiquity in the neotropics (i.e., probably older than the five languages in our analysis) that they can be considered, for historical linguistic purposes, to be neotropical. In other words, the plant vocabulary of Proto-Tupí-Guaraní, in principle, could have had names for these species.

Only species for which names in three or more of the five languages were obtained are included in the analysis. This criterion guarantees that each species occurs in at least two of the three ecological regions; it also limits any possible effects of linguistic borrowing, which would be most likely to occur among the proximate pairs of languages (the K/T and the Ar/As pairs).

As field collections were being made, it began to appear that the pattern of similarity and dissimilarity in plant names between these Tupí-Guaraní languages was at least partly a function of the degree of domestication of plants

(Balée 1989). Patterns of plant nomenclature appear to segregate traditionally domesticated and nondomesticated plants. These patterns may be summarized as follows: (1) life-form heads (for example, K *mɨra, ka'a, sɨpo*) are not incorporated into names for traditional domesticates; (2) animal morphemes are incorporated into names for traditional domesticates only when the animals are not ecologically associated with the plants themselves; (3) "obscure" plant names (i.e., names that do not incorporate plant morphemes, such as K *akuši-nami* "agouti-ear," which refers to a small forest shrub in the coffee family) do not denote traditional domesticates; (4) morphemes referring to divinities (such as K *kurupir*) and to the state of being "false" or "similar" (K *-ran,* Ar *-rĩ,* As *-rána,* T *-ran,* W *-lã*) are only incorporated into plant names that do not refer to traditional domesticates (Balée 1989).

Three basic kinds of plant species can be identified in terms of degree of domestication: nondomesticates, semidomesticates, and domesticates. Nondomesticates typically occur in primary well-drained forest, archaic vine forests, or swamp forests. These are zones where contemporary human interference in species composition and dominance is, or recently has been, negligible. Although some nondomesticates may sporadically occur in zones of recent human interference, such as old swiddens and old fallows, they do not appear to gain dominance other than in fairly undisturbed forests. Nondomesticates are wild species.

Semidomesticates, in contrast, do not generally appear to become ecologically dominant without human interference, usually by horticultural fires or by the seemingly random tossing away of viable seeds. A few of these species (such as *Annona montana* Macf. var. *marcgravii* 'araticum' and *Theobroma grandiflorum* Schum. 'cupuaçu'—see Appendix 2) may be deliberately planted and carefully protected from time to time by individuals from one or more of the five societies, but such management lacks cross-cultural regularity. The category of semidomesticates corresponds to that of "protected plants" in Berlin et al. (1973, 146). In addition, most of the semidomesticates in Appendix 2 are disturbance indicators, that is, their presence tends to indicate former·sites of human habitation and horticulture. Semidomesticates are generally found in swiddens of all ages and old fallows.

Neotropical plant domesticates (Appendix 3) are completely dependent on human management for their long-term propagation; most, if not wholly incapable of setting seed, are producers of minuscule quantities of viable seed. These species are often parthenocarpic as a result of human interference. The genotypes of domesticates have been altered by human intervention over long periods of time.

To measure the degree of similarity in plant names between two languages, we consider pairs of words, such that any word in language A corresponds to a word in language B for the same species. The number of such pairs that are similar and the number that are dissimilar phonologically are then tabulated, the ratio between them being the degree of similarity.

In order to define similarity adequately, it is necessary to distinguish *literal* plant words from *metaphorical* or *descriptive* (henceforth metaphorical) plant words, a distinction that proves to be of crucial analytical importance. In our usage, literal plant words are those that contain a literal plant morpheme; they may contain other morphemes as well. *Literal plant morphemes* are here defined as those that have as their sole referent a specific class of plants, excluding general life form morphemes, such as "tree" or "herb." The word *pine* in English, for example, refers only to specific trees—the association between the word and its referents is purely arbitrary. The terms *jack pine, white pine,* and *red pine* are also literal since they contain the literal morpheme "pine." Likewise, in the Tupí-Guaraní languages under study, the words for an ingá tree found in old fallows (*Inga capitata* Desv. —from example 6, Appendix 2) are literal in the five languages: Ar, *iña-pəkə-'i,* 'L-long-tree'; As, *kururu-iɲja,* 'toad-L'; K, *iɲja-hu-'ɨ,* 'L-big-tree'; T, *tapi'i-riɲja-'ɨw,* 'tapir-L-tree'; and W, *iɲja-mulua-ya,* 'L-pregnant-owner,' since they all incorporate the literal morpheme *iña/iɲja,* which we gloss as 'L.' Two literal plant words are considered to be similar if their literal plant morphemes are similar, regardless of the other morphemes occurring in the word. Thus, the three words for "ingá" in this example, upon being systematically compared, constitute three pairs (Ar/As, Ar/K, and As/K) of similar, literal plant words. In our usage, *metaphorical* names are those that (a) do not contain a literal plant morpheme or (a) do contain a literal plant morpheme that is being used only metaphorically (i.e., the class of plants designated by the whole metaphorical name is not included in the class of plants designated by the literal morpheme). For example, in folk English, *dogwood* is an example of a metaphorical plant term, since neither *dog* nor *wood* refers to a specific plant, as does *pine.* The term *poison oak* is also metaphorical, since it is not botanically a kind of oak (which, in folk English, when applied to species of the genus *Quercus,* is otherwise a literal plant term). Likewise, in the Tupí-Guaraní data, the K word for *Tapirira guianensis* Aubl., *tayahu-mɨra,* 'white-lipped peccary-tree,' is metaphorical, since its constituent morphemes do not denote a specific plant and the W word for *Conceveiba guianensis, a'ɨ-miniyu,* 'sloth-cotton,' is metaphorical because this tree of the spurge family is not a kind of cotton. The relation between a metaphorical plant term and its referent is, in a sense, less arbitrary than that of a literal term to its referent, because some culturally given interpretation of the plant intervenes between the metaphorical term and its referent.

It is more complicated to judge the similarity of metaphorical plant terms since these may contain several morphemes, and some degree of arbitrariness is unavoidable. Two metaphorical terms are deemed similar (1) if they share two morphemes that are similar in sound and in meaning (e.g., K *yaši-sipo-pe*, 'tortoise-vine-flat,' and T *iwipo-pew*, 'vine-flat') or (2) if one of the principal nominal components is similar in sound and in meaning, excluding life-form morphemes or common plant part morphemes (e.g., T *zani-ro-'iw*, 'oil-bitter-tree,' W *yani*, 'oil,' referring to the crabwood tree of the mahogany family, *Carapa guianensis* Aubl.).

Phonetic resemblance between forms must be apparent for them to be considered similar (such as *iña* and *iŋa*, 'ingá,' above). Given the number of languages involved in this study, the lack of descriptive work on two of the languages (Ar and As), the uncertainty of some phonetic details, and the limited size of the corpus, we cannot, in general, reconstruct the Proto-Tupí-Guaraní forms with certainty and then identify borrowings by the fact that they do not show the same systematic sound correspondences as do the recon-structable words.

Borrowing, however, appears to have been very minimal. Berlin et al. (1973, 152) also observed that borrowing of plant words between Tzeltal-Tzotzil, which are very closely related Mayan languages, was a "relatively rare occurrence." In addition, as a general principle, names for domesticates would be the most likely of the three categories of plant names to be bor-rowed, yet these names strongly tend to reconstruct in Proto-Tupí-Guaraní (Aryon Rodrigues, personal communication, letter, 1988). It is very doubtful that much borrowing occurred, since a society would have had to lose the domesticate as well as its name and then regain the domesticate together with a new name. It seems unlikely this would have happened often. Second, if borrowings were extensive from language A to language B, one would expect these two languages to be conspicuously more similar to each other than is either to languages C, D, and E. But among these Tupí-Guaraní languages, no such significant pairings were found. There has been, however, minor Portuguese influence (K *kuyer-'i* and T *wira-kuzer*, 'spoon-tree,' from *colher*, K *kanei-'i-tuwir*, 'resin-tree-white,' from *candeia*, and the words for "wild cacao" and "cacao"). It should be noted that the referents of these words are of neotropical origin. The similarities between the languages for these words probably reflect independent borrowing from Portuguese in the remote past.

Similarity between literal plant terms must, in general, be due to their retention in the languages since splits in the protolanguage. This is probably also the general cause of resemblances between metaphorical terms, though in some cases resemblance may be due to independently similar cultural interpretations of the plant. No effort is made here to exclude these, because there are no clear means of identifying such cases and their contribution to the overall proportion of similarity is certainly extremely limited.

Results

The results show clearly that the more intensively managed plants have higher rates of similarity in their names from one language to the other. Combining data from all ten pairs of languages:

ALL WORD PLANT CATEGORY	PAIRS	SIMILAR	DISSIMILAR
Nondomesticates	441	136 (30.8%)	305 (69.2%)
Semidomesticates	278	164 (59.0%)	114 (41.0%)
Domesticates	198	159 (80.3%)	39 (19.7%)

The differences between the three categories of plants—nondomesticates, semidomesticates, and domesticates—in terms of degree of similarity (30.8%, 59%, and 80.3%, respectively) are very significant (chi^2 = 146.483, 2 df, p < .0001). In other words, lexical similarity between the ten pairs of languages very significantly increases along a scale of increasing human domestication of plants (see fig. 16.1).

The results also indicate that the type of plant name, whether literal or metaphorical, is also strongly influenced by the degree of domestication:

ALL PLANT CATEGORY	WORDS*	LITERAL	METAPHORICAL
Nondomesticates	323	137 (42.4%)	186 (57.6%)
Semidomesticates	175	128 (73.1%)	47 (26.9%)
Domesticates	113	110 (97.3%)	3 (2.7%)

*Fourteen indeterminate words are excluded.

The differences between the proportions of metaphorical words in the three categories of plants (57.6%, 26.9%, and 2.7%) are very significant and show that these words were taken from fundamentally different samples (G heterogeneity = 143.482, p < .0001). In other words, the proportion of metaphor-

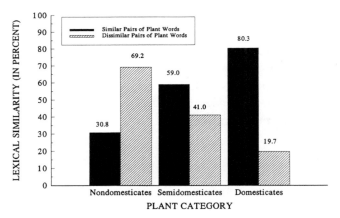

Figure 16.1. Lexical similarity by plant category.

ical words declines considerably as a function of increasing plant domestication (see fig. 16.2).

Another important finding is that the literal plant terms are much more
similar from language to language than are metaphorical terms. Overall, the
similarity of pairs of literal words compared to metaphorical words is:

	SIMILAR	DISSIMILAR	TOTAL
Literal Word Pairs	393 (77.0%)	118 (23.0%)	511 (100%)
Metaphorical Word Pairs	49 (23.2%)	162 (76.8%)	211 (100%)

(The fact that the percentage of similar literal word pairs is almost exactly
the same as the percentage of dissimilar metaphorical word pairs is a coincidence, not a mistake). It is important to note that the overall proportions of
similarity of literal plant name pairs for each of the three plant categories are
not significantly different (68% for nondomesticates, 78.6% for semidomesticates, and 80.8% for domesticates).

The ratio of literal to metaphorical plant words, combining words from all
plant categories, is not significantly different between the five languages (chi^2
= 1.7, df = 4, p > .05).

Discussion

The above results are generally in accord with the hypothesis that cultural
importance influences the retention of plant names in sister languages (Berlin
et al. 1973):

Degree of cultural importance of plants ⟶ *Degree of retention of names of plants*

But our results suggest that this process can be further elucidated by recognizing as analytical variables (1) the degree of plant domestication (domesticated, semidomesticated, nondomesticated); (2) a widespread nomenclatural pattern among these languages, in which words for traditional domesticates tend to be literal, words for nondomesticates tend to be metaphorical, and words for semidomesticates tend to lie between these extremes; and (3) the much higher stability of literal, as opposed to metaphorical, plant names.

In this model, the types of names that the nomenclatural pattern assigns to domesticates tend strongly to be literal, the types assigned to semidomesticates show an increasing proportion of metaphorical terms, and the majority of those assigned to nondomesticates are metaphorical. For some reason, literal terms are more stable over time and hence are more apt to be similar from language to language. That is, synchronic cultural factors of degree of plant domestication and the plant naming system combine with the linguistic properties of names and diachronic linguistic processes to produce similarity and variation in plant vocabulary:

(1) Synchronic Factors:
Degree of plant domestication + Nomenclatural system ⟶ Proportions of literal vs. metaphorical names

(2) Diachronic Processes:
Differential retention of proportions of similarity and literal/metaphorical names ⟶ Similarity among names

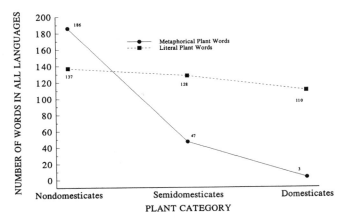

Figure 16.2. Metaphorical vs. literal plant words in the five languages.

When the data of the Mayan study by Berlin et al. (1973) are reanalyzed in the above terms, it appears that the retention of plant words in the Mayan languages follows the same patterns found for Tupí-Guaraní. Using the glosses of Tzeltal plant words given in a later publication (Berlin et al. 1974), it can be determined that, of the Tzeltal plant names cognate with Tzotzil names, seventy-nine are literal and only thirty-two are metaphorical, indicating a high rate of cognacy for literal terms.

Combining the categories of cultivated and protected plants, on the one hand, and those of wild-useful and wild-useless plants on the other (tables 1–4 in Berlin et al. 1973) to reach a valid statistical sample, we arrive at the following proportions for the 111 cognate sample of the two Mayan languages:

cultivated/protected: 43 (37 literal and 6 metaphorical)
wild: 68 (42 literal and 26 metaphorical)

The ratio of literal to metaphorical cognates (6.2 to 1) in the first category is about 4 times higher than the corresponding ratio (1.6 to 1) for the combined "wild" category. This difference is very significant at $p < .01$, $chi^2 = 7.0$, $df = 1$. Clearly, the more managed plants are receiving literal names at a much higher rate than the less managed plants, as in the case of the Tupí-Guaraní languages. In addition, as with these Tupí-Guaraní languages (Balée 1989), a nomenclatural pattern that lexically distinguishes between cultivated and noncultivated plants has been explicitly noted for Mayan speakers of the Yucatan peninsula (Marin et al. 1976, 472).

Once again combining cultivated and protected plants on the one hand, and useful/useless wild plants on the other (see table 5 in Berlin et al. 1973, 161) to reach a statistically meaningful sample, we find that of the 52 word pairs in the first group, 43 are cognates, whereas of the 205 word pairs in the "wild" group, only 68 are cognates. That is, the Mayan managed plants have a cognacy rate about two and one-half times higher than that of the wild plants, the same pattern as that of Tupí-Guaraní.

The question remains whether plant utility, aside from degree of plant domestication, as we have defined it, would more economically explain the proportion of similar plant words among the five Tupí-Guaraní languages in our sample. We quantified the uses of nondomesticated species (see Prance et al. 1987) for the K. The uses were (1) food, (2) construction material, (3) tool, weapon, utensil or container, (4) medicine, and (5) adornment. Fuel and game food were excluded as uses, since these are extremely widespread among forest species. Each use is of two types: major or minor. A major use has a value of 1.0, a minor use, 0.5, and no use, 0 (cf. Turner 1989).

The value of plant utility as a predictor of literal as opposed to metaphorical plant names, which are predictors of cognacy and retention, was tested within the nondomesticated plant category, where the factor of use can be separated from that of degree of plant domestication. Of the nondomesticated plants with a high use value, thirteen are metaphorical and twelve are literal. Of the nondomesticates with a low use value, thirty-seven are metaphorical and thirty are literal. The differences are not great and are not statistically significant. The usefulness of a plant, therefore, at least within the nondomesticated category, is not shown to be a predictor of whether its name will be literal or metaphorical, and, by inference, whether its name will be retained.

Why are literal plant terms more stable? One hypothesis is that of Alphonse de Candolle (stated later, in somewhat different form, by Zipf's law [Berlin 1992, 259]): they are shorter. Although there may be some truth in this, it is an incomplete explanation, since the shorter metaphorical words in our sample (having only one morpheme excluding any life-form or common plant part morpheme) do not seem to have a higher similarity rate than the longer words (two or three morphemes, excluding any life-form or common plant part morpheme). Another possibility is that the literal terms endure because of their arbitrariness—the metaphorical terms involve a cultural interpretation of the plant that is susceptible to change.

In spite of the strong correlations observed in the section on results, some degree of unpredictability and possibly still unidentified factors, at work in determining naming patterns, remain. For example, some nondomesticated species (in particular, several palms) show stable literal names. It is not yet clear what causes such exceptions.

The general patterns explained above, however, appear also to be present in the Mayan Tzeltal and Tzotzil as well as in the Tupí-Guaraní languages studied. Perhaps this is the general case in egalitarian, horticultural societies. It would be instructive to compare these observed patterns with those of state societies and foraging societies. Further research might also examine whether similarity and variation in other semantic fields, such as birds, fish, or mammals, can be analyzed along the same general principles.

APPENDIX I

Examples of Names for Nondomesticated Plant Species in Five Tupí-Guaraní Languages[1]

1. *Anacardium giganteum* Hancock ex Engl. (Eng. "wild cashew"; Port. "cajuí"): *akayu-'ɨ*, 'L-tree' (K); *akazu-'ɨw'ete*, 'L-tree-true' (T); *akay-u*, 'L-big' (W). Obs.: Three of three possible pairs are similar. All names are literal.

2. *Tapirira guianensis* Aubl. (Port. "tatapiririca"): *təkəré-me'e-'a-'i*, '?-some-fruit-tree' (Ar); *tayahu-mɨra*, 'white-lipped peccary-tree' (K): *tata-piririk-'ɨw*, 'fire-crackling-tree' (T); *tata-pilili*, 'fire-cracking' (T). Obs.: One (T/W) of six possible pairs is similar. All names are metaphorical.

3. *Capparis* sp. (Eng. "caper tree"): *yapə-tā'i*, 'crested oropendola-spicy-tree' (Ar); *ɨwɨra-tái*, 'tree-spicy' (As); *sawɨya-mɨra*, 'rat-tree' (K). Obs.: None of the three possible pairs is similar. All names are metaphorical.

4. *Conceveiba guianensis* Aubl.: *iŋa-i-úna*, 'Inga-tree-black' (As); *arapuha-mɨra*, 'red brocket deer-tree' (K); *wɨra-kɨ'ɨw-ran*, 'tree-chili pepper-similar' (T); *a'ɨ-miniyu*, 'sloth-cotton' (W). Obs.: None of the six possible pairs is similar. All names are metaphorical.

5. *Sapium marmieri* Huber (Eng. "tallow tree"): *ɨka-'i*, 'latex-tree' (Ar); *yuwa-'ɨwa*, 'bird lime-tree' (As); *wakura-mɨra-hu*, 'nighthawk-tree-big' (K). Obs.: None of three possible pairs is similar. All names are metaphorical.

6. *Psychotria poeppigiana* M. Arg. (Port. "mata cavalo"): *akuči-wirā*, 'agouti-tree' (Ar); *yawči-iŋga*, 'tortoise-Inga' (As); *tapi'ika'a*, 'tapir-herb' (K); *ka'a-rahɨ*, 'herb-poison' (T). Obs.: None of six possible pairs is similar. All names are metaphorical.

7. *Simaba cedron* Planch. (Port. "serve p'ra tudo"): *ari-kara-'ɨwa*, '?-yam-tree' (As); *pere-pusan-'ɨ*, 'skin eruption-remedy-tree' (K); *akuči-wɨra*, 'agouti-tree' (T). Obs.: None of three possible pairs is similar. All names are metaphorical.

8. *Ampelocera edentula* Kuhlm.: *yači-pápe-'i*, 'tortoise-claw-tree' (Ar); *ɨwɨ-payé*, 'earth-shaman' (As); *tapi'iākwāpe-'ɨ*, 'white bearded manakin-tree' (K). Obs: None of three possible pairs is similar. All names are metaphorical.

9. *Rinorea passoura* (DC.) Kuntze: *yanə-'i*, 'spider-tree' (Ar); *wayaw-a'ɨy*, 'guava-seed' (As); *pɨwa-'i*, 'arrow point-tree' (K); *pɨwa-'ɨw* 'L-tree' (T). Obs.: One (K/T) of six possible pairs is similar. All names are metaphorical.

10. *Minquartia guianensis* Aubl. (Port. "acariquara"): *yɨwoy-'ɨ*, 'boa constrictor-tree' (K); *wakari-'ɨw*, 'kind of fish-tree' (T); *wakali-'ɨ*, 'kind of fish-tree' (W). One (T/W) of three possible pairs is similar. All names are metaphorical.

APPENDIX 2

Examples of Names for Semidomesticated Plant Species in Five Tupí-Guaraní Languages[2]

1. *Spondias mombin* L. (Eng. "hog plum"; Port. "tarerebá"): *akāya-'i*, 'L-tree' (Ar); *kayuwa-'ɨwa*, 'L-tree' (As); *taper-'ɨwa-'ɨ*, 'old village-fruit-tree' (K); *tawera-'ɨw*, 'old village-tree' (T); *akaya*, 'L' (W). Obs.: Four of the ten possible pairs are similar (Ar/As, Ar/W, As/W, K/T). Two (K and T) of the names are metaphorical.

2. *Annona montana* Macf. var. *macrgravii* (Eng. "soursop"; Port. "araticum"): *tayəhə-'ə-'i*, 'white lipped peccary-fruit-tree' (Ar); *arašiku-'i*, 'L-tree' (K); *aračiku-'ɨw*, 'L-tree' (T). Obs.: One (K/T) of three possible pairs is similar. One (Ar) of the names is metaphorical.

3. *Didymopanax morototoni* (Aubl.) Decne & Planch. (Eng. "matchwood"; Port. "morototó"): *murete-təwi-'i*, 'L-?-tree' (Ar); *moroto-'ɨ*, 'L-tree' (K); *molototo*, 'L' (W). Obs.: Three of three possible pairs are similar. All names are literal.

4. *Maximiliana maripa* (Corr. Serr.) Drude (Port. "inajá"): *náya-'i*, 'L-tree' (Ar); *inayá*, 'L' (As); *inaya-'ɨ*, 'L-tree' (K); *naza-'ɨw*, 'L-tree' (T); *inaya*, (W) [L]. Obs.: Ten of ten possible pairs are similar. All names are literal.

5. *Hymenaea parvifolia* Huber (Eng. "copal tree"): *yúta-'i*, 'L-tree' (Ar); *yeta-'ɨwa*, 'L-tree' (As); *yeta-'ɨ*, 'L-tree' (K); *zuta-i-'ɨw*, 'L-small-tree' (T); *yɨta-'i*, 'L-tree' (W). Obs.: Ten of ten possible pairs are similar. All names are literal.

6. *Inga capitata* Desv. (Port. "ingá"): *iña-pəkə-'i*, 'L-long-tree' (Ar); *kururu-iŋja*, 'toad-L' (As); *iŋja-hu-'i*, 'L-big-tree' (K); *tapi'i-riŋja-'ɨw*, 'tapir-L-tree' (T); *iŋja-mulua-ya*, 'L-pregnant-owner' (W). Obs.: Ten of ten possible pairs are similar. All names are literal.

7. *Eugenia patrisii* Vahl. (Port. "pitanga"): *me'e-'a-'i*, 'some-fruit-tree' (Ar); *arākwā-mɨra*, 'little chachalacha-tree' (K); *iwaū-'ɨw*, 'fruit-black-tree' (T); *ɨwa-pitā*, 'fruit-red' (W). None of six possible pairs is similar. All names are metaphorical.

8. *Theobroma grandiflorum* Schum. (Port. "cupuaçu"): *kəpi-'i*, 'L-tree' (Ar); *kɨpɨ-hu-'ɨ*, 'L-big-tree' (K); *kupi-'a-'ɨw*, 'L-fruit-tree' (T); *kapɨai*, 'L' (W). Obs.: Six of six possible pairs are similar. All names are literal.

9. *Fleurya aestuans* (L.) Gouv. (Eng. "stinging nettles," Port. "urtiga"): *pinə* , 'L' (Ar); *pɨnú*, 'L' (As); *purake-ka'a*, 'electric eel-herb' (K). Obs.: One (Ar/As) of three possible pairs is similar. One name (K) is metaphorical.

10. *Lantana camara* L. (Eng. "lantana"): *ñéma-'i*, 'nothing-tree' (Ar); *kanami-ran*, 'Clibadium sylvestre* (a domesticated fish poison)-similar' (K); *ərəkwə-wɨra*, 'little chachalacha-tree' (T); *yakale-pili*, 'caiman-aromatic plant' (W). Obs.: None of six possible pairs is similar. All names are metaphorical.

APPENDIX 3

Examples of Names for Domesticated Plant Species in Five Tupí-Guaraní Languages[3]

1. *Anacardium occidentale* L. (Eng. "cashew"; Port. "caju"): *akayú*, 'L' (Ar); *akayu*, 'L' (K); *akazu*, 'L' (T); *akayu*, 'L' (W). Obs.: Six of six possible pairs are similar. All names are literal.

2. *Xanthosoma* sp. (Eng. "cocoyam"; Port. "tajá"): *taya*, 'L' (K); *taza*, 'L' (T); *tā-sī*, 'L-thorny' (W). Obs. Three of three possible pairs are similar. All names are literal.

3. *Crescentia cujete* L. (Eng. "calabash tree"; Port. "cuieira"): *kəi*, 'L' (Ar); *kuyá*, 'L' (As); *kwi*, 'L' (K); *kwi*, 'L' (T); *kwi*, 'L' (W). Obs.: Ten of ten possible pairs are similar. All names are literal.

4. *Bixa orellana* L. (Eng. "annatto"; Port. "urucum"): *irikə*, 'L' (Ar); *urukú*, 'L' (As); *uruku*, 'L' (K); *uruku*, 'L' (T); *uluku*, 'L' (W). Obs.: Ten of ten possible pairs are similar. All names are literal.

5. *Neoglaziovia variegata* L. (Port. "carauá"): **kɨrawã**, 'L' (Ar); **kurawa**, 'L' (As); **kɨrawa**, 'L' (K); **kurawa**, 'L' (T); **kulawa**, 'L' (W). Obs. Ten of ten possible pairs are similar. All names are literal.

6. *Cucurbita moschata* (Lam.) Poir. (Eng. "crookneck squash"; Port. "jerimum"): **yurumū**, 'L' (Ar); **yerimū**, 'L' (As); **yurumū**, 'L' (K); **zurumū**, 'L' (T); **asikala**, 'L' (W). Obs.: Six (Ar/As, Ar/K, Ar/T, As/K, As/T, K/T) of ten possible pairs are similar. All names are literal.

7. *Dioscorea trifida* L. (Eng. "yam"; Port. "inhame"): **karã**, 'L' (Ar); **kará**, 'L' (As); **kará**, 'L' (K); **kará**, 'L' (T); **kalá**, 'L' (W). Obs.: Ten of ten possible pairs are similar. All names are literal.

8. *Gossypium barbadense* L. (Eng. "cotton"; Port. "algodo"): **mɨniyu**, 'L' (Ar); **miniyú**, 'L' (As); **maneyu**, 'L' (K); **manizu**, 'L' (T); **mɨnɨyu**, 'L' (W). Obs.: Ten of ten possible pairs are similar. All names are literal.

9. *Musa X paradisiaca* L. (Eng. "plantain"; Port. "banana"): **pátsitsi**, 'L' (Ar); **pako**, 'L' (As); **pako**, 'L' (K); **pako**, 'L' (T); **pako**, 'L' (W). Obs.: Six (As/K, As/T, As/W, K/T, K/W, T/W) of ten possible pairs are similar. All names are literal.

10. *Zea mays* L. (Eng. "maize"; Port. "milho"): **awatsi**, 'L' (As); **awači**, 'L' (As); **awaši**, 'L' (K); **awači**, 'L' (T); **awasi**, 'L' (W). Obs.: Ten of ten possible pairs are similar. All names are literal.

NOTES

This is a shorter and somewhat revised version of Balée and Moore (1991). The reader wishing to examine all the data on which the arguments of this paper are based should also consult the longer version. We would like to thank Dr. Manuel Ayres of the Universidade Federal do Pará in Belém for very helpful advice on the statistical analysis.

1. Botanical species' names and English or Portuguese folk names (when known) are followed by the indigenous names, given in boldface. Morpheme-by-morpheme glosses, enclosed within single quotation marks, follow each indigenous name. Hyphens indicate morpheme boundaries. The letter L in a gloss indicates a literal plant morpheme. The language code for each indigenous name follows the gloss.

2. See n. 1 above.

3. See n. 1 above.

REFERENCES

Alcorn, J. B.
1984   *Huastec Mayan ethnobotany.* Austin: University of Texas Press.
Balée, W.
1989   Nomenclatural patterns in Ka'apor ethnobotany. *Journal of Ethnobiology*
            9 (1): 1–24.

Balée, W., and D. Moore.
1991   Similarity and variation in plant names in five Tupí-Guaraní languages
            (eastern Amazonia). *Bulletin of the Florida Museum of Natural History*
            (Biological Sciences) 35 (4): 209–62.

Bendor-Samuel, D. H.
1966   *Hierarchical structures in Guajajara*. Ph.D. diss., University of London.

Berlin, B.
1992   *Ethnobiological classification*. Princeton, N.J.: Princeton University
            Press.

Berlin, B., D. E. Breedlove, R. M. Laughlin, and P. H. Raven
1973   Cultural significance and lexical retention in Tzeltal-Tzotzil ethno-
            botany. In *Meaning in Mayan languages*, edited by M. S. Edmonson,
            143–64. The Hague: Mouton.

Berlin, B., D. E. Breedlove, and P. H. Raven
1974   *Principles of Tzeltal plant classification*. New York: Academic Press.

Boudin, M. H.
1978   *Dicionário de Tupi moderno*. Vols. 1 and 2. São Paulo: Conselho Estadual
            de Artes e Ciências Humanas.

Cronquist, A.
1968   *The evolution and classification of flowering plants*. Boston: Houghton
            Mifflin.

Gould, S. J.
1980   *The panda's thumb*. New York: W. W. Norton.

Grenand, P.
1980   *Introduction a l'étude de l'univers Waypi: Ethnoécologie des Indiens du Haut-
            Oyapock (Guyane Française)*. Paris: SELAF.

Heiser, C. B.
1979   *The gourd book*. Norman: University of Oklahoma Press.

Léry, J.
1960   *Viagem à terra do Brasil*. Translated by S. Milliet. São Paulo: Livraria
            Martins Editora.

Lisboa, C.
1967   História dos animais e árvores do Maranhão. Lisbon: Publicações
            do Arquivo Histórico Ultramarino e Centro de Estudos Históricos
            Ultramarinos.

Marin, A. B., A. B. Vazques, and R.M.L. Franco
1976   Nomenclatura etnobotnica Maya: Una interpretación taxonómica.
            Instituto Nacional de Antropologia e Historia, Centro Regional del Sureste:
            36. Mexico City: Coleccion Científica.

Nicholson, V.
1982   *Breve estudo da língua Asurini do Xingu, no. 5*. Brasília: Summer Institute
            of Linguistics.

Posey, D. A.

1983   Indigenous ecological knowledge and development of the Amazon. In *The dilemma of Amazon development,* edited by E. F. Moran, 225–57. Boulder, Colo.: Westview Press.

Prance, G. T., W. Balée, B. M. Boom, and R. L. Carneiro.

1987   Quantitative ethnobotany and the case for conservation in Amazonia. *Conservation Biology* 1 (4): 296–310.

Rodrigues, A. R.

1984–85   Relaçes internas na família lingüística Tupí-Guaraní. *Revista de Antropologia* 27/28:33–53.

Rogers, D. J., and S. G. Appan

1973   Manihot, manihotoides (euphorbiaceae). *Flora Neotropica monograph* 13. New York: Hafner Press.

Smole, W.

1980   *Musa* cultivation in pre-Columbian South America. *Geoscience and Man* 21:47–50.

Sousa, G. S.

1974   *Notícia do Brasil.* São Paulo: Departamento de Assuntos Culturais do MEC.

Storey, W. B.

1976   Papaya, *Carica papaya* (Caricaceae). In *Evolution of crop plants,* edited by N. W. Simmonds, 21–24. London: Longman.

Turner, N. J.

1988   The importance of a rose: Evaluating the cultural significance of plants in Thompson and Lilloet interior Salish. *American Anthropologist* 90 (2): 272–90.

Vasconcellos, S.

1865   *Chronica da companhia de Jesu no estado do Brasil.* Lisbon: A. J. Fernandes Lopes.

Viveiros de Castro, E.

1992   *From the enemy's point of view: Humanity and divinity in an Amazonian society.* Translated by C. V. Howard. Chicago: University of Chicago Press.

PART V   ADAPTATION TODAY

17

Becoming Indians

The Politics of Tukanoan Ethnicity

JEAN E. JACKSON

This chapter is a discussion of how an indigenous rights movement among Tukanoans of southeastern Colombia is affecting their notions about themselves and their culture. I argue that the concept of culture as conventionally understood does not help us understand these changes because several assumptions underlying it do not apply. I suggest that both anthropologists and activists promoting the preservation of "Indian culture" can at times unwittingly collaborate in misrepresenting what is actually going on.

To the degree that modern Amazonian Indian groups can and do choose to remain distinctively "ethnic" as they are increasingly incorporated into modern society, their distinctiveness changes in its essential nature. Even if the content of their ethnicity—the characteristics that make the group different from other sectors of society—appears to be identical with cultural forms from earlier periods, the underlying meaning is so altered that we cannot say these forms are the same (see Barth 1969). Part of the difficulty we may have describing situations like this stems from a conventional concept of culture based on a quasi-biological analogy in which a group of people are seen as "having" or "possessing" a culture somewhat in the way an animal species has fur or claws. In addition, people are thought of as acquiring culture slowly, during their childhoods, as part of their development. The culture they acquire existed before them and is seen as their legacy; they are not creating or inventing it. While culture is understood to change over time, this is seen as gradual process; in the case of rapid change, acculturation is said to occur, with one group seen as losing some of its culture. Thus, similar in some respects to the way one's genes are inherited, culture is inherited, even though culture is seen as superorganic.[1] To suggest that people are at times less passive about their culture, that they do create and invent it, is difficult without sounding negatively judgmental—unless "create" is understood as a long-term process. People who are seen as engaging in inventing culture tend to be spoken of in negative terms, the implication being that the culture resulting from these operations is not really authentic.[2] In sum, for the most part culture is simply not considered to be something constructed or modified by individuals, and in this sense it is opposed to history.[3]

I argue in this chapter that defining culture in a truly dynamic and agential way will help us better understand those South American Indian groups who are increasingly being incorporated—but not assimilated—into the dominant societies surrounding them.

An ethnic federation in the Vaupés territory of Colombia is used as a springboard for these discussions. Descriptions of Tukanoan[4] (as the indigenous inhabitants of the Vaupés are called) culture in the Indian rights and indigenist[5] press allow us to draw some inferences about how Tukanoan culture is conceived of by non-Tukanoan Colombian Indians and others interested in promoting indigenous rights. Hence, the Vaupés provides a provocative case study for this discussion because of the material available that shows how Tukanoans are beginning to be instructed by outsiders, both whites and Indians, on what it means to be an Indian.

In a sense, then, in this chapter I look at Tukanoans not so much as Indians who have culture or who comprise a culture, but as a people who are acquiring culture—"Indian" culture. Although clearly Tukanoans already are Indians, in this sense they are also *becoming* Indians (see Jackson 1991a).

In addition to being an analytic term, *culture* can, like so many words in the anthropological lexicon, be used for polemical, ideological, propagandistic purposes, especially when imbued with positively valued moral connotations. If culture is defined in terms of things, tangible or intangible—the blueprints in people's heads for making artifacts, for interacting with one another, for making sense of their world—one can talk about how Tukanoans can "lose" their culture as they are increasingly incorporated into Colombian society. A picture can be drawn of a people deracinated, deprived, "without their culture." This is the view taken by various organizations involved in protecting indigenous groups, many American and Colombian anthropologists, and others knowledgeable about and interested in the Tukanoan situation.[6]

Although the culture-as-things (material and mental) model is useful for some purposes (I use it below for describing how the entire Vaupés in many respects is a single cultural system), it falters when one delves into the processes of how ethnic groups acquire new cultural forms or asks about why traditional forms are retained or dropped. For this we need a concept of culture more equipped to deal with the fact that cultural forms can radically change in meaning even though they appear to remain the same. As noted above, one of the problems with the "culture-as-things" model is that it sometimes assumes, incorrectly, that continuities between earlier patterns and present-day ones have been produced by the same cultural and societal processes. Another problem is that the model is overly static. It tends to downplay the agential, processual, and social interactional (see Bourgois 1988, 329) aspects of culture. Finally, it can promote a misreading of the circumstances of a given threatened people by overly focusing on the peril of "losing culture" rather than on other, perhaps more grave, dangers, such as loss of land base. I am not suggesting that "losing one's culture" never has negative consequences, but simply emphasizing that, in addition to being an analytic term, "culture" is often used in highly politicized contexts and that, while these political meanings are linked to the term's analytical, less political meanings, the two must be kept separate.

If we see culture as something dynamic, something that people use to adapt to changing social conditions, and as something that is adapted in turn, we have a more serviceable sense of how culture operates over time, particularly in situations of rapid change. At times it is helpful to see culture less like an animal's fur or claws and more like a jazz musician's repertoire. The pieces the musician plays come out of a tradition, but improvisation also occurs, and the choices made by the musician about the performance take into consideration the acoustical properties of the hall, the properties of the instrument(s) played, and the inferred inclinations of fellow musicians and the audience. This analogy stresses the agential aspects of culture; we cannot speak of a jazz musician as "having" jazz, and for the most part speaking of people as "having" culture occludes the interaction between those people and their traditions. The analogy stresses the interactional aspects of culture; the musician engages an audience and fellow musicians, just as to an important extent a culture exists because a "we" and a "they" are interacting. This may also turn out to be a more genuinely respectful view of present-day indigenous groups in their struggles to preserve their self-respect, autonomy, and a life with meaning (see Cowlishaw 1987, 221).

Wolf provides a useful characterization of this alternative approach to "culture": "In the rough and tumble of social interaction, groups are known to

exploit the ambiguities of inherited forms, to impart new evaluations or val-
ences to them, to borrow forms more expressive of their interests, or to create
wholly new forms to answer to changed circumstances" (1982, 387). This
notion is particularly useful for understanding the present-day Tukanoan
case, particularly with respect to indigenous-rights organizing, because it allows us to consider the possibility that, at times, Tukanoans are not to be
seen as continuing some of their traditional cultural forms so much as appropriating them as a political strategy.

Sources for this chapter include twenty-eight formal interviews conducted
in Colombia during March, 1987 and June-July, 1989. I also engaged in a
number of informal conversations with native leaders, change agents, residents (both Tukanoan and white) of Mitú, the capital of the Vaupés, and with
individuals in Bogotá who are knowledgeable about Colombian indigenous-
rights organizing and development efforts among Colombian Indian groups.
All interviewees characterized themselves as concerned about the autonomy
and overall well-being of Colombian Indians. Continuing archival work in
the Vaupés and Bogotá and dissertation fieldwork in 1968–70 have provided
other sources of information.

The Vaupés

The Vaupés is in the Colombian sector of the central northwest Amazon, a
region including both Colombian and Brazilian territory, roughly the size of
New England, on the Equator. Tukanoans, who number about twenty thousand, traditionally lived in multifamily longhouses, one per settlement, on
or near rivers. Longhouses, as well as the more recent settlement pattern of
nucleated villages, are separated from one another by two to ten hours' canoe
travel. During this century four to eight nuclear families would inhabit a
longhouse, and present village size ranges anywhere from 15 to 180 persons.
Population density is quite low, at most .3 inhabitants per k^2 (PRORADAM
1979). The men of a settlement hunt, fish, and clear swidden fields in which
the women grow bitter manioc and other crops.

The units of traditional Vaupés social structure, in ascending order of
inclusion, are the local descent group, the clan or sib, the (ideally) exogamous language group, and the poorly understood phratry. (This is a simplified
description; the Cubeo and Makuna are exceptions in some crucial respects.)
The language group is a named, patrilineal-descent unit composed of from
six to more than thirty clans (see Sorensen 1967). Distinguishing features
are (1) the language and name; (2) separate founding ancestors and distinct
roles in the origin myth cycle; (3) the right to ancestral power through the

use of certain linguistic property such as sacred chants; (4) the right to manufacture and use certain kinds of ritual property; and (5) a traditional association with certain ceremonial or near-ceremonial objects. Membership is permanent and public; the one fact known about an individual before anything else is his or her language group.

Although I am presenting this as a description of "traditional" Tukanoan culture, it is my belief that Tukanoan linguistic exogamy is an extremely dynamic and relatively recent institution, the result of indirect pressure from colonization efforts elsewhere in Colombia, Venezuela, and Brazil (see Gómez-Imbert n.d.; Jackson 1983, 164–78). Documentary and archeological information is so scarce for either the pre-Columbian or early colonial periods that we cannot assume much about earlier social or political structures. Population density was almost certainly greater (see Goldman 1963; Koch-Grünberg 1903–5; Reichel-Dolmatoff 1971).

Although varying internally in some traditional customs, ecology, and degree of acculturation, the Vaupés is a single society in many respects. This homogeneity derives from a similarity of observable phenomena, ecological and social, and from the similarities in Tukanoans' models of their world. Furthermore, Tukanoans themselves see themselves as parts of an interacting whole. Many apparent examples of cultural diversity in the Vaupés are actually mechanisms helping to unify the settlements of the region. Multilingualism is an example: the various languages, somewhat like different uniforms in a football game, facilitate the interaction by serving as emblems of the participating groups.[7]

The earliest explorers were the conquistadors looking for the famed "Dorado de Los Omagua" in the first half of the sixteenth century. The first mission, a Carmelite one, was established in 1852 in the Brazilian Vaupés, but the first permanent missions were not established until 1914, at Monfort and Teresita on the Papurí River, by the Dutch Catholic Monfortian Congregation. Salesians built Yavaret in 1929, and in 1949 the Order of St. Javier founded the Prefectura Apostólica de Mitú, which has administered all Catholic missions since then. Protestantism appeared in the 1940s and has had a significant impact in the region, largely through the efforts of the near-legendary New Tribes Mission evangelist, Sophia Muller, and the Summer Institute of Linguistics/Wycliffe Bible Translators (see below). Except for the Pirá-Paraná region, most children were attending residential mission schools by the mid-sixties. Currently, education is managed by both the Prefecture and the Ministry of Education, and most teachers are Tukanoans. Also by the mid-sixties, except for the more traditionally minded, all Tukanoans had adopted Western clothing. Some aspects of native dress are currently being

promoted in the schools, and Tukanoan men will don some ritual paraphernalia for ceremonies; the degree to which these are mainly dancing and
chanting ceremonies as opposed to more sacred ones depends on how far
from Mitú the settlement hosting the ceremony lies.

The rubber boom early in the century, through its forcible recruitment of
labor, the introduction of epidemics, and the substantial dislocation of settlements, greatly disrupted Tukanoan life. With very few exceptions, all non-
Indians in the Vaupés have always lived in or near Mitú, the capital, on the
Vaupés river. Since the creation of the Vaupés *resguardo* (reservation; see
below), any non-Tukanoan needs to obtain permission to travel outside of
Mitú's environs; with the exception of missionaries, no non-Indian can reside in Tukanoan territory.[8]

CRIVA

The Regional Council of Vaupés Indians (CRIVA) is an ethnic federation (see
R. Smith 1985) representing some thirty-five named groups in the Vaupés
territory. It encompasses a number of local units, some formed on language-
group lines (e.g., Union of Cubeo Indians [UDIC]) or regions (e.g., Union of
Indians of the Acaricuara Zone [UNIZAC]). CRIVA, in turn, belongs to the
National Colombian Indian Organization (ONIC).

Space limitations prohibit placing CRIVA in its proper context. To understand its founding and evolution would require a more thorough discussion
than I can offer of the local Vaupés scene and of the people elsewhere in
Colombia who create the legislation and make the policies that affect the
region's inhabitants. Comprehending the current Tukanoan situation requires knowing about the history of land reform and Indian-white struggles
elsewhere in the country. Interest groups whose members have had an impact
on indigenous organizing in the Vaupés include people attached to the numerous governmental welfare and development agencies in Mitú; other government agents (e.g., the military police); missionaries; guerrillas; coca paste
traffickers;[9] anthropologists; and representatives of national and international
indigenous organizations. Although all non-Indians live in or just outside
Mitú, a town of some six thousand inhabitants, *colonos* (homesteaders) and
other non-Indians (for example, the owners of *almacenes*, or general stores),
also play an important role.

CRIVA is of importance to this chapter's topic because the interviews I had
with some of its members, along with some of the documents CRIVA has
written provide examples of how ideas about Indian identity and culture
from the exterior can influence a local Indian community.

However, the topic of how Tukanoans are becoming more politicized and self-conscious about their identity and culture cannot be comprehensively understood simply by examining CRIVA. For example, an increased interest in messianic movements can be seen as an alternative response to ideas introduced from outside (Hugh-Jones 1981; Wright and Hill 1986).

CRIVA was founded in 1973 with the backing of the Prefectura Apostólica del Vaupés, the Catholic mission headquarters in Mitú. Another organization influencing CRIVA's development is ONIC (National Organization of Colombian Indians) and a few of its member organizations, in particular the Regional Council of Cauca Indians (CRIC). Government agencies, in particular the Department of Indian Affairs, and Colombian anthropologists have been involved in CRIVA's activities as well.

CRIVA has had, and continues to have, problems. Almost all of the individuals I interviewed supplied evidence that the organization has not succeeded in gaining the allegiance and trust of its members. Most interviewees commented that CRIVA overly orients itself towards Mitú and the outside—towards non-Indians in the region and in Bogotá, and to non-Tukanoan Indians.

The vast majority of Tukanoans are substantially less politicized than active CRIVA members, and many Tukanoans are indifferent or hostile to the organization. For the most part, Tukanoans living far from Mitú are not actively involved in CRIVA, and many apparently do not respect the leaders or the positions they espouse. We can say that most Tukanoans are less self-consciously indigenist than active CRIVA members, and of those who are interested in indigenous-rights organizing, some are not sure that CRIVA best represents their interests in situations of Indian–non-Indian conflict.

Thus, no claim is being made that active CRIVA members typify Tukanoans in general. They may represent the Tukanoan of tomorrow, or they may not—the region is changing so rapidly that it is hard to predict what the future will look like.

Although this chapter is not an analysis of the difficulties CRIVA has encountered, a summary of reasons why it is so weak is necessary for understanding its cadet position vis-à-vis non-Tukanoans. The main factors are (1) no urgent threat to Tukanoan lands or other natural resources; (2) over-dependence on non-Tukanoans; (3) internal divisiveness; (4) the effects of coca paste trafficking; and (5) co-optation and marginalization of leaders, resulting in their losing legitimacy in the eyes of their constituents.

In the 1970s, the Colombian government instituted wide-ranging legislation affecting Indians that included regularization of Indian land claims into *reservas* (reserves) and *resguardos* (reservations). A *reserva* is land owned by the state with usufruct rights given to the inhabitants. A *resguardo* entails collective ownership of land by the Indian community. A resguardo containing 3,354,097 hectares (Arango and Sánchez 1989, 115) was established in the Vaupés in 1982. That so much territory has been ceded to so few Indians, with virtually no pressure coming from the Indians themselves, is indeed remarkable. It reflects an extremely unstable national political situation (see Brooke 1990b, 10; Riding 1987; Youngers 1990, 5) and a policy implemented by a fundamentally weak national government that attempts to win hearts and minds in the countryside and thus prevent leftist guerrilla groups from gaining more converts.[10] Some of the more militant highland Indian groups played a role in these developments, as well as some well-publicized scandals involving Indian atrocities. During this time Indian organizing, with the participation of international indigenous-rights organizations, led to the establishment of many pro-Indian organizations, and a great deal of discussion in the national press about Colombian Indians, their current status, and probable future.

What is important to note is that not only is there virtually no land pressure currently in the Vaupés, Tukanoans now have a vast resguardo that they administer but which they played virtually no role in obtaining (see Brooke 1990a, 6). Hence, one of the important factors that can aid organizing, a perceived mutual threat to land or other natural resources, is missing in the history of CRIVA. Although Tukanoans face many dangers and suffer from discrimination, compared to Indians elsewhere in Colombia and the hemisphere, they have not had to contend with such grave perils as land invasions, assassinations, or imprisonment and torture of Indian activists. One interviewee commented: "We have a problem here because these are people who didn't even *know* they owned the land. . . . obtaining the resguardo was an artificial event. . . . The Sikuani *won* their territory, whereas many people in the Vaupés don't even know what a resguardo is."

A second factor is over-dependence on non-Tukanoans. CRIVA has been treated paternalistically by virtually all the outsiders it has interacted with. The role of outsiders working with local Tukanoan leaders—priests, government agents, anthropologists, representatives of national and international Indian rights organizations, lawyers promoting civil and human rights legislation, and so forth—is extremely complex. These various interest groups have divergent goals, and although many sincerely want what is best for Tukanoans, one result of so many outsiders playing a role in the formation and evolution of CRIVA has been CRIVA's inability to grow up. As an interviewee said: "very weak . . . these Indians don't have representation in the communities, they are in the hands of the mestizos and don't have direct contact with the communities. They were formed in the mission and have interests unsuited to the communities' interests. . . . they are more interested in their own personal development."

Another knowledgeable individual said that CRIVA was initially promoted by the Catholic Church because it was seen as an alternative to the leadership found in the traditional settlement, a leadership less in tune with the church's interests than CRIVA would be. One Bogot interviewee, very much involved in indigenous grass roots projects and knowledgeable about the Vaupés remarked: "The priests say 'you have to organize.' And they [CRIVA] organize, but the priests said that in order to continue managing the people. Thus, although they [CRIVA leaders] are artificial officials, this corresponds to the interests of the mission."

Another activist in Bogotá commented that outsider Indians who travel to the Vaupés say, "we're going to work with the *gente de base* [the people of the base communities]." "But they're bureaucrats, they speak Spanish, they manage the white world. Now, it's true the local people may have to learn to manage the white world, but they must do so for their *own* interests."

A lawyer in Bogotá involved in Indian land claims cases characterized CRIVA leaders: "They are waiting for those in power to do something—now it's waiting for a response from the government, tomorrow waiting for an investigator to give them money. It's not an *Indian* organization at all. Like most Indian organizations, it is conceived and made rational with the rationality of the white."

Another factor is the problem of internal divisions. The local Catholic mission played a decisive role in creating CRIVA and undoubtedly sees its promotion of the organization as an answer to the many critics who have accused missionaries of creating divisions in Tukanoan society. Certainly, all who know the Vaupés have witnessed instances of the Prefecture's employing divide-and-conquer tactics over the years in its struggles against its evangelical Protestant rivals. And any new divisions probably build on already existing fault lines, such as the splits between old and young, proacculturation and traditionalist, and Mitú-oriented and backwoods. There is also some rivalry among language groups. Despite romantic claims of Tukanoan harmony and homogeneity in the national and local indigenist press, the Vaupés has never been known for its cohesion and unanimity.

In the late 1970s, many Tukanoans quickly acquired large amounts of cash and trade goods through coca. Although this bonanza has hardly been a blessing for Tukanoans in the long run, the results of this kind of white-Indian interaction are far different from the results of white-introduced epidemics, colono-induced violence, land invasions, and so on that have occurred elsewhere in the country. To some extent the rapid change and easy cash that coca trafficking brought to the region resulted in many Tukanoans' feeling even less militant about protecting their land and customs, and even more inclined to interact with the white world than before. Various interviewees commented that Tukanoan Indian-rights organizing was as much a response to coca as anything else. One subgroup of CRIVA was described as little more than a coca growers' guild, concerned with regulating prices, the amount of land whites could cultivate, and the amount of *mordida*, or payoff, to local (and sometimes federal) authorities.

The final factor is the fact that participating in ethnic federations like CRIVA often brings about a degree of bureaucratization, co-optation, and marginalization of leaders vis-à-vis more traditional sectors. This process puts CRIVA leaders in a bind: to some degree, the more efficient and effective they become at garnering goodies offered by the system, the more suspect and illegitimate they become to their constituencies.

The Acquisition of Indian Culture from Outsiders

Various interest groups in the Vaupés have recently found it useful to pay attention to traditional Tukanoan culture—as they conceive of it—and even to promote it. A general fear expressed by both Catholic clergy and government agents I interviewed is of creating too much dependency in Tukanoans. For example, one development agent said "you need the idea of self-sufficiency. And Tukanoans are moving more and more towards centralization and dependency on outside products." This is, of course, the classic development bind. What is interesting in the Vaupés case is that this concern results in these individuals taking a critical view of CRIVA for not being traditional *enough*. Non-Indians in Mitú are criticizing an Indian-rights movement for being too caught up in the white world and for not caring enough about preserving Tukanoan culture or developing genuine grass roots activism. One would expect the opposite kind of criticism.

Non-Indians who suddenly see virtues in Indian traditionalism probably do not come to think this way out of a recently acquired respect for lifeways different from their own. Two other factors probably influence their thinking along these lines: the guerrilla threat, and the inability of the local Catholic mission and the government to develop the region in a major way.

Most non-Indians in the Vaupés are worried about Indian-guerrilla alliances, and are thus comforted by the idea of traditionalist Tukanoans spurning guerrilla arguments about joining forces against a common enemy.[11] Most knowledgeable people recognize that the Revolutionary Armed Forces of Colombia (FARC), the oldest and largest guerrilla group in the country, has significantly different objectives than do Indian guerrilla groups. Indeed, some Andean Indians have mobilized to violently oppose national political fronts seeking to use popular movements as a springboard towards insurrectional, revolutionary actions. In the Sierra Central some especially violent clashes have occurred, and confrontations, including assassinations of Indian leaders by members of FARC and similar groups, are regularly reported in the Indian-rights press. The current leftist dialogue apparently recognizes this division: it is no longer couched in terms of how best to incorporate the Indian movement into the popular revolutionary movement, as was the case earlier. One interviewee commented: "The FARC wants democracy [in the areas it controls], yes, but with them as the heads. This is unacceptable to Indian leaders anywhere in the country." Another commented that whereas FARC says "Yes, we respect Indian culture," when push comes to shove they say, "the *comandante* commands here, and not the Indian chief."

However, attempts continue to be made to unite the Indian and non-Indian revolutionary movements, including some efforts to this end in Mitú. FARC has a permanent presence in the "zone of influence" of Mitú, and white residents affirm that some successful proselytization of Tukanoans has occurred. The FARC sometimes plays a Robin Hood role when Tukanoans complain of bad debts and the government Indian Affairs representative is unsuccessful at clearing the books. A FARC member will tell the debtor that he must pay up, leave the territory, or be killed. Although in general FARC does not consider Indians to be their worst enemies, Tukanoans nonetheless suffer from its presence. After a FARC raid on Mitú in April, 1988, river traffic was severely curtailed, and a military base was established, resulting in a substantial increase in illness—including venereal disease—among Tukanoans.

Another reason some non-Tukanoans in Mitú see advantages to promoting Indian traditionalism far more than was the case twenty years ago has to do with the welfare and development programs being promoted in Mitú. Everyone has stories of failed projects because Tukanoans did not like cement floors, latrines, beds, and so on. All of the interviewees I spoke with in Mitú commented that the correct approach was one that, yes, bettered Tukanoan lives but also somehow kept them in their ambient ("mejorar su vida pero no quitarles de su elemento").

A crucial factor in this is that very little work is to be found in Mitú (more precisely, very little money is available for work needing to be done). In addition, many whites resent present-day Tukanoans, and wax nostalgic for earlier times, when Indians knew their place and were not *atrevidos* (insolent) and drunk. Some non-Indians as well as Tukanoans in the region feel that *all* of the Vaupés's publicly elected officials should be Tukanoan because the population is 95 percent Indian. A few non-Indians see this as a world turned upside down and hence, are more likely to think kindly of Tukanoans returning to longhouse life, in their "elemento," rather than living in Mitú and appointed to offices like secretary of education (a position held by a Tukanoan in 1987). A town official commented that the Indian in his ambient is a good thing, that shaman medicines are better than white medicines, and that basically, what non-Indians have done is complicate Tukanoan lives, create needs that cannot be met, and in general, commit psychological genocide. Another interviewee favorably compared the paternal authority of a traditional Tukanoan headman to the out-only-for-themselves attitudes of politicians in Mitú. And another interviewee, in charge of many development projects, also took a traditionalist line and commented that all the bad debts non-Indians have saddled Tukanoans with is a good idea because then, they will know not to count on the daily-wage market and will continue to be economically self-sufficient. Tukanoans will mistrust non-Indians and stay in their settlements rather than migrating to Mitú, where there is no work. And Tukanoans must learn to be generally mistrustful of non-Indians so that "when the subversives (guerrillas) come in with money and communism, they will mistrust them." One priest sarcastically commented that the only way Tukanoans learned about the modern economy was in coca trafficking: "Production, redistribution, transport . . . la coca was the only example. And of course there was a market."

Thus, whereas twenty years ago non-Indians spoke of teaching Tukanoans the dignity of work and the value of saving money, clearly many factors have contributed to a changed position, apparently held by many non-Indians in the region, namely, that Tukanoans face grave dangers by acculturating too rapidly.

Catholic missionary publications at times support the preservation of culturally distinct groups and at times even espouse a socialist solution of Colombia's problems. In the Vaupés, the Prefecture has promoted publication of various booklets about the culture and geography of the Vaupés, including lexicon, mythology, and maps—materials with absolutely no Christian religious content.

One knowledgeable individual commented on the changes the local Catholic mission has gone through with respect to traditional Tukanoan culture: "The mission wanted to replace the longhouse. Before, there was interest in centralization. Fifteen years ago . . . the help from the state, from the Church was negating Indian identity. But now, to reinforce Indian identity we have to decentralize, to return to the longhouse, to pay attention to traditional language, clothing, rites, exchange of women."

Protestant missionaries have not promoted Indian rights, partly because they have not had the dialogue with Colombian and foreign anthropologists that Catholic clergy have (see Jackson 1993b).[12] Although not promoting the formation of groups like CRIVA, the Summer Institute of Linguistics/Wycliffe Bible Translators (SIL) does present an image of an organization dedicated to studying indigenous language and culture, promoting bilingual education, and creating a corps of indigenous leaders to take over proselytization when the linguist teams depart.

In part due to the rivalry between the Prefecture and groups like New Tribes Mission and SIL, in the last twenty years the local Catholic mission has tried to appear supportive of Indian rights from an enlightened, left-leaning, tradition-respecting, anthropologically informed position. It began to overlook such previously disapproved-of traditional practices as dancing, drinking manioc beer, and taking the hallucinogen *banisteriopsis*, in part because these activities are anathema to evangelical Protestants. The Prefecture has sponsored "Indian weeks" in which ceremonies and dances are performed—a complete reversal from its position of twenty years ago regarding Tukanoan ceremonies. The Colombian Catholic Church responded to criticism from outsiders by forming its own Missionary Colombian Anthropological Center, launching a publication, *Etnia*, in 1965, and opening an ethnographic museum in Bogotá in 1973.

Another major non-Tukanoan source of input about Indian culture to which Tukanoans are being exposed derives from the interaction between CRIVA members and activist Indians from similar organizations elsewhere in Colombia who visit the Vaupés or who confer with CRIVA officials during visits they make to Bogotá. As indicated above, although CRIVA began as the creation of the Prefecture, it soon began to change, as a result of the increasing coca market and interaction with outside Indian-rights organizations.

An example of the collaboration between CRIVA members and outsiders is a book written by a Tukanoan, Jesús Santacruz, on *Principios Fundamentales del Consejo Regional Indígena del Vaupés* (*Fundamental Principles of CRIVA*). It contains any number of incorrect ethnographic observations, very probably due to misinformation from Catholic missionaries and non-Tukanoan Indians. Publications written by CRIVA members in their newsletter, *La Voz de la Tribu* and in ONIC's newsletter *Unidad Indígena*, provide evidence that these individuals are coming to accept an outsider view of Tukanoans and their traditions, a view congruent with non-Tukanoan notions of what it means to be an Indian and even what it means to be a tropical forest Indian. For example, one article speaks of Tukanoans longing for unity, longing to stop distinguishing among tribes and clans (in *Unidad Indígena*, 1976, no. 12, 8). A CRIVA leader remarked to me that "The people wanted to end with the sense of isolated groups, such as Desana, Cubeo, and move towards unity, so that all the groups could reunite like brothers. To look for unity." Whereas, from the point of view of CRIVA, factionalism along language group or clan lines is indeed divisive, I very much doubt if most Tukanoans are ready to stop distinguishing among themselves this way. This is a remarkably different notion of brotherhood than the traditional patrilineal one.

Some basic characteristics of Tukanoan society are distorted or not mentioned in these publications. For example, an article in *Unidad Indígena* describes Vaupés groups: "To each tribe corresponds a territory whose limits are clearly recognized and respected; in keeping with tradition and mythology, this territory is communal property of the entire tribe" (1976, no. 17, 6–7). The article continues: "Each culture conserves almost all of its own characteristics; each tribe speaks its own language, and owing to the contact between the different tribes, the result is that in general each person speaks three, four or more different languages" (ibid.). An association between land and language group in the Vaupés does exist, especially in an ideal, symbolic sense. But although language groups are found in some areas of the Vaupés and not others, and this is explained in the origin myths, land ownership is not thought of in terms of an exclusive, inalienable title to land; certainly, the boundaries are not precisely delineated. Local settlements are often intermingled with respect to language group affiliation; sometimes, a settlement's closest neighbors belong to other language groups. It is also interesting that the article does not mention the basis for so much contact: language exogamy. In this quotation, language is viewed in the conventional sense as a marker of a distinct cultural entity, a "tribe," which it most certainly is not. In another issue of the paper a romantic picture of communally worked land is given: "The communities . . . conserve, each one, its territory, which is communal property of all the tribe, and they work it communally. They live from the abundant fruits that the jungle gives them spontaneously and from hunting" (*Unidad Indígena*, 1976, no. 14, 11).

Land is not worked communally in the Vaupés. These and other quotations from CRIVA and ONIC publications show, by their ethnographic inaccuracies, a systematic bias, a desire to present a particular view of tropical-forest Indians. It is a simplified, romantic, idealized image that glosses over or ignores confusing or inconvenient factors such as language exogamy, even though this is a fundamental organizing principle of Tukanoan social structure.

Such quotes provide a glimpse of a new Indian identity and culture, one provided by outside-derived images and, in part, by outside political aims. For example, to assert tribal communal ownership of clearly demarcated lands is to have a strong arguing position in potential future battles over land rights. What is interesting is how Tukanoans are learning to say these things about themselves, as the Santacruz book and pages of *La Voz de la Tribu* confirm. And equally interesting is that these lowland Indians are receiving some of these new images from fellow *Indians*—representatives of ONIC, representatives of the American Indian Movement (AIM), and other pro-Indian groups. Many examples of this process can be found among Native Americans in the U.S.A. and Canada who have acquired feather warbonnets or drums their ancestors never used, but which now are important because they signal pan-Indian identity. What is of value in the Vaupés material is that we are observing the beginnings of this process.

Rethinking Culture Change

What I have just described is what I referred to above as the process of "becoming an Indian." But how can we describe this process using our conventional notions of "culture"? Tukanoans are not passive recipients of efforts to change them. Part of their active response is their experiencing—living—the very real conflicts between many of their traditional cultural forms and those of the incoming dominant ideology. We have seen examples of a new wrinkle in the messages from this ideology: a heralding of the desirability of Tukanoans' remaining the way they are in some important respects. But "remaining the way they are" nevertheless involves significant change on the part of Tukanoans, paradoxical though it may seem, because definitions of who they are derive so extensively from their increasing interaction with non-Tukanoans.

We have seen that Tukanoans who are influenced by the national Indian-rights movement are hearing and incorporating into their self-image several notions foreign to their traditional understandings of themselves and their society. CRIVA faces a dilemma because it tries to represent tropical-forest Indians to an outside world while occupying a marginal and relatively powerless status in Mitú and within the national Indian movement. Although to some extent Tukanoans are seen as more authentically Indian than some other Colombian Indian groups, because of CRIVA's relative lack of political savvy within ONIC, instruction about what being an authentic Indian means is for the most part not entrusted to Tukanoans. CRIVA may in the future develop political clout and organizational savoir-faire to help them survive within externally imposed political structures. When traditional political forms and expectations differ extensively from the new ones, however, the members of an activist group can experience the conflict and confusion resulting from fence-straddling and the marginality of biculturalism. Tukanoans, coming out of relatively fluid, dispersed local communities, have little knowledge of centralized political structures, with their bureaucracies and cash-based economies. The means for achieving an active role in deciding their own destinies, making collective decisions following the new rules, and learning to negotiate with outside groups is not a part of the traditional Tukanoan political repertoire (see Jackson 1984).

Traditional cultural forms that are retained are not necessarily the "same" if their meaning has changed. This might seem so obvious as not to warrant comment, but such a point is often forgotten because anthropologists, indigenists, and others are interested in discovering the connections between current traditions and earlier ones. But "culture" is not necessarily an analytic, purely descriptive term in these circumstances; rather, it is often a politically loaded one. If a ritual evolves from something Tukanoans do entirely for one another into something they do for outsiders, or if Tukanoans perform a ritual for themselves because it fosters a self-image that has been inspired by outsiders, then despite superficial similarities that these new rituals might have with traditional rituals, they are not traditional in some important respects.

We can speak of a ritual having been folklorized when it occurs because the participants' involvement in the larger society significantly influences why the ritual is performed and why particular traditional ritual forms have been retained. As noted above, it is difficult to talk about this type of transformation, whether of a ritual or of Indian culture in general, except in deprecatory terms. Simply to talk of "becoming an Indian" suggests something inauthentic, insincere, as does the word "folklorize."

As Tukanoans are increasingly embedded in Colombian culture and society, they will increasingly come to define themselves in terms of the larger society, even though this definition is not the simple one of "how fast are we amalgamating?" We are seeing the very beginnings of a process of folklorization of some aspects of culture among the more acculturated Tukanoans who participate in the local indigenous-rights movement. They are finding out what it means to be Tukanoan in a new way, one different from the way Tukanoans revised their self-concepts over the past two centuries in interactions with whites. Young Tukanoans who reside in Mitú and its environs are learning from outsiders not only how to be Indian but also to some extent how to be Tukanoan. The pages of CRIVA's newspaper that describe Tukanoan traditions in ethnographically incorrect fashion are a harbinger of a transformed Tukanoan identity. That this transformed identity receives some of its form, language, and content from other *Indians* in no way changes the basic process of what I am calling folklorization.

An important change occurs when, because a vastly more powerful cultural system is making significant inroads into an indigenous culture, the members of that culture become aware of themselves as a *culture*—here contrasted to being aware of themselves as a distinct *people*, which, I would maintain, is how indigenous cultures conceive of the differences between themselves and their neighbors in precontact situations. A further refinement, a distinction difficult to characterize, is that whereas to some extent indigenism begins with the very first contact with a radically different culture, *Indigenism*—indigenism with a capital *I*, self-conscious indigenism, along with self-conscious culture—begins when a group of people begin to appropriate notions of who they are *from* the intrusive dominant culture, albeit in contradistinction to it.[13] This is now occurring in the Vaupés. The analogy about unselfconscious rituals versus folklorized ritual—ritual whose meaning is derived in part from the fact that the audience includes people from vastly different cultures—is useful. The same point can be made about "authentic" North American Indian handiwork intended primarily for the non-Indian market: to some extent it is the market and the federal government, not the Indians, that determines standards of authenticity and excellence (see Belkin 1988). No Tukanoan spoke of *nuestra cultura* ("our culture") in the late 1960s in this self-conscious sense, although at that time many complained bitterly about non-Indians. But Tukanoans are now beginning to speak in this fashion.

As noted above, it is difficult to describe this contrast without introducing judgmental notions (e.g., "authentic" vs. "derivative"). I do not want to give the impression that I am judging some cultural traits as better than others simply because they are traditional as opposed to newly introduced. I do believe there are criteria with which to make such judgments, but they have to do with the effects of such preserved or new traits on the well-being of the group in question—and sometimes this is difficult to assess, even in hindsight, partly because as anthropologists we often play the dual roles of analyst and advocate. We form opinions about what is valuable and what should be jettisoned in the Tukanoan and Colombian cultural systems. In this sense we, no less than others, are political actors.

Conclusions

Questions about evolving Tukanoan culture illustrate some of the problems faced by anthropology in defining and analyzing cultural units, in particular when trying to assess change from one type (e.g., a somewhat isolated and bounded "tribal culture") to another (e.g., an "ethnic group," a group of people fairly thoroughly embedded in a larger unit). I have argued that we are seeing the beginnings of a process of folklorization of various Tukanoan cultural traits. Perhaps in the future we shall see the commoditization of them; elsewhere in the hemisphere various interest groups, including indigenous groups themselves, package and promote "Indianness." The cultural forms that are retained from earlier traditions can therefore totally change in meaning, as when traits are retained, cast aside, or redefined as part of a self-conscious awareness and promotion of a particular kind of Indian identity as a political strategy.

Since resemblances between earlier forms of Tukanoan culture and later forms may be spurious, conceiving of a culture in terms of traits that persist over time can be misleading. If the underpinnings of a new, partially folklorized Tukanoan culture are quite different, if the criteria for membership serve different purposes and are oriented to different audiences, then we cannot conceive of this culture simply in terms of a continuous stream that, while evolving, has had an underlying identity over the decades. We need to think of culture change over relatively short periods of time in a more dynamic fashion rather than as either the "same" or "amalgamated" or "lost." We need to see Tukanoans and others as creating and improvising culture in addition to possessing culture. And we need to create and invent models and metaphors that analyze this process in nonderogatory terms.

The northwest Amazon has always presented thorny problems to those who adopt and promote "cookie-cutter" models of society and culture. Tukanoans continue to play this provocative, and, although at times exasperating, extremely worthwhile role.

NOTES

This chapter was originally a paper delivered in 1989 and revised in 1990; the ethnographic data and analysis offered here should be understood to apply to the situation up to that time. In the intervening years some significant changes have taken place at both the national and local levels, in particular the creation of a new Colombian Constitution in 1991 that contains many articles dealing with Colombia's Indian communities. Some of these changes are discussed in Jackson 1991a, 1991b, 1992, 1993a, 1993b, and n.d.a.

The research for chapter is part of an on-going research project concerned with changing identity among Tukanoans of Colombia. I am grateful to the MIT Provost's Fund for funding a trip to Colombia in March, 1987, the Dean of Humanities and Social Sciences Fund for funding a trip to Colombia in June and July of 1989, and to both for support for archival research. My thanks to all in Bogotá and the Vaupés who have so willingly given of their time and energy. My appreciation also to the Anthropology Departments of the National University and the University of Los Andes, the Office of Indian Affairs, and the Colombian Anthropology Institute. Thanks also to the participants at the 1987 Bennington South American Indian Conference who commented on an earlier oral version, and the participants at the Wenner-Gren conference in Novo Friburgo in June, 1989. Readers of previous drafts who kindly offered suggestions include Jaime Arocha, Charles Hale, Darna Dufour, Christian Gros, James Howe, Stephen Hugh-Jones, Theodore Macdonald, Anna Roosevelt, David Stoll, and Robin Wright.

1. Some of the literature on ethnicity offers similar critique. Vincent, for example, suggests that we have a "too stolid perception of ethnic groups as permanent component units" (1974, 376) and asserts that "ethnic ties are not primordial ties—the assumed givens of a society and their actual realized organizations in any situation have to be demonstrated" (1974, 377). Barth notes that "our habits of speech may hark back to the days of Wissler and Kroeber, when a culture was a trait list of customs" (1982, 79). Poyer states flatly that "primordialist theories are no longer supportable" (1988, 472)—but see A. Smith 1986.

2. See Kahn (1981, 43), who notes how hard it is to avoid taking ethnicity as a given, a natural phenomenon rather than an ideology that needs to be explained. Surely one source of this difficulty is the moral opprobrium that attaches to depictions of people choosing their culture in some fashion—note the negative connotation of Kahn's "ideology." Many writers argue that embedded in the idea of ethnicity is the notion of permanence, but that this is only "putative," a similarly potentially deprecatory term. A number of writers on ethnicity discuss the malleability of criteria for membership, which "can be narrowed or broadened in boundary terms in relation to the specific needs of political mobilization" (Cohen 1978, 385–86). Such analyses can be felt as a slap in the face of a given group who is making a claim to land or other resource on the basis of common origins and tightly defined criteria for membership (see Jackson 1989).

3. Small-scale tribal groups that are seen as still retaining their culture are considered to be "without history," as Cowlishaw nicely puts it (1987, 221). Also see Wolf 1982.

4. "Tukanoan" refers to all riverine indigenous inhabitants of the Vaupés. Makú, forest-dwellers who also differ in other respects, are not included (see Silverwood-Cope 1975). Although many Tukanoans live on the Brazilian side of the border, this paper considers only those in Colombian territory.

5. Indian-rights consciousness in Colombia goes back to the 1920s when, with the effects of the Bolshevik Revolution, the Latin American communist movement spoke about the Indian proletariat and adopted a vision of a "Great Indo-American nation" (Pineda Camacho 1984, 211–12). I should note that I often use *Indian* for

the Spanish *indígena*. The Spanish cognate, *indio*, is a highly pejorative term, which is not the case in English, despite some writers who prefer *Native American*. But *Native American* connotes Indians of the U.S.A. and Canada. It is worth emphasizing, however, that any difficulties encountered in any group nomenclature (e.g., "native," "Indian," "white," "ladies") are relevant to the purpose of this paper. Justifying use of a given term by aesthetic and conventional-use arguments is not meant to imply that problems of nomenclature are not of great political and moral significance.

6. For a critique of this point of view with regard to the effects of the introduction of white trade goods, see S. Hugh-Jones 1992.

7. For more comprehensive treatments of Tukanoan ethnography, see Århem 1981; Chernela 1992; Goldman 1963; C. Hugh-Jones 1979; S. Hugh-Jones 1979; Jackson 1983; Reichel-Dolmatoff 1971.

8. For further information on the history of the region, see Goldman 1963; S. Hugh-Jones 1979, 1981; Reichel-Dolmatoff 1971; Wright 1981.

9. Coca paste is an intermediate stage between coca leaf harvesting and processing and the production of cocaine per se, which, to my knowledge, does not occur in the Vaupés.

10. See "Programa Nacional de Desarrollo de las Poblaciones Indígenas" (National Program for the Development of Indian Populations), and former president Belisario Betancur's *El Indígena: Raíz de Nuestra Identidad Nacional* ("The Indian: Root of our National Identity").

11. And it is true that a leftist victory in Colombia would not guarantee an Indian utopia—whatever that might look like. If we examine other nations that have experienced leftist (progressivist or socialist) governments, whether by election, coups, or revolutions, the circumstances of fourth world groups within them has not necessarily improved from previous situations.

12. Relations between SIL and Colombian anthropologists and linguists have generally been poor. Foreign Protestant organizations tend to assume an antileft and progovernment stance at odds with many of the country's social scientists. In 1975–76, many Colombians who had carried out investigations in the Vaupés entered a campaign to have SIL leave the country. This alliance among national Indian rights leaders, Colombian social scientists, and the church was bitterly resented by SIL (see Cass 1981; *Micronoticias* 1978, M-54; and Stoll 1982).

13. I am grateful to Stephen Hugh-Jones for his well-thought-out views on this topic.

REFERENCES

Arango Ochoa, R., and E. Sánchez Gutierrez
1989   *Los pueblos indígenas de Colombia (población y territorio)*. Bogotá: Departamento Nacional de Planeación.

Århem, K.

1981   *Makuna social organization: A study in descent, alliance and the formation of corporate groups in the north-western Amazon*. Uppsala: Uppsala Studies in Cultural Anthropology 4.

Barth, F.

1982   Problems in conceptualizing cultural pluralism, with illustrations from Somar, Oman. In *The prospects for plural societies*, edited by D. Maybury-Lewis, 77–87. Washington, D.C.: American Ethnological Society.

Barth, F., editor

1969   *Ethnic groups and boundaries*. Boston: Little, Brown.

Belkin, L.

1988   Of Indian roots, and profits as well. *New York Times*, 29 September, A18.

Betancur, B.

1984   *El indígena: Raíz de nuestra identidad nacional*. Colombia: Dirección General de Integración y Desarrollo de la Comunidad, División Asuntos Indígenas, Ministerio de Gobierno.

Bourgois, P.

1988   Conjugated oppression: Class and ethnicity among Guaymi and Kuna banana workers. *American Ethnologist* 15 (2): 328–48.

Brooke, J.

1990a   Tribes get right to 50% of Colombian Amazon. *New York Times*, 4 February, 6.

1990b   Assassins wiping out Colombia party. *New York Times*, 1 April, 10.

Cass, J.

1981   Just Bible translators? Colombians have doubts. *Boston Sunday Globe*, 8 March, 16.

Chernela, J.

1992   *The Wanano of the Brazilian Amazon: A sense of space*. Austin: University of Texas Press.

Cohen, R.

1978   Ethnicity: Problem and focus in anthropology. *Annual Review of Anthropology* 7:379–403.

Cowlishaw, G.

1987   Colour, culture and the Aboriginalists. *Man* 22 (2):221–37.

Goldman, I.

1963   *The Cubeo: Indians of the northwest Amazon*. Illinois Studies in Anthropology, no. 2. Urbana: University of Illinois Press.

Gómez-Imbert, E., and S. Hugh-Jones

n.d.   "Introducción al estudio de las lenguas del Piraparaná." In *Estudio preliminar del atlas etnolingüístico de Colombia*. Bogotá: Instituto Caro and Cuervo, forthcoming.

Hugh-Jones, S.

1979   *The palm and the Pleiades: Initiation and cosmology in northwest Amazonia.*
            Cambridge: Cambridge University Press.

1981   Historia del Vaupés. *Maguaré: Revista del Departamento de Antropología*
            (Universidad Nacional de Colombia) 1 (June): 29–51.

1992   Yesterday's luxuries, tomorrow's necessities: Business and barter in north-
            west Amazonia. In *Barter, exchange and value: An anthropological ap-
            proach,* edited by C. Humphrey and S. Hugh-Jones, 42–74. Cambridge:
            Cambridge University Press.

Jackson, J.

1983   *The fish people: Linguistic exogamy and Tukanoan identity in northwest
            Amazonia.* Cambridge: Cambridge University Press.

1984   The impact of the state on small-scale societies. *Studies in Comparative
            International Development* 19 (2): 3–32.

1989   Is there a way to talk about making culture without making enemies?
            Dialectical Anthropology 14 (2): 127–44.

1991a   Being and becoming an Indian in the Vaupés. In *Nation-States and
            Indians in Latin America,* edited by Greg Urban and Joel Sherzer, 131–
            55. Austin: University of Texas Press.

1991b   Hostile encounters between Nukak and Tukanoans: Changing ethnic
            identity in the Vaupés, Colombia. *Journal of Ethnic Studies* 19 (2): 17–40.

1992   Constructing and contesting Indian culture: Shaman schools and ethno-
            education in the Vaupés, Colombia. Paper presented in symposium,
            Indigenous identity and ideology: A zone of contention. American
            Anthropological Association Annual Meetings, San Francisco.

1993a   El concepto de "nación indígena": Algunos ejemplos en las Américas.
            In *La Construcción de Las Américas. Memorias del VI Congreso de Antro-
            pología en Colombia,* edited by Carlos Uribe, 218–42. Bogotá: Univer-
            sidad de los Andes.

1993b   Vaupés indigenous rights organizing and the emerging ethnic self. In
            *Discourses and the Expression of Personhood in South American Inter-Ethnic
            Relations,* edited by Jonathan D. Hill. Bennington: *South American
            Indian Studies* 3:28–39.

n.d.a   Culture, genuine and spurious: The politics of Indianness in the Vaupés,
            Colombia. *American Ethnologist,* in press.

Kahn, J.

1981   Explaining ethnicity: A review article. *Critique of Anthropology* 16
            (4, Spring): 43–52.

Koch-Grünberg, T.

1903–5   Zwei Jahre unter den Indianern. Reisen in Nordwest-Brasilien. 2 vols.
            Berlin: Ernst Wasmuth.

Micronoticias
1978   Declaración del comité de profesores del departamento de antropología de la Universidad Nacional sobre el Instituto Ligüístico de Verano. Julio-Agosto, M-54: 2–4.

Pineda Camacho, R.
1984   La reivindicación del índio en el pensamiento social Colombiano (1850–1950). In *Un siglo de investigación social: Antropología en Colombia*, edited by J. Arocha and N. Friedemann, 197–252. Bogotá: Etno.

Poyer, L.
1988   Maintaining "otherness": Sapwuahfik cultural identity. *Amercian Ethnologist* 15 (3): 472–85.

Programa Nacional de Desarrollo de las Poblaciones Indígenas (Program for the Development of Indian Populations), Department of National Planning, 1984. Bogotá.

PRORADAM (Proyecto de Radargramétrico del Amazonas)
1979   La Amazonía Colombiana y sus Recursos. Bogotá: República de Colombia.

Reichel-Dolmatoff, G.
1971   *Amazonian cosmos: The sexual and religious symbolism of the Tukano Indians*. Chicago: University of Chicago Press.

Riding, A.
1987   Truce between Colombia and rebels is unravelling. *New York Times*, 10 August, A-11.

Santacruz, J.
1985   *Princípios fundamentales del Consejo Regional Indígena del Vaupés*. Comisaría Especial del Vaupés.

Silverwood-Cope, P. L.
1990   *Os Makú: Povo cacador do noroeste da Amazônia*. Brasília: Editora Universidade de Brasília.

Smith, A. D.
1986   *The ethnic origins of nations*. Oxford: Basil Blackwell.

Smith, R.
1985   A search for unity within diversity: Peasant unions, ethnic federations, and Indianist movements in the Andean republics. In *Native peoples and economic development: Six case studies from Latin America*, edited by T. Macdonald, 5–38. Cambridge, Mass.: Cultural Survival.

Sorensen, A. P. Jr.
1967   Mutlilingualism in the northwest Amazon. *American Anthropologist* 69: 670–82.

Stoll, D.
1982   *Fishers of men or founders of empire? The Wycliffe Bible Translators in Latin America*. London: Zed/Cultural Survival.

Unidad Indígena
1976   Conclusiones del tercer congreso del Consejo Regional Indígena del
              Vaupés. April, no. 12:8.
1976   Las comunidades indígenas en Colombia: Comunidades de la selva.
              June, no. 14:11.
1976   El Vaupés: Geografía. November, no. 17:6–7.
Vincent, J.
1974   The structuring of ethnicity. *Human Organization*, 33 (4, Winter):
              375–79.
Wolf, E.
1982   *Europe and the people without history.* Berkeley and Los Angeles: Univer-
              sity of California Press.
Wright, R.
1981   *History and religion of the Baniwa Peoples of the upper Rio Negro Valley.* 2
              vols. Ann Arbor, Mich.: University Microfilms.
Wright, R., and J. Hill
1986   History, ritual, and myth: Nineteenth-century millenarian movements
              in the northwest Amazon. *Ethnohistory* 33 (1): 31–54.
Youngers, C.
1990   Body count. *Nation*, 2 July, 5.

Index

Achagua tribe, 61

Achuar longhouse(s), 231–33

Achuar men: and control of marriages, 236–39; initiation rites of, 240–41; tankamash for, 231–33; use of weapons by, 227–28

Achuar tribe: *aujmatin* ceremony of, 232; gender hierarchy in, 233–34; household structure of, 208; and male-female role differentiation, 229–30; male initiation in, 240–41; marriage and family organization in, 236–39; and pattern of warfare, 226–27; settlement patterns of, 205–7, 227; slash-and-burn horticulture of, 207; structure of work expenditure, 211–19; subsistence for, 227–28; traders, shamen, and warriors, 234–35; work processes of, 207–11

Achuar women: and birth-spacing, 228–29; *ekent* for, 231–32; as subordinates to males, 236–39; subsidiary work of, 230–31

Afonso Pena, President, 108

Agriculture: in cerrado region, 252–54; nomadic, of Kayapo people, 277–78

Aguaruna Jivaro, diet and nutritional status of, 162–63

Aguaruna tribe, 204, 226

Agüero, O., 297

Aisuari, 84

Alcohol dependence, fostered by trade, 68

Altimarano. *See* de Espinosa

Altimira encounter, 281

Alto Xingu tribes, diet and nutritional status of, 164–65

Amazon, Brazilian, settlement in, 81–82, 96–97. *See also* Settlement patterns; Brazilian Amazon; Amazonia

Amazon, lower, early pottery-age sites in, 7

Amazon, upper, chiefdoms in, 86–88

Amazon floodplain, 249; European occupation of, 80; hierarchical groups in, 88–90; sociopolitical organization in, 79–94

Amazonia: cerrado region of, 249–69; cultural and biological evolution in, 13–17; density of early settlement in, 96; early explorers of, 96–97; hierarchical groups in, 88–90; hunting and fishing in, 177–200; immigrant population in, 107; language distributions in, 343–46; millenarian episodes in, 287–311; problems and research directions, 90–92, 126; settlement patterns in, 5, 79–86

Amazonian anthropology: academic barriers, hindrance in, 17–18; implications for ethnology of, 10–11, 56–57; population size and, 177–80; research methods in, 3, 22–23, 79–90

Amazonian environment: geologic and climatic nature of, 4–5; and population densities, 177–80

Amazonian exploration: documentation of, 80–81; population decline and, 81, 96–113

Amazonian Indians: current health status of, 136–37; deculturation and destabilization of, 95–116; demographic studies of, 125–31; diet adequacy of, 166–69; diet and nutritional status of, 151–75; health and demography of, 123–49; health of, 16; historical perspective on, 124–25; homeostasis as a cultural system for, 203–22; response to Europeans of, 11–13

Amazonian language(s): features of, 354–55; genetic relatedness of, 346–56; groups in lowland South America, 345 (fig.); linguistic exogamy/endogamy in, 344; measuring similarity and variation in, 366–71; shared linguistic features of, 354–56; Tupí-Guaraní family of, 363–80. See also Genetic relatedness of language

Amazonian millenarian movements, 288–304; Ashaninka of Central Peru and, 291–93; Canela and, 294–96; Kapon and Pemon and, 297–98; links between pre- and postcontact episodes, 303–4; Orden Cruzada and, 296–97; Tukanoan and Arawakan and, 293–94

Amazonian occupation: chiefdom societies in, 8–9; early foragers in, 6–8; prehistoric evidence of, 5–6, 9–10, 97, 124–25; tribal and village horticulturalists in, 8

Amazonian seasonality: differing levels in, 5; and protein intake, 166–67

Amazonian Synthesis: Wenner-Gren International Conference, 22

Amerindia: ancient vs. modern, 35–37; European contact and extinction of, 42–44, 96–113; male dominance in, 44

Amerindian economies: European trade and, 44–46; exchange systems in, 37–38, 84; food surpluses in, 36–37

Amerindian modes of leadership, 39

Amerindian polities: of the Amazon and Orinoco, 33–48; ceramic distribution in, 34–35; linguistic distribution in, 33–34

Anthropology, need for integrated evaluation in, 46–47

Anthropometric statistics, 152–53, 167

Aparia, 81–82, 86

Appan, S. G., 367

Arawakan Indians, 38; language of, 354; of Upper Rio Negro region, 293–94

Araweté language, 364

Archaelogical sites: of Bororo in Vermelho River basin, 318; ceramic remains in, 100; density of, 98; in Orinoco floodplain, 59

Archaeological and Ethnoarchaeological Project of São Lourenço River Basin, 336

Archaeological perspective, of the eastern Bororo, 315–42

Århem, K., 182, 184, 186, 189, 191, 192, 402n

Arigao Bororo, 333

Arvelo-Jiménez, N., 11

Ashaninka (Campa): millenarian fervor in, 291–93; and struggle with Shining Path, 292

Asurini do Xingu language, 364

Atahualpa, Juan Santos, 300; as leader of Ashaninka revolt, 291–93

Autochthonous control, by ethnic groups, 56–57

Bakairi (Carib), as Bororo neighbors, 322

Baleé, W. L., 19, 257, 290, 363, 374

Banner, Eva, 282n

Banner, Horace, 282n; and Kayapó contact, 272

"Battle for Rubber," 109

Baumgartner, J., 168, 169

Beckerman, S., 15, 178–91, 227, 258

Bedoya, E., 125

Behrens, C. A., 132, 162, 183, 192

Belém-Brasilia highway, 109

Benefice, E., 162

Bep names, of Kayapó, 276

Bergman, R. W., 136, 182, 183, 185, 186, 188, 189, 190, 191

Berlin, B., 132, 374

Berlin, E. A., 132, 162, 163, 209

Beta Analytic (United States), 337n

Betendorf, J. F., 91, 92

Bichiwung (Pichiwon), prophet of Hallelujah movement, 297–98

Black, D. P., 126, 132, 136, 164

Black, F. L., 126, 132, 133, 136, 164, 188

Blowguns, of Achuar tribe, 207

Bororo, Eastern, from an archaeological perspective, 315–42. See also Bororo tribe(s).

Bororo house(s): men's clubhouse as, 328; traditional layout of, 326–28

Bororo territory, great diversity in, 320–21

Bororo tribe(s), 250; archaeological evidence of, 330–34; cessation of ceramic making by, 329; chronological occupational sequence of, 319; demographic aspects of, 323–24; division into East and West, 319;

fieldwork with, 317; history, an emic view of, 329–30; and large village tradition, 257–58, 321; shamans' position in, 321–22; traditional territory of, 320–23

Bororo villages: ceremonial activities in, 328; and social order, 324–25

Botanical referents, for Amazonian language study, 365

Boza, F. V., 168, 169

Brainerd, B., 350

Brazil, central, Bororo area of, 315–42

Brazilian Amazon: deculturation and destabilization of, 95–116; settlement in, 81–82

Brazilian Indians, pre- and postcontact situations and, 271–86

Brazilian societies, study of, 250

Brieger, F. G., 253, 254

Brown, M. F., 17, 18

Bugos, P. E., 131

Cachoeira Porteira, 97

Callegari-Jacques, S. M., 128

Campbell, L., 357

Campos, R., 189

Canela (Ramkokamekra), of Maranhão, Brazil, 294–96

Cantella, R., 133

Captaincy of São Jose do Rio Negro, 103

Carbon 14 dating, 97

Carib(s), 38; and bypass of traditional trade routes, 61–62; centers of exchange, 67 (fig.); ethnohistorical reconstruction of society of, 59; geographic location of, 62 (fig.); internecine conflict among, 43; language of, 354; location of, 62 (fig.); politics of elites and Spanish, 42–43; routes in eighteenth century, 63 (fig.), 64 (fig.), 65 (fig.), 66; and trading-military policy, 39

Carmelite mission, in Brazilian Vaupés (1852), 387

Carneiro, R. L., 124, 164, 165, 211, 229

Carneiro da Cunha, M., 295, 296
Casey, H. L., 132
Cashinahua tribe, "population policy" of, 130
Cass, J., 402n
Castelo Branco, F. Caldeira, and Portuguese colonization, 100–101
Cayapo. *See* Kayapó
CEDI/PETI, 114
Centerwall, W. R., 132
Ceramic artifacts, in Bororo ceremonies, 329
Ceremonial activities: agriculture in, 252–54; of Kayapó, 273; population in historical, 257–58; vegetation of, 251–52; in villages, archaelogical evidence for large, 257–58
Cerrado region: forest fields in, 255–56; gathering in, 255–57; hunting in, 254–55; settlement patterns in, historical, 257–58; subsistence and social ties in, 258–59. *See also* Brazil, Central
Chaga's disease and Leishmaniasis, 133–34
Chagnon, N. A., 125, 126, 127, 128, 132, 136, 209
Chaim, M. Matos, 257
Chantre y Herrera, J., 89, 90
Chaves, G. M., 134
Chernela, J. M., 134, 402n
Chiefdoms, in Amazonia, 8–9; areas of, 38–39; European alliances with, 43; importance of progeny in, 39–40; settlement patterns and, 86–88
Christianity, indigenization of, in millenarian movements, 299–300
"Christos," of Upper Rio Negro Region, 293–94
Clark, G. A., 133
Clark, K. E., 182, 183, 187
Clastres, H., 288, 290, 300
Clastres, P., 288, 290, 299
CNPq/CIPA, 125
Coca, as Tukanoan cash source, 391–92, 394
Cockburn, T. A., 132, 133

Cohen, E. L., 135
Cohen, R., 402n
Coimbra, C.E.A., Jr., 132, 134, 135
Cole, J.W.L., 350
Colichon, A., 133
Colinvaux, P. A., 206
Colonization: Brazilian, failure of, 110–11; Portuguese, aspects of, 100–101
Colson, A.J.B., 297, 298
Companhia Geral do Comércio do Grão Pará e Maranhão, 103
Comrie, B., 350
Conselho Nacional de Pesquisa (CNPq), 336
Contemporary demographic studies, 126–32
Copal trees, naming comparison for, 364
Correa, C. G., 115
Corrego Grande, 317
Coudreau, H., 272
Cowlishaw, G., 402n
Criollo merchants, and debt/peonage, 67–68
CRIVA: approval by Catholic Church of, 391; as ethnic federation in Vaupés, 388; and interaction with other activists, 395; as weak organization, 389
Crocker, C. J., 305n
Crocker, W. H., 294, 295, 305n
Cross-field research, for Bororo sites, 334–36; use of in Amazonia, 3
Cross-sex identification, 239–40
Cruxent, J. M., 8
Cuibas, diet and nutritional status of, 155
Cultura apropiada, 56
Cultura autonoma, 56
Cultura enajenada, 56
Cultural control, by ethnic groups, 56–57
Cultura propia, 56
Culture, as dynamic adaptive behavior model, 385–86
Culture-as-things model, misreading of patterns by, 385
Curripacos: diet and nutrition of, 156–57, 159

da Cruz, José Francisco, 296–97
Da Matta, R., 15
da Rocha, F. J., 164
de Acuña, C., 35, 48, 80–91, 96
de Aguado, P., 36
Dean, W., 109, 116
de Aquirre, L., 96
de Azevedo, J. L., 96, 116
Debt peonage, 67–68
de Candolle, Alphonse, 363, 375
de Carvajal, G., 80–91, 96
de Castel Branca, F. C., 100, 102
de Espinosa, A. V., 83, 84, 85
de Goeje, C. H., 38
de Heriarte, M. 79
de la Cruz, L., 79–85
De Lima, P. E., 165
de Mendonça, Furtado F. X., 102, 103
Demographic information, difficulty in
    obtaining, 126
Demographic studies, contemporary, 126–
    32
Denevan, W. M., 48, 124, 125–26, 177,
    211, 226, 245, 271
de Oliveira, A. E., 116
de Orellana, F., 80, 87, 95; first Amazon
    voyage (1541), 96
Depopulation, Indian: Kayapó by
    epidemics, 281–82; since World War II,
    125
de Rojas, A., 95, 96
Descimentos, 116n; resettlement of Indians
    by, 101–5
Descola, P., 17, 205, 206, 207, 212
de Souza, A. F., 84
de Souza Ferreira, J., 84
Destabilization, of Amazonia, 11–13
de Ursúa, P., 96
Devereux, G., 136
Diamond mining, 108
Diet and nutritional status: of Alto Zingu
    tribes, 164–65; of Amazonian peoples,
    151–75, 166–69; changes with
    acculturation, 169–70; comparisons of
    historical and living, 15; of Curripacos

group, 156, 159; guidelines in assessing,
    151–52; of Mekranoti, 163; of Piapocos,
    Pieaoas, Guahibos, and Cuibas, 155–
    56; of Trio and Wajana groups, 154–55;
    of Tukanoan group, 159, 161; of
    Waorani, Siona-Secoya, Jivaro, and
    Shipibo, 162–63; of Xavante, 165–66;
    of Yanomami group, 156
Diogo Nunes. See Drummond
di Paolo, R., 116
Disease-contact typology, 273–74
Diseases in Amazonia: chronic, 135;
    introduced, 132–37; Kayapó history of,
    271–74
Dixon, C. F., 134
Dobyns, H. F., 124
Domesticated plant species names, in
    Tupí-Guaraní, 377–78
Donnelly, C. J., 135
Downs, W. G., 126, 133, 136
Dricot, J. M., 169
Dricot-D'ans, C., 169
Drummond, C., 83, 84
Dufour, D. L., 15, 132, 136, 226
Dutch Catholic Monfortian Congregation,
    387
Dyen, I., 350

Early, J. D., 126, 127, 130, 131
East-west men's house, ngá-be, 275
Eaton, J. W., 130
Economic system(s), of the Achuar, 207–
    11
Edmundson, G., 38
Edsall, G., 132, 133
Ekent, role of, defined, 231
Embleton, S. M., 350, 351, 353, 357n,
    358n
Emic vision, of Bororo elders, 317–18
Environment, in Amazonia, 4–5
Environmental destruction: for
    colonization, 125; health affect
    of, 137–38
Epidemics, disintegration of Amerindia
    from, 43; disintegration of Bororo tribe

from, 320; Kayapó history of, 212–74; population decimation and, 81, 102. *See also* Diseases, Depopulation
Erdtmann, B., 134
Erickson, C., 10
Ethnocentricity, of European writers, 99
Ethnohistorical transition, in Amazonia, 11–13
Ethnology, of Amazonian Indians, 10–13
Etymology, in language, defined, 346
European conquest: and historic distortions, 99; impact of, on Guiana Shield peoples, 55–78; impact on Amazonia of, 11–13, 124–25; impact on cerrado populations of, 260–62
European contact: millenarian movements prior to, 288–304; and extinction of Amerindia, 42–44, 281–82; impact on Northern Kayapó of, 271; Indian population disintegration and, 80; Jivaroan warfare before, 227; two periods of, 80
European trade, and Amerindian ethnogenesis, 44–46
Evans, A. S., 126, 132, 133
Evans, C., 35, 36, 115
Eveleth, P. B., 165
Exchange systems, in Aisuari territories, 84

Fajans, S. S., 135
FAO/WHO, 159, 161
FAO/WHO/UNU, 153, 154
FARC, debt collection by, 393
FARC-Indian alliance, concern in Vaupés about, 392–93
Faron, L. C., 324
Fearnside, P. M., 125
Ferguson, R. B., 261
Ferro-Luzzi, A., 162
Fertility and natality, control of, 125. *See also* Infanticide
Fertility rates, of Xavante and Yanomamo, 127
Fields, K., 289
Figueiredo, N., 116

Fire, used as tool in cerrado, 251–52
Fishing: and hunting, variability in, 180–81; rates of return from, 181–87
Fitzcarrald, Carlos, 292
Flacklam, R. R., 134
Flavin, C., 125
Fleming-Moran, M., 135
Flowers, N. M., 12, 126, 127, 131, 133, 136, 166, 182, 188, 255
Floyd, J. C., 135
Food resources, in early Amerindian economies, 36–37
Foragers, early, in Amazonia, 6–8
Forest fields, in cerrado region, 255–56
Franco, M.H.L.P., 19
Franco, R.M.L., 374
Fritz, S., 80, 83, 85, 87, 92
Fry, R. E., 289
FUNAI, to replace SPI, 337
Fundação de Amparo a Pesquisa do Estado de São Paulo (FAPESP), 336
Fundação Nacional do Índio (FUNAI), 320, 337
Fundamental Principles of CRIVA, by Jesus Santacruz, 395, 397

Gabbay, Y., 132
Garden size (Achuar): and daily female time expenditure, 216 (table); as function of social status, 212; and production area compared, 217
Gardner, G., 261
Garson, A. G., 59
Gathering, in cerrado region, 255–57
Gê tribes, manioc used by, 252–53; use of meat and maize by, 254
Geerdink, R. A., 135, 154
Gelber, M. G., 242
Gender egalitarianism, in hunter-gatherer societies, 225
Gender hierarchy, in Achuar society, 233–34
Genetic relatedness of language: comparative method for, 346–47; and distributions in Amazonia, 343–61;

glottochronology to assess, 347–51; and linguistic controversy, 343–44; spatial and temporal methods for, 353–54; spatial methods to assess, 351–53. *See also* Amazonian language
Geology and climate, in Amazonia, 4–5
Gerszten, E., 132
Getulio Vargas, 108–9
Giaccaria, B., 255, 261
Gimbutas, M., 358n
Glanville, E. V., 135, 154
Gleason, N. N., 133
Glottochronology, problems inherent in, 348–49
Gómez-Pompa, A., 125
Goldman, I., 130, 184, 402n
González Tarbes, M. de la G., 73
Gorotire: expulsion of missionaries from, 276–77, 277–78; Kayapó village of, 272, 275
Gottsberger, G., 277
Gragson, T., 182, 188, 189, 192
Grange, J. M., 133
Great Aparia, 82
Greenberg, J. H., 343, 349, 357n
Greene, D., 131, 132
Gross, Daniel, 263
Gross, D. R., 165, 182, 188, 211, 250, 261, 262
Guahibos, 155
Guajará, D.A.R., 116
Guajibo tribe, 61
Guato, as Bororo neighbors, 322
Gudschinsky, S. C., 349
Guerras justas, 115n
Guevara, S., 125
Guggenheim Foundation, 304
Guiana Shield, Paleoindian occupation in, 6
Guiradet, Herbert, 283n
Gurgel, J.T.A., 253
Gurupi/Turiacu river basins, Ka'apor and Tembé language in, 364
Guyano, regional organization of, 40–41

Hackett, C. J., 132
"Hallelujah" movement, in Circum-Roraima region, 297–98
Hames, R. B., 125, 136, 188, 189, 190, 191, 203, 209
Hancock, G. A., 134
Hannoverisches Landesamt für Bodenforschung (Germany), 337n
Harner, M. J., 234, 238
Harris, D. R., 251
Hartado, M., 188
Harvard growth standards for anthropometric statistics, 152–53
Hasegawa, I., 132
Hawkes, K., 188, 191
Health status, of native Amazonians, 132–36
Healy, G. R., 134
Hecht, S. B., 125
Heckenberger, Michael, 337
Heide, A., 255, 261
Helminthiasis, 134
Hemming, J., 34, 293, 302
Henle, G., 132
Heply, G. R., 134
Hern, W. M., 16, 126, 127, 132, 133–34
Hershkovitz, P., 254
Hierarchical groups, in Amazonia, 88–90
Hierholzer, W. H., 126, 132, 133, 136, 164
Highways, and modern development, 109–10
Hilbert, P. P., 115
Hill, J. D., 287–305
Hill, K., 180, 188, 191, 192
Hill, M. C., 133
Historical perspective, on Amazonian Indians, 124–25
Hockett, C. F., 349
Hodge, L., 136
Holmberg, A. R., 131
Holmes, R., 156, 169
Homeostasis, Jivaro people and, 203–24
Huambisa, 204
Hugh-Jones, C., 402n

Hugh-Jones, P., 164, 165
Hugh-Jones, S., 293, 294, 401n, 402n
Hunter-gatherers: in Amazonia, 6–8;
    earliest dates of, 97; gender
    egalitarianism of, 225; seasonal
    aggregation of, 258–59; transition to
    agriculture by, 331–32
Hunting: in cerrado region, 254–55; rates
    of return by, 182 (table), 187–93, 188
    (table); seasonal aggregation for, 258–
    59; by shotgun, 203
Hunting and fishing: among Achuar tribes,
    207–8; in interfluvial/riverine areas,
    214; and population constraints, 179;
    and protein return, 178–79
Hymes, D. H., 352

Ideology and social organization, as
    research barriers, 17
Indians: alliances with guerrillas, 392–93;
    attacks by, 261; decimation and
    deculturation of, 96–115;
    disintegration of, 80–94; in lowland
    South America, 20–21 (fig.); relations
    with whites, 301–3; rights, and Federal
    Constitution (1988), 115; social and
    cultural change among, 113–15; wage
    labor of, and entrada, 68, 70
Indigenism, defined, 399
Infanticide, 129–31; Bororo practice of,
    320; Tapirape tribe and, 125; Xavante
    tribe and, 127
Interdisciplinary research: in Amazonia,
    14–23; Kayapó ideal for, 271–72
Interfluvial routes of the Orinoco Basin,
    72–73
Interlocked soft corn, Xavante maize
    variety of, 253–54
Intermarriage, to "civilize" Indians, 103
Intertribal domination, in Amazonia, 91
Iruri, 88
Irvine, D., 184

Jackson, J. E., 12, 184
James, A. T., 350

James, W.P.T., 152
Jansen, A., 152
Jantz, R. L., 130
Jelliffe, D. B., 153
Jivaroan Achuar. See also Achuar
Jivaroan people: Achuar of Ecuador, 204;
    and resistance to intrusion, 227; Shuar,
    Aguaruna, and Huambisa dialect groups
    of, 226; trading chains of, 234–35
Johnson, R., 7
Johnston F. E., 128, 130
Junk, W. J., 4
Junqueira, P. C., 126

Ka'apor language, 364
Kagan, I. G., 134
Kahn, J., 401n
Kamiko, Venancio Aniseto, as "Christo"
    in Upper Rio Negro region, 293–94
Kane (disease), 274
Kaplan, H., 188
Kaplan, J., 130, 135, 136
Kapon, millenarian movements among,
    297–98
Kari'ña. See Carib
Kayapó, Gorotire: use of forest fields by,
    255
Kayapó, Mekranoti group, 250
Kayapó Project (1982), and collection of
    information, 279–80
Kayapó (Southern), as Bororo neighbors,
    322; and mule train attacks, 262
Kayapó tribe: Amazonian synthesis for,
    271–86; disease and effects on, 273–74;
    dispersal and deculturation of, 275–79;
    history, 272; ideal for interdisciplinary
    research, 271–72; and large village
    tradition, 257–58; nomadic agriculture
    of, 277–78; and restructure of society,
    280–81
Kee-khwei, 300; as messianic figure, 294–
    96
Keiter, F., 126
Kelekna, P., 15, 17
Kelley, M. A., 133

Kelley, P. M., 162, 189–90, 191
Kensinger, K. M., 128, 130
Kern, Dirse, on population density, 98
King, G., 130, 135, 136
Klein, H. E. Manelis, 19
Kokrajmoro, measles epidemic in, 273
Kracke, W., 301
Kroeber, A. L., 349
Kurland, J. A., 258

Lamm, S. H., 132, 136, 164
Land reforms, by Colombian government,
    389–90
Language: oppositional hypotheses for, 19,
    22; study in Amazonia, 363–80
Language in Amazonia: botanical referents
    for study of, 365; cross-discipline
    research with, 353; distribution, 343–
    46, 345 (fig.); measuring similarity and
    variation in, 366–71; morphological
    characteristics of, 354–55
Larrick, J. W., 130, 135, 136, 162
Lathrap, D. W., 34, 82, 115, 125, 211, 347
Laughlin, R. M., 374
Lawrence, D. N., 134
Lee, J. A., 134
Lee, R. V., 126
Leigh, C., 36
Lévi-Strauss, C., 18, 239, 250, 323, 335
Lexical similarity in Tupí-Guaraní
    languages, 371–72; by plant category,
    372 (fig.)
Lexicostatistics, 347–49; defined, 357n
Lian-Chen, J. F., 132
Liebhaber, H., 132
Língua geral, prohibition of, 104
Linguistic analysis: of Amazonian lifeways,
    19, 22; priorities for future, 355–56;
    historical and comparative, in Amazon,
    355
Linguistic features, of Amazonian
    languages, 354–56
Linguistic paleontology, and problems of
    diffusion/drift, 351–53
Linn, P. R., 305n

Lipschutz, A., 124
Lisansky, J., 125
Lithics: from Bororo sites, 331; early dates
    of, 6; rock art, Pleistocene, 7
Liu, K.-B., 5
Lizot, J., 156, 182, 189, 209
Lobaton, Guillermo, and the MIR, 292
Locations of indigenous groups, 154 (fig.)
Longhouses, multifamily, Tukanoans and,
    386
Lopes, D., 98
Lowenstein, F. W., 135
Lucas, L., 132, 136, 164

Machifaro, 83
Magalhaes, M. P., 7
Magalis, J. H., 5
Maize: cultivation by Achuar, 206;
    interlocked corn variety of, 253–54; as
    protein source, 179; as staple of
    Araweté, 365; as staple of Bororo and
    Xavante, 252
Malaria, 133, 273
Male dominance, in Amerindia, 44
Male-female role differentiation, in
    Achuar tribes, 229–30
Manioc: as Achuar staple, 208–9; beer, as
    Achuar staple, 232; cultivation of, 97;
    in diets, 167; cyanide in, 168–69
Marajó Island, cattle raising on, 108
Maranca, S., 7
Markell, E., 209
Markell, E. K., 162, 163, 209
Martin, P. S., 124
Martius, C.F.P. von, 253
Maybury-Lewis, D., 126, 127, 128, 131,
    250–60
Mayer, A. J., 130
Mayhall, J., 130, 135, 136
Mayna tribe, 226
McCarthy, L. M., 131
McDowell, N., 305n
Measles (Rubeola), 132; in Kayapó
    villages, 273
Meat hunger, 36

Medical anthropology, integration of
historical and living, 14
Medina, E., 252
Meggers, B. J., 35, 36, 80, 115, 124, 132,
184, 211
Mekranoti, diet and nutritional status of,
163–64. See also Kayapó
Melancon, T. F., 125
Mendoza, D., 132
Métraux, A., 80, 86, 124, 289, 337n
Metzger, D., 189
Migliazza, E. C., 358n
Millenarian movements: in Amazonia,
287–311; and Indian-White relations,
301–3; integration of Christian symbols
in, 299–300
Miller, E. T., 6
Miller, M. C., 5
Miller, R. T., 133
Milton, K., 132, 189
Missionary activity, in Amazonia, 101–2
Mission of Santa Anna Nova, 272
Modern development plans, and negative
Amazonian impact, 111–12
Moore, D., 19, 363, 364
Moore, L. L., 134
Morães, M.A.P., 134
Morales Méndez, F., 56–59
Moreira Neto, C. de A., 115, 116
Morey, R. V., 189
Movement of the Revolutionary Left
(MIR), 292
Muller, Sophia, New Tribes Mission
evangelist, 387
Murphy, R. F., 130, 184
Murphy, Y., 130
Museu Goeldi, as research sponsor, 97–98
Myers, T. P., 115, 124
Mythology, in Bororo society, 329–30

National Endowment for the Humanities,
304
Native Amazonians. See Amazonian
Indians
Native Communities Law (Peru), 292

NCHS, standards for anthropometric
statistics, 152–53
NCHS percentiles, mean standard of
Amazonian compared, 155 (fig.)
Neel, J. V., 126–36, 165, 166, 358n
Nimuendajú, C. U., 252, 287, 323
Niswander, J. D., 166
Nobre, C., 125
Nomadic agriculture, of Kayapó, 277–78
Nondomesticated plant species names,
among Tupí-Guaraní, 375–76
Novoa, R. D., 183
Nowaczynski, W., 135
Nuevo descubrimiento, 35
Nunes de Mello, J. A., 134
Nutritional status, anthropometry to
assess, 152–53

Oiapoque River Basin, Waypi language in,
364
Oliva, O., 126
Oliveira, A. G. de, 11
Oliver, W. J., 135
Omagua, 82–83
Omran, A. R., 131
Onchocerciasis, 134
Opton, E. M., 132, 133
Orden Cruzada, 296–97
Order of St. Javier, 387
Orellana, R., 80, 87
Orihel, T. C., 134
Orinoco Basin: biomes of, 57; colonial
towns in, 63–64; interfluvial routes of,
72–73
Orinoco polities, defense of, 58
Orinoco regional interdependence, 55–78
Ortiz Moreno, M. E., 162
Osmundsen, Lita, 22
Oviedo y Valdes, G. F., 86

Panday, J. P., 19
Papuri River, mission sites on (1914), 387
Parakanã Indians, development and, 112
Paresi (Arawak), as Bororo neighbors, 322
Pastaza phase pottery, 206

Paterniani, E., 253
Pau d'Arco Kayapó, large villages of, 272
Pek, S., 135
Pemon, millenarian movements among, 297–98
Pereira de Queiroz, M. I., 290
Pest, J. W., 134
Peters, J. F., 126, 127, 130, 131
Pezie, K. A., 132
Pezzia, A., 132
Piapoocos, diet and nutritional status of, 155
Piaroas, diet and nutritional status of, 155
Picchi, D. S., 188
Pimentel Barbosa reservation, 257, 258
Pineda Camacho, R., 401n
Pinheiro, F. P., 126, 132, 133
Piperno, D. R., 206
Pires de Campos, A., 319
Plant morphemes, literal: defined, 369
Plant names, metaphorical: defined, 369
Plant nomenclature: segregation by domesticity, 367–68; similarity in domesticated, 371–72; in Tupí-Guaraní languages, 363–80
Polygamy, exogamous vs. endogamous, 41. See also Polygyny
Polygynous nuclear family, as Achuar tradition, 205
Polygyny: in Achuar tribe, 236–39; statistics on, 128 (Table); Xavante and Yanomamo practice of, 127
Pombaline policy, 102–3
Population: advances, health affect of, 138; constraint(s), hunting/fishing yields as, 179; estimates, early, 125–26
Porras, P., 206
Porro, A., 11, 82, 97
Porto Trombetas, 97
Portuguese colonization, 100–101
Posey, D. A., 12, 17, 132, 253, 255, 256, 272–81
Postel, S., 124
Poyer, L., 401n
Prance, G. T., 162

Prehistoric occupation, in Amazonia, 5–11
Productivity, of Achuar tribe, 208–11
Projeto Carajas, 98
Projeto Radambrasil, 4
PRORADAM (Proyecto de Radargramétrico del Amazonas), 386
Protein: capture, 36, 272; limitation hypothesis, 178; maize as source of, 179
Puberty, Achuar, and initiation rites, 240–41
PVEA, 109
Pyka-tô-ti village: abandonment of, 274

Quiripa, 73

Radioisotopic Institution (Japan), 337n
Ralegh, W., 40
Ramos, A. R., 125
Rapajos River, and Santarém culture, 100
Redford, K. H., 187
Redmond, E., 9
Regan, J., 296
Regional Council of Vaupés Indians. See CRIVA
Reichel-Dolmatoff, G., 387, 402n
Reid, H., 189
Reis, A.C.F., 115n
Religion and power, in Amazonia, 92
Renard-Casevitz, F. M., 221
Renfrew, C., 47, 351, 353, 358n
Renvoise, B. S., 256
Research strategies, for Amazonia, 3; archival search and oral history in, 73; epistemology important to, 22–23; interdisciplinary requirements for, 14–17; perspectives for future Bororo, 334–36; in study of Bororo tribe, 316–19
Resgatado (rescued), plight of Indians as, 101–2
Resgates, 115n
Resguardo, Vaupés Tukanoan reservation (1982), 388, 390
Revolutionary Armed Forces of Colombia. See FARC

Ribeiro, D., 272
Ribeiro, F. da Paula, 259
Rice, as Xavante staple, 254
Richards, V. A., 126
Ritter, M. L., 182, 188
Rivet, P., 38
Robinson, J. G., 187
Rodrigues, A. R., 370
Rogers, D. J., 367
Romanoff, S., 190
Roosevelt, A. C., 35, 48, 59, 94, 97, 98,
    115, 124, 131, 211, 263, 289
Ross, E. B., 132, 163, 209, 211
Rubin, G., 239

Saffirio, J., 125
Saignes, T. H., 221
Salzano, F. M., 126–37, 164, 165
Sankoff, D., 350
Santacruz, J., 393, 397
Santacruz, Jesus, 395
Santarém-Monte Alegre, earliest dates
    from, 6
Sapir, E., 352
Savanna: as biome of Orinoco basin, 57;
    part of cerrado as, 251
Schmitz, I., 6, 7
School of American Research, 304
Schwaner, T. D., 134
Scott, J. C., 303
Segregation of male/female activity, 239–
    40
Sellers, P., 125
Semidomesticated plant species names, in
    Tupí-Guaraní, 376–77
Service, E. R., 91
Servico de Proteção ao Índio (SPI), Indian
    reservations established by, 320
Settlement patterns: of Achuar tribe, 205,
    205–7; in Amazonia, 5, 96–99; of
    Bororo tribe, 324–25; chieftanship
    and, 86–88; density of early, 96, 124;
    tribal territories and, 80–90; of
    Tukanoans, 386–88
Setz, E.Z.F., 184, 188

Shaman(s): as Achuar male occupation,
    235; in Bororo society, 321–22
Shapiro, J., 230
Shavante (Macro-Gê family), as Bororo
    neighbors, 322
Shell, O. A., 186
Shining Path, 292
Shipibo, diet of, 163
Shipibo-Conibo population, 126
Shuar tribe, 204, 226
Shukla, J., 125
SIL, and rivalry with CRIVA, 395
Silveira, M. I. de, 98
Silverman, Sydel, 22, 263
Silverwood-Cope, P., 184, 189, 192, 401n
Simoes, M. F., 97, 115
Simon, P., 36
Simons, M., 125
Siona-Secoya, diet and nutritional status
    of, 162
Siskind, J., 130, 184
Smith, A. D., 401
Smith, N.J.H., 98, 183, 187
Smith, R. C., 125
Social ranking, in millenarian movements,
    300–301
Social structure: of central Brazilian
    groups, 258–60; of Tukanoans, 386–
    87, 396
Sorensen, A. P., 34
Sottneck, F. O., 134
South American Indian Languages
    Documentation, 356
Spielman, R. S., 135
Spielmann, K. A., 331
Sponsel, L. E., 189
Stahl, F. A., and Ashaninka crisis cult,
    292
Stature of Amazonian adults, compared to
    NCHS percentiles, 155 (fig.)
Stearman, A. M., 125
Steward, J. H., 124, 323, 324
Stiles, H. M., 135
Stocks, A., 183, 185, 192, 193
Sulzer, A. J., 133

Summer Institute of Linguistics/Wycliff Bible Translators. See SIL
Sussenbach, T., 187
Swadesh, M., 347, 348, 349, 350, 351
Sweet, D. G., 115

Tadarimana village, 317; housefloor layout in, 327 (fig.); house size in, 323–24; site map of, 326 (fig.)
Taylor, A. C., 205, 206, 220
Taylor, K. I., 124
Taylor-Descola, A. C., 221
Teixeira, P., 80, 83, 86, 95–96, 100; voyage of (1639), 95–96
Tembé language, 364
Tenbrink, M. S., 135
Tepe Tede'wa, "fish people" and red maize, 254
Terra Sem Mal ("Land Without Evil"), migrations to, 290
Tessman, G., 126
Test list(s), for glottochronology, 348–49
Thatcher, V. E., 134
Thomas, D. J., 297, 306n
Thomson, L. A., 135
Thornton, R., 124, 133
Tournon, J., 132
Treece, D., 125
Trekking: Bororo practice of, 322; cerrado people and, 255–57
Tukanoan Indians: and ethnic federation in the Vaupés, 384; ethnicity, politics of, 383–406; social structure of, 386–87, 398–99; of Upper Rio Negro region, 293–94
Tukanoan reservation, at Vaupés Resguardo (1982), 388, 390
Tukuna tribe, 287
Tupac Amaru revolutionary movement, 292
Tupí-Guaraní: caraia (godmen) of, 290–91; five linguistic subgroupings of, 365; millenarian movements of, 289–90; and plant names over time, 363–80

Tupí-Guaraní language: compared to Carib, 355; examples of domesticated plant names in, 377–78; examples of nondomesticated plant names in, 375–76; examples of semidomesticated plant names in, 376–77; lexical similarity by plant category in, 372 (fig.); metaphorical vs. literal plant words in, 373 (fig.); phonetic resemblance in forms in, 370–71
Turner, T., 237, 275

UDIC, 388
Udjy (sorcery), 274; present day accusations of, 275
Uhl, C., 182, 183
Union of Cubeo Indians. See UDIC
United States Center for Health Statistics (NCHS), expedition of, 80. See also NCHS
Universidade Federal do Pará (Belém), 378
Ursúa-Aguirre, 80, 81, 83, 84

van der Merwe, N. J., 350
Vasquez, F., 81, 82, 83
Vaupés, as home of Tukanoans, 386–88
Vermelho River, first settlement on, 333–34
Vermelho River Basin: as Bororo sampling area, 318–19; villages in, 321
Verswijver, G., 272, 275, 282n
Vickers, W. T., 162, 186, 187, 190, 203, 209, 255
Vincent, J., 401n
Vinhas de Queiroz, M., 302
Vocabulary, measuring similarity and variation in, 366–71
Vázquez-Yanes, C., 125

Wagley, C., 124, 125
Walker, G. F., 130
Wallace, G. D., 132, 133
Walls, K. W., 133
Waorani, 162
Warfare, and Achuar tribe, 226–27

War of the Tupinambas, 102
Warren, J., 133
Warrior, as Achuar male occupation, 235–36
Waypi language, 364
Weight-for-height in school children and adults, 160 (fig.)
Weinstein, E. D., 135, 165
Weiss, K. M., 127, 128
Wenner-Gren Conference, 22, 263; "Amazonian Synthesis: An Integration of Disciplines, Paradigms and Methodologies," 260
Werner, D., 164, 182, 192
Werner, D. W., 260
West, B. S., 132, 133
Wheeler, E. F., 167
Whitehead, N. L., 260, 261
Whiting, B., 240
Whiting, J., 240
Whitten, N. E., 125, 222
WHO Working Group, 152, 153
Wickham, Henry, 107
Wilbert, J., 350
Wilson, B., 291
Wilson, J., 36
Wolf, E., 385–86, 401n
Women foragers, and birth control, 228
Women horticulturalists, and birth-spacing, 228–29

Work expenditure (Achuar), vs. potential productivity, 211–12
Wright, R., 402n
Wright, R. M., 287, 293, 294, 302
Wüst, I., 250, 257

Xarae, as Bororo neighbors, 322
Xavante tribe, 250; diet and nutritional status of, 165; and large village tradition, 257–58; maize as primary food of, 254; rice as staple of, 254; trekking by, 256
Xingu, River, 97
Xingu River Basin, Araweté and Asurini languages in, 365

Yanomami tribe: diet and nutritional standards of, 156, 209, 210 (Table)
Yao, political structure of, 40–41
Yapu, diet and nutritional status of, 161
Yavaret Mission (Salesians), 387
Yellow fever, 133, 273
Yoffee, N., 358n
Yost, J. A., 130, 135, 136, 162, 189–90, 191

Zarzar, A., 205n
Zerries, O., 330
Zucchi, A., 48

About the Editor

ANNA ROOSEVELT is an anthropologist with interests in human ecology and cultural evolution. For about twenty years she has carried out field research in lowland South America. In 1988 she received a MacArthur Fellowship for her interdisciplinary research in Amazonia. Her research, funded also by the National Science Foundation and the National Endowment for the Humanities, has been published in *Nature, Science,* and other journals, and she is the author of books including *Moundbuilders of the Amazon: Geophysical Archaeology on Marajo Island, Brazil, Parmana: Prehistoric Manioc and Maize Cultivation Along the Amazon and Orinoco,* and *Excavations at Corozal, Venezuela.* Roosevelt is Curator of Archaeology at the Field Museum of Natural History and Professor of Anthropology at the University of Illinois at Chicago.